Artificial Intelligence

Express Learning Series

Shivani Goel
Assistant Professor
Computer Science and Engineering Department
Thapar University
Patiala, Punjab

PEARSON

Delhi • Chennai

ISBN 978-81-317-8747-2

First Impression

Published by Dorling Kindersley (India) Pvt. Ltd., licensees of Pearson Education in South Asia.

Head Office: 7th Floor, Knowledge Boulevard, A-8 (A), Sector 62, NOIDA, 201 309, UP, India.
Registered Office: 11 Community Centre, Panchsheel Park, New Delhi 110 017, India.

Typeset by Chennai Publishing Services
Printed in India by HT Media Ltd., Noida

Contents

Preface

Artificial intelligence (AI) is a vast and universal field. It is the field which emphasized the need of many challenging researches in computer science. These include playing games intelligently, imitating a human expert, recognition of speech and processing of vision like an intelligent human being.

This book on Artificial Intelligence aims to provide comprehensive material on this subject to undergraduate and graduate students in computer science. The book has been written keeping in mind the syllabi designed for courses on AI in various technical universities in India. The book can serve as a reference book for the AI course since it covers all topics in AI in easy question answer form. This book covers a number of examples on each topic to provide a good understanding of each topic.

The main topics covered in the book include game playing, natural language processing, uninformed and informed searches, knowledge representation schemes like semantic networks, frames, scripts , conceptual dependencies, CYC etc. Other topics covered are uncertainty handling, expert systems, natural language processing, genetic algorithms, pattern recognition, intelligent agents, neural networks fuzzy logic. Two languages for AI are covered in the book namely, List processing and PROLOG. Pseudo algorithms for various methods and techniques are included wherever required to improve the understanding.

Acknowledgements

First of all, I thank GOD for giving me motivation and energy to write this book.

Next I would like to thank all my Gurus who have blessed me with their valuable teachings and shown me the correct path to proceed in life.

I would like to thank my parents for bringing me up with all love and care and teaching good manners and values. Their encouragement has been a constant source of motivation for writing this book. This book is indeed dedicated to my parents Mrs Usha Goel and Mr Ramesh Chand Goel.

Very special thanks to my loving husband Deepak and my daughters Gariyasi and Prakriti for all their support in completing this book. I would like to thank my family members and my friend Vineeta Bassi who have helped in every possible way in completing this book.

I would also like to thank all my students who have give positive feedback about my teaching on subject AI and encouraged me to write a book on AI.

I would also like to take this opportunity to express my gratitude to everyone who, directly or indirectly contributed to the successful completion of the book.

Shivani Goel

[illegible] most widely used [illegible]

[illegible]

[illegible]

[illegible]

[illegible]

[illegible]

[illegible]

[illegible]

1

Introduction to AI Problems

1.1 INTRODUCTION

Artificial intelligence (AI) began in earnest with the emergence of modern computer during 1940s and 1950s. These computers were capable of storing large amounts of information and hence knowledge. The processing speed of these computers was very high. This gave an idea to the researchers to make these think intelligently like human being. The advantages were twofold. First, the processing speed and accuracy could be more of these intelligent systems than humans. Second, they could emulate some of the human capabilities. But the task was not that easy. The human brain is very complex and is capable of acting in an intelligent way using a number of interconnected concepts like memory, understanding, knowledge acquisition, and updation, including all possibilities of likelihoods of occurrence of various events and recognition of various inputs from the outside world and processing. The AI programs have different areas defined for handling and incorporating all of these concepts. All of these have evolved and developed over time one by one and still the research is continuing to handle these complications of handling intelligence in machines. There are many ways of implementing AI in machines. The simplest was to use game playing. A number of other simpler problems were solved using the concepts of AI. The expert systems and intelligent agents are the examples of programs running on machine and exhibiting intelligence. The best example of AI implementation in machines is the development of a robot that can think and decide like a human. It uses many problem-solving techniques and is capable of learning of its own.

Q. What do you understand by AI?

Ans. Artificial intelligence consists of two words: "Artificial" and "Intelligence". Intelligence is something that is related to human beings and a person who is intelligent has the chance to win in the games of life, solve the problems of life more efficiently than those who have less intelligence. The computer is the artificial medium created by human being for solving various types of complex problems with high speed and accuracy. The software programs running on the computer makes it intelligent. AI is the branch of computer science that studies how to make computer intelligent like a human being.

Q. Explain historical foundations of AI.

Ans. In 1961, Newell and Simon built a general problem solver which could think humanly in problem solving. In 1978, Bellman suggested automation of activities like decision making, learning, etc., which involve human thinking. In 1985, Haugeland proposed the concept of machines with minds, i.e., which could think. In 1990 and 1991, Kurzweil, Rich and Knight proposed of building machines which could act like human and perform intelligent tasks. In 1985, Charniak and McDermott and Winston (1992) proposed to build the machines which could think rationally, i.e., they could do computations by perceiving, reasoning, and then acting in a rational way. This involved thinking at mental level. Schalkoff (1990) and Luger and Stubblefield (1993) proposed for building of system which could also act rationally. This involved automation of intelligent computations

Q. What are AI problems?

Ans. The starting work in the field of AI was on solving formal tasks such as game playing and theorem proving. Next was commonsense reasoning which includes reasoning about physical objects and their relationships to each other like performing symbolic manipulations of logical expressions, etc. Then visual perception and natural language understanding were used for simulating the human intelligence in vision perception and speech recognition in machines. Other problems are financial analysis, medical diagnosis, engineering design and planning, scientific analysis, etc.

Q. What is an AI technique?

Ans. There are two parts of an AI technique:

(a) the knowledge representation which is used to capture the knowledge about the real world and

(b) the search algorithm which is used to find the solution to the problem.

In an AI technique, knowledge should be represented in such a way that it can be understood by people who must provide it. It should be able to capture generalizations in knowledge, i.e., group important properties together so that it can be used in many situations. It should be made easy to modify the knowledge to correct the errors and to reflect the changes in the domain. Different types of AI problems have different type of knowledge representation and different algorithm for solving it.

Q. What is the architecture of AI machine?

Ans. An intelligent agent is an example of an AI machine. The architecture of intelligent agent is the architecture of AI machine. Main parts of the architecture include actuators for producing outputs, sensors for taking inputs, environment in which the machine is to operate and the performance measures against which the AI machine is to take decisions.

Q. What are the applications of AI, i.e., what are the areas of simulation of sophisticated and intelligent behavior in real life?

Ans. There are many areas in which intelligent behavior is simulated. These include:

In daily life for all users:

- Computer games
- Credit card verification in e-commerce/fraud detection
- Customer relationship management
- Intelligent user interfaces
- Medical diagnosis systems
- Regulating/controlling hardware devices and processes (e.g., in automobiles)
- Voice/image recognition

- Scheduling systems (railways, airlines, hotels, manufacturing)
- Web search engines/web spiders
- Web personalization and recommender systems (collaborative/content filtering)
- Personal agents
- Pattern recognition (face recognition, handwriting recognition, fraud detection and prevention)

For technical users

- Spell/grammar checkers
- Context sensitive help systems
- Error detection/correction in electronic communication
- Program verification/compiler and programming language design
- Data mining and knowledge discovery in databases

Q. What are the characteristics of AI applications?

Ans. An AI application has the following characteristics:

1. Ability to act intelligently as human
2. Ability to simulate functioning of human brain
3. Ability to adapt and learn as an intelligent human
4. Ability to process symbols and natural language like humans
5. Ability to perform an intelligent action

1.2 TURING TEST

Q. Explain Turing test and its origin

Ans. In 1950, Alan Turing proposed the "Turing Test" for determining whether a machine can think or not. To conduct this test, two persons and the machine to be evaluated are evaluated. One person plays the role of the interrogator, who is in a separate room from the computer and the other person is the one whose performance is compared with the machine. The interrogator can ask questions to both the person and the machine by typing without seeing them. However, the interrogator knows them only as A or B and aims to determine which one is the person and which one is the machine. The interrogator also receives the typed responses from both. The goal of the machine is to fool the interrogator into believing that it is the person. If the machine succeeds at this, then we will conclude that the machine can think.

1.3 PRODUCTION SYSTEM

Q. Define a production system.

Ans. A production system is a way to describe the operations that can be performed in search for a solution to a problem. A production system consists of:

1. *A set of rules*: A rule consists of a left side and a right side. The left side determines the conditions which must be true if the rule is to be applied and the right side describes the operation or action to be performed if the rule is applied. The set of all possible rules are stored in a production system.

2. One or more databases that contain whatever information is appropriate for the particular task. Some parts of the database may be permanent, while other parts of it may only contain the solution of the current problem.
3. A control strategy that specifies the order in which the rules will be compared to the database. It also specifies the way of resolving the conflicts in case many rules can be applied at the same time.
4. A rule applier which will apply the rules and find the solution to the problem at hand.

Q. What are the various types of production system?

Ans. There are four definitions of classes of production systems

1. *Non-monotonic production system*: In a production system when there are many rules applicable at a time, then we can select any one of them at the current time. If this selected rule when applied does not lead to a solution, then the non-monotonic production system does not allow the application of rest of the rules applicable to be applied now.
2. *Monotonic production system*: In a production system when there are many rules applicable at a time, then we can select any one of them at the current time. If this selected rule when applied does not lead to a solution, then the monotonic production system allows the application of any of the rules (i.e., applicable but not applied) which could have been applied at last time to be applied now.
3. *Partially commutative production system*: This is a production system with the property that if the application of a particular sequence of rules transforms state x into state y, then any possible different sequence of those rules that is allowable also transforms state x into state y.
4. *Commutative production system*: This is the production system that is both monotonic and partially commutative.

Q. What are production system languages? Give examples.

Ans. Production system languages are the programming languages which are designed for easy construction of rule-based production systems. These are either supporting backward chaining or forward chaining or both. Examples of production system languages are:

-**PROLOG (Programming in logic)** which uses backward chaining and logic statements only, but it has no mechanisms for handling uncertainty.

-**OPS5 (Official Production System)** used to develop many expert systems, including the ability to encode certainty factors or other forms of uncertainty like probabilities. It uses forward chaining.

-**SOAR (State, Operator and Result)** used to develop SOAR project for handling operations in intelligent agents. It supports all features of OPS5 and chunking.

-**CLIPS (C language Integrated Production System)**: It is written in C but looks like LISP. It supports both forward and backward chaining.

-**Jess**: This language emerged when CLIPS was re-written in Java with GUI capabilities.

-**Lisa:** a rule engine written in LISP

1.4 PROBLEMS IN AI

Q. What are the example problems solved in AI?

Ans. The problems to be solved in AI are the ones that are performed by human beings and which involve intelligence. *Examples*: playing games, learning a new language, recognizing any pattern, solving theorems, performing various searches, understanding, and planning.

Q. Define problem state space.

Ans. It represents the set of all possible states which can be taken in solving a problem. States represent both the initial states, intermediate states, and goal states.

Explanation-Traveling salesman problem: Suppose the following information is given about the distance between various cities. The start city is A.

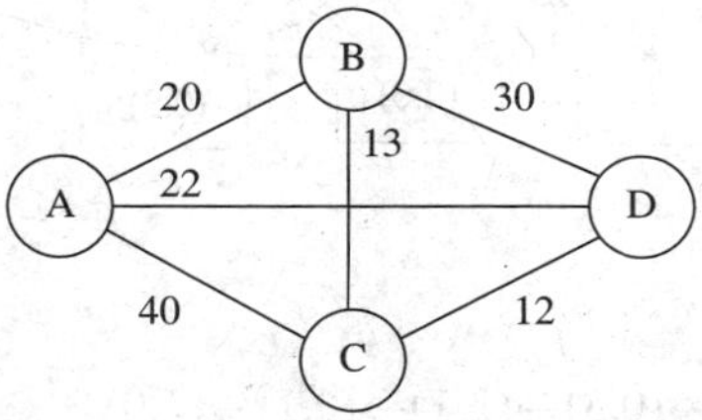

The possible routes with their possible distances are to be calculated and the one with the minimum distance is to be selected by the traveling salesman.

The possible routes are:

1. A→B→C→D→A with distance1 = 20 + 13 + 12 + 22 = 67
2. A→B→D→C→A with distance2 = 20 + 30 + 12 + 40 = 102
3. A→C→B→D→A with distance3 = 40 + 13 + 30 + 22 = 105
4. A→C→D→B→A with distance4 = 40 + 12 + 30 + 20 = 102
5. A→D→C→B→A with distance5 = 22 + 12 + 13 + 20 = 67
6. A→D→B→C→A with distance6 = 22 + 30 + 13 + 40 = 105

The two routes with minimum distance 67 KM are A→B→C→D→A and A→D→C→B→A.

Q. Define Traveling salesman problem and its state representation.

Ans. A salesman has a list of cities, each of which he must visit exactly once. There are direct roads between each pair of cities on the list. To find the route, the salesman should follow the shortest possible round trip that both starts and finishes at any one of the cities. The state is represented as the pair of any two cities and the distance between them. The solution is the minimum total distance between the start city and all the other cities traveled at least once and back to start city.

Q. Define water jug problem and its state representation.

Ans. Here we have given two jugs with different capacities, one is an X-Liter jug and the other is a Y-Liter jug. Neither has any measuring marker on it. There is a pump that can be used to fill the jugs with water. How can we get exactly L Liters of water into the Y-Liter jug? The state is represented as the tuple $<x,y>$ where x represents the integer amount of water in X-Liter jug and y represents water in Y-Liter jug. The solution is the sequence of steps taken from start state to goal state with the list of all rules applied.

Explanation-Water jug problem: Suppose the capacity of the two jugs is 2 liters and 3 liters. The goal is to get exactly 1liter of water in 2 liter jug. The state space for it is shown in figure below:

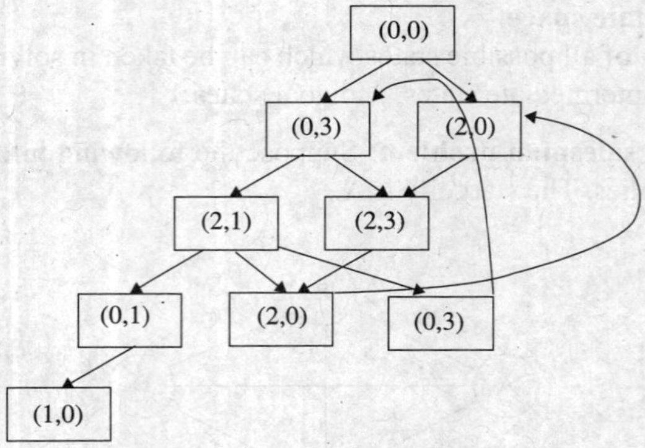

The solution steps will be (0,0)→(0,3)→(2,1)→(0,1)→(1,0).

Q. Define Blocks world problem and its state representation.

Ans. In blocks world problem, there are *N* number of blocks resting on table with a particular sequence. They are required to be arranged in desired sequence. The available moves are: we can place a block whose top is empty on the table. We can place a block on the top of another block whose top is empty. The state is represented using a sequence of blocks in current positions. The solution is the sequence of actions taken to get the goal state from the desired state.

Explanation - Blocks world problem: Suppose there are three blocks with labels as A,B and C. The required arrangement of the blocks is shown in goal state and the initial arrangement of blocks is shown in start state.

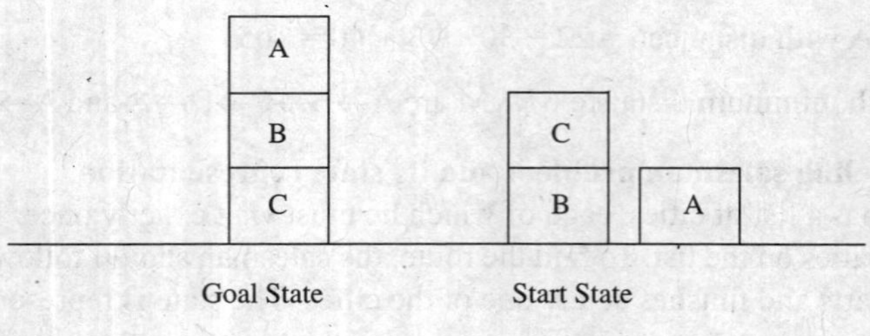

By applying the possible operators, the start state is to be converted into goal state. The solution for the blocks world problem is:

1. Place block C on the table.
2. Put block B on top of block C.
3. Put block A on top of block B.

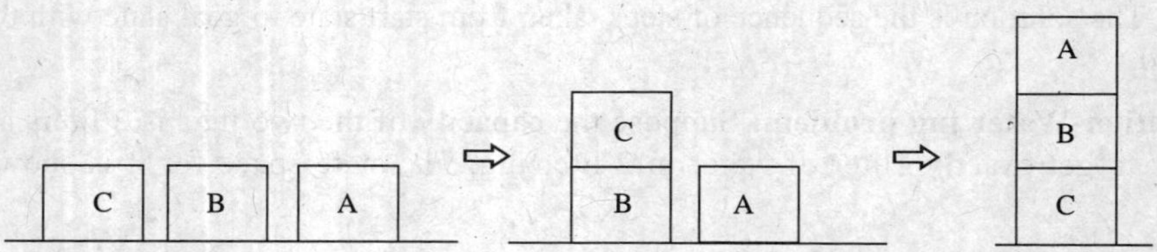

Problem State space:

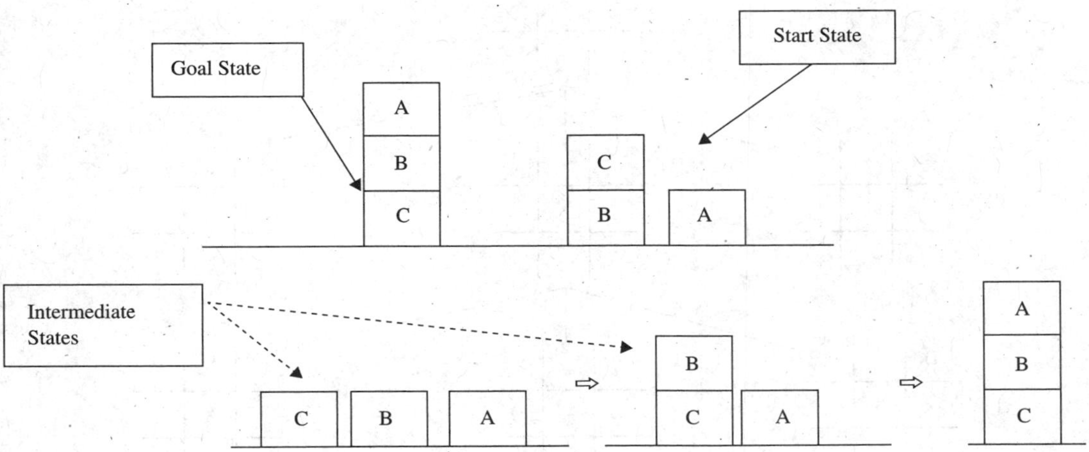

Q. Define 8-puzzle problem and its state representation.

Ans. The 8-puzzle is a square tray in which are placed eight square tiles. The remaining ninth square is uncovered or unnumbered. Each tile has a number on it. A game consists of a starting position and a specified goal position. The goal is to transform the starting position into the goal position by sliding the tiles around. Its state is represented as a 3 × 3 matrix for storing the tiles positions. The solution is to show the sequence of tiles moved in order to get start state to goal state.

1	2	3
8		4
7	6	5

Q. Define Tic-Tac-Toe problem and its state representation.

Ans. It is a two-player game where one player called MAX marks a letter X and the opponent called MIN marks a letter 0. There is a 3 × 3 grid where the two players put their letters. The player who is able to first mark his three letters in a complete row or a complete column or a complete diagonal wins the game. The state is represented by the positions occupied by the letters by the two players in 3 × 3 grid along with other empty places. The start state is the empty grid. The solution here is a goal state which indicates win for either of the player (three Xs indicate winning for MAX and three 0s indicate winning for MIN).

Explanation-Tic Tac Toe problem: Initially the grid is empty. Say it is MAX player's turn. He can mark at any of the 9 places, the three of which are shown below. In the next move, suppose MAX marks the X in the middle of the grid. Then there are eight options for MIN to put a 0, three of which are shown below. The two players take their turns one by one trying to win and not letting the opponent win.

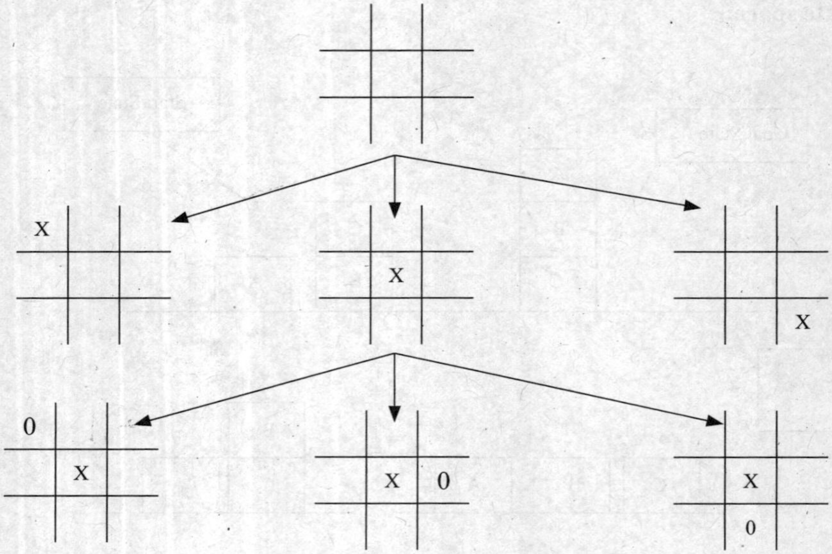

Any intermediate state could be

0	X	
	X	0
	0	X

A winning state for MAX could be

0	X	
	X	0
	X	0

Q. Define Towers of Hanoi problem and its state representation.

Ans. Somewhere near Hanoi, there is a monastery whose monks devote their lives to a very important task. In their courtyard are three tall posts. On these posts is a set of **n** disks, each with a hole in the center and each of a different radius. When the monastery was established, all of the disks were on one of the posts, each disk resting on the one just larger than it. The monk's task is to move all of the disks to one of the other pegs. Only one disk can be moved at a time and all the other disks must be on one of the pegs. In addition, at no time during the process may a disk be placed on top of a smaller disk. The third peg can be used as a temporary resting place for the disks. What is the quickest way for the monks to accomplish their mission? The state can be represented as the sequence of disks in order of size on all the three pegs. The solution is the sequence of disk movement between pegs in order to get from start state to goal state.

Explanation- Towers of Hanoi problem: Suppose there are 3 disks numbered 1,2,3. The disk 1 is the smallest, disk 2 is medium and disk 3 is largest in size. The condition that can be checked at any time is disk2>disk1, so disk2 cannot be placed on disk1. Disk3>disk2, so disk3 cannot be placed on disk1 or disk2. Initially these are resting on Peg1.the goal is to move these to Peg3. Peg2 is used as the intermediate peg.

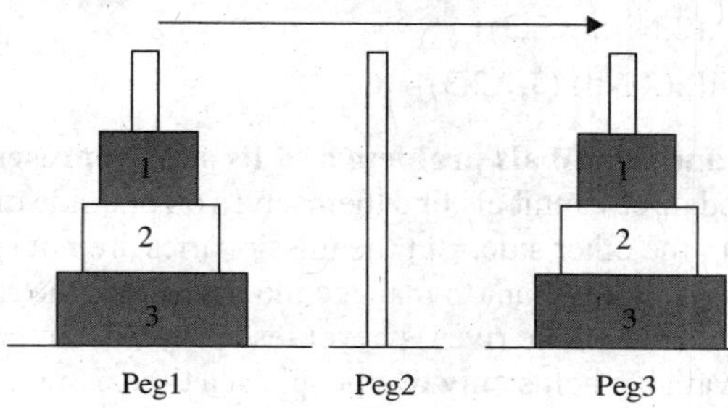

The possible state space for this problem in shown in figure below:

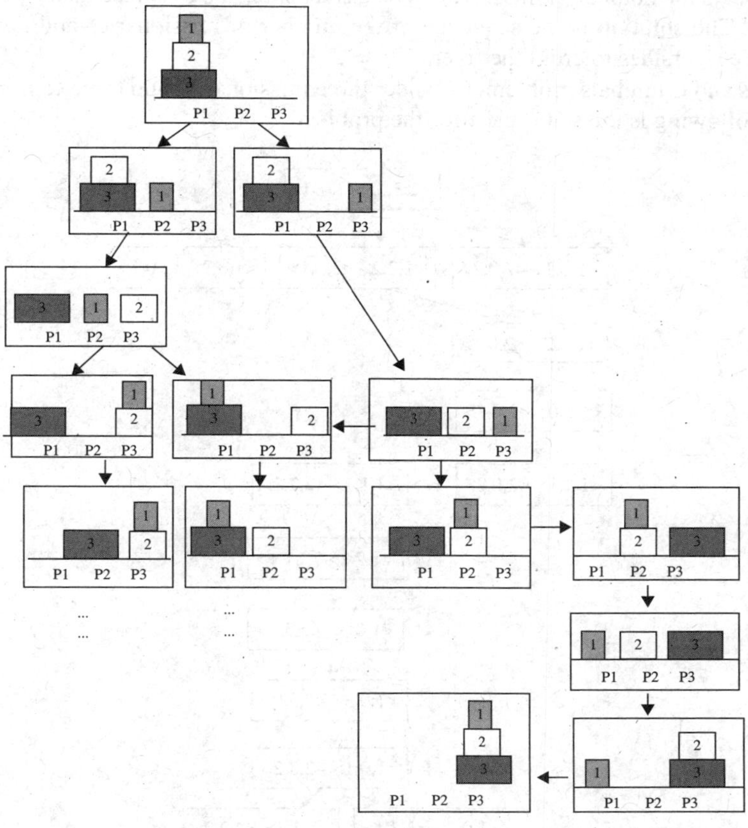

The state is represented as a the tuple (peg_number , sequence of disks). The solution steps and states are :

1. Place disk1 on Peg3 ((1,2,3),(2,Nil),(3,1))
2. Place disk2 on Peg2 ((1,3),(2,2),(3,1))
3. Place disk1 on Peg2 ((1,3),(2,1,2),(3,Nil))

4. Place disk3 on Peg3 ((1,Nil),(2,1,2),(3,3))
5. Place disk1 on Peg1 ((1,1),(2,2),(3,3))
6. Place disk2 on Peg3 ((1,1),(2,Nil),(3,2,3))
7. Place disk1 on Peg3 ((1,Nil),(2,Nil),(3,1,2,3))

Q. Define missionaries and cannibals problem and its state representation.

Ans. Three missionaries and three cannibals find themselves on one side of a river. They have agreed that they would all like to get to the other side. But the missionaries are not sure whether they can trust the cannibals or not. So the missionaries want to manage the trip across the river in such a way that the number of missionaries on either side of the river is never less than the number of cannibals who are on the same side. The only boat available holds only two people at a time. How can everyone get across the river without the missionaries risking being eaten? The state is represented as 3 tuple <rs, *m*, *c*>, where rs represents the river sides which can be either 1 (starting side of the river) or 2 (destination side of the river), *m* represents the number of missionaries on a river side, and *c* represents the number of cannibals on a river side. The solution is the sequence of the number of missionaries and number of cannibals moved along the riversides to cross the river.

Missionaries and Cannibals problem: Consider three missionaries and three cannibals on one side of the river. The following is the state space for the problem:

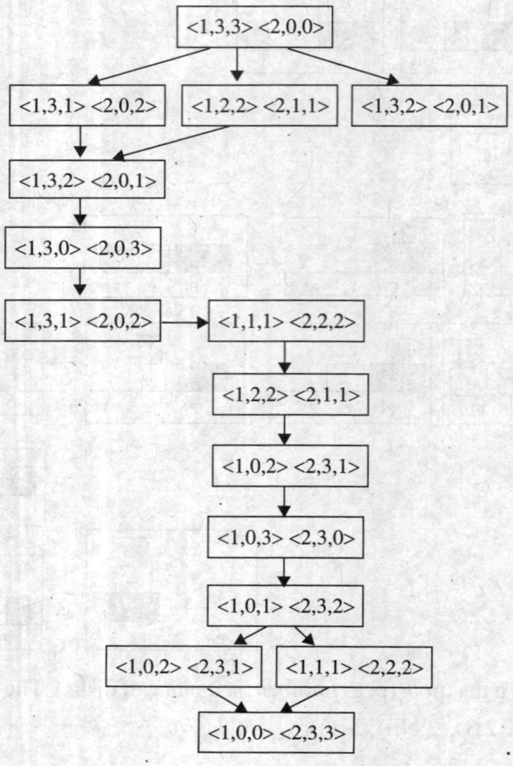

Q. Define monkey and banana problem and its state representation.

Ans. A hungry monkey finds himself in a room in which a bunch of bananas is hanging from the ceiling. The monkey, unfortunately, cannot reach the bananas. However, in the room, a chair and a stick are available. The ceiling is just the right height so that a monkey standing on a chair could knock the bananas down with the stick. The monkey knows how to move around, carry other things around, reach for the bananas and wave a stick in the air. What is the best sequence of actions for the monkey to take to acquire bananas? The state is represented as predicates like can get (monkey, banana), on (monkey, chair), etc. The solution is the sequence of steps taken by the monkey in order to get the bananas from the ceiling.

Monkey banana problem

Each state is represented by 4 variables:

- the position of the monkey : possible values are door, window, middle, any position(P)
- the position of the box : possible values are under the banana, middle, any position(P)
- if the monkey is on the box: possible values are yes or no
- if the monkey has the banana: possible values are yes or no

The allowed moves are:

1. Monkey can walk from current position M to any position P
   walk(P): from (M, B, no, no) to (P, B, no, H). Here H is variable that will be true when the monkey will hold the banana.
2. Monkey can push the box from current position M to any position P. This will change the position of the monkey as well as the position of the box.
   push(P): from (M, M, no, H) to (P, P, no, H).
3. Monkey can climb up the box. His position will remain unchanged.
   climb: from (M, M, no, H) to (M, M, yes, H).
4. Monkey can grasp the banana.
   grasp: from (middle, B, yes, no) to (middle, B, yes, yes).

The initial state is : monkey is at the door and the box is in the middle of the room: (door, middle, no, no).
The set of goal states is (*, *, *, yes). Here * indicates that any value will be a part of the solution.
The solution steps are:

1. walk(middle) : (middle, middle, no, no).
2. climb : (middle, middle, yes, no).
3. grasp : (middle, middle, yes, yes). Hence goal is achieved.

Q. Define theorem proving.

Ans. A number of axioms are given along with a question. The user needs to relate the axioms in any particular sequence to find answer to the solution. The state is represented as the number of axiom matched starting from the goal state, i.e., the theorem to be proved and the new axiom generated to be proved. The solution steps continue in this fashion till no further axiom is left to be proved.

Theorem proving example:

Consider the given set of axioms:

1. All post graduate (PG) students have a specialization.
2. Ashu has specialization commerce.
3. Shikha has specialization management.
4. All undergraduate (UG) students who pass exam register themselves for post graduation.
5. All undergraduate (UG) students who pass exam become post graduate students.

To prove: Shikha has passed her under graduate exam.

Proof:

I. If we start from axiom 4, Shikha would have passed her under graduate exam if she had registered herself for post graduation.
There is no axiom which supports this fact. So we ignore this solution and start again.

II. If we start from axiom 5, Shikha would have passed her under graduate exam, if she's a post graduate student.
From 1, Shikha would have been a post graduate student, if she has a specialization.
From 3, it is proved, that Shikha has a specialization in management and hence is is post graduate student and this implies that she has passed her undergraduate exam.

The sequence of steps taken is:

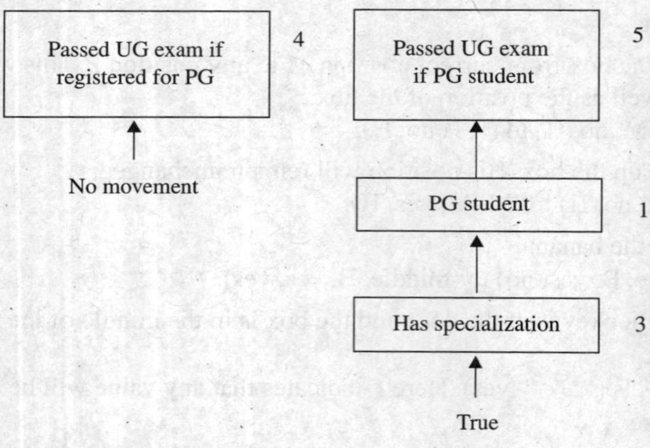

Q. Define the relationship between classes of production systems and classes of problems.

Ans. For any solvable problem, there exist an infinite number of production systems that describe ways to find solutions. Partially commutative and monotonic production systems are useful for solving ignorable problems. Theorem proving and water jug problems are examples of this type of problems. Non-monotonic and partially commutative systems are useful for problems in which changes occur but can be reversed and in which order of operations is not critical. This is usually the case in physical manipulation problems, such as robot navigation on a flat plane or 8-puzzle problem. Production systems that are not partially commutative production systems are useful for many problems in which irreversible changes occur. The order in which they are performed can be very important in determining the final output. Chemical synthesis and game playing like chess, tic-tac-toe are examples. Non-partially commutative production systems are less likely to produce the same node many times in the search process. We can solve problems like playing the game of bridge by using non-partially commutative and non-monotonic production system.

1.5 PROBLEM CHARACTERIZATION

Q. Write various ways of characterizing a given problem.

Ans. In order to choose the most promising method for a particular problem, it is necessary to analyze the problem along several key dimensions:

1. Can we predict the problem's universe, i.e., the set of all possible states? If yes, it will be easy to search through the entire state space and if not, then problem is difficult for handling.
2. Is the state space a huge one? If yes, it needs efforts to search through the state space but if it is small, then we can even exhaustively search for the solution.
3. Do we need a large amount of knowledge to solve the problem? If yes, we first need to gain all the knowledge and represent in a useful manner, only then we can search or find the solution. If not, then problem solving is relatively easy.
4. Can we decompose the problem into a set of (nearly) independent but smaller or easier subproblems? If yes, the problem solving may be easy by focusing on smaller subproblems one by one instead of handling a complex problem.
5. Is it possible that we can ignore the steps taken to find a solution in a particular direction or it is possible that we can undo the steps taken which are not leading us to the solution? If not, then we need to be careful while selecting the step and use some planning before taking a step. If yes, then the problem is relatively easy to handle. But still it needs the alternate steps ready to be used.
6. Do we need a solution as a state of the world or as a path to a goal state? It is easier to look for a state as solution but for finding a path, more effort is required.
7. Do we need a solution which is best in comparison to all other possible solutions or we can stop on finding any path? If yes, then it needs generation of all the solution paths first and then choosing the best path or some measures of ensuring that the path we have found is definitely best. If there is no such restriction, then it is much easier to handle.
8. Can a computer that is simply given the problem returns the solution, or will the solution of the problem require interaction between the computer and a person? It is easier to write a program in computer and let it find the answer as compared to interacting throughout with the computer.

SOLVED EXAMPLES

Q. Give example of a decomposable problem and a non-decomposable problem.

Ans. Decomposable problem: Integration problem is decomposable into smaller subproblems. Suppose we want to solve the problem of computing the expression

$\int (x^2 + \sin x + 3)\, dx$

We solve this problem by breaking it down into three smaller problems $\int x^2\, dx$, $\int \sin x\, dx$ and $\int 3\, dx$ and then finding their sum. Each of these can be solved using a small collection of specific rules of integration. Here, the process of problem decomposition can be exploited by a simple recursive integration program. At each step, the integrator checks to see whether the problem it is working on is immediately solvable. If so, the answer is returned directly. If the problem is not easily solvable, the integrator checks to see whether it can decompose the problem into smaller problems. If it can, it creates those problems and calls itself recursively on them. Sometimes blocks world problem may have decomposable problem. For example, consider the block world problem:

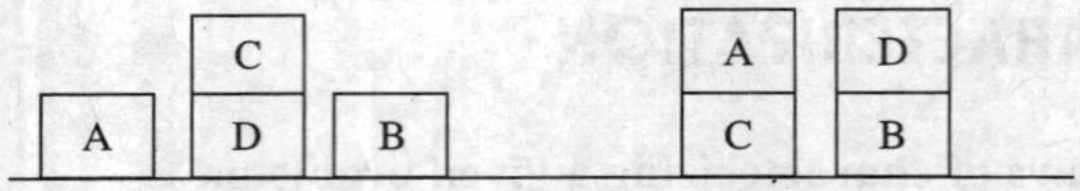

Start state   Goal state

This problem is separate into four subproblems, one for each component of the goal.
ON(A,C) and ON(D,B) and ONTABLE(C) and ONTABLE(B).
Non-decomposable problems are 8-puzzle, water jug, missionaries and cannibals, card games, etc.

Q. Give example of a problem whose steps can be ignored.

Ans. Theorem proving is a problem whose steps can be ignored. We proceed by first proving a lemma that we think will be useful. Eventually we realize that the lemma is no help at all. Then there is no need to worry as we can just proceed as we should have been in the first place. All we have lost is the effort that was spent in exploring unsuccessful path.

Q. Give example of a problem whose steps can be undone.

Ans. 8-puzzle problem: Now suppose in solving the 8-puzzle problem, we make a stupid move, say move a tile into a wrong place. Then we can backtrack and undo the last move and move further. Mistakes can still be recovered from but not quite as easily as in the theorem proving problem. An additional step must be performed to undo each incorrect step. The control mechanism for an 8-puzzle solve must keep track of the order in which operations are performed so that the operations can be undone one at a time if necessary.

Q. Give example of a problem whose steps cannot be undone.

Ans. Game playing like tic-tac-toe or chess playing program are such problems where we cannot undo the changes after making a stupid move. Thus, the steps are irrecoverable. These can be solved by planning before taking a step.

Q. Give example of a problem whose universe is predictable.

Ans. Universe means the set of all possible moves that can occur in solving any problem. Based on this we can have certain-outcome problem which means that it is possible to plan an entire sequence of moves and be confident that we know what the resulting state will be. Example of this type of problems is 8-puzzle problem.

Q. Give example of a problem whose universe is unpredictable.

Ans. Universe means the set of all possible moves that can occur in solving any problem. Based on this we can have uncertain-outcome problem which means that it is difficult to know an entire sequence of moves. Example: card games like playing bridge. In this type of problems even planning is difficult. So we need to go for plan revision to take place as the plan is carried out and the necessary feedback is provided.

Q. Give example of a problem whose solution is a state.

Ans. The problem of finding a consistent representation of a sentence in natural language processing is an example where the solution is a state. For example, to find the consistent representation for the sentence "The bank manager ate a hot dog," the state of each word is required to be bound for the correct meaning of this sentence. The bank here is not a river bank but a financial institution. The hot dog is not an animal dog which is hot but a dish named hot dog.

Q. Give an example of a problem where good solution to the problem is obvious without comparison to all other possible solutions

Ans. These types of problems are known as any path problem. These problems can be solved in a reasonable amount of time by using heuristics that suggest good paths to explore. If the heuristics are not perfect, the search for a solution may not be as direct as possible, but that does not matter.

Consider the problem of answering questions based on a database of simple facts:

1. A student will get degree only if he/she registers as a student and pass his/her exam.
2. Ashima has registered herself as a student.
3. Ashima has passed her exam.
4. A student will get degree if he/she has GATE score more than 90%.
5. Ashima has GATE score 95%.

Suppose the question to be answered is "Will Ashima get a degree?" By representing each of these facts in a formal language, such as predicate logic, and then using formal inference methods, we can fairly easily derive an answer to the question. We can follow any of the below path:

Solution path 1: 2 and 3 are true hence from 1, Ashima will get a degree.

Solution path 2: From 4 and 5, Ashima will get a degree.

Q. Give an example of best path problem.

Ans. These types of problems are known as best path problem. These are computationally harder than any path problems. Here the heuristic used should be the one which could not miss the best solution.The heuristic is a function which defined the value of the function based on which we are to select the move. Acts an example, the distance travelled so far by the salesman is the heuristic function used in traveling salesman problem. So a more exhaustive search will be performed. In case of the traveling salesman problem, the best path with shortest distance will be any one and not any one. Thus we need to find that path only and no other path will be the solution.

Q. Give an example of a problem where good solution to the problem is not obvious without comparison to all other possible solutions

Ans. These types of problems are known as best path problem. These are computationally harder than any path problems. Here the heuristic used should be the one which could not miss the best solution. So a more exhaustive search will be performed. In case of the traveling salesman problem, the best path with shortest distance will be any one and not any one. Thus we need to find that path only and no other path will be the solution.

Q. Give example of a problem whose solution is a path.

Ans. Water jug problem: For this kind of problem, we need to report the path that leads to that state. You are given two jugs, an 8-Liter one and a 3-Liter one. Neither has any measuring marker on it. There is a pump that can be used to fill the jugs with water. How can you get exactly 2 Liters of water into the 8-Liter jug?

The state space for this problem can be represented as a set of ordered pairs of integers (x,y), where x represents the number of Liters of water in the 8-Liter jug and y represents the number of Liters of water in the 3-Liter jug ($x = 0,1,2,3,4,5,6,7,8$ and $y = 0,1,2,3$).

Start state is (0,0) and goal state is $(2,n)$ for any value of n (i.e., any amount of water in 3-Liter jug). The set of rules (operators) are give below:

1. Fill the 8-Liter jug: if $x < 8$ then $(x,y) \rightarrow (8,y)$
2. Fill the 3-Liter jug: if $y < 3$ then $(x,y) \rightarrow (x,3)$
3. Pour some water out of 8-Liter jug: if $x > 0$ $(x,y) \rightarrow (x-d,y)$
4. Pour some water out of 3-Liter jug: if $y > 0$ $(x,y) \rightarrow (x,y-d)$
5. Empty the 8-Liter jug on the ground: if $x > 0$ then $(x,y) \rightarrow (0,y)$
6. Empty the 3-Liter jug on the ground: if $y > 0$ then $(x,y) \rightarrow (x,0)$
7. Pour water from the 3-Liter jug into the 8-Liter jug until the 8-Liter jug is full

If $(x + y) \geq 8$ and $y > 0$ then $(x,y) \rightarrow (8,y-(8-x))$

8. Pour water from the 8-Liter jug into the 3-Liter jug until the 3-Liter jug is full

   If $(x + y) \geq 3$ and $x > 0$ then $(x,y) \rightarrow (x-(3-y),3)$

9. Pour all the water from the 8-Liter jug into the 3-Liter jug

   If $x + y \leq 3$ and $x > 0$ then $(x,y) \rightarrow (0,x + y)$

10. Pour all the water from the 3-Liter jug into the 8-Liter jug

    If $x + y \leq 8$ and $y > 0$ then $(x,y) \rightarrow (x + y,0)$

11. Pour 2 Liters from the 3-Liter jug into the 8-Liter jug

    $(0,2) \rightarrow (2,0)$

12. Empty the 2 Liters in the 8-Liter jug on the ground

    $(2,y) \rightarrow (0,y)$

In order to describe the operators completely, we had made some assumptions not mentioned in the problem statement. We have assumed that we can fill a jug from the pump, we can pour water out of a jug onto the ground, we can pour water from one jug into another and there are no other measuring devices available. Now we need a control strategy that loops through a simple cycle in which some rule whose left side matches the current state is chosen, the appropriate change to the state is checked to see if it corresponds to a goal state. As long as it does not, the cycle continues. One such sequence for water jug problem is given below:

Liters in the 8-Liter jug	Liters in the 3-Liter jug	Rule applied
0	0	
		1
8	0	
		8
5	3	
		6
5	0	
		8
2	3	

Hence we have got 2 Liters in 8-Liter jug. We can get many other sequences of steps for finding the solution of the water jug problem depending on the control strategy used.

Q. Give an example of a problem which needs huge knowledge for solving it?

Ans. Game playing problem like playing chess need a huge knowledge. All the possible states, initial state, all intermediate states and final states(total of about 10^{120}) must be stored in the knowledge base. All the rules for choosing the next step should be stored and checked before making a move. Since a move once taken cannot be reverted back, procedure for planning and look ahead should be a part of the program. Hence a huge knowledge is needed. Similarly, natural language processing need a huge knowledge for solving these problems as the rules and vocabulary of any natural language is very vast and it must be included in AI program.

Q. Give an example of a problem which needs huge knowledge for solving it?

Ans. Game playing problem like playing chess or natural language processing need a huge knowledge for solving these problems.

Q. Give an example of a problem which does not need huge knowledge for solving it?

Ans. Problem like 8-puzzle or blocks world does not need huge knowledge for solving it, only the knowledge of operators is required. There are only four operators possible in 8-puzzle, i.e. move left, move right, move up or move down. In case of blocks world, the operators are placing one block on the top of the other block whose top is clear, making the top of a block clear by removing the block on its top and third one, placing any block on a table.

Q. Give an example of a problem which does not need huge knowledge for solving it?

Ans. Problem like 8-puzzle or blocks world does not need huge knowledge for solving it, only the knowledge of operators is required.

Q. Give an example of a problem which needs human intervention for solving it?

Ans. Speech recognition is an application in AI which needs human intervention. Here the speech recognition program is required to recognize the input given by the human. A program takes one input and responds according to the interpretation of speech by it. Then it again needs next input so that it can produce the next output and so on.

Q. Give an example of a problem which needs human intervention for solving it?

Ans. Speech recognition is an application in AI which needs human intervention. Here the Speech recognition program is required to recognize the input given by the human.

Q. Give an example of a problem which does not need human intervention for solving it?

Ans. 8-puzzle is an example which does not need any human intervention for solving it. The human will input only initial state and final state and the program will find the solution. The AI program is to show all the intermediate states generated by taking moves and finally the final state.

Q. Give an example of a problem which does not need human intervention for solving it?

Ans. 8-puzzle is an example which does not need any human intervention for solving it. The human will input only initial state and final state and the program will find the solution path.

MULTIPLE CHOICE QUESTIONS

Select the most appropriate answer to the questions:

1. Which production systems are useful for solving theorem proving?
   (a) Partially commutative, non-monotonic (b) Not partially commutative, monotonic
   (c) Partially commutative, monotonic (d) Not partially commutative, non-monotonic
2. Which production system is useful for solving monkey and banana problem?
   (a) Partially commutative, non-monotonic (b) Not partially commutative, monotonic
   (c) Partially commutative, monotonic (d) Not partially commutative, non-monotonic
3. Which production system is useful for solving chemical synthesis problem?
   (a) Partially commutative, non-monotonic (b) Not partially commutative, monotonic
   (c) Partially commutative, monotonic (d) Not partially commutative, non-monotonic
4. Which production system is useful for chess playing?
   (a) Partially commutative, non-monotonic (b) Not partially commutative, monotonic
   (c) Partially commutative, monotonic (d) Not partially commutative, non-monotonic
5. 8-Puzzle is an example of which type of problem?
   (a) Ignorable (b) Recoverable

(c) Irrecoverable (d) All of these

6. Which of the problem has an unpredictable universe?
   (a) 8-puzzle (b) Bridge
   (c) Blocks world (d) Chess
7. Which of the following problems has state as a solution?
   (a) 8-puzzle (b) Blocks world
   (c) Water jug (d) None of these
8. Which of the following is any path problem?
   (a) Theorem proving (b) Chess
   (c) 8-Puzzle (d) All of these
9. Which of the following problems is decomposable?
   (a) 8-puzzle (b) Integration
   (c) Blocks world (d) None of these
10. Which of the following is best path problem?
    (a) 8-puzzle (b) Traveling salesman problem
    (c) Chess (d) None of these

Answers: 1. c 2. a 3. b 4. d 5. b 6. b 7. d 8. d 9. b 10. b

EXERCISES

1. Consider the following problems. Define its state representation and problem characteristics.
   (a) monkey and banana
   (b) missionaries and cannibals
2. You are given two jugs, a 5-Liter one and a 3-Liter one. Neither has any measuring marker on it. There is a pump that can be used to fill the jugs with water. How can you get exactly 2 Liters of water into the 5-Liter jug?
3. Categorize the following problems into ignorable, recoverable, or irrecoverable problems:
   (a) Water jug (b) 8-Puzzle
   (c) Chess (d) Theorem proving
4. Consider the given axioms:
   (a) Marcus was a man
   (b) Marcus was born in 1840
   (c) Marcus was a Pompeian
   (d) All Pompeians died when volcano erupted in 1879
   (e) No man lives longer than 100 years
   (f) It is now 2011

   Answer the question: Is Marcus dead now? Show that it is any path problem.

2

Search Algorithms

2.1 INTRODUCTION

In all AI problems, the algorithm needs to find a solution to a particular problem starting from a given initial state to reach goal state(s). Every problem has certain set of operators that can be used to move from one state to another. The set of all possible states including initial, goal, and intermediate states are known as a state space. The algorithm is required to search for a sequence of steps to be taken to find solution to the AI problem. So, search is the characteristic of all AI problems. The goodness of a search technique or method can be judged by the time taken by it to find a solution and the space required for storing the intermediate states as well as the solution path. This is done using big O notation measuring the time and space complexity of any search algorithm. We should know about the time and space complexity of the algorithm before selecting it for current problem to be solved. The search can be divided into two types: blind and informed.

Blind search occurs when we do not have any information about the direction in which we are going while searching. This is also called uninformed search. In these types of search, the nodes in the state space are explored mechanically until a goal is found or a failure occurs or the space is exhausted or certain time limit has reached. Examples of uninformed search algorithms are generate and test, depth-first search (DFS), breadth-first search (BFS), and DFS with iterative deepening.

When some information is available to guide the search through all possible states, the search algorithm is called an informed search. This information can be in the form of cost of each path to goal stated by means of a function called heuristic function. These include both the exact costs and the estimates of the costs in finding a solution through the current node. Branch and bound search, beam search, simple hill climbing, steepest ascent hill climbing, best-first search, greedy best-first search, A* algorithm, and A* algorithm with iterative deepening are examples of informed search methods. Some desirable properties of heuristic search algorithms are admissibility, optimality, completeness, and dominance.

Some of AI problems can be decomposed into subproblems and then they can be solved independently. In order to solve these problems, AND-OR graphs can be used. AO* algorithm can be used to solve these type of problems. In order to handle constraints in AI problems, constraint satisfaction and means ends analysis methods are used.

2.2 UNINFORMED SEARCH ALGORITHMS

Q. Explain DFS in AI.

Ans. Depth-first search is performed by moving downward in depth-first fashion in a search tree. The leftmost branch is explored first till either the goal node is found or the leaf node is reached. If the goal is found and only one goal was to be found, then the search terminates by giving the solution from root node to the goal node. Otherwise, backtracking is done for the elements from the right of the leaf node till the root node in the tree. If we reach the root node during backtracking and still the goal is not found, then the search continues again from the next leftmost branch which is not yet explored and then elements on right side from the bottom of the tree again up to root. It terminates as soon as the goal is found or till the complete search tree is explored to report all the solutions. DFS is implemented using a queue. The newly generated children are placed at the head of the queue so that they will be chosen first. The algorithm for DFS is

1. Place the starting node s on the queue.
2. If the queue is empty, then return failure and stop.
3. If the first element on the queue is a goal node g, then return success and stop. Otherwise,
4. Remove and expand the first element from the queue and place all the children at the **front** of the queue.
5. Return to step 2.

Explanation-Depth first search: Suppose the goal node is node I. Let us consider the graph given below.

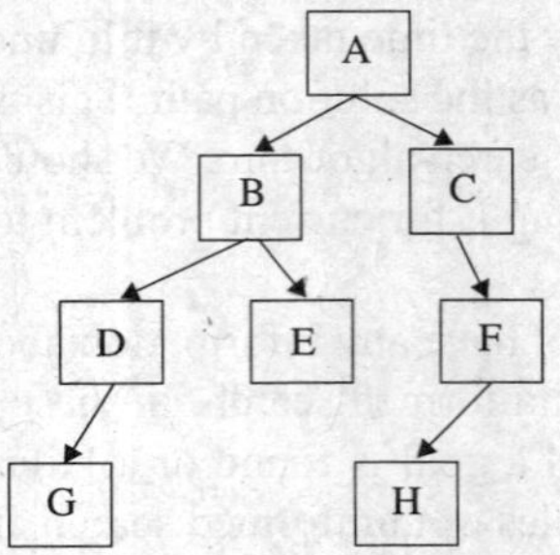

The starting node s is A. The initial queue is {A}.

Node A is removed from the queue and checked if it is the goal node. Since, it is not the goal node, the children of A, i.e. nodes B and C are put in the queue. The queue becomes {B, C}.

The first node in the queue i.e. node B is removed from the queue and checked if it is the goal node. Since, it is not the goal node, the children of B, nodes D and E are put in front of the queue. The queue becomes {D, E, C}.

The first node in the queue i.e. node D is removed from the queue and checked if it is the goal node. Since, it is not the goal node, the child of D, node G is put in front of the queue. The queue becomes {G, E, C}.

The first node in the queue i.e. node G is removed from the queue and checked if it is the goal node. Since, it is not the goal node, and there is no child of this node, the next node in the queue is checked i.e. node E. It is also not the goal node and their there is any child of this node.

The first node in the queue i.e. node C is removed from the queue and checked if it is the goal node. Since, it is not the goal node, the child of C, node F is put in front of the queue. The queue becomes {F}.

So the next node in the queue i.e. node F is checked. Since, it is not the goal node, the child of F, nodes H is put in the queue. The queue becomes {H}.

The next node in the queue i.e. node H is checked. Since, it is not the goal node and there is also no child of this node, so the list becomes empty. The breadth first search stops and reports no solution found.

The order of traversal of the nodes using depth first search is A→B→D→G→E→C→F→H.

In case the goal node is G, then the search would stop at G with traversal as A→B→D→G and the path would be A→B→D→G. This is found be tracking the parents of the goal node back to start node.

In case the goal node is E, the search would stop at E with traversal as A→B→D→G→E and the path would be A→B→E. This is found be tracking the parents of the goal node back to start node. Thus depth first search may or may not find the shortest solution.

In case the goal node is E, the search would stop at E with traversal as A→B→C→D→E and the path would be A→B→E. This is found be tracking the parents of the goal node back to start node. Thus breadth first search finds the shortest path to the solution.

Q. Explain BFS in AI.

Ans. Breadth-first search is performed by exploring all nodes at a given depth before proceeding to the next level. The space required for BFS is high if the branching factor (the average number of children of a node in the search tree) is large. Still it is used because it will always the shortest path to goal because we are exploring all nodes at one level before going to the next level. So, no goal is left at lower levels. It uses a queue structure to hold all generated but still unexplored nodes.

The algorithm for BFS is

1. Place the starting node s on the queue.
2. If the queue is empty, then return failure and stop.
3. If the first element on the queue is a goal node g, then return success and stop. Otherwise,
4. Remove and expand the first element from the queue and place all the children at the **end** of the queue.
5. Return to step 2.

Explanation- Breadth First Search: Suppose the goal node is node I. Let us consider the graph given below.

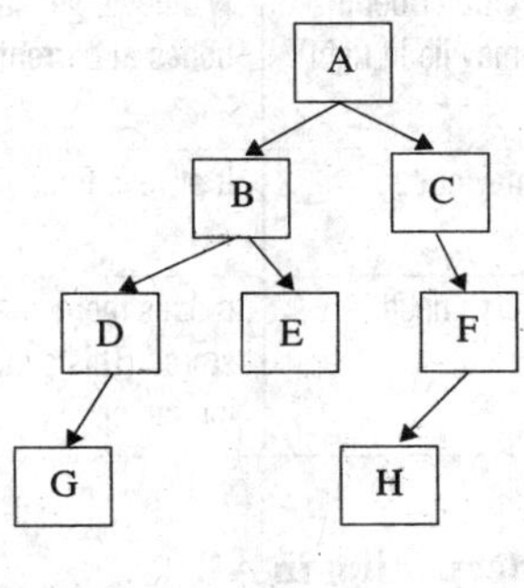

The starting node s is A. The initial queue is {A}.

Node A is removed from the queue and checked if it is the goal node. Since, it is not the goal node, the children of A, i.e. nodes B and C are put in the queue. The queue becomes {B, C}.

The first node in the queue i.e. node B is removed from the queue and checked if it is the goal node. Since, it is not the goal node, the children of B, nodes D and E are put in the queue. The queue becomes {C, D, E}.

The first node in the queue i.e. node C is removed from the queue and checked if it is the goal node. Since, it is not the goal node, the child of C, node F is put in the queue. The queue becomes {D, E, F}.

The first node in the queue i.e. node D is removed from the queue and checked if it is the goal node. Since, it is not the goal node, the child of D, node G is put in the queue. The queue becomes {G, E, F}.

The first node in the queue i.e. node G is removed from the queue and checked if it is the goal node. Since, it is not the goal node, and there is no child of this node, the next node in the queue is checked i.e. node E. It is also not the goal node and their there is any child of this node.

So the next node in the queue i.e. node F is checked. Since, it is not the goal node, the child of F, nodes H is put in the queue. The queue becomes {H}.

The next node in the queue i.e. node H is checked. Since, it is not the goal node and there is also no child of this node, so the list becomes empty. The breadth first search stops and reports no solution found.

The order of traversal of the nodes using breadth first search is A→B→C→D→E→F→G→H.

In case the goal node is G, then the search would stop at G and the path would be A→B→D→G. This is found be tracking the parents of the goal node back to start node.

Q. What are the advantages and disadvantages of DFS and BFS?

Ans. The DFS finds a solution quickly. It only stores the nodes at the current branch so the space requirement for DFS is less. It can be used to find all possible solutions. The space complexity of DFS is $O(b*d)$ where b is the branching factor of the search tree and d is the depth of the search tree while the time complexity is $O(b^d)$. The disadvantage of DFS is that it can be caught in a blind alley in finding the solution in a wrong direction along a high depth. The DFS may not find the optimal solution. BFS is sure to find the optimal solution. The space requirement for BFS is more since it needs to store all the nodes at level n before starting searching the solution at level $n + 1$. The space and time complexity of BFS is $O(b^d)$. This is very high when the branching factor for a search tree is large.

Comparison table for DFS and BFS

Depth First Search	Breadth First Search
Explores all nodes in depth first fashion	Explores node in breadth first fashion
May get caught in a blind alley i.e. searching at a greater depth in left part of the search space while the solution may lie in right part	Will never get caught in a blind alley because it explores all nodes at current level first i.e. at lower depths
It may find the first solution found which may or may not be optimal	It always finds the optimal solution if one exists
It uses less space because only nodes at current path need to be stored	It uses more space as all the nodes at current level needs to be stored. This space will increase with an increase in the branching factor.

Q. Explain DFS with iterative deepening in AI.

Ans. In order to solve the problem of blind alley, there is need to control the search at higher depth in DFS. So, DFS with iterative deepening is used in which the level of depth is fixed for searching the solution. It is also known as depth limited search. The search is started with a small depth say 2 or 3. If the solution is not found, then the level of depth is increased by one and search is performed again in a depth-first fashion. Thus, this deepening of depth continues till a solution is found.

Explanation- Depth first search with iterative deepening(DFSID): Suppose the goal node is node I. Let us consider the graph given below.

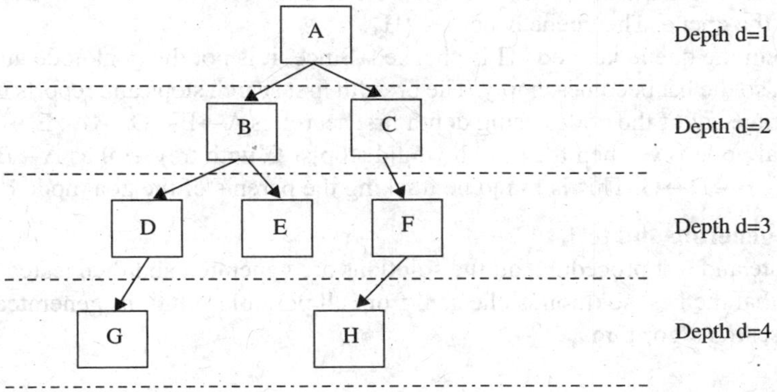

At depth d = 1, the starting node s is A. The initial queue is {A}. Since it is not a goal node, the DF-SID stops as the queue becomes empty and there is no goal found.

At depth d = 2, the starting node s is A. The initial queue is {A}. Node A is removed from the queue and checked if it is the goal node. Since, it is not the goal node, the children of A, i.e. nodes B and C are put in the queue. The queue becomes {B, C}. The first node in the queue i.e. node B is removed from the queue and checked if it is the goal node. Since, it is not the goal node, the next node C is checked if it is the goal node. The DFSID stops as the queue becomes empty and there is no goal found.

At depth d = 3, the starting node s is A. The initial queue is {A}. Node A is removed from the queue and checked if it is the goal node. Since, it is not the goal node, the children of A, i.e. nodes B and C are put in the queue. The queue becomes {B, C}. The first node in the queue i.e. node B is removed from the queue and checked if it is the goal node. The children of B, nodes D and E are put in front of the queue. The queue becomes {D, E, C}. The first node in the queue i.e. node D is removed from the queue and checked if it is the goal node. The queue becomes {E,C}. Since it is not the goal node, the next node in the queue i.e. node E is checked if it is the goal node. The queue becomes {C}. Since it is not the goal node, the next node in the queue i.e. node C is checked if it is the goal node. The child of node C i.e. node F is put in front of the queue. The queue becomes {F}. Now the node F is checked if it is the goal node. Since it is not the goal node and the queue becomes empty, so DFSID stops.

If the goal node is E, then the search will stop at depth d = 3 with the traversal as A→B→D→E. The path to goal will be A→B→E. Thus shortest path will be found by DFSID.

At depth d = 4, the starting node s is A. The initial queue is {A}.

Node A is removed from the queue and checked if it is the goal node. Since, it is not the goal node, the children of A, i.e. nodes B and C are put in the queue. The queue becomes {B, C}.

The first node in the queue i.e. node B is removed from the queue and checked if it is the goal node. Since, it is not the goal node, the children of B, nodes D and E are put in front of the queue. The queue becomes {D, E, C}.

The first node in the queue i.e. node D is removed from the queue and checked if it is the goal node. Since, it is not the goal node, the child of D, node G is put in front of the queue. The queue becomes {G, E, C}.

The first node in the queue i.e. node G is removed from the queue and checked if it is the goal node. Since, it is not the goal node, and there is no child of this node, the next node in the queue is checked i.e. node E. It is also not the goal node and their there is any child of this node.

The first node in the queue i.e. node C is removed from the queue and checked if it is the goal node. Since, it is not the goal node, the child of C, node F is put in front of the queue. The queue becomes {F}.

So the next node in the queue i.e. node F is checked. Since, it is not the goal node, the child of F, nodes H is put in the queue. The queue becomes {H}.

The next node in the queue i.e. node H is checked. Since, it is not the goal node and there is also no child of this node, so the list becomes empty. The breadth first search stops and reports no solution found.

The order of traversal of the nodes using depth first search is A→B→D→G→E→C→F→H.

In case the goal node is G, then the search would stop at G with traversal as A→B→D→G and the path would be A→B→D→G. This is found be tracking the parents of the goal node back to start node.

Q. Explain generate and test.

Ans. In generate and test procedure, all the solutions are generated and then tested for best solution. This is to ensure that the best solution is checked from all possible solutions generated. It is also called British Museum search algorithm.

Algorithm:

1. Generate a possible solution. For some problems, this means generating a particular point in the problem space. For others, it means generating a path from a start state.
2. Test to see if this is actually a solution by comparing the chosen point or the endpoint of the chosen path to the set of acceptable goal states.
3. If a solution has been found, then report it and quit. Otherwise, return to step 1.

It is a DFS procedure because complete solution must be generated before it can be tested. All the solutions need to be generated but they can be generated randomly. It is exhaustive search through the solution space.

Flow chart for Generate and Test

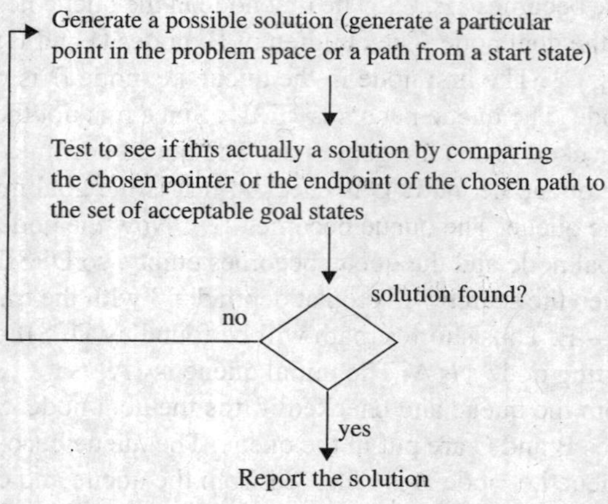

2.3 INFORMED SEARCH ALGORITHMS

Q. Define a heuristic function. How does heuristic search adds information in search?

Ans. A heuristic function is a function that provides an estimate of how much the current state is away from the goal state. This can provide direction for search by selecting the state that is nearest to the goal state by comparing the heuristic values of all current states.

As an example, consider the 8-puzzle. The heuristic functions can be :

(i) number of tiles misplaced from their required position in 3X3 matrix

(ii) number of tiles placed correctly according to their required position in 3X3 matrix

(iii) number of places each tile is placed away from its required position in 3X3 matrix

Q. Explain simple hill climbing problem solving in AI.

Ans. Hill climbing is a variant of generate and test method in which the feedback from the test procedure is used to help the generator decide which direction to move in the search space. It is like DFS where the most promising child is selected for expansion. The test function is augmented with a heuristic function that provides an estimate of how close a given state is to a goal state, the generate procedure can exploit it to find a good solution.

Algorithm for simple hill climbing:

1. Evaluate the initial state. If it is also a goal state, then return it and quit. Otherwise, continue with the initial state as the current state.
2. Repeat until a solution is found or until there are no new operators are left to be applied in the current state:
   (a) Select an operator that has not yet been applied to the current state and apply it to produce a new state.
   (b) Evaluate a new state:
      (i) If it is a goal state, then return it and quit.
      (ii) If it is not a goal state but it is better than the current state, then make it the current state.
      (iii) If it is not better than the current state, then continue in the loop.

Flow chart for Simple Hill Climbing

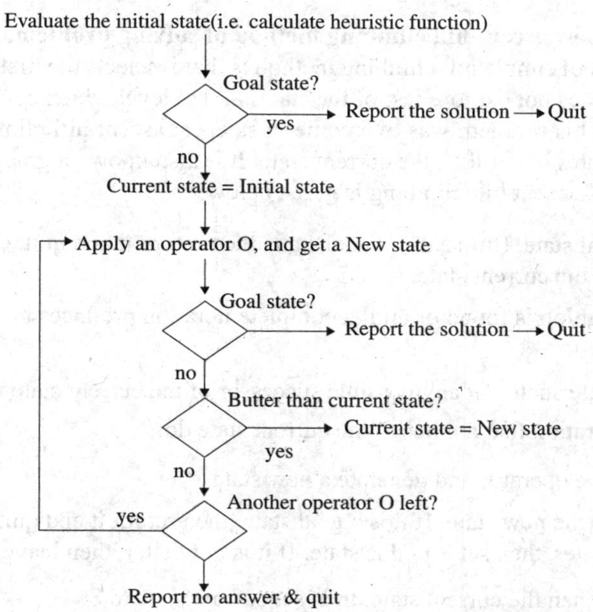

Explanation Simple Hill Climbing: Consider the solution state space shown in figure below:

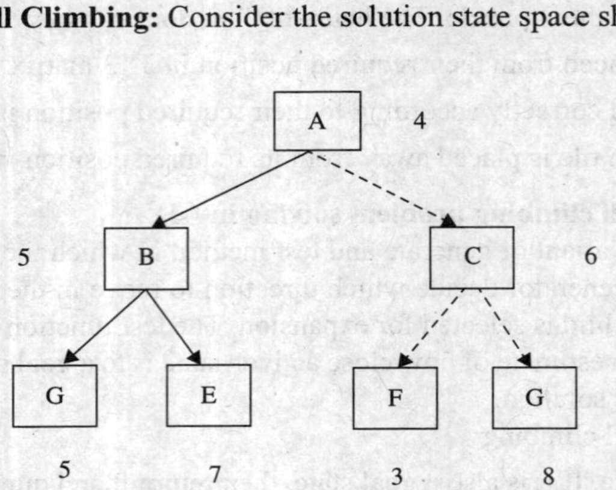

Here the start state is A with a heuristic function value 4. Suppose the better state is the one whose heuristic value is greater than its parent state. First successor B is generated by applying one operator to A. The heuristic function value of state B is 5. This is better than A. Hence the other successor C will not be generated using simple hill climbing. Now B will be considered as current state. Since it is not a goal state, its successor D will be generated by applying an operator. The value 5 of heuristic function of D may be better if we consider value equal to parent node as better. In that case, D is examined and if it is a goal state, it is reported as a solution, otherwise the algorithm returns failure. In case the value should be more than the parent in order to be considered better, D is not a better state. Then successor E of state B will be generated with heuristic function value as 7. Then it is examined whether it is a goal state or not. If yes, answer will be reported else the algorithm returns failure. If G was the optimal solution or goal state, it is not examined using simple hill climbing.

Q. Explain steepest ascent hill climbing method of solving problem.

Ans. The drawback of simple hill climbing method is that it selects the first state which is better than the current state and does not explore rest of the states at that level which could be even better than the selected better state. This problem was overcome in steepest ascent hill climbing that selects the best among the children states better than the current state. It is also known a gradient search.
Algorithm for steepest-ascent hill climbing is given below:

1. Evaluate the initial state. If it is also a goal state, then return it and quit. Otherwise, continue with the initial state as the current state.
2. Repeat until a solution is found or until a complete iteration produces no change to the current state:
   (a) Let S be a state such that any possible successor of the current state will be better than S.
   (b) For each operation that applies to the current state do:
      (i) Apply the operator and generate a new state.
      (ii) Evaluate the new state. If it is a goal state, then return it and quit. If not, compare it to S. If it is better, then set S to this state. If it is not better, then leave S alone.
   (c) If S is better than the current state, then set current state to S.

Flow chart Steepest Ascent Hill Climbing:

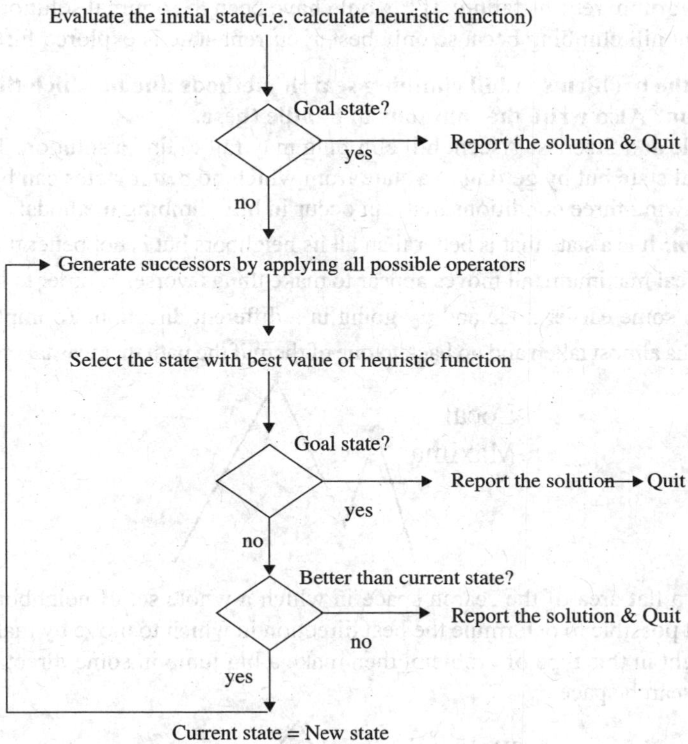

Explanation Steepest Ascent Hill Climbing: Consider the solution state space shown in figure below:

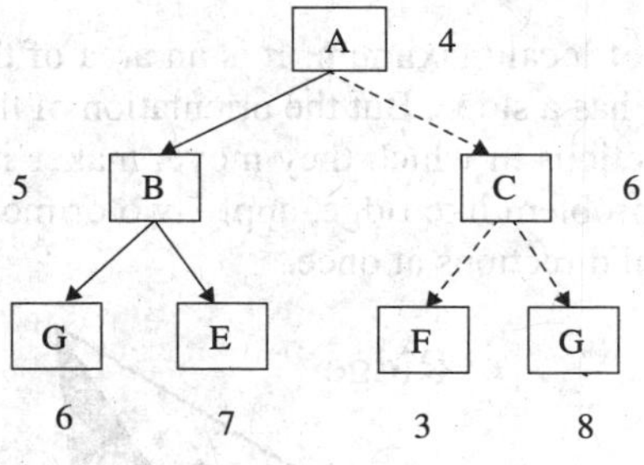

Here the start state is A with a heuristic function value 4. Suppose the better state is the one whose heuristic value is greater than its parent state. First both the successors B and C will be generated by applying operators to A. The heuristic function value of state B is 5 and that of C is 6. Both are better than A and C is best of both B and C. So C will be considered as current state. Since it is not a goal state, its successor F and G will be generated by applying the possible operators. The value 8 of heuristic function of G is better than C. So, it is examined whether it is a goal state or not. If yes, answer will be reported else the algorithm returns failure. If E would have been the optimal solution, it is not examined using steepest ascent hill climbing because only best at current state is explored further.

Q. What are the problems in hill climbing search methods due to which they may fail to find the solution? Also write the solutions to handle these.

Ans. Both Simple and Steepest-Ascent hill climbing may fail to find a solution. They may terminate not by finding a goal state but by getting to a state from which no better states can be generated. This is because of the following three conditions that can occur in hill climbing methods:

(a) ***A local maximum:*** It is a state that is better than all its neighbors but is not better than some other states farther away. At a local maximum, all moves appear to make things worse. In order to handle this situation, we can backtrack to some earlier node and try going in a different direction. To implement this strategy, maintain a list of paths almost taken and go back to one of them if the path that was taken leads to a dead end.

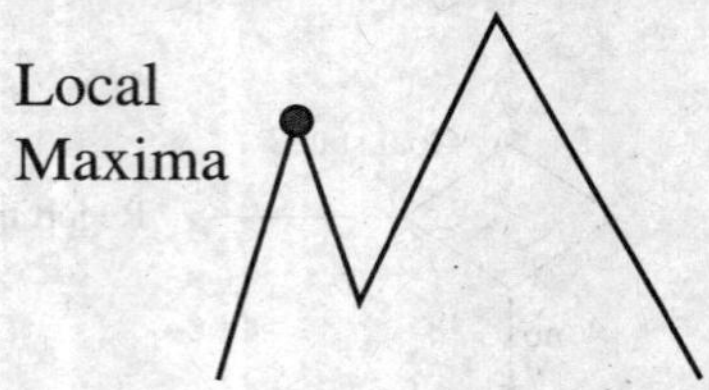

(b) ***A plateau:*** It is a flat area of the search space in which a whole set of neighboring states have the same value. It is not possible to determine the best direction in which to move by making local comparisons. If we are caught in this type of problem, then make a big jump in some direction to try to get to a new section of the search space.

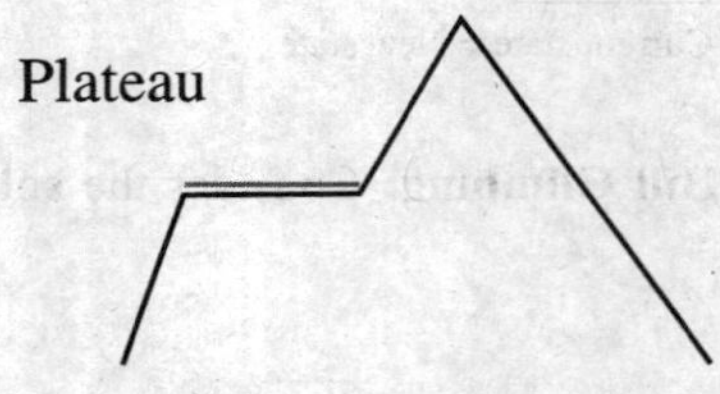

(c) ***A ridge:*** It is a special kind of local maximum. It is an area of the search space that is higher than surrounding areas and that itself has a slope. But the orientation of the high region, compared to the set of available moves and the directions in which they move, makes it impossible to traverse a ridge by single moves. In order to get a problem like ridge, apply two or more rules before doing the test. This corresponds to moving in several directions at once.

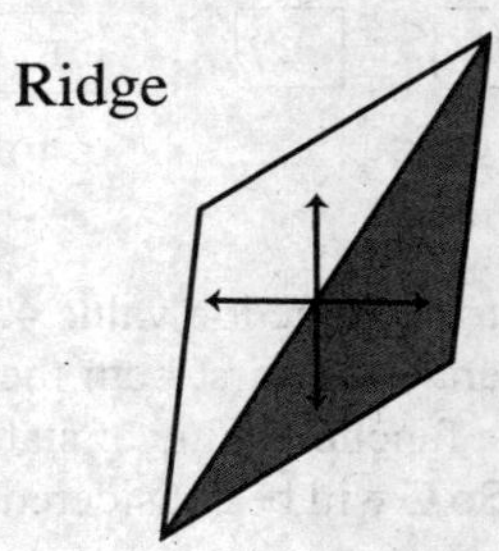

Q. Explain branch and bound search.

Ans. The branch and bound search strategy applies to problems having a graph search space where two nodes can have more than one alternative paths. Using branch and bound strategy, all the path lengths, i.e., costs are selected from a node to all generated nodes are saved. Then the new path lengths will be compared with all old ones and the shortest path will be chosen for expansion. This way, any path to a goal node is certain to be a minimal length path.

The algorithm used in branch and bound search is as follows:

1. Place the start node of zero path length on the queue.
2. Until the queue is empty or a goal node has been found:
   (a) Determine if the first path in the queue contains a goal node.
   (b) If the first path contains a goal node, then exit with success.
   (c) If the first path does not contain a goal node, then remove the path from the queue and form new paths by extending the removed path by one step.
   (d) Compute the cost of the new paths and add them to the queue.
   (e) Sort the paths on the queue with lowest cost paths in front.
3. Otherwise, exit with failure.

Q. Explain beam search.

Ans. Beam search is a heuristic search algorithm in which W number of best nodes at each level is always expanded. It uses BFS to build the search tree. At each level of the tree, it generates all successors of the states at the current level, and sorts them in order of increasing heuristic values, but considers only W number of states with best heuristic values at each level and ignores the rest. W is called the width of the beam search. If the branching factor is B, then only W*B nodes will be considered at each level. If width is infinite then no states are pruned and hence it is same as BFS, otherwise there is risk that the goal state may be pruned. So, it cannot guarantee to find the optimal solution.

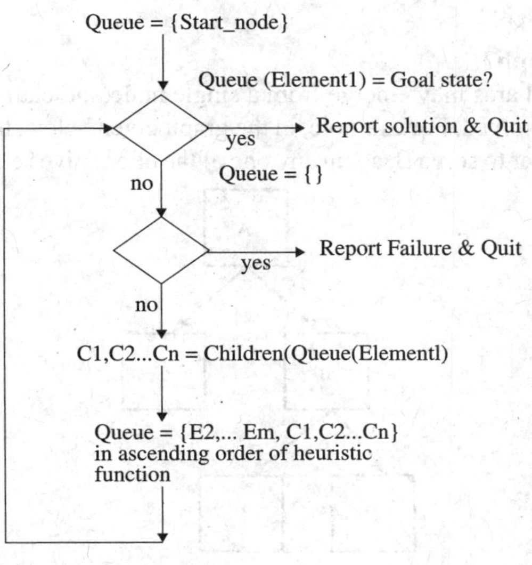

Q. Explain best-first search.

Ans. In order to solve a problem in AI, a directed graph is required in which each node represents a point in the problem space. OR graph can be used since each of its branches represents an alternative problem solving path. The main aim of using best-first search algorithm is to combine the advantages of BFS and DFS. The advantage of BFS is that the optimal path lies at upper levels rather than in depth of the tree. The advantage of DFS is to save the space in storing all the nodes at one level before going to the next level. Also, it eliminates the disadvantage of steepest ascent hill climbing that it selects only the best among the current level and still leaves other nodes unexplored. In order to keep track of the nodes that have been visited, i.e., whose nodes have been generated and which are still to be explored. The algorithm of best-first search uses the following steps:

1. Place the starting node Start on the queue of node.
2. If the queue of nodes is empty, then return failure and exit.
3. If the first element on the queue of nodes is a goal node G, then return success and exit. Otherwise,
4. Remove the first element from the queue, expand it and compute the estimated goal distances for each child. Place the children on the queue of nodes and re-arrange all the elements in the queue in ascending order corresponding to goal distance from the front of the queue.
5. Go to step 2.

The best-first search algorithm is useful due to following reasons:

1. It combines the advantages of breadth first search (BFS) and depth first search (DFS). It can take the direction of search in either breadth wise or depth wise. It uses the advantage of BFS, i.e. it finds optimal path at upper levels of the tree. It uses the advantage of DFS in saving the space in storing all the nodes only in current branch.
2. It eliminates the disadvantage of steepest ascent hill climbing (SAHC). SAHC selects only the best node at the current level and does not explore other nodes later. The best first search selects node best node at current level and also keeps track of the nodes that have been visited but are still unexplored.

The algorithm is shown below:

Q. What is an OR graph?

Ans. In an OR graph, several arcs may emerge from a single node, indicating a variety of ways in which the original problem may be solved. For example, in the graph given below, there are two alternative ways of solving A, B, and C. In order to solve B, again any one of the alternatives can be taken, i.e., either D or E.

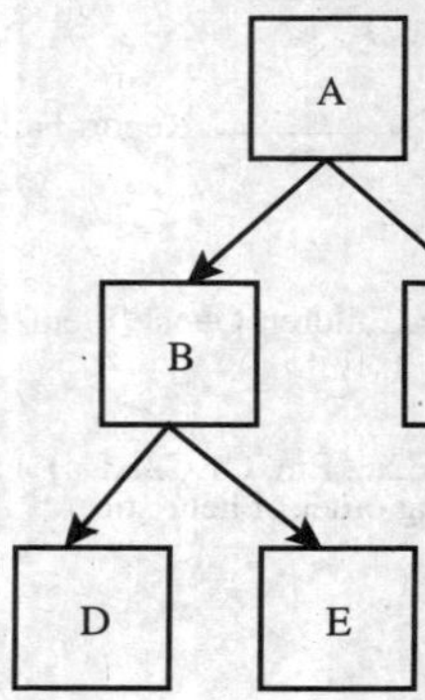

Q. What is an AND-OR graph?

Ans. AND-OR graph (or tree) is useful for representing the solution of problems that can be solved by decomposing them into a set of smaller problems, all of which then must be solved. This decomposition generates AND arcs. So, if both AND arcs and OR arcs are present in the graph (or tree), then it is called AND-OR graph (or tree). For example, in the graph given below, there is an AND arc between nodes B and C. This means, in order to solve A, both B and C will have to be solved. However, in order to solve node B, any one of the alternative, either D or E can be chosen as there is an OR arc between them.

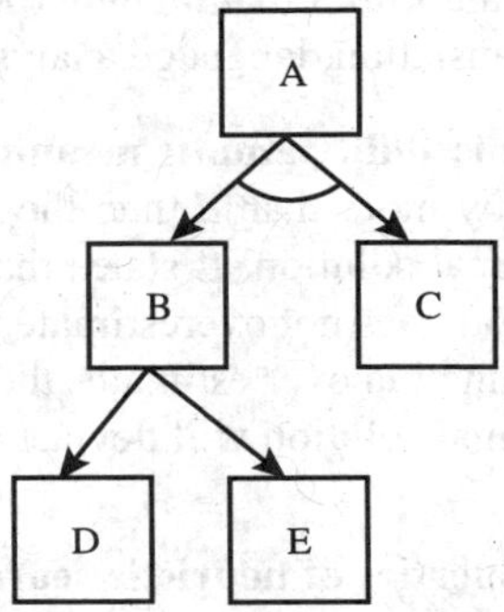

Q. Explain greedy best-first search.

Ans. Greedy best-first search tries to expand the node that is closest to the goal assuming it will lead to a solution quickly. Here, the implementation strategy is expanding the "most desirable" node into the fringe queue and sort the queue in decreasing order of desirability. For example, consider the straight-line distance heuristic which states expand the node that appears to be closest to the goal. It can also get stuck in loops and there is no guarantee of optimal solution.

Q. State A* algorithm and its applications.

Ans. Best-first search is a simplification of A* algorithm. It was given by Hart *et al*. The A* search method is an informed search method that uses a heuristic function of the form:

$$f^*(n) = g^*(n) + h^*(n)$$

Here, $g^*(n)$ is the estimate of the cost of getting to the node n from the start node. $h^*(n)$ is the estimate of the cost from node n to the goal node. The * indicates the estimates of the corresponding true values $f(n) = g(n) + h(n)$. For state space tree problems, $g^*(n) = g(n)$ since there is only one path and the distance $g^*(n)$ will be known to be the true minimum from the start to the current node n. This is not true in case of graphs because alternate paths from start node to n may exist.

Two lists are maintained in this algorithm: OPEN and CLOSED. Nodes on the OPEN list are the ones that have been generated but not yet expanded. It is a priority queue. The nodes on the CLOSED list are the ones that have been expanded and whose children are available to the search procedure.

The algorithm for A* is as follows:

1. Place the starting node s on the list OPEN.
2. If the list OPEN is empty, then stop and return failure.
3. Remove the node n from the list OPEN that has the smallest value of $f^*(n)$. Return success and stop if it is a goal node. Otherwise, go to step 4.

4. Expand n, generating all of its successors $n`$ and place $n$ on list CLOSED. For every successor $n`$ if $n`$ is not already on lists OPEN or CLOSED attach a back pointer to $n$, compute $f^*(n`)$ and place it on the list OPEN.
5. Each $n`$ that is already on OPEN or CLOSED should be attached to back pointers that reflect the lowest $g^*(n`)$ path. If n` was on the list CLOSED and its pointer was changed, then remove it and place it on the list OPEN.
6. Return to step 2.

There are several applications of A* algorithm that include routing problems, resource planning problems, speech recognition, machine translation, language analysis, robot motion planning, etc.

Q. State graceful decay of admissibility and its meaning.

Ans. If h' rarely overestimates h by more than d then the A* algorithm will rarely find a solution whose cost is d greater than the optimal solution. It states that the A* algorithm will find an optimal solution provided the heuristic function does not overestimate the optimal cost.

It also means that if the heuristic function over estimates the cost, then A* algorithm will not be able to find the optimal solution. The optimal solution will deviate atleast by the amount the cost was overestimated by the heuristic function.

Q. Explain some desirable properties of heuristic search algorithms.

Ans. There are many desirable properties of heuristic search algorithms:

1. *Admissibility*: Algorithm A is admissible if it is guaranteed to return an optimal solution when one exists.
2. *Completeness*: Algorithm A is complete if it always terminates with a solution when one exists.
3. *Dominance*: Let A1 and A2 be admissible algorithms with heuristic estimation functions $h1^*$ and $h2^*$, respectively. A1 is said to be more informed than A2 whenever $h1^*(n) > h2^*(n)$ for all n. A1 is said to dominate A2.
4. *Optimality*: Algorithm A is optimal over a class of algorithms if A dominates all members of the class.

Q. Explain iterative deepening A*.

Ans. Iterative-deepening A* (IDA*) works as follows: at each iteration, perform a DFS, cutting off a branch when its total cost $(g + h)$ exceeds a given threshold. This threshold starts at the estimate of the cost of the initial state, and increases for each iteration of the algorithm. At each iteration, the threshold used for the next iteration is the minimum cost of all values that exceeded the current threshold.

Steps in iterative deepening A* algorithm are

1. Set threshold value = the heuristic evaluation function value of the start state.
2. Perform a DFS to find the solution path. During searching, any branches that have value of the heuristic evaluation function more than the Threshold value are to be pruned/eliminated for search. If the solution path is found, then return it and quit. Otherwise, go to step 3.
3. Update the Threshold value by the minimum amount it was exceeded during the previous step.
4. Go to step 2.

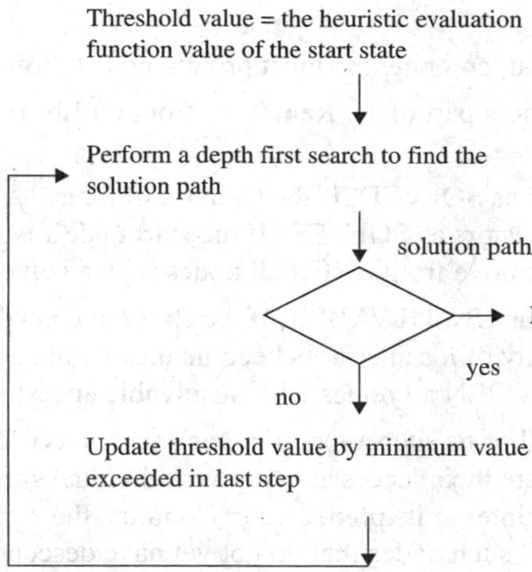

Q. Differentiate between best first, greedy best first, and A* algorithms.

Ans. Best-first search is a general heuristic search where minimal cost nodes are expanded first. Greedy best-first search is best-first search with the estimated cost to reach the goal as a heuristic measure. It is faster than uninformed search but cannot guarantee optimal solution and is not complete. A* search algorithm is the best-first search with path cost so far and the estimated path cost to goal. It combines the advantages of uniform cost and greedy searches. It is complete, optimal, and optimally efficient.

Best First Search	Greedy Best First Search	A* search algorithm
It is a general heuristic search where minimal cost nodes are expanded first	It is best-first search with the estimated cost to reach the goal as a heuristic measure	It is the best-first search with path cost so far and the estimated path cost to goal. It combines the advantages of uniform cost and greedy searches.
	It is faster than uninformed search but cannot guarantee optimal solution and is not complete.	It is complete, optimal, and optimally efficient.

2.4 PROBLEM REDUCTION

Q. Explain AO* algorithm and its applications.

Ans. AND-OR graphs are useful for certain problems where the solution involves decomposing the problem into smaller problems. This is also called problem reduction. Here, the alternatives often involve branches where some or all must be satisfied before we can progress. As in the case of the A* algorithm, we use the OPEN list to hold nodes that have been generated but not expanded and the CLOSED list to hold nodes that have been expanded. It requires that nodes traversed in the tree be labeled as SOLVED or UNSOLVABLE in the solution process to account for AND node solutions which require solutions to all successor nodes. A solution is found when the start node is labeled as SOLVED. The steps in AO* algorithm are

1. Place the start node s on OPEN.
2. Using the search tree constructed thus far, compute the most promising solution tree T_0.
3. Select a node n that is both on OPEN and a part of T_0. Remove *n* from OPEN and place it on CLOSED.
4. If *n* is a terminal goal node, then label *n* as SOLVED. If the solution of *n* results in any of *n*'s ancestors being solved, label all the ancestors as SOLVED. If the start node *s* is solved, exit with success where T_0 is the solution tree. Remove from OPEN all nodes with a solved ancestor.
5. If *n* is not a solvable node, then label *n* as UNSOLVABLE. If the start node is labeled as UN-SOLVABLE, then exit with failure. If any of *n*'s ancestors become unsolvable because *n* is label from unsolvable as well. Remove from OPEN all nodes with unsolvable ancestors.
6. Otherwise, expand node *n* generating all of its successors. For each such successor node that contains more than one subproblem, generate their successors to give individual subproblems. Attach to each newly generated node a back pointer to its predecessor. Compute the cost estimate *h** for each newly generated node and place all such nodes that do not yet have descendents on open. Next, recomputed the values of *h** at *n* and each ancestor of *n*.
7. Return to step 2.

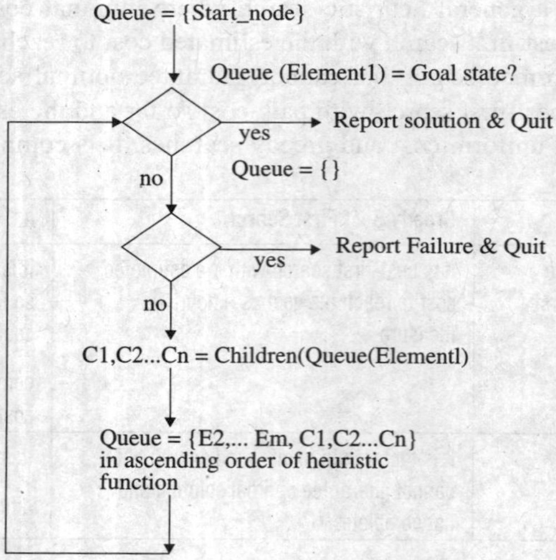

Q. Explain the method of Means End Analysis.

Ans. Means ends analysis relies on a set of rules that can transform one problem state into another. The left side of the rule describes the preconditions: the conditions that must be met for the rule to be applicable. The right-hand side of the rules indicates those aspects of the problem state that will be changed by the application of the rule. A separate data structure called a difference table indexes the rules by the differences that they can be used to reduce. The means ends analysis process centers around the detection of differences between the current state and the goal state. Once such a difference is isolated, an operator that can reduce the difference must be found. But that operator cannot be applied to the current state. So, we set up a subproblem of getting to a state in which it can be applied. This kind of backward chaining in which operators are selected and then subgoals are set up to establish the preconditions of the operators is called operator subgoaling. If the subgoals are such that we can apply the operator, then it is easy to solve the subproblems rather than the original problem. Thus, the effectiveness of the operator is that it is able to reduce the difference. We can also assign priority levels to the differences so that the higher priority difference can be considered before the lower priority ones.

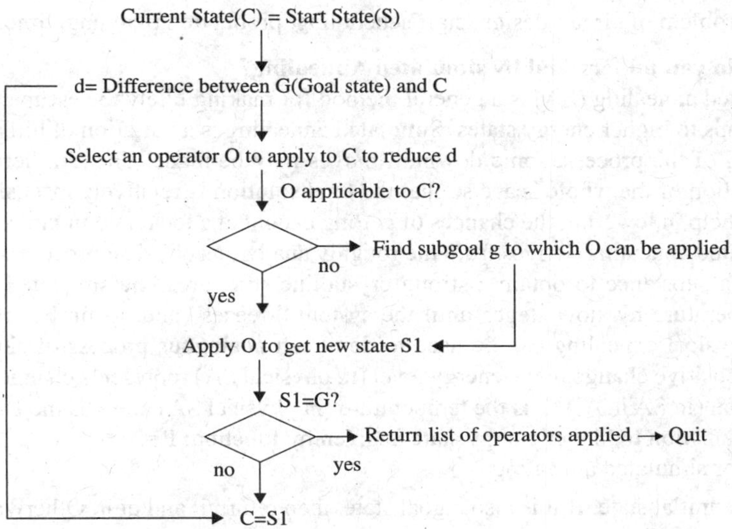

Q. What do you understand by constraint satisfaction? Give one application.

Ans. Constraint satisfaction is a search procedure that operates in a space of constraint sets. The initial state contains the constraint that is originally given in the problem description. A goal state is any state that has been constrained "enough" where "enough" must be defined for each problem. In order to define a constraint satisfaction problem (CSP), following should be specified:

Inputs: $<V, D_V, C_V>$

V: It is the set of variables $v_1, v_2, \ldots$ in the CSP

D_V: It specifies the domain for each variable – dom(v_i) in the CSP

C_V: It indicates all the constraints on values of variables in the CSP

Outputs: It is a model where assignment of values to variables are done so that all values val(v_i) are in dom(v_i) and all the constraints are satisfied.

It is a two-step process. First, all initial constraints are identified and propagated as far as possible throughout the system. Then, if there is still not a solution, then we need to search. We make a guess about something and add as a new constraint in the set of constraints. Then again, we propagate this new constraint to find the solution. The level of constraints can make the search easier or difficult. A unary constraint involves only a single variable ($variable_1 \neq value_1$), a binary constraint involves two variables ($variable_1 \neq variable_2$) and high-order constraints involve three or more variables ($variable_1 > variable_2$) Λ ($variable_2 < variable_3$) Λ ($variable_4 \neq variable_3$).

Q. Give examples of problems which can be represented as CSPs.

Ans. There are many problems in various areas in real life that can be represented as CSP.

1. Artificial intelligence: problem of temporal reasoning.
2. Bioinformatics: problem of sequence alignment.
3. Computer graphics: problem of geometric coherence.

4. Control theory: problem of controllers for sensory based robots.
5. Database systems: problem of constraint databases.
6. Operation research: problem of optimization.
7. Real life: problem of circuit design, staff scheduling, production planning, time table, etc.

Q. What do you understand by simulated Annealing?

Ans. Simulated annealing (SA) is a general method for making likely the escape from local minima by allowing jumps to higher energy states. Simulated annealing is a variation of hill climbing in which, at the beginning of the process, some downhill moves may be made. The aim here is to do an early detailed exploration of the whole space so that the final solution is relatively insensitive to the starting state. This may help in lowering the chances of getting caught at a local maximum, a plateau or a ridge. The term simulated annealing derives from the roughly analogous physical process of **heating** and then **slowly cooling** a substance to obtain a strong crystalline structure. The simulated annealing process lowers the temperature by slow stages until the system "freezes" and no further changes occur. The properties of physical annealing can be used to define an analogous process of simulated annealing. Here, ΔE is the positive change in the energy level (in physical SA) represents change in the value of the objective function (in SA in AI). T is the temperature (in physical SA) and k is the Boltzmann constant. Probability of transition to higher energy state is given by function: $P = e^{-\Delta E/kt}$.
The algorithm for simulated annealing is

1. Evaluate the initial state. If it is also a goal state, then return it and quit. Otherwise, continue with the initial state as the current state.
2. Initialize BEST_TILL_NOW to the current state.
3. Initialize T according to the annealing schedule.
4. Loop until a solution is found or until there are no new operators left to be applied in the current state.
   (a) Select an operator that has not yet been applied to the current state and apply it to produce a new state.
   (b) Evaluate the new state. Compute:
   $$E = (\text{value of current}) - (\text{value of new state}).$$
      (i) If the new state is a goal state, then return it and quit.
      (ii) If it is not a goal state, but it is better than the current state, then make it the current state. Also, set BEST_TILL_NOW to this new state.
      (iii) If it is not better than the current state, then make it the current state with probability p'. Generating a random number generator to produce a number in the range [0, 1]. If the number is less than p', then the move is accepted. Otherwise, do nothing.
   (c) Revise T as necessary according to the annealing schedule.
5. Revise BEST_TILL_NOW as the answer.

It is necessary to select an annealing schedule that has three components:

(a) Initial value to be used for temperature.
(b) Criteria that will be used to decide when the temperature will be reduced.
(c) Amount by which the temperature will be reduced.

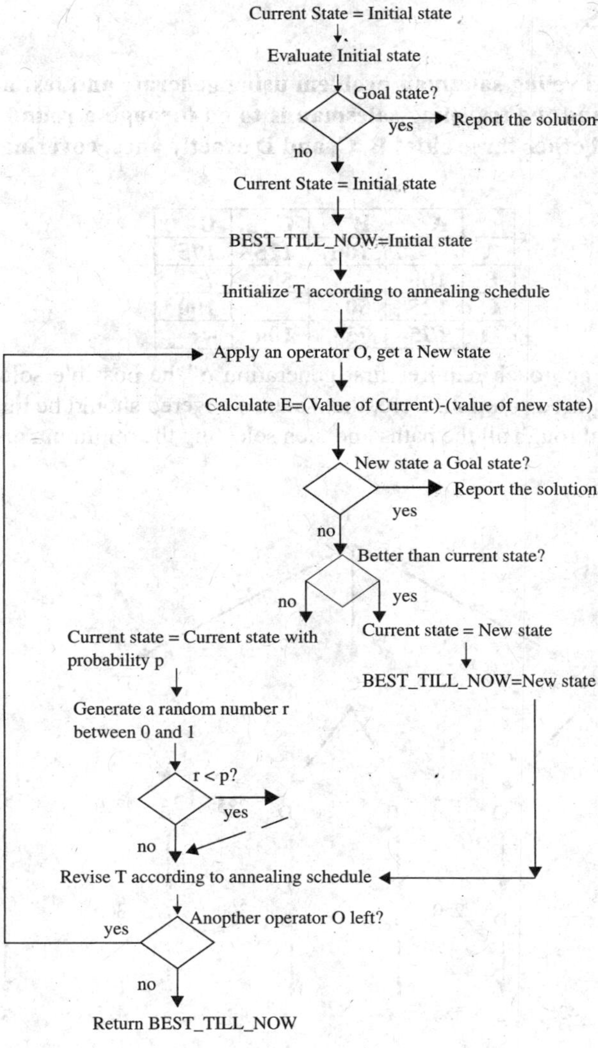

Q. What is the difference between simulated annealing and hill climbing?

Ans. There are three differences between simulated annealing and hill climbing methods:

Simulated Annealing	Hill Climbing
The annealing schedule must be maintained	There is nothing as annealing schedule
Moves to worse states may be accepted	Move to worse state is not accepted
It is good idea to maintain, in addition to the current state, the best state found so far.	Best state found so far is not maintained

SOLVED EXAMPLES

Q. Solve the given traveling salesman problem using generate and test method. Assume the source city is A and the traveling salesman is to go through a round trip from city A to city A, visiting all other three cities B, C, and D exactly once, covering minimum possible distance path.

	A	B	C	D
A	-	100	125	175
B	100	-	50	75
C	125	50	-	100
D	175	75	100	-

Ans. Generate and test approach requires first generation of the possible solution to the problem and then to test if it is a required solution. Here, the distance covered should be minimum that requires checking distance covered through all the paths and then selecting the minimum distance path. The tree generated for this is

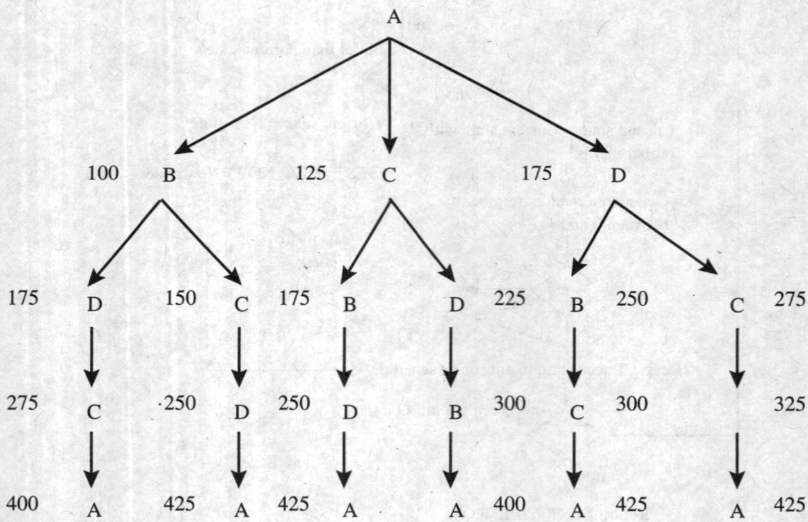

It shows there are two possible paths where the distance is minimum:
A→B→D→C→A and A→C→D→B→A with a total distance of 400.

Q. Find the solution to 8-puzzle problem using DFS algorithm.

Initial state

2		3
1	8	4
7	6	5

Goal state

1	2	3
8		4
7	6	5

Ans. The search space tree for the above problem is shown below:
The DFS sequence will be A→B→E→J→K

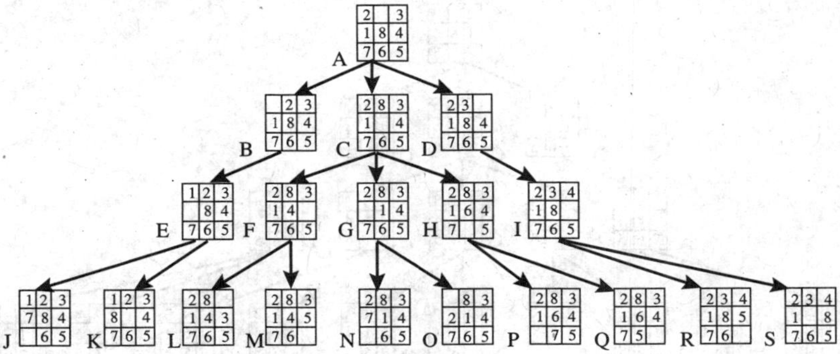

Figure 2 State Space Search Tree for 8-Puzzle Problem

The solution path is A→B→E→K.

Q. Solve the above problem using DFS with iterative deepening.

Ans. We start from second level, i.e., the list of first successor nodes.

At depth = 2

The nodes generated during traversal of the search tree are A→B→C→D.

No goal found. So, increase the depth of search.

At depth = 3

The nodes generated during traversal of the search tree are A→B→E→C→F→G→H→DI.

No goal found. So, we again increase the depth of search.

At depth = 4

The nodes generated during traversal of the search tree are A→B→E→J→K, and this is the goal node. So, the solution is found and the solution path is A→B→E→K.

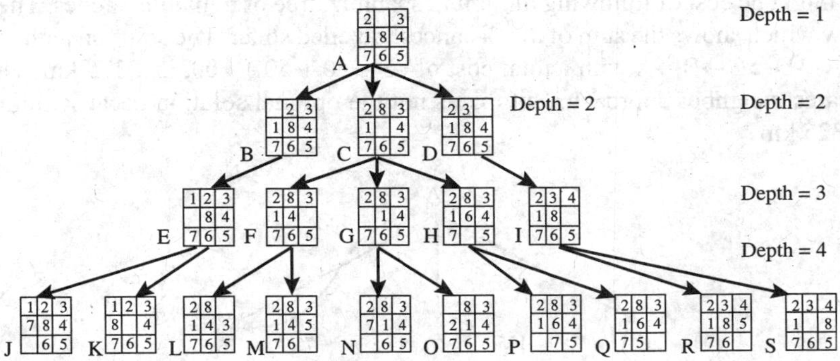

Q. Find the solution to 8-puzzle problem using BFS algorithm.

Initial state

2		3
1	8	4
7	6	5

Goal state

1	2	3
8		4
7	6	5

Ans. The search space tree for the above problem is shown in figure below.

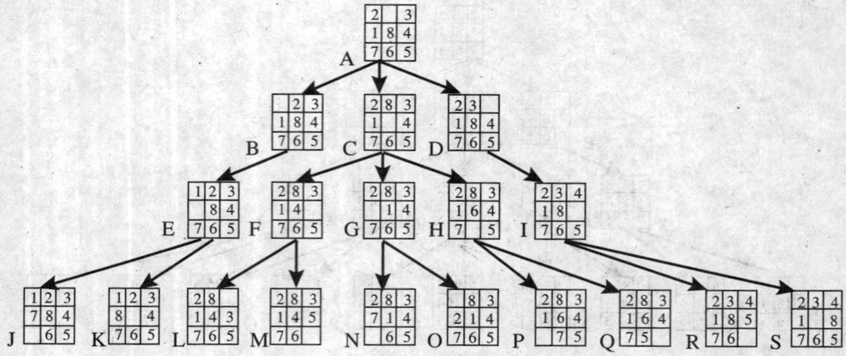

The DFS sequence will be A→B→C→D→E→F→G→H→I→J→K.
The solution path is A→B→E→K.

Q. Solve the given traveling salesman problem using branch and bound search algorithm. Assume the source city is A and the traveling salesman is to go through a round trip from city A to city A, visiting all other three cities B, C, and D exactly once, covering minimum possible distance path.

	A	B	C	D
A	-	200	125	75
B	200	-	50	75
C	125	50	-	50
D	75	75	50	-

Ans. Branch and bound search might use DFS by considering the cost so far is sum of costs of chosen edges. Bound might be cost of following minimum spanning tree of remaining nodes. The complete tree is shown below which shows the sum of the distances travelled so far. The solution path taken by branch and bound is A→D→C→B→A with a total cost of 75 + 50 + 50 + 200, i.e., 375 km. This approach is also called nearest neighbor approach. But this is not the optimal solution because minimum distance possible was 325 km.

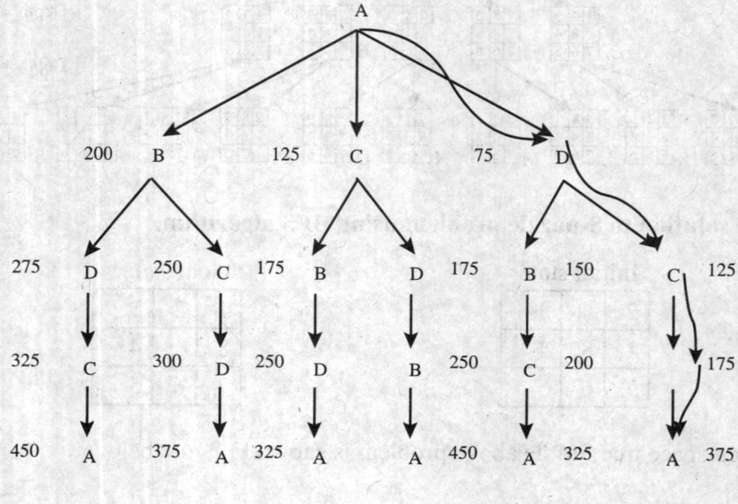

Q. Find the solution path to the blocks world problem using simple hill climbing method. State the heuristic used.

Initial state	Goal state
A	D
D	C
C	B
B	*A*

Ans. The available moves are follows: We can place a block whose top is empty on the table. We can place a block on the top of another block whose top is empty.

Suppose we use the following heuristic function: Add one point for every block that is resting on the thing it is supposed to be resting on. Subtract one point for every block that is sitting on the wrong thing. Using this function, the goal state has a score of 4. The initial state has a score of 0 (1(D) + 1(C)–1(B)–1(A)). There is only one move from initial state, place A on the table. Then, the heuristic value is 2 (1(D) + 1(C) + 1(A)–1(B)). Since it is a better state, the hill climbing method will accept that move.

Istate1		Goal state
		D
	D	C
	C	B
A	*B*	*A*

From this new state, there are two possible moves, leading to the two states:

Istate2			Goal state
			D
			C
		C	B
A	*D*	*B*	*A*

Score: (1(C)–1(D)–1(B) + 1(A)) = 0

Istate3		Goal state
		D
		C
D	C	B
A	B	*A*

Score: (1(C)–1(D) + 1(A)–1(B)) = 0

Here, the hill climbing method will halt because all these states have lower score than the current state. The process has reached ***a local maximum***. To solve this problem, it is necessary to disassemble a good local structure because it is in the wrong global context.

Suppose we use the new modified heuristic function: For each block that has the correct support structure (i.e., the complete structure underneath it is exactly as it should be), add one point for every block in the support structure. For each block that has an incorrect support structure, subtract one point for every block in the existing support structure.

Using this function, the goal state has the score 6 (0(A) + 1(B) + 2(C) + 3(D)). The initial state has the score of –6 (–3(A)–0(B)–1(C)–2(D)). Moving A to the table yields a state with a score of –3 (0(A)–

0(B)–1(C)–2(D)). The next two states are follows: Istate2 (score: –1) and Istate3 (score –2). This time simple hill climbing will choose move Istate2 which is the correct one.

	D
	C
	B
A D B C	*A*
Istate4	Goal state

Score: (0(C)–0(D)–0(B) + 0(A)) = 0 (better than Istate2 score –1)

	D
	C
B	B
C D A	*A*
Istate5	Goal state

Score: (0(C)–0(D) + 1(B) + 0(A)) = 1 (better than Istate4 score 0)

	D
C	C
B	B
D A	*A*
Istate6	Goal state

Score: (2(C)–0(D) + 1(B) + 0(A)) = 2 (better than Istate5 score 1)

D	D
C	C
B	B
A	*A*
Istate7	Goal state

Score: (2(C) + 3(D) + 1(B) + 0(A)) = 6 (Goal state)

Solution path: Initial state → Istate1 → Istate2 → Istate4 → Istate5 → Istate6 → Istate7

A D C → B	D C → A B	C → A D B	→ A D B C	B → A D C	C B → A D	D C B A

Q. Find the solution to 8-puzzle problem using steepest ascent hill climbing. State the heuristic function used.

Initial state

2		3
1	8	4
7	6	5

Goal state

1	2	3
8		4
7	6	5

Ans. The heuristic used is number of tiles misplaced from the goal position. The goal can be treated as the 3 × 3 matrix and the numbered tiles are matched against there position in the goal matrix.

1	2	3
4	5	6
7	8	9

The calculation is done as follows: The numbered tile 1 should be placed at first row and first column, i.e., at position 1 in the goal matrix but it is also placed at second row and first column, i.e., position 4 in the initial state. So, it is counted as misplaced tile. Similarly, the numbered tiles 2 and 8 are not in their required positions, i.e., 2 and 4, respectively. So, these all will be counted as misplaced tiles. The numbered tile 5 should be placed at third row and third column, i.e., at position 9 in the goal matrix and it is also placed at position 9 in the initial state. So, it will not be counted as misplaced tiles. Similarly, the numbered tiles 3, 4, 6, and 7 are at their correct positions in the initial states. So, these will not be counted as misplaced tiles. The correct positioning of the empty tile may also be included in calculations, but it is not included here to reduce the calculations. So, the total number of misplace tiles for the initial state is 3(f*(A)). In a similar way, the heuristic function value is calculated at each node. The following figure shows the steps taken during steepest ascent hill climbing method for solving the above 8-puzzle problem.

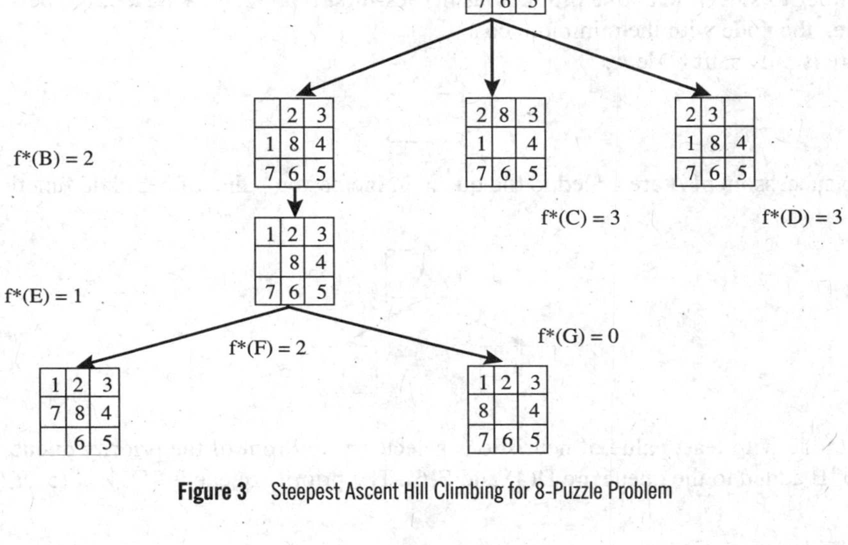

Figure 3 Steepest Ascent Hill Climbing for 8-Puzzle Problem

Solution path: A→B→E→G.

Q. Suggest some other heuristics that can be used for 8-puzzle problem.

Ans. A number of heuristics can be used for solving 8-puzzle problem:

(a) Number of tiles placed at correct positions as in goal state. In this case, the node with increasing value will be considered better.

(b) +1 for each tile at its correct position (i.e., as in the goal state) and –1 for each tile at its wrong position (i.e., not as in the goal state). This is not a good heuristic because it will cause problems like local maxima and plateau.

(c) The number of places each numbered tile is away from its goal position (i.e., difference between rows and columns between current and goal positions)

Q. Consider the search tree shown below. Find the solution path using to goal node G using best-first search.

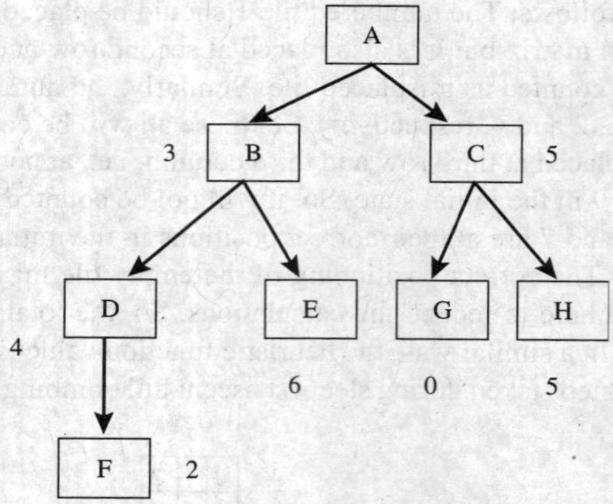

Ans. In order to solve the above problem using best-first search, at each step, the best successor is expanded, i.e., the node with the minimum cost.

Step 1: There is only start node A.

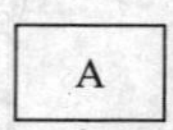

Step 2: Two successors of A are added to the queue in increasing value of heuristic function: B(3) and C(5).

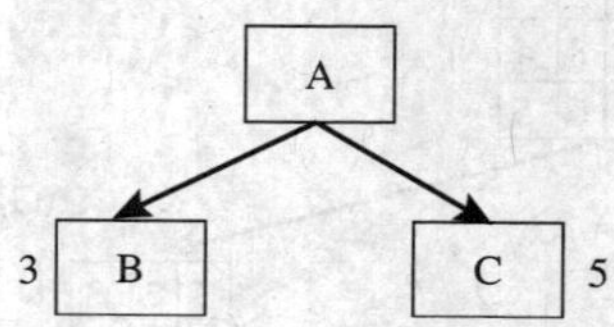

Step 3: The node with least value of heuristic is selected from front of the priority queue, i.e., B. The successors of B added to the queue are D(4) and E(6). The priority queue is {D(4), C(5), E(6)}.

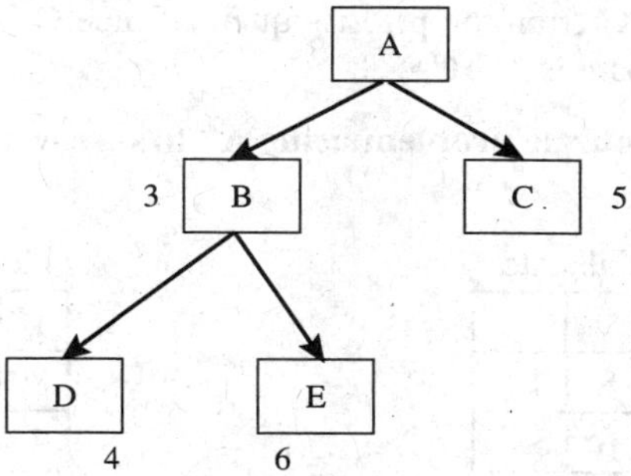

Step 4: The node with least value of heuristic is selected from front of the priority queue, i.e., D. The successor of D, i.e., F(2) is added to the priority queue. The new priority queue is {F(2), C(5), E(6)}.

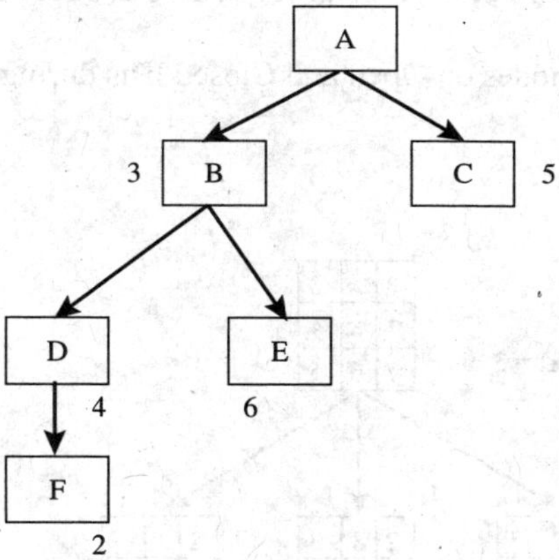

Step 5: The next node expanded is F. Since there is no successor of F and it is also not the goal node, the next node in the priority queue, i.e., C is expanded. The successors of C added are G(0) and H(5). The priority queue is {G(0), H(5), E(6)}.

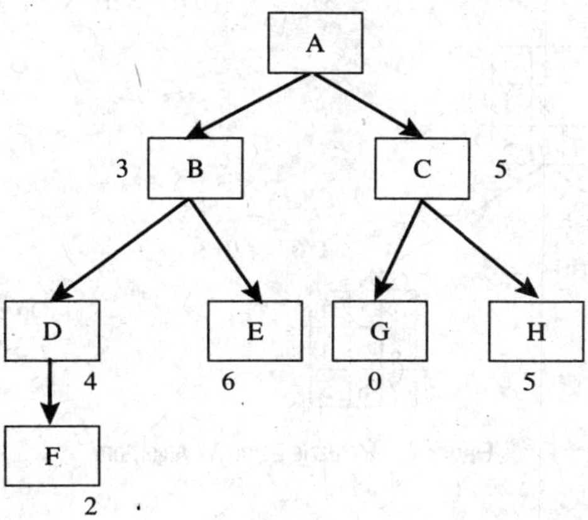

Step 6: Next node expanded is G from the priority queue. Since G is the goal node, no node will be further expanded. The solution path is A→C→G.

Q. Find the solution to 8-puzzle problem using A* first search algorithm. State the heuristic function used.

Initial state

2		
1	8	4
7	6	5

Goal state

1	2	3
8		4
7	6	5

Ans. The heuristic h^* = Number of tiles misplaced from the goal position. The cost of going from start node to current node is the number of steps taken to reach current node from start node. It is taken as g which is incremented by 1 for each level starting with 0 at start node. The heuristic function value is $f^* = h^* + g$.

The following figure shows the nodes on Open and Closed lists during A* for solving the above 8-puzzle problem.

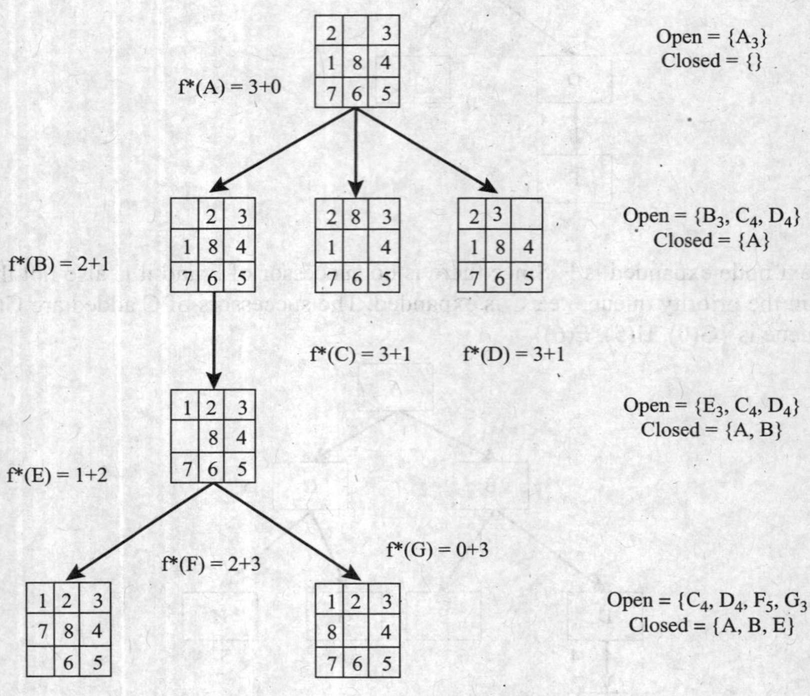

Figure 4 8-Puzzle Using A* Algorithm

Solution path: A→B→E→G.

Q. Find the solution path to solve problem A using AO* algorithm for the tree given.

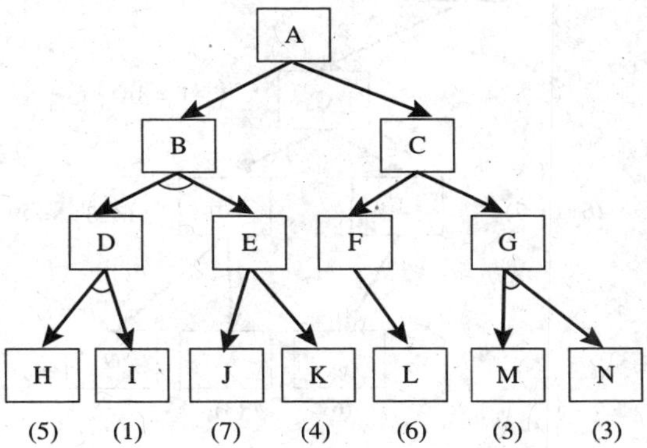

Ans. The above problem contains both AND and OR arcs. At each step, the least cost node will be chosen for expansion. The values will be propagated up from the leaf node to parent node to indicate the cost of solving that node.

Step 1: The cost of solving A through B is 16. In order to solve B, both D and E need to be solved. In order to solve D, both H and I need to be solved. So, the cost of solving D is 8 which is calculated as the sum of the cost of solving H(5) + cost of solving I(1) + cost of these 2 arcs (2). There are two ways to solve E, either through J with cost 8(7 + 1) or through K with cost 5(4 + 1). So, least cost path E is chosen. Thus, total cost of solving B is cost of solving D(8) + cost of solving E(5) + cost of these two arcs (2), i.e., 15. So, if A is solved through B, then the total cost is 16 (15 + 1).

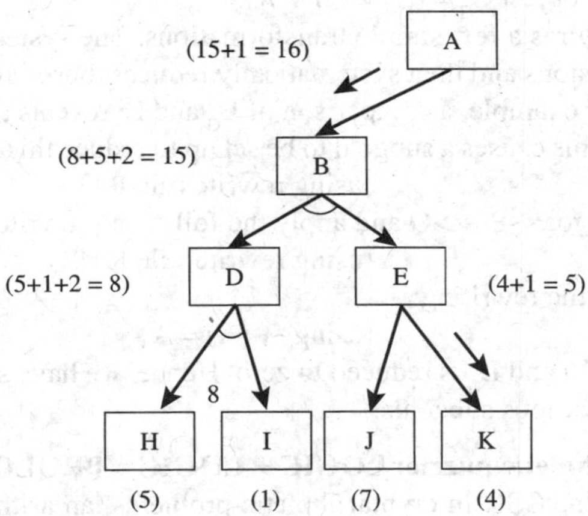

Step 2: The second option is to solve A through C. C can be solved either through F or G. The cost of solving F is 7 which is sum of solving L(6) and the cost of one arc, i.e., 1. The cost of solving G is 8 which is the sum of cost of solving M(3) and cost of solving N(3) and the cost of these two arcs, i.e., 2. The least cost path for solving C is 8 through F. the cost of solving A through C is 9 (8 + 1).

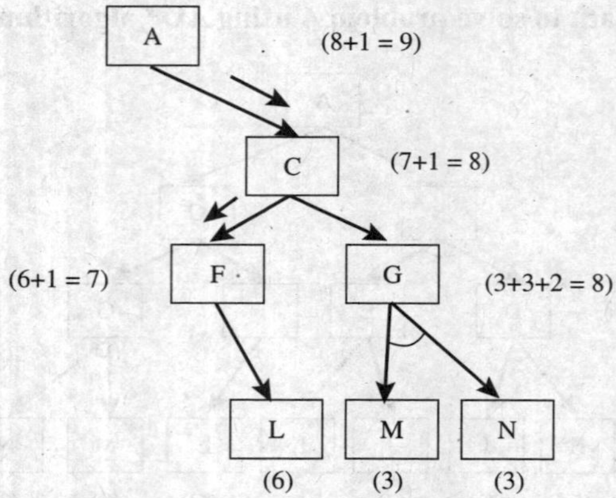

Step 3: The least cost path for solving A is through C with cost 9 which is less than cost of solving A through B, i.e., 16. So, the solution through C will be selected.
The solution path is A→C→F→L.

Q. Give an example of a problem which can be solved using Means End Analysis.

Ans. Let we assume the General problem Solver operators are rewrite rules of the following form:
R1: (A V B)→(B V A)
R2: (A & B)→(B & A)
R3: (A→B)→(~B→~A)
R4: (A→B)→(~A V B)
As a simple example, we suppose General problem Solver is given the initial propositional logic object L_i = (R V (~P→Q)) and goal object L_G = ((P V Q) V R).
To determine L_G from L_i requires a few simple transformations. The system first determines the difference between the two expressions and then systematically reduces these differences until L_G is obtained from L_i or failure occurs. For example, a comparison of L_G and Li reveals the difference that R is on the left in Li but on right in L_G. This causes a subgoal to be set up to reduce this difference. Li is rewritten as:
Li_1 = ((~P→Q) V R) {using rewrite rule R1}
Next, we try to solve the subgoal ~P→ >Q and apply the following rewrite rule R4:
Li_2 = ((~~P V Q) V R) {using rewrite rule R4}
First subgoal still requires some rewriting:
Li_3 = ((P V Q) V R) {using ~~(A) = A}
Now the difference between Li and L_G is reduced to zero. Hence, we have solved the problem by reducing the differences between various subgoals.

Q. Solve the cryptarithmetic puzzle: LOGIC + LOGIC = PROLOG

Ans. Let we first define this CSP. In cryptarithmetic problems, an arithmetic equation is given. Instead of digits, alphabets are written in the equation. The digits from 0 to 9 can be assigned to all the alphabets. Constraints are that no two alphabets can have the same value and the values assigned should satisfy the given arithmetic equation.

```
  C4 C3 C2 C1
   L O G I C
  +L O G I C
  P R O L O G
```

Initial state:

Initially rules for propagating constraints generate the following additional constraints:

1. 2C = G or 2C = G + 10
2. G is even
3. C1 + 2I = O or C1 + 2I = O + 10
4. C2 + 2G = L or C2 + 2G = L + 10
5. C3 + 2O = O or C3 + 2O = O + 10
6. C4 + 2L = R + 10 and P = 1 or C4 + 2L = R and P = 0.

Now this list of initial constraints is complete, now we need to generate some more constraints based on some guess. Let we guess for the value which is used in many places and that letter is O. There are two possible values for O, either O = 0 with C3 = 0 and C4 = 0 or O = 9 with C3 = 1 and C4 = 1. Let us take O as 0. Then, the initial set of constraints is modified as follows: O = 0, C3 = 0, C4 = 0, I = 5, C1 = 0, C2 = 1, C < 51`. 2C = G, C < , C1 = 0.

3`. C1 = 0, 2I = 0 + 10, i.e., I = 5, C2 = 1

4`. 1 + 2G = L, C3 = 0

Again, we are to make a guess. Let we take P = 1

6`. C4 = 0, 2L = R + 10, L > 5

Again let us take G = 4

C = 2, L = 1 + 8 = 9, R = 8.

The solution is L = 9 O = 0 G = 4 I = 5 C = 2 P = 1 R = 8.

```
 9 0 4 5 2
+9 0 4 5 2
1 8 0 9 0 4
```

Q. Give example of map coloring problem in constraint satisfaction.

Ans. Map coloring problem is to color the nodes of the graph so that no two adjacent nodes are the same color.

Formal definition is

Variables (V): nodes

Domains (D_V): same for each variable for every i, dom(v_i) = the set of colors

Constraints (C_V): mathematically, a set of permissible tables, i.e., for every pair of variables x and y, a table for all the allowed values of x and y.

Example: Color a very simple graph with three nodes, two edges, and two colors red and yellow.

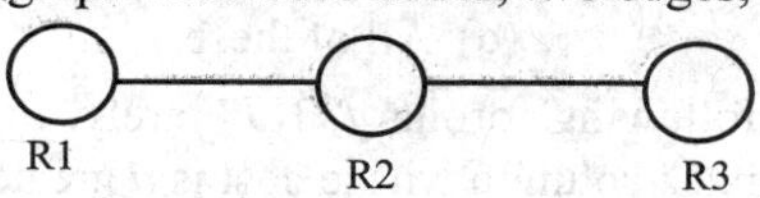

Formal representation is V: {R1, R2, R3}

D_V: dom(R1) = {red, yellow}

dom(R2) = {red, yellow}

dom(R3) = {red, yellow}

C_V:

R1	R2
Red	Yellow
Yellow	Red

R2	R3
Red	Yellow
Yellow	Red

Solution:
The solutions can be found by using natural join operator:

R1	R2
Red	Yellow
Yellow	Red

$\bowtie$

R2	R3
Red	Yellow
Yellow	Red

=

R1	R2	R3
Red	Yellow	Red
Yellow	Red	Yellow

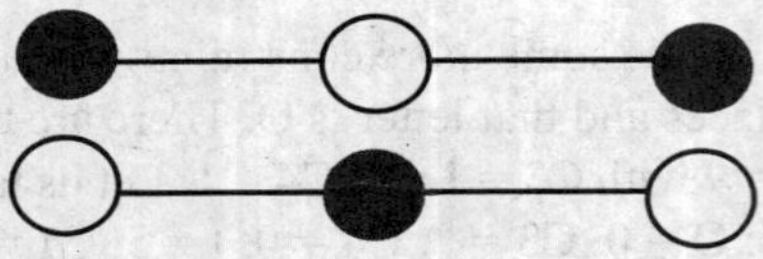

MULTIPLE CHOICE QUESTIONS

Select the most appropriate answer to the questions:

1. The time taken to search through N cities using generate and test approach for travelling salesman problem is proportional to which of the following?
   (a) (N-1)! (b) N!
   (c) N*(N-1) (d) None of these
2. Which of the following is often used when a good heuristic function is available for evaluating states but when no other useful knowledge is available?
   (a) DFS (b) BFS
   (c) Hill climbing (d) All of these
3. Steepest ascent hill climbing takes what time in selecting a move as compared to simple hill climbing?
   (a) Less (b) More
   (c) Equal (d) None of these
4. What is a flat area of the search space called in which a whole set of neighboring states have the same value?
   (a) Local maxima (b) Plateau
   (c) Ridge (d) All of these
5. What is the condition for the following corollary? If *h'* rarely ___________ h by more than d then the A* algorithm will rarely find a solution whose cost is *d* greater than the optimal solution?
   (a) Overestimates (b) Underestimates
   (c) Guesses (d) None of these
6. In A* algorithm, nodes on which list are the ones that have been generated but not yet expanded?
   (a) Closed (b) Main
   (c) Open (d) All of these

7. The nodes on which of the following list are the ones that have been expanded and whose children are available to the search procedure?
   (a) Closed (b) Main
   (c) Open (d) All of these
8. The A* algorithm finds which of the solution if one exists?
   (a) Good (b) Better
   (c) Optimal (d) None of these
9. Which of the following graphs are useful for solving decomposable problems?
   (a) AND (b) OR
   (c) Directed (d) AND-OR
10. In Means End Analysis, the effectiveness of the operator is that it is able to which of the following to the difference?
   (a) Increase (b) Improve
   (c) Reduce (d) Iterate.

Answers: 1. b 2. c 3. b 4. b 5. a 6. c 7. a 8. c 9. d 10. c

EXERCISES

1. Consider an example of problem where branching factor is very high. Will BFSwork better in this case than DFS? Justify your answer.
2. Consider the traveling salesman problem with the following distances:

	A	B	C	D
A	-	100	120	170
B	100	-	150	170
C	120	150	-	150
D	170	170	150	-

   If the starting city is B, then find the path for minimum distance during a round trip. Use any heuristic method.
3. Which of the hill climbing variant gives better solution and which method takes less time in selecting the moves?
4. Solve the following Blocks world problem using DFS.

Initial state	Goal state
A	D
D	C
C	B
B	*A*

5. Solve the following 8-puzzle problem using simple hill climbing. State the heuristic used.

Initial state

2	3	
1	8	4
7	6	5

Goal state

1	2	3
8		4
7	6	5

6. Solve the following 8-puzzle problem using best-first search. State the heuristic used.

Initial state

1		3
4	2	5
7	8	6

Goal state

1	2	3
4	5	6
7	8	

7. Solve the cryptarithmetic puzzle:

```
   S E N D
 + M O R E
 =M O N E Y
```

3

Game Playing

3.1 INTRODUCTION

Game playing is a challenging task for Artificial Intelligence (AI) researchers. Performance of the human expert utilizes a vast amount of domain-specific knowledge and procedures. Such knowledge allows the human expert to generate a few promising moves for each game situation. In contrast, when selecting the best move, a program playing the game exploits brute-force computational speed to explore as many alternative moves and consequences as possible. As the computational speed of modern computers is increasing, the game programs are succeeding. Also the game playing was a good domain for machine intelligence as it provided a structured task and limited knowledge. For playing the game, the only knowledge required was about the rules of playing a particular game and then measuring the success or failure. There are many games for which successful programs have been developed in AI. These include playing chess, checkers, tic-tac-toe, 8-puzzle, Grundy's game, go, backgammon, and Othello. The best example is Deep Blue's win over Gary Kasparov in chess.

Q. Explain the history of game playing.

Ans. Game playing is an area that is fascinating for AI researchers. In 1950, Claude Shannon described the mechanisms for playing chess in a research paper. In 1953, Charles Babbage designed analytical engine to play chess. He also designed the engine for playing tic-tac-toe. After this, Alan Turing described a chess-playing program. In 1960, Arthur Samuel succeeded in building the first significant, operational game playing program for checkers. The program could play checkers and learn from its mistakes and improve its performance.

Q. Give examples of various games which can be played on computer. Give the main features used in solving these.

Ans. There are many games which can be played using computers. These can be divided into single-player, two-player, or multiplayer games. Single-player games include 8-puzzle, 15-puzzle, etc. Two-player games include chess, checkers, Go, Othello, backgammon, tic-tac-toe, Nim, etc. Multiplayer games which involve more than two players include card games like Bridge, etc. All of these have different goals and hence different AI techniques can be used to solve these. However, one thing is common that the game tree which needs to be generated to find the solution for the game. The characteristics considered for specifying each game include knowledge representation scheme used, the timing and space requirements, and the algorithm used for finding the optimal solution.

The history is summarized below:

1960's : SpaceWar, First computer games and Chess
1970's: Pong, Space Invaders, Galaxian, tic tac toe
1980's: Karate Champ, Pac Man
1990's: Madden Football, Dune II, WarCraft, Battlecruiser 3000AD, Deep Blue
2000's: Black and White, Collin McRae Rally 2

3.2 THE MINIMAX SEARCH PROCEDURE

Q. What is adversarial search?

Ans. Game playing is different in many respects from other search problems. First, the moves are not in player's hands. It is difficult to predict the opponent's moves. Second, since there are two players, there is always a time limit or there is a chance of opponent's win, it is advisable to select approximate move instead of waiting for the optimal move. Adversarial search is used in game playing which uses heuristic search. One example is minimax search.

Q. Explain minimax search procedure.

Ans. The minimax algorithm is a specialized search algorithm which returns the optimal sequence of moves for a player in a zero-sum game. The initial state is the board position and information on which player moves first. The successor function returns a list of (move, state) pairs which each indicate a legal move and the resulting state. The terminal test determines when the game is over. Ending states are called terminal states. The utility function assigns a numeric value to the terminal states. For example, if the options are win, lose, or draw, the terminal values might be +1, −1, and 0, respectively. These states and legal moves form the game's search tree.

Q. How the move is selected using minimax algorithm?

Ans. Given a minimax search tree, the optimal strategy can be determined by examining the minimax value of each node. This value indicates the utility (for MAX) of being in a certain state, assuming both players play optimally. The minimax value of the terminal state is its own utility. Given a choice, MAX chooses to move to a state of maximum value and MIN chooses a state of minimum value. The minimax algorithm computes the minimax decision for the current state by recursively computing the minimax values of each successor state. The recursion proceeds to the leaves of the game tree, and then the minimax values are backed up through the tree to give the final value.

The steps taken are:

1. Generate the search tree from the current position till the depth d of the tree which is selected as d-ply search.
2. Compute the static evaluation function, i.e., heuristic value of the leaf nodes at depth dz.
3. Propagate the values till the current position on the basis of the payer:
   (a) If it is the turn of MAX player, generate the successors of the current position, apply minimax to each of the successors, and return the maximum of the results.
   (b) If it is the turn of MIN player, generate the successors of the current position, apply minimax to each of the successors, and return the minimum of the results.

Q. Explain how the two players are represented and how do they take moves.

Ans. In a two-player game, searching for an optimal move is difficult because the moves of the other player must be taken into account when deciding a sequence of moves. Two players are considered: MAX (representing the player wishing to win) and MIN (representing the opponent that should not be allowed to win). During the game, MAX makes a move in the initial state. MIN makes its move from all possible responses resulting from MAX's moves. MAX chooses move from the states resulting from every possible response generated by MIN's moves, and so on. An optimal solution will only be reached if the opponent is assumed to be infallible. In the game tree that results from the minimax algorithm, each level represents a move by either MAX or MIN, called a ply.

Suppose the first move is to be taken by player MAX. He is to select a move from steps B and C from the start state A . He is to select the maximum of the two. But he will not select unless he sees the next moves by the opponent player MIN. The player MIN will select the minimum values. Among D and E nodes, he will select node D as it has the minimum value 5. Among F and G nodes, he will select node G as it has the minimum value 3 as shown in figure below:

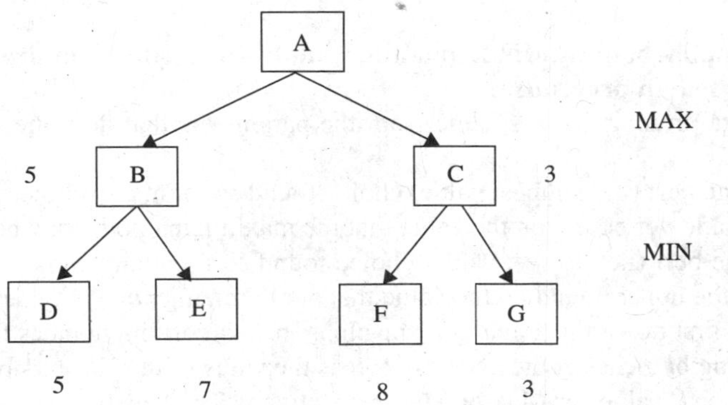

Now player MAX can select the maximum value among nodes B and C which is node B with value 5. So the move selected by player MAX will be B as shown in figure below:

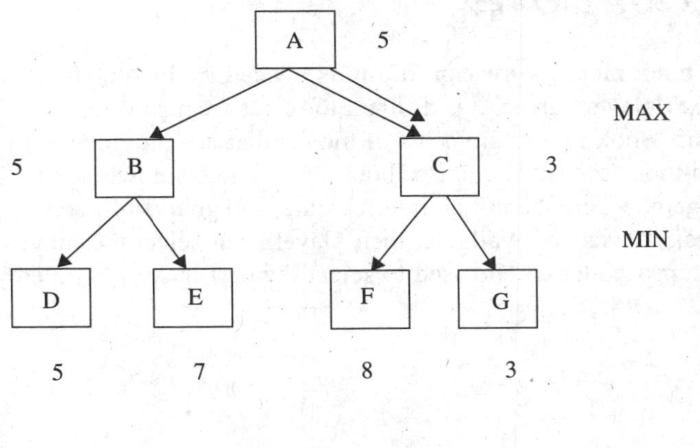

3.3 REFINEMENTS IN MINIMAX SEARCH PROCEDURE

Q. What are the various ways to improve the performance of minimax search procedure?

Ans. There are four refinements which can help in improving the performance of minimax search procedure. These are

(a) Adding alpha–beta cutoffs
(b) Using book moves
(c) Using secondary search
(d) Waiting for quiescence
(e) Using iterative deepening

3.4 ADDING ALPHA–BETA CUTOFFS

Q. What is alpha–beta cutoff? Explain how alpha–beta cutoffs improve the performance in minimax search procedure?

Ans. Alpha–beta pruning gets its name from the parameters that describe values it uses to decide what to prune:
α = the value for the best (i.e., highest value) choice found so far at any choice point along the path for Max. It represents a lower bound on the value that the maximizing node may be assigned.
β = the value of the best (i.e., lowest value) choice found so far at any choice point along the path for Min. It represents the upper bound on the value that a minimizing node may be assigned.
As it moves depth-first down the game tree, the alpha–beta algorithm updates the values of α and β. It prunes the remaining branches at the node as soon as the value of the current node is found to be worse than the current α or β value for Max or Min, respectively. The benefits are that the pruning does not affect final result and good move ordering improves the effectiveness of pruning. If there is perfect ordering, time complexity of minimax with alpha–beta pruning is $O(b^{m/2})$, i.e., doubles depth of search which can be carried out for a given level of resources.

3.5 USING BOOK MOVES

Q. What is a book move? How can minimax procedure be improved using book moves?

Ans. In some multiplayer games, it is difficult to select the next move simply by seeing the current game configurations. Book moves are a list of moves that are provided with the game so that players can select from those easily. The use of book moves adds knowledge to the players. Chess is an example of such a game where the initial, intermediate, and goal configurations can be specified using book moves. If book moves are available, then players can select the moves in a better way. Then, the minimax search procedure can be used to select the best move possible by calculating the utility values.

3.6 USING SECONDARY SEARCH

Q. What is secondary search? How can it improve minimax search procedure?

Ans. In an n-ply game, a game tree is explored to an average depth of n levels for selecting a move. Though a good move is selected at this level, but it may still not prove be a good move later and may result in horizon effect. So, it is advisable to extend the search to one or two more levels so that we can be sure that there will be no horizon effect. This may not be very costly to do a secondary search as compared to selecting a move early and failing later due to the horizon effect. Example of secondary search was used by the DEEP THOUGHT chess computer which uses singular extensions. This uses expanding the critical best leaf node so far one extra ply.

Q. What is horizon effect?

Horizon means some place where it seems there is nothing beyond that in sky. The horizon effect is a problem many games, where the number of possible states or positions is immense and computers can only feasibly search a small portion of it, typically a few steps called ply down the game tree. This is done using techniques such as minimax or alpha-beta pruning. However, evaluating a partial tree may give a misleading result. This is because when we feel that we cannot see any states farther away as if horizon is reached, but actually there are many more. When a significant change exists just over the 'horizon' of the search depth, i.e. beyond the selected depth for search, horizon effect is observed. It can be mitigated by extending the search algorithm with a quiescence search which gives the search algorithm ability to look beyond its horizon for a certain class of moves of major importance to the game state, such as captures. For example, if we see more than two ply in selecting a move using minimax, we may eliminate horizon effect in tic-tac-toe.

3.7 WAITING FOR QUIESCENCE

Q. What is quiescence? How it can help in improving minimax search procedure?

Ans. In a game tree, finding a stable step is called quiescence. In a game search, one needs to wait when to stop going deep into the tree. This is called waiting for quiescence. It can help in avoiding the horizon effect because the player waits for a stable step and then select it. Then minimax can be used to find the utility value. The chances of success will increase because there is some surety of the step to do not prove bad in next levels and hence minimax will improve.

3.8 USING ITERATIVE DEEPENING

Q. How can iterative deepening be applied to minimax search procedure?

Ans. Iterative deepening is applied to minimax in order to search for finding the shortest solution path to the goal state in game playing. Here, rather than searching to an n-ply, the minimax is applied to a depth of 1-ply, 2-ply, then 3-ply, and so on till the solution to goal node is not found through the current node. It can better be applied to single-agent search to solve problems like 8-puzzle.

Iterative deepening A* algorithm is used successfully to find the optimal solution to 15-puzzle problem in reasonable time and space requirements.

Q. State the IDA*.

Ans. Steps in iterative deepening A* algorithm are:

1. Set threshold value = the heuristic evaluation function value of the start state.
2. Perform a depth-first search to find the solution path. During searching, any branches which have value of the heuristic evaluation function more than the threshold value are to be pruned/eliminated for search. If the solution path is found, then return it and quit. Otherwise, go to step 3.
3. Update the threshold value by the minimum amount when it was exceeded during the previous step.
4. Go to step 2.

3.9 ALTERNATIVE TO MINIMAX SEARCH

Q. What are the alternatives for searching in game playing other than minimax search procedure?

Ans. The basic assumption in using minimax search algorithm is that the opponent is assumed to be equally intelligent as the player. So the best or optimal move is assumed to be taken by the opponent. This may not be the situation at all times. A slightly less promising node may be taken by the opponent, which may help in the winning of the player. But it is difficult to select the steps which are less than best moves using game playing algorithms.

3.10 REFERENCES ON SPECIFIC GAMES

Q. Define rules for playing checkers.

Ans. Checkers is a two-player game played on a checkered 8 × 8 square board. There are 12 dark color pieces and 12 light color pieces. Each player gets 12 pieces of the same color which are placed on the dark squares of the board in three rows. The objective of the game is to remove all pieces of the opponent from the board or by leading the opponent to such a situation where the opponent is left with no legal moves. The row closest to a player is called the king row. The pieces in the king row are called kings, while others are called men. Kings can move diagonally forward as well as backward. Men can move only forward. If one player jumps over the pieces of the opponent diagonally, then that piece of the opponent is removed. When men pieces jump over king pieces of the opponent, they transform into kings and can move backward and forward.

Q. Explain how Samuel's checkers program learns to play checkers?

Ans. It uses minimax search procedure to explore game trees. Due to time constraints, it can search only up to a limited depth according to the current situation. When it cannot search beyond a certain depth, then it applies the static evaluation function to the current board position and uses this score to continue its search of the game tree. It propagates the calculated values to the root of the tree to select the best move possible. The stored value at this position can be used when that node appears at some other part of the game tree. This reduced the efforts in searching. In order to store the value, the board positions were indexed by the number of pieces. In order to reduce the number of values required to be stored, some generalization should be used. This was done in checkers program by only storing the positions where white is to move.

Q. Define rules for playing chess.

Ans. Chess is played on a checkered board with 64 squares arranged in an 8 × 8 square. There are total 32 pieces of two colors, i.e., 16 black pieces and 16 white pieces. Each player is given 16 pieces of one color and the opponent gets 16 pieces of other color. Sixteen pieces have special shapes and represent different roles. These include one king, one queen, two knights, two rooks, two bishops, and eight pawns. Each of these pieces moves in a unique manner. The winner of the game is the player who is first to remove the opponent's king from the board. The player who takes white pieces is given the first turn. The player takes turn alternatively by moving any one piece to either an unoccupied space or taking the place of the opponent's piece by removing it. There is one situation which both players should avoid called checkmate, where the opponent's king is under immediate attack. Knowing all the possible winning configurations and thinking of the opponent's moves in deciding player's best move is a challenging task.

Q. Define rules for playing Othello.

Ans. Othello is a two-player board game which is played on an 8 × 8 square with pieces which are shaped like coins and have two distinct bi-colored sides (light and dark). The original name of the game is Reversi. Each player can select a face. The objective is to make your pieces constitute a majority of the pieces on the board at the end of the game by turning over as many of the opponent's pieces as possible. The player choosing the dark face gets first chance. He can place another dark piece in such a position that there exists at least one straight line occupied between the new piece and another dark piece with one or more light pieces in between. This will cause all the light pieces to turn dark. Similarly the opponent can capture dark pieces and turn them into light.

SOLVED EXAMPLES

Q. Consider the tree given below. Calculate the value at the root of the tree using minimax algorithm.

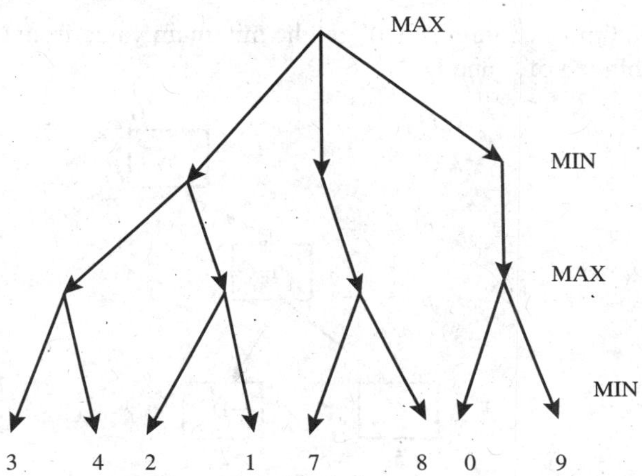

Ans. From the leaf nodes, as it is MAX's turn, so, maximum values will be propagated up and at MIN's turn, minimum values will be propagated up.

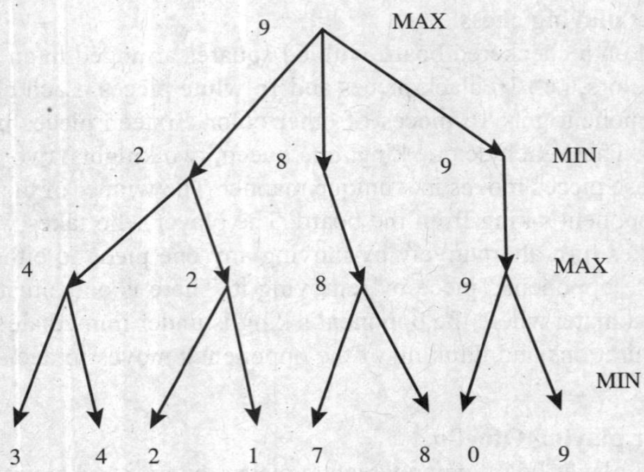

Q. Consider again the game tree shown below. Calculate the value at the root of the tree using minimax algorithm. Perform alpha–beta pruning to show which nodes will be pruned.

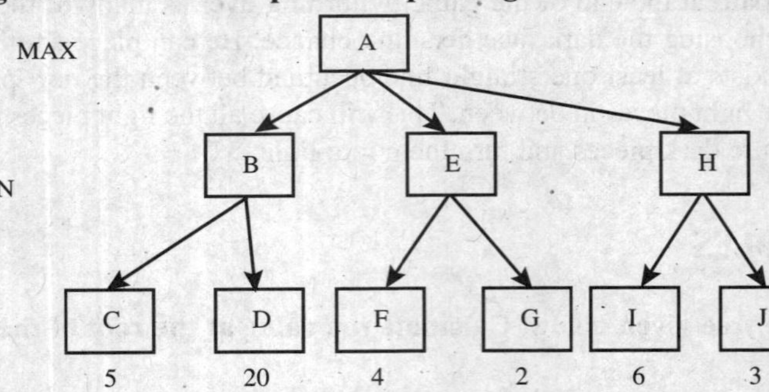

Ans. First of all, the leftmost children B will get the minimum value from C and D. Here, the MIN node will choose the minimum of C and D, i.e., 5.

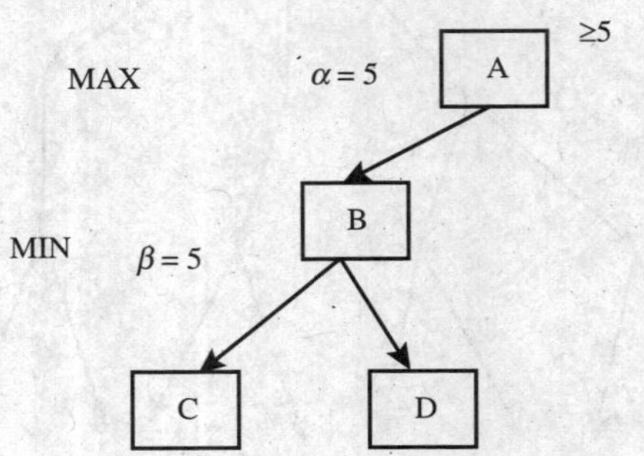

Here, β is 5 which means value of β cannot increase than 5. The initial value propagated up the tree at MAX node A will be 5 so, the value of α will be equal to or more than 5. At the next level, the next node of A, i.e., E will be expanded.

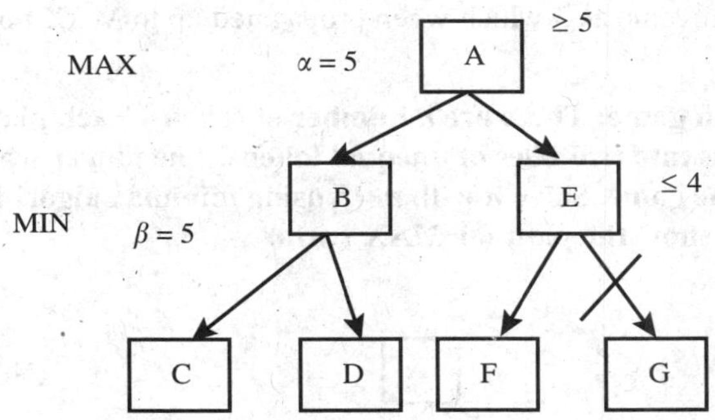

Node E gets the value through F as 4. Since it is a MIN node, the value at E will be either 4 or less than 4 but cannot be more than 4. This will not cause any increase in the value of A which is to select the MAX value and value of α cannot be less than 4. So the other branches of E are α pruned. Next, the third node H will be expanded.

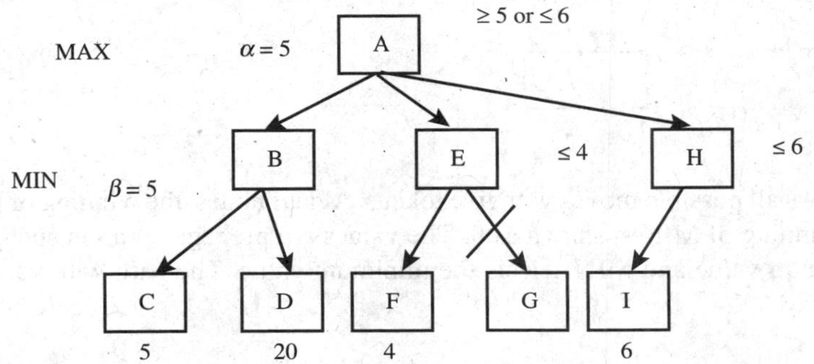

Node H gets first value from I, i.e., 6. Since, it is more than α, the chances are that if this is the minimum value at H, the value of α may increase to 6. So it will not be pruned and the next successor will be generated.

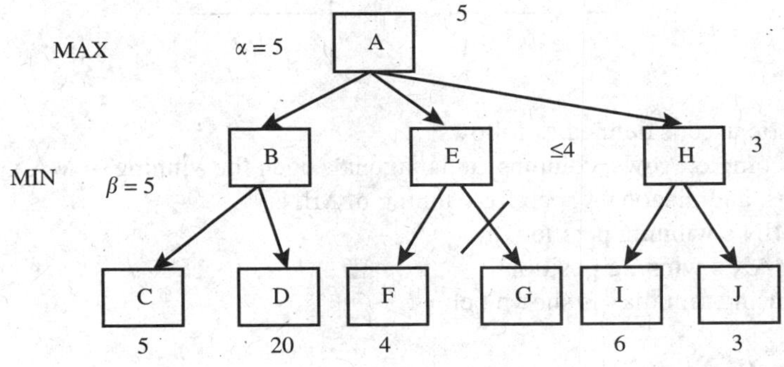

Node H gets the minimum value as 3 which when propagated up to MAX node A does not change the value, i.e., 5.

Q. Consider the Nim game: There are *n* number of tokens. Each player is required to divide the pile of tokens into two piles of unequal tokens. The player who cannot divide any pile further looses the game. Solve it with *n* = 5 using minimax algorithm. Assume MAX takes first move. Also show the path for MAX's win.

Ans.

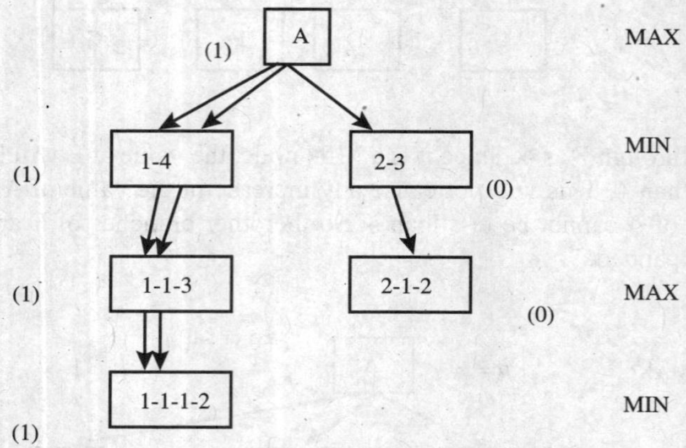

Here, the tree shows all possible moves with five tokens. At leaf nodes, the winning of MAX is indicated by value 1 and winning of MIN is shown as 0. The values are propagated up in such a way that MAX selects the maximum value and MIN selects the minimum value. The path with value 1 indicates the winning move for MAX.

Q. Consider TIC-TAC-TOE. Assume that MAX puts an X and MIN puts a 0. Calculate the next step of MAX using minimax search procedure. State the heuristic used.

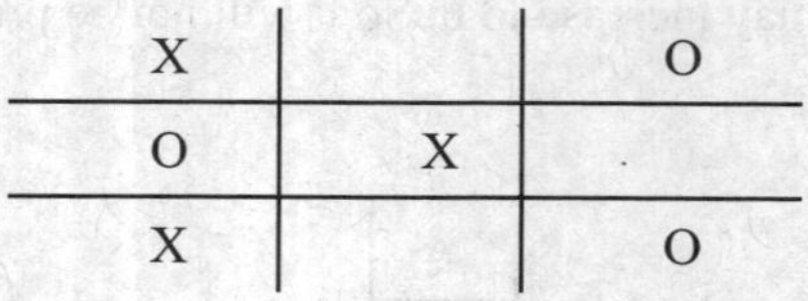

Ans. The heuristic used is defined as follows:
H(n) = Number of complete rows, columns, and diagonals open for winning of MAX– Number of complete rows, columns, and diagonals open for winning of MIN.
H(n) = −100, for MIN's winning position
H(n) = +100, for MAX's winning position
The complete tree using minimax is shown below:

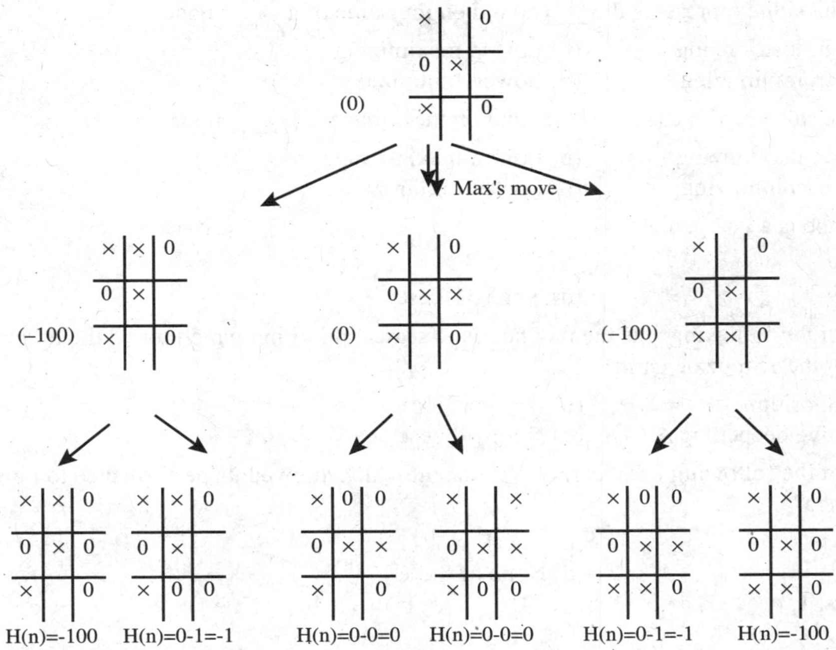

MULTIPLE CHOICE QUESTIONS

Select the most appropriate answer to the following questions:

1 Expanding a node below a certain depth more than *n* in *n*-ply search is called:

(a) Horizon effect (b) Quiescence
(c) Secondary search (d) All of these

2. What occurs when a node appears to be good at a certain depth but proves to be bad in next level?

(a) Horizon effect (b) Quiescence
(c) Secondary search (d) All of these

3. When search is carried out of the best node after a particular level to see if it is stable is called:

(a) Horizon effect (b) Quiescence
(c) Secondary search (d) All of these

4. Minimax search procedure is similar to which of the following search?

(a) Breadth first search (b) Depth first search
(c) Depth first search with limited depth (d) None of these

5. Which of the following is an alternative approach to solving game trees?

(a) A* algorithm (b) B* algorithm
(c) AO* algorithm (d) None of these

6. The alpha value represents the ___ bound on the value of a _____node.
   (a) Upper, maximizing (b) Lower, maximizing
   (c) Upper, minimizing (d) Lower, minimizing
7. The beta value represents the ___ bound on the value of a _____ node.
   (a) Upper, maximizing (b) Lower, maximizing
   (c) Upper, minimizing (d) Lower, minimizing
8. Tic-tac-toe is a ___ game.
   (a) 1-ply (b) 2-ply
   (c) *n*-ply (d) None of these
9. Which of the following was the first heuristic search algorithm which found the optimal solution paths for the 15-puzzle game?
   (a) A* algorithm (b) B*algorithm
   (c) Iterative deepening A* (d) None of these
10. Which of the following uses learner component which allowed its performance to improve with experience?
   (a) Chess (b) Checkers
   (c) Go (d) None of these

Answers. 1. c 2. a 3. b 4. c 5. b 6. b 7. c 8. b 9. c 10. b

EXERCISES

1. Consider the following game tree in which static scores are from first player's point of view who is to take move A and is maximizing player. What move he should take from state A?

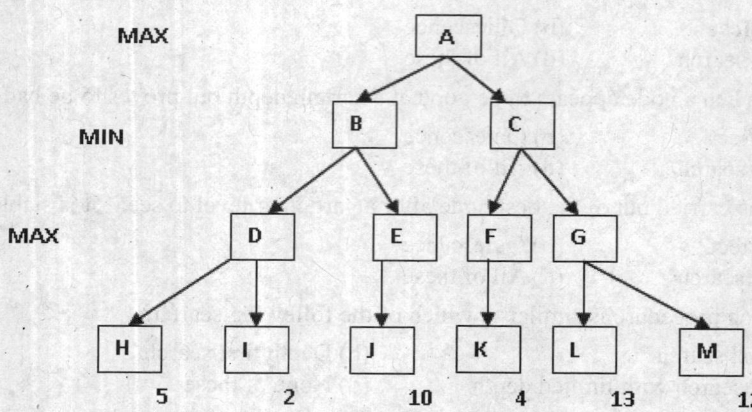

2. In the game tree shown in Q1, perform alpha–beta pruning to indicate which nodes would not need to be examined?

3. Select the next move for MAX using minimax (putting an X).

	O	O
	X	
X		

4. Use alpha–beta pruning for selecting the move in Q3.
5. Solve Nim game with seven tokens.
6. Show the path for winning of MAX in Q5 supposing MAX takes the first turn.
7. Try to find the rules for playing Go game.

4 Knowledge Representation

4.1 INTRODUCTION

To perform a task, systems need a representation of the domain knowledge. There are many different forms in which knowledge can be represented. There are mainly two kinds of entities to be represented in knowledge. These are facts, i.e., the things which are always true in the world and the representation of these facts in some formalized way so that we can manipulate them in the way required for the current problem. The representation of knowledge in natural language is easy to understand but is difficult for use in Artificial Intelligence (AI) programs. So, it may need to be translated into formal representation. This representation may be logical which can be done using propositional and predicate logic for representation of knowledge. The first-order predicate knowledge represents the way of doing it. It may be symbolic representation of domain objects, concepts, and attributes. For example, rules, semantic networks, frames, schemas, and conceptual dependencies (CDs), etc., can be used to represent symbolic knowledge in the domain. There is some domain that is sub-symbolic, which includes distributed representation of objects, concepts, and attributes in the world. This can be done using neural nets, etc.

4.2 KNOWLEDGE REPRESENTATION

4.2.1 Representations and Mappings

Q. What do you understand by knowledge representations and mappings?

Ans. In order to solve problems, some mechanism is needed for representing the knowledge. Consider for example, solving a problem using any programming language, say C. How do we start? The first is a problem statement in English (say, write a program in C to find factorial of a number). Then we write a program in C language using syntax of C so that manipulation can be done. That is the internal representation. Then whatever is the result of the program, say some output or error message etc, we again need to interpret that in English in order to understand.

Similarly in artificial intelligence, we can represent initial knowledge using any knowledge representation (KR) method. This is called forward representation mapping. Then the manipulation or processing will be done using that KR method. Now in order to understand the final facts or output, we need to represent again in English. This is called backward representation mapping. Thus, the knowledge can be structured at two levels: the knowledge level where facts are described and at the symbol level for internal manipulation. The process of representation mapping is shown in figure below:

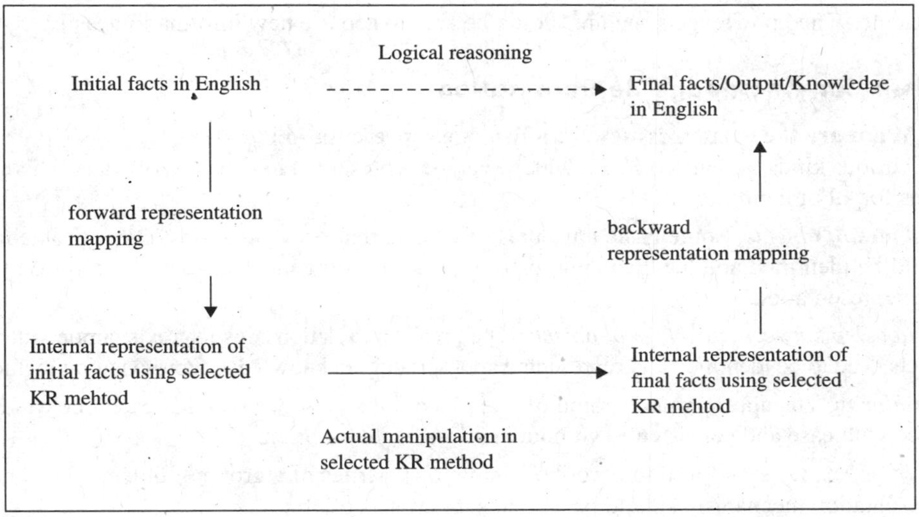

Q. Give an example of representation mapping.

Ans. Consider the given set of axioms: All elephants have trunks. Jumbo is an elephant.

In forward representation mapping, we convert it into predicate clauses as:

$\forall$: elephant(e) $\rightarrow$ has (e, trunk).

elephant(Jumbo).

From these two, it can be inferred using deduction: has (Jumbo, trunk).

Now, it order to understand this inference from the given axioms, backward representation mapping is needed which states the inference in English as: Jumbo has a trunk. Thus, it is necessary to convert from English to predicate and then from manipulated results in predicate to English.

4.2.2 Approaches to Knowledge Representation

Q. What are the various approaches to knowledge representation?

Ans. A good system for the representation of knowledge in a particular domain should possess the following four properties:

1. *Representational adequacy*: The knowledge representation scheme should have the ability to represent all of the kinds of knowledge that are needed in that domain, i.e., all the ways of representation should be adequate to represent the knowledge in the domain.
2. *Inferential adequacy*: The knowledge representation will be successful if we can infer something useful from the represented knowledge. So a knowledge representation scheme should be able to manipulate the representational structures in such a way as to derive new structures corresponding to gain new knowledge from old knowledge.
3. *Inferential efficiency*: The knowledge about a system could be vast. While drawing inferences,

some additional information may prove to be useful for better direction of inferring in some useful ways. The knowledge representation scheme should have the ability to incorporate additional information to infer efficiently along with the required knowledge structure.

4. *Acquisitional efficiency*: Any system grows with time. The knowledge needs to be added or updated frequently. The knowledge structure should be able to acquire new information easily.

4.2.3 Issues in Knowledge Representation

Q. What are the various issues in knowledge representation?

Ans. Various kinds of real-world knowledge can be represented in a variety of ways. There are several issues for all of them:

1. *Attributes of objects*: Some basic attributes of objects that occur in almost every problem domain should be identified and handled appropriately in each of the mechanisms we propose for knowledge representation.
2. *Relationship between attributes of objects*: The important relationships that exist among attributes of objects need to be identified and represented appropriately in knowledge representation method used.
3. *Granularity*: The appropriate division of one object into sub-object so that each one can be represented with ease and consistently without any loss of information.
4. *Sets of objects*: A set is used to describe common properties of a group of objects. The knowledge representation mechanism should be able to support sets of objects.
5. *Accessing the relevant part of a large knowledge base*: When a large amount of knowledge is stored in a database, the knowledge representation scheme used should allow methods to access the relevant parts quickly and with ease.

4.2.4 Procedural versus Declarative Knowledge

Q. How the procedural knowledge differ from declarative knowledge?

Ans. There are two ways in which procedural knowledge is differ from procedural knowledge.

1. A declarative knowledge is one in which knowledge is specified using facts and rules but the method of using this knowledge is not specified. A separate program is required to specify the steps for using the declarative knowledge.
2. In procedural representation, the way to use the knowledge is embedded along with the knowledge itself. In order to use a procedural representation, it needs to be augmented with an interpreter which will follow the instructions specified in the knowledge. The process used for finding the answer depends on the interpreter, in which way it uses the control information.

4.2.5 The Frame Problem

Q. Define frame problem in AI.

Ans. In any problem, there are a number of related things represented as facts. In order to get the solution, a sequence of steps is required to be selected by any algorithm. Only some facts change as a result of rule application by any algorithm and there are some parts of the facts which do not change by the rule application. The problem of representing the facts that change as well as those that do not change is known as the Frame problem. In order to support this kind of reasoning, some systems make use of an explicit set of axioms known as ***frame axioms***. The frame axioms describe all the things that do not change when a particular rule or operator is applied in state I to produce next state i+1. In order to do this, at each node, an indication of the specific changes that can be made to that node are stored. This indication is called a state variable. This could represent location, time, or anything which did not change.

The example is color of an object which does not change when the place of an object is changed using transfer function. This can be represented as : If color of object o is c at location location1, then even at location location2, the color of object o is c again. In predicate logic, it can be written as:

color(o,location1,c) □ transfer(o, location1,location2) → color(o, location2, c).

here Λ represents an AND operator.

4.3 FORMALIZED SYMBOLIC LOGIC

4.3.1 Propositional Calculus

Q. How do we represent knowledge using propositional calculus?

Ans. Propositional calculus is a system that deals with the method used for manipulation of the symbols according to some rules. The alphabet set of propositional calculus is given as:

(a) A set of propositional symbols or variables, P, Q, R called atoms.

(b) Logical constants true (T) and false (F).

(c) Two parentheses "(" and ")"

(d) A set of logical operators called connectives:

Λ – And (represents conjunction), returns T if both atoms are true, otherwise false

V – Or (represents disjunction), returns F if both atoms are false, otherwise true

~ – Not (represents negation), returns T of atom if false and false otherwise

→ – Implies (represents conditional if-then), P → Q returns F if only P is true and Q is false

↔ – Equivalence (biconditional), returns T if both atoms have same truth values, false otherwise

The expressions are evaluated from left to right.

The precedence of the operators in decreasing order of priority is: () ~ Λ V → ↔ .

The truth table given below indicates the meaning of the logical operators:

P	Q	~P	P Λ Q	P V Q	P → Q	P ↔ Q
T	T	F	T	T	T	T
T	F	F	F	T	F	F
F	T	T	F	T	T	F
F	F	T	F	F	T	T

(e) A set of equivalence relations or laws: These are used to reduce a given formula to another or derive a new formula. These can be verified using truth table:

Commutative laws:	P Λ Q ≅ Q Λ P	P V Q ≅ Q V P
Associative laws:	(P Λ Q) Λ R ≅ P Λ (Q Λ R)	(P V Q) V R ≅ P V (Q V R)
Double negation:	~ (~P) ≅ P	
Distributive laws:	P Λ (Q V R) ≅ (P Λ Q) V (P Λ R)	P V (Q Λ R) ≅ (P V Q) Λ P V R)
De Morgan's laws:	~(P V Q) ≅ ~P Λ ~Q	~ (P Λ Q) ≅ ~ P V ~ Q

Adsorption laws:	$P \wedge (P \vee Q) \cong P$	$P \vee (P \wedge Q) \cong P$
	$P \vee (\sim P \wedge Q) \cong P \vee Q$	$P \wedge (\sim P \vee Q) \cong P \wedge Q$
Law of contradiction:	$P \wedge \sim P \cong$ False	
Law of excluded middle:	$P \vee \sim P \cong$ True	
Laws of impotency:	$P \wedge P \cong P$	$P \vee P \cong P$

Q. What is a tautology?

Ans. A formula α is called a tautology if and only if α is true for all interpretations.
For example: The formula $A \vee \sim A$ is a tautology as it is true under all interpretations.

Q. What are the rules of inference?

Ans. There are two rule of inference:

1. *Modus ponens*: If P and $P \rightarrow Q$ is given to be true, then we can infer that Q is true.
   P: It is a holiday
   Q: The school is closed
   $P \rightarrow Q$: If it is a holiday then the school is closed
   If P and $P \rightarrow Q$ is given to be true, then we can say Q (the school is closed)
2. *Modus tollens*: If ~Q and $\sim P \rightarrow \sim Q$ are given to be true, then we can infer that ~P is true. If the school is not closed then we can infer that it is not a holiday.

4.3.2 Predicate Calculus

Q. Discuss theory of first-order predicate logic

Ans. First-order predicate logic (FOPL) models the world in terms of objects, which are things with individual identities, properties of objects that distinguish them from other objects, relations that hold among sets of objects; functions, which are a subset of relations where there is only one value for any given input. Examples of objects are students, employees, chairs, etc. Examples of relation are brother-of, smaller_than, visits, etc. Examples of properties are blue, square, pale, large, etc. Examples of functions are best-friend, one-more-than, etc. For examples , if objects are students and instructors, examples of relation are studies_in, teaches etc. Examples of properties are undergraduate, postgraduate, artificial intelligence (subject name) etc. Examples of functions are best-student, number_of_subjects, etc.

Q. How can we represent simple facts in first-order predicate logic?

Ans. The real-world facts can be represented as logical propositions written as well-formed formulas (wffs) in propositional logic. Symbols represent objects, properties, or relations in the real world. Propositional calculus symbols are formed of the following:

1. The set of all uppercase letters of the English alphabet
2. The set of digits from 0 to 9
3. The underscore character (_)
   Example: It is drizzling. In propositional calculus, it is represented as DRIZZLING.
   It is dry. In propositional calculus, it is represented as DRY.
   If it is drizzling, then it is not dry. In propositional calculus, it is represented as a rule:
   DRIZZLING $\rightarrow \neg$DRY.

Q. How can we define a sentence in predicate calculus?

Ans. Every atomic sentence is a sentence. An atomic sentence is defined as a predicate constant of arity *n*, followed by *n* terms, t1, t2..., t*n* enclosed in parentheses and separated by commas. Atomic sentence is also called atomic expression, atom, or proposition.

1. If s is a sentence, then its negation ~s is also a sentence.
2. If s1 and s2 are sentences, then their conjunction s1 $\wedge$ s2 is also a sentence
3. If s1 and s2 are sentences, then their disjunction s1 V s2 is also a sentence
4. If s1 and s2 are sentences, then their implication s1 $\rightarrow$ s2 is also a sentence
5. If s1 and s2 are sentences, then their equivalence s1 $\equiv$ s2 is also a sentence
6. If X is a variable and s is a sentence, then $\forall$ X s is a sentence
7. If X is a variable and s is a sentence, then $\exists$ X s is a sentence

Q. What are the two quantifiers in predicate calculus?

Ans. In predicate calculus, we can use variables. When a variable appears as an argument in a sentence, it refers to unspecified objects in the domain. First-order predicate calculus includes two symbols, the variable quantifiers $\forall$ (universal quantifier) and $\exists$ (existential quantifier) that constrain the meaning of a sentence containing a variable. A quantifier is followed by a variable and a sentence, such as:

$\exists$ X mother (X, Prakriti). There exists some X who is mother of person named Prakriti.

$\forall$ X likes (X, resting). X like resting, is true for everybody, i.e., we can substitute any value for X and likes (X, resting) will be true.

Relation between sentences involving $\forall$ and $\exists$ using De Morgan's laws:

$(\forall x) \sim P \cong \sim (\exists x) P$

$\sim(\forall x) P \cong (\exists x) \sim P$

$(\forall x) P \cong \sim (\exists x) \sim P$

$(\exists x) P \cong \sim (\forall x) \sim P$

Q. How can we represent class membership and class inclusion in predicate logic?

Ans. This is done using predicates ***isa*** and ***instance***. The predicate ***isa*** represents the relationship of class inclusion, while predicate ***instance*** represents class membership relationship.

Consider the two facts: Penguin is a bird. Pingu is a penguin. There are two classes in the first statement. One is the bird and the other is the penguin. The objects of class penguin inherits all the attributes of the class bird. Thus, there exists a class membership relation between penguin and bird and it can be written as:

class(penguin, bird).

In the second fact, Pingu is an object of class penguin. Thus, there is an instance relation between class penguin and object Pingu and it can be written as:

instance(Pingu, penguin).

Q. How can we include computable functions and predicates in predicate calculus?

Ans. For simple computations like less than or greater than, it is not possible to add set of facts indicating infinite number of values for these indicating true values. For example, greater-than (13,12) or greater-than (11,10), greater-than (12,11), and so on. But these simple computations may be needed in representing the real-world knowledge about the objects. So it is advisable to use computable predicates which clear the meaning of the computation being done. If these also involve some calculations first, these become computable functions as they will first return the value of the function and then the computation of the predicate will be performed. For example, greater-than (5–2, 1) will first calculate the function value 5–2 = 3 and then compute greater-than (3,1) which is true. The result of the predicates will be either true or false. For example, if lt represents lesser-than, then lt (4,3) will return false because 4 is not lesser-than 3 while lt (2,3) will return true.

4.3.3 Comparison of Proposition and Predicate Calculus

Q. What are the differences between predicate and propositional calculus?

Ans. The main difference between predicate and propositional calculus is that there are no variables in propositional calculus while predicate calculus have variables. There is no unification required in propositional calculus because there are no variables, but we need to unify variables with either constants or other variables during resolution.

Predicate calculus	Propositional calculus
• Variables can be represented using ptredicate calculus	• No variables are allowed in propositional calculus
• During resolution, unification is required as variables are involved	• During resolution, no unification is required since there are no variables

4.4 DEDUCTION

4.4.1 Forward and Backward Reasoning

Q. Explain the forward and backward reasoning.

Ans. When a search procedure is used to find the answer to any problem, it involves identifying a path through a problem space from an initial configuration to a goal state. There are two possible directions for searching or reasoning:

(a) *Forward reasoning or data driven reasoning* (*move forward from start to goal state*): In this type of reasoning, the search tree has initial configuration(s) at the root of the tree. The next level of the tree is generated by finding all the rules whose left sides match the root node and using their right sides to create the new configurations. The next level of the tree is generated by taking each node generated at the previous level and applying it to all of the rules whose left sides match it. This search process is continued until a configuration that matches the goal state is generated.

(b) *Backward reasoning or goal driven or goal directed reasoning* (*move backward from goal to initial state*): In this type of reasoning, the search tree has goal configuration(s) at the root of the tree. The next level of the tree is generated by finding all the rules whose right sides match the root node and using their left sides to create the new configurations. The next level of the tree is generated by taking each node generated at the previous level and applying it to all of the rules whose right sides match it. This search process is continued until a node is found which matches the initial state is generated.

Forward reasoning can be used for finding a solution to water jug problem where we start from a start state and move towards the goal state.

Backward reasoning can be used in proving a theorem where we know the theorem and we try to prove all axioms to be true for this theorem i.e. we finally move to initial states.

Q. What are backward chaining rule systems and backward chaining rule systems tautology?

Ans. Backward chaining rules systems are used for goal-directed problem solving. Here the rules encode knowledge about how to achieve particular goal. Forward chaining rule systems encode knowledge about how to respond to certain input configurations. When we reason either starting from goal or axioms, it is called backward or forward reasoning, respectively.

Q. What are the factors which decide which reasoning should be used for finding the solution to the current problem?

Ans. Both forward and backward reasoning methods explore the same number of paths in finding the solution. The suitability of the reasoning mechanism used depends on the requirement of the user and the problem type as given below:

1. *The number of states:* If there are many possible goal states and fewer initial states, then it is difficult to start reasoning from one of the goal state as it may not be the desired one. Similarly, if there are many possible initial states but fewer goal states then it is difficult to start with any initial state which may not prove to be fruitful and need backtracking again. So it is advisable that the direction should to move from the smaller set of states (either initial or goal) to the larger one so that the solution can be found in less time.
2. *Justification of reasoning to user:* If the user wants a justification how we reached the goal state as in case of medical diagnosis system, we should move backward from goal state (i.e., disease) to initial states (i.e., the symptoms given by the user). If we want to prove a mathematical problem of integration, we should move backward from the given integration equation and find the required solution. In order to find the solution path to a Traveling salesman problem, the solution should be found using forward reasoning.
3. *Branching factor:* The branching factor of tree indicates the average number of nodes that can be reached directly from a single node or it is the average number of children of any node in a tree. This depends on the possible number of rules which can match the rule (either from left side or right side). If the branching factor keeps on increasing, it will be difficult to find the solution. So the direction should be towards a lower branching factor. For example, if a disease is to be diagnosed, only a specific set of symptoms should be present while, for even a single symptom, there are a large number of diseases possible. So we should move in a backward direction where the branching factor will converge for a particular disease.
4. *Event initiating problem solving:* There is always a condition which states there is a need for problem solving. For example, if there is a query from a user to solve a particular theorem, then the goal is needed to be proved from a given set of axioms, hence backward reasoning should be taken as problem solving method. In case, it is finding a solution to a game like 8-puzzle or chess, the forward reasoning should be used to find the answer.

Q. When do you think the forward and backward reasoning be combined together?

Ans. Sometimes some aspects of a problem are handled by forward chaining and other aspects by backward chaining as in case of medical diagnosis. First, the doctor or expert system uses backward chaining to find the disease of the patient and then uses forward chaining to give the prescription. The form of the rules indicates whether both forward and backward reasoning can be applied or not. If both left and right sides contain pure assertions, then forward chaining can match the assertions on the left side of a rule and add to the state description the assertions on the right side. But of arbitrary procedures are allowed as the right sides of rules, then the rules will not be reversible.

4.5 THEOREM PROVING

4.5.1 Theorem Proving Using Wang's Algorithm

Q. How can we prove a theorem using Wang's algorithm?

Ans. Wang's algorithm is a means of proving theorems in the propositional calculus.

1. Write the premises separated by commas, followed by an arrow (→), and then the theorem to prove.

   Example: p, ~ q ∧ r → p ∧ ~q
2. If a formula is negated, remove the "~" and move the formula to the opposite side of the arrow.

   Example: p, ~(q ∧ r) → p ∧ r is changed to: p → p ∧ r, q ∧ r
3. If any formula on the left has the format "(alpha and beta)," replace this with "alpha, beta," similarly, any formula on the right with format (alpha v beta) can be replaced with "alpha, beta".

   Example: p, p ∧ q → r, s is changed to: p, p, q → r, s

   and p, q → r v p is changed to: p, q → r, p
4. Any formula "(alpha v beta)" on the left must be turned into two lines, one containing alpha, and the other beta. Both lines must be proved. Likewise for and on the right.

   Example: p v q, r, s → q v p is changed to the two lines:

   p, r, s → q v p

   q, r, s → q v p
5. If at any point the same formula appears on both sides of an arrow, that line is proved (succeeds).
6. If none of: v, or ~ is left anywhere in a line, and condition (5) has not been met, then the line cannot be proved, the theorem is invalid.

4.5.2 Inferencing

Q. What is inferencing? How can we infer something given a set of facts?

Ans. In predicate calculus, in order to prove a goal, rules of inference are used to transform the goal into another goal (or sub goals) that can in turn be transformed, and so on, until there are no unsatisfied goals remaining.

Example: Consider the given set of axioms: Ashima, Alisha and Alya are members of Ladies club. All Ladies club members are either housewives are working women. Working woman like driving. Alya and Ashima like to drive. Is Alya a working woman?

These can be represented in predicate as:

1. member(Ashima, Ladies_club).
2. member(Alisha, Ladies_club).
3. member(Alya, Ladies_club).
4. ∀ x: member(x, Ladies_club) ∧ ~house_wife(x) → working_woman(x).
5. ∀ y: working_woman(y) → likes (y, Driving).
6. Likes(Alya, Driving).
7. Likes(Ashima, Driving).

Now in order to answer the goal query: Is Alya a working woman? It is first represented in predicate as: working_woman(Alya).

In predicate calculus, in order to prove a goal, rules of inference are used to transform the goal into another goal (or sub goals) that can in turn be transformed, and so on, until there are no unsatisfied goals remaining.

working_woman(Alya).

This will be true if sub goal: likes(Alya, driving) is true as given is rule 5.

This is true as given in rule 6. Hence, it is true that Alya is a working woman.

Q. Explain the process of matching.

Ans. In order to search a solution, there is a need to choose a rule and apply that to produce the next node in the tree. There can be many possible rules which can be applied to the current node. Select the rule which matches with the preconditions of all the applicable rules and the current state is known as matching.

Q. Explain the rules for matching.

Ans. There are many rules for matching.

1. *Indexing:* Use the current state as an index into the rules and select the matching ones immediately. This will reduce the time in exploring all possible rules unnecessary.
2. *Matching with variables:* In case the preconditions in rules are not states as exact descriptions of particular situations, then the matching can be done using unification.
3. *Complex and approximate matching:* When the preconditions of a rule specify required properties that are not states explicitly in the description of the current state. In this situation, a separate set of rules must be used to describe how some properties can be inferred from others. In case the preconditions match approximately with the current situation, more complex matching is required.

Q. Explain the approaches to resolve a conflict during matching.

Ans. During matching, when there is situation for which many rules are applicable, this is called a conflict. As only one rule can be applied at the moment, so this conflict should be resolved and only one appropriate rule should be selected for application. There are three approaches to conflict resolution. They are as follows:

1. Assign a preference based on the action that the matched rule would perform
2. Assign a preference based on the objects that matched
3. Assign a preference based on the rule that matched.

Q. What are the problems faced in using inference rules for proving a goal?

Ans. There are certain issues when we use rules of inference for proving a goal. First, it is difficult to solve all the sub goals when there are many AND arcs possible, it takes more time even for solving simple theorem. Second, the representation of the axioms in the form people are comfortable is complex for representation and proving the goals.

4.6 RESOLUTION IN LOGIC

Q. Explain the method of resolution for proving the facts or finding answers to queries.

Ans. The method of resolution works on the logic that in order to prove, P, it is easy to prove ~P to be false. Thus by double negation ~(~P) will prove P to be true. This is called refutation. Resolution is a procedure that is efficient in proving the goals as compared to inference because it represents all the statements into a very convenient standard form called clausal form and it uses chaining backward from the theorem to be proved to the axioms.

Q. Write the resolution algorithm.

Ans. The steps in resolution in propositional/predicate calculus are as follows:

1. Convert all given set of propositions to clause form
2. Negate the goal and convert result to clause form and the result to the clauses obtained in step 1.
3. Repeat until either a contradiction occurs or no progress can be made:
   (a) Select two clauses call these parent clauses
   (b) Resolve the clauses using disjunction if any pairs of literal L or ~L occur in the two parent clauses, pick one and eliminate it from the result
   (c) If the result is empty then the contradiction has been found, otherwise add the result to the set of clauses.

Q. Write the algorithm to convert predicate to clause form during resolution.

Ans. The steps for converting the clauses in predicate form to clausal form are given below:

1. Eliminate → using "a → b" is same as ~a ∨ b
2. Reduce scope of ~ to a single term using De Morgan's laws (e.g., ~(a Λ b) is ~a V ~b)
3. Standardize variables so each quantifier binds a unique variable (e.g., ∀x:P (x) V ∀x:Q (x) becomes P (x) V ∀y:Q (y))
4. Move all quantifiers to the left without changing their relative order
5. Eliminate all existential quantifiers
6. Since all remaining variables universally quantified drop the ∀ prefix
7. Use distributive property to convert expression into conjunction of disjuncts (e.g., this makes (a Λ b) V c become (a V c) Λ (b V c))
8. Create separate clause corresponding to each conjunct (each of which must be true)
9. Standardize apart the variables in the clauses generated by the previous step so that no two clauses refer the same two variables
   Steps 1, 2, 7, and 8 are common in both propositional and predicate calculus.
   Steps 3, 4, 5, 6, and 9 will be used in predicate calculus only because it contains variables.

Q. Write the algorithm for unification during resolution.

Ans. In predicate calculus, variables need to be unified with either constants or other variables, so unification is used in predicate calculus only. In general, the unification algorithm is given below for unifying any literals L1 and L2.

If L1 or L2 are both variables or constants then

- If L1 and L2 are identical then return NIL
- If L1 is a variable then if L1 occurs in L2 then return FAIL, else return substituting L2 for L1
- If L2 is a variable then if L2 occurs in L1 then return FAIL, else return substituting L1 for L2
- Return FAIL
- The unification should return fail if the initial predicate symbols in L1 and L2 are not identical or if they have different numbers of arguments.

4.7 STRUCTURED KNOWLEDGE

Q. What are weak slot and filler structures used for knowledge representation in AI?

Ans. Weak slot and filler structures enable real-world objects modeled as entities, the properties of relations between objects are easy to define and attribute values can be retrieved quickly using indexing. These are called weak slot and filer structures because these do not consider the content of the representation in detail. In slot and filler structures, the slot represents the pair: an attribute and its value. A filler is a value that a slot can take which could be a numeric, string (or any data type) value, or a pointer to another slot. Semantic nets or networks and frames are two types of weak slot and filler structures used in AI.

4.7.1 Semantic Networks

Q. How is knowledge represented in a semantic net?

Ans. In a semantic network, the concepts or objects are represented using directed graph. Entities are represented as rectangular boxes called nodes (vertices of the graph). A concept is treated as set or a subset. The relation between concepts is stored by edges (labeled arcs) which interconnect the nodes. The edges can represent a subclass relation (isa), an instance relation, an object (size, length, etc.), or a property of an object (small, 75, etc.). For example, human is a set of all humans and a boy is subset of the set human.

(a) *Representation of 2-ary predicates:* In the simplest form, 2-ary predicates can be represented in semantic networks by representing the two arguments as the entities and predicate as the relation between the entities. For example, consider the following information: Every person is a mammal. Every person has parts face and body. Vishal is a person. These can be represented as (Figure 4.1):

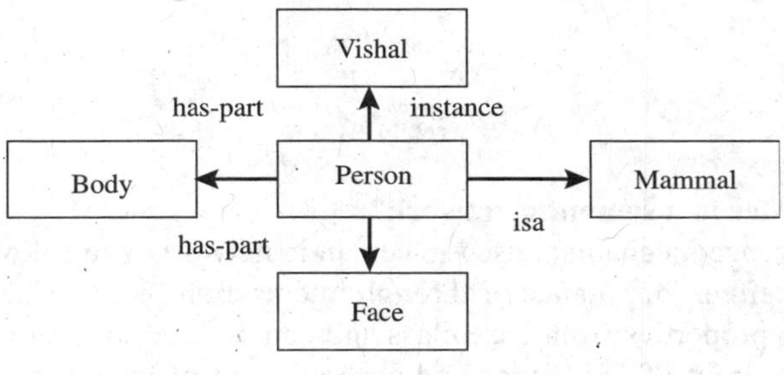

Figure 4.1

These values can also be represented in logic as:
Every person is a mammal: *isa (person, mammal)*
Every person has parts face and body: *has-part (person, face) Λ has-part (person, body)*
Vishal is a person: *instance (Vishal, person)*,
isa and *instance* represent inheritance in semantic networks. *isa* depicts a class and subclass relationship while *instance* is used to represent the relationship between a class and its object.

(b) *Representation of 3-ary predicates:* As it is clear from the representation of 2-ary predicates in semantic network, 3-ary predicates should be represented as 2-ary predicates and adding a new node to represent the predicate. The relation of all the three arguments to the 3-ary predicate node is represented as separate 2-ary predicates. For example, consider the sentence: partnership (Sachin, Sehwag, 250). (Figure 4.2)

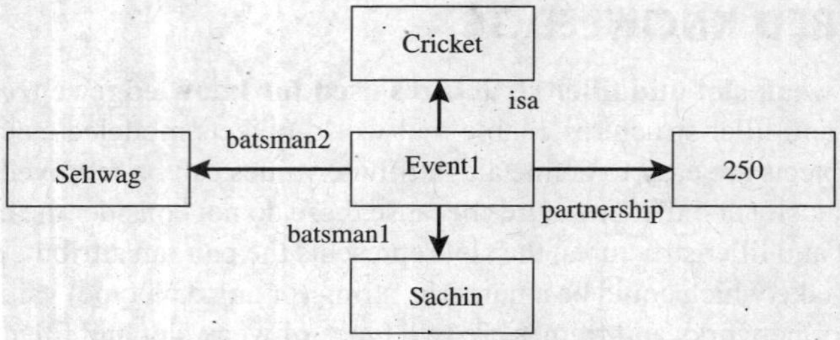

Figure 4.2

(c) *Representation of n-ary predicate*: Similar to 3-ary predicates, various parts of *n*-ary predicate can be represented in pairs as 2-ary predicates and then additional nodes can be added to relate these all. The semantic network can be extended in any directions possible to represent the attributes and relationships of all entities. For example, Raghav gave a chalk to the teacher. Here the main event is giving and all the other entities are related to this (Figure 4.3). The semantic network for representing this sentence is:

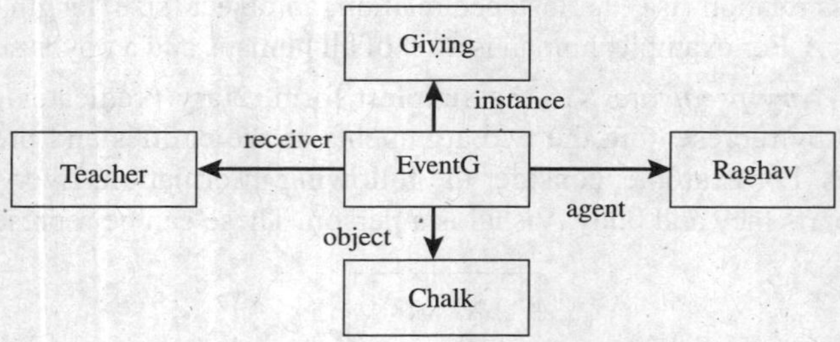

Figure 4.3

Q. How can we infer in a semantic network?

Ans. The basic inference mechanism used in semantic network is to follow links between nodes. This can be done using either inheritance or through intersection search. The subclasses and objects of a class inherit all the properties from base class and can be used in inference. Using intersection, the activations are spread out of two nodes and at their point of intersection, the inference can be found. For example, given the semantic network, we can infer that Vishal has parts face and body through inheritance. For intersection search, consider the following semantic network representing the sentence.

In making certain inferences we will also need to distinguish between the link that defines a new entity and holds its value and the other kind of link that relates two existing entities. Considering the example given, where the marks of two students are depicted and we also wish to compare them.

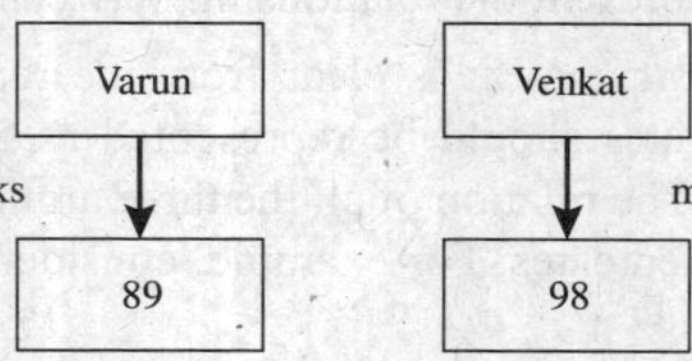

Figure 4.4 Marks of two students

If we want to compare them, we need extra nodes for the concept as well as its value.

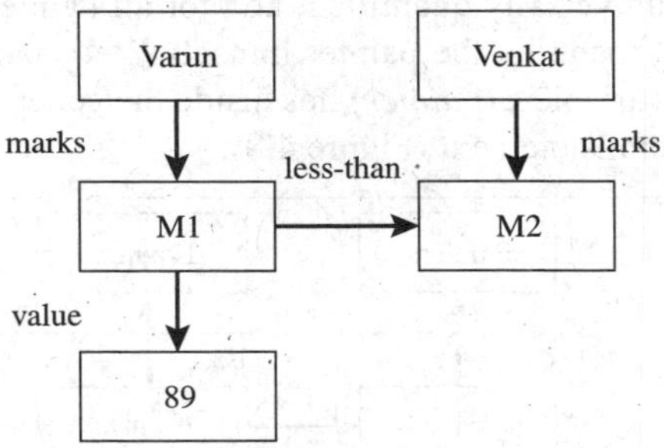

Figure 4.5 Comparison of two marks

Q. What are partitioned semantic nets? What is their use?

Ans. There are two uses of partitioned semantic networks.

1. Semantic networks in general do not support variables which can be universally or existentially quantified. This can be done using partitioned semantic networks. In order to do the partitioning, the semantic network is broken into **spaces** which consist of groups of nodes and arcs and regard each **space** as a node. There is a special class named general class, GS. A node g will be an instance of this special class. Every attribute in the partitioned semantic network will have at least two attributes: a form which states which relation is being asserted and one or more connections which are linked to the nodes representing either universally quantified (using for all, i.e., ∀) or existentially quantified (using for some, i.e., ∃).Consider the sentence: The painter loves the painting. This is partitioned semantic network which can be drawn as:

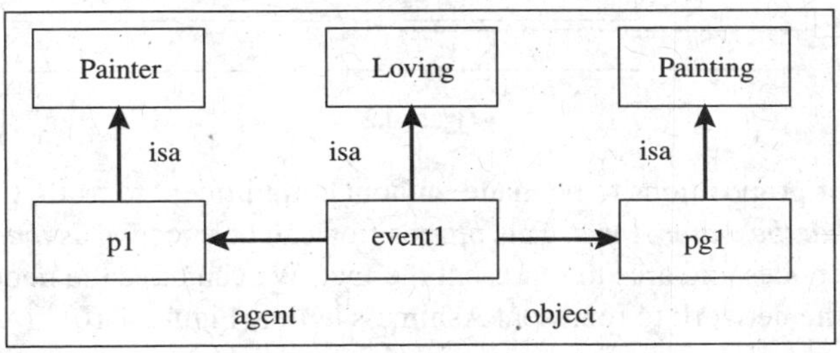

Figure 4.6

Every painter loves a painting (Figure 4.6).

This can be represented as $\forall x$ *painter (x)*$\rightarrow \exists y$: *painting (y)* Λ*loves (x, y)*

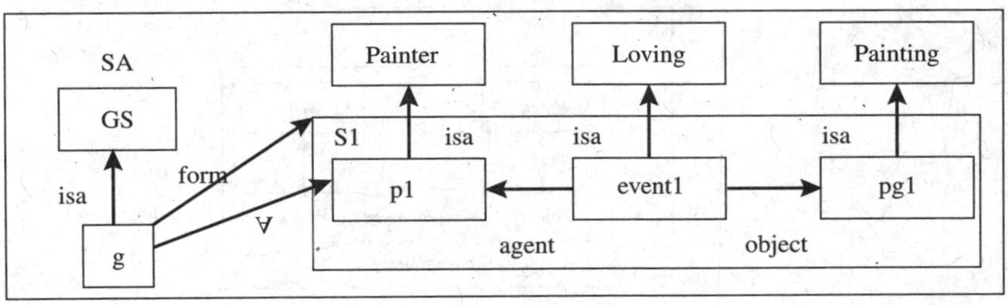

Figure 4.7

Now, consider the sentence: Every painter loves his painting. (Figure 4.7)

Here the variable painter is universally quantified, i.e., for all painters and y is existentially quantified, i.e., the particular painting made by the painter himself. Two spaces will be constructed for this network, one for each x, y. The variable x (*painter*) lies inside the general statement and y (*the painting*) lies outside the form of the general statement (Figure 4.8).

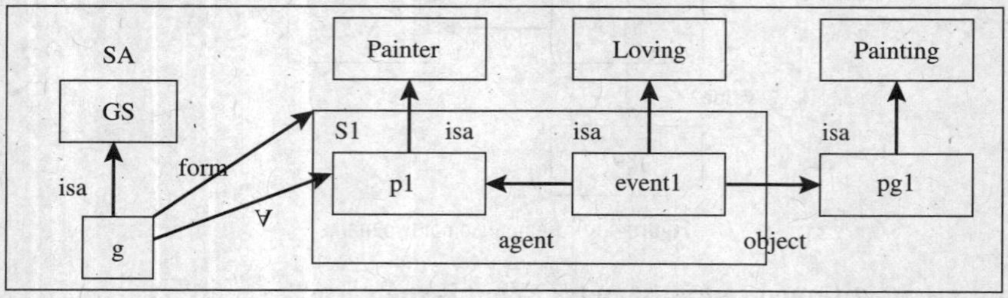

Figure 4.8 Partitioned network

Now if the sentence is every painter likes all paintings. Then both x and y are universally quantified. (Figure 4.9) The partitioned semantic network for this is:

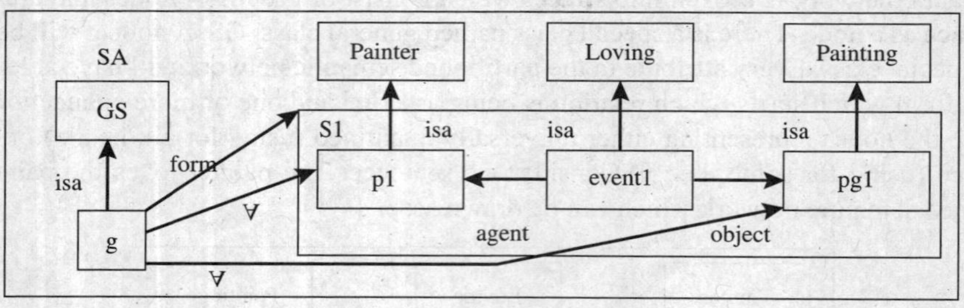

Figure 4.9

2. They also allow for propositions to be made without commitment to truth. Consider the following: *Ashima believes that the water is wet.* This proposition can be encoded as *the water is wet* in a *space* and within it have nodes and arcs to represent the fact. We can have the nodes and arcs to link this *space*, the rest of the network to represent Ashima's belief (Figure 4.10).

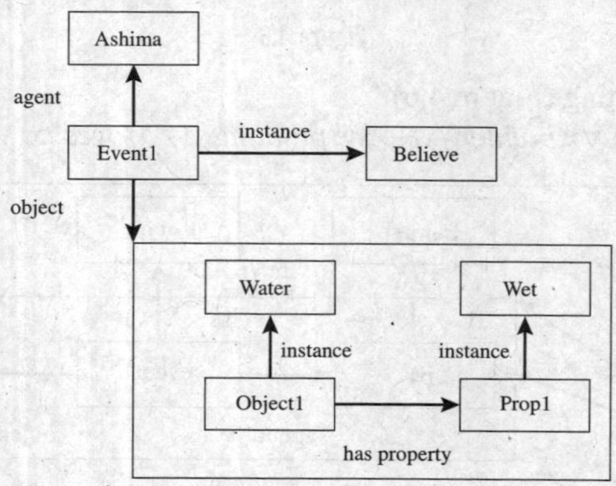

Figure 4.10 Partitioned network

4.7.2 Frames

Q. How can we represent knowledge using frames?

Ans. A *frame* is a collection of attributes or slots and associated values that describe some real-world entity. Frame use data structure (records) to represent the knowledge represented in semantic networks. These can be considered as an extension to semantic nets when complex structure is to be represented. Frames can be understood using set theory.

Each frame represents the node in a semantic network as a class (i.e., a set of elements), or an instance (i.e., an element of a class) and each relation as a slot.

Class is either super class or meta class for all classes, i.e., every class *isa* Class. Slot is the meta class of all slots.

Every class has cardinality as essential attribute which indicates the number of elements in that set. The *isa* attribute possesses a transitivity property. Both *isa* and *instance* have inverses which are called subclasses or all instances. Cardinality is specified for all base classes. The attributes and values which are common to all the instances of a class are represented in a frame. A * is used to indicate the attributes which can be inherited by the subclasses of that class.

A slot maps from elements of its domain, i.e., class to elements of its range, i.e., values. There are many attributes which are attached with each slot.

(a) *Instance*: it relates the slot to its class
(b) *Definition*: The definition or value for definition of the slot
(c) *Default*: It specifies the default value of any element in the slot if any other value is not specified
(d) *Domain*: The domain of the elements of the slot
(e) *Range*: It specifies the class of which elements of range must be elements
(f) *Range-constraint*: It specifies the logical expression that constraints the range of the elements. If it is absent, then it is assumed to be TRUE
(g) *To-compute*: In case the value of the slot is to be computed, the procedure is written for deriving its value
(h) *Single-valued*: In case the slot computes a function, it must return only a single value, otherwise many values can be returned. The default value is assumed to be true if it is not specified as false
(i) *Inverse*: It contains the inverse of the slot useful in reasoning
(j) *Transfers-through*: Lists other slots from which values for this slot can be derived through inheritance.

Q. What are the reasoning actions that can be performed using frames?

Ans. The frame–system interpreter can perform the following reasoning actions:

(i) *Relating the definition*: Propagation of definition values along *isa* and *instance* links to relate all information (using definition attribute)
(ii) *Inheritance*: Inheriting all values including default values to slots related (using transfers through and default attributes)
(iii) *Legality of value*: This is done to verify that the value of the slot is legal (using range-constraint and single-valued attribute)
(iv) *Consistency check*: This is done to verify that the slot makes sense for the frame when a slot value is added to a frame (using domain constraint attribute)
(v) *Maintaining consistency*: When one value of slot may be updated, its inverse should also be updated to maintain consistency (using inverse attribute)

(vi) *Computation of a value for a slot*: Using to-compute and transfers through attributes, the value for a slot can be computed.

4.8 STRONG SLOT AND FILLER STRUCTURES

Q. What are strong slot and filler structures in AI?

Ans. The structures used for representing knowledge which need specific rules to be specified explicitly (i.e., strongly) are called strong slot and filler structures.

4.8.1 Conceptual Dependencies

Q. How can we represent knowledge using Schank's conceptual dependency?

Ans. Conceptual dependency originally developed by Schank et al. to represent knowledge acquired from natural language input. The goals of this theory are as follows

- To help in the drawing of inference from sentences
- To be independent of the words used in the original input
- That is to say: For any two (or more) sentences that are identical in meaning there should be only one representation of that meaning

Conceptual dependencies provide a structure into which nodes representing information can be placed, a specific set of primitives and at a given level of granularity. Sentences are represented as a series of diagrams depicting actions using both abstract and real physical situations. The actions are built up from a set of primitive acts which can be modified by tense. The mood can also be included in the representation.

Q. What are the primitive acts in a conceptual dependency?

Ans. Examples of primitive acts given by Schank and Abelson used in conceptual dependency are:

ATRANS – Transfer of an abstract relationship. E.g., give, donate, take.
PTRANS – Transfer of the physical location of an object. E.g., go, walk, run.
PROPEL – Application of a physical force to an object. E.g., push.
MTRANS – Transfer of mental information. E.g., tell.
MBUILD – Construct new information from old. E.g., decide.
SPEAK – Utter a sound. E.g., say, speak.
ATTEND – Focus a sense on a stimulus. E.g., listen, watch.
MOVE – Movement of a body part by owner. E.g., punch, kick.
GRASP – Actor grasping an object. E.g., clutch, grasp.
INGEST – Actor ingesting an object. E.g., eat, smoke, drink.
EXPEL – Actor getting rid of an object from body. E.g., vomit, cry, sweat.

The following six primitive conceptual categories provide building blocks which are the set of allowable dependencies in the concepts in a sentence.

PP – Real-world objects
PA – Attributes of objects
ACT– Real-world actions
AA – Attributes of actions
T – Times

LOC – Locations

Q. How do we represent different tenses and moods in conceptual dependencies?

Ans. The use of tense and mood in describing events is represented using the following modifiers. The action is represented by ⇔ which takes two arguments, one is the actor and the other is the action. In the example given here, actor is bird and action is fly which is represented as PTRANS.

Modifier	Example	Usage syntax in CD
blank – present tense	The bird flies.	Bird ⇔ PTRANS
f – future tense	The bird will fly.	F Bird ⇔ PTRANS
p – past tense	The bird flew.	P Bird ⇔ PTRANS
? – interrogative	Does the bird fly?	? Bird ⇔ PTRANS
	Will the bird fly?	f? Bird ⇔ PTRANS
	Did the bird fly?	p? Bird ⇔ PTRANS
/– negative	The bird will not fly.	f/ Bird ⇔ PTRANS
	The bird did not fly.	p/ Bird ⇔ PTRANS
c – conditional	The bird flies if it is sunny.	Pl refer to solved examples as it involves complex conceptualizations
delta – timeless	Ostrich cannot fly.	/ Ostrich ⇔ PTRANS
k – continuing	The bird is flying.	K Bird ⇔ PTRANS
	The bird will be flying.	f k Bird ⇔ PTRANS
	The bird was flying.	p k Bird ⇔ PTRANS
ts – start transition	The bird has started flying.	ts Bird ⇔ PTRANS
	The bird will start flying	f t_s Bird ⇔ PTRANS
tf – finished transition	The bird has stopped flying.	t_f Bird ⇔ PTRANS
	The bird will stop flying.	f t_f Bird ⇔ PTRANS

The bird flies if it is sunny.

Sunny

C ⇑

Bird ⇔ PTRANS

Q. Explain all conceptual dependencies.

Ans. Following are the semantic rules for the formation of dependency structures:

1. This rule specifies the relation between an actor PP and the event ACT caused by him/her. Double arrows (⇔) indicate *two-way* links between the actor (PP) and action (ACT).

   Examples: Bird flew

		p
PP ⇔ ACT	Bird flew	Bird ⇔ PTRANS

2. This rule specifies the relationship between two PPs one of which is a subset of other.

   Example: Joe is a PP and he is a student.

PP ⇔ PP	Joe is a student	Joe ⇔ student

3. This rule specifies the attribute PA of an actor PP.

   Example: A beautiful girl.

PP ← PA	A beautiful girl	Girl ← Beautiful

4. The rule below indicates the relationship between an actor PP and the object O of the action ACT performed by him/her.

   Example: John pushed the door. Here, the action is pushing and the object that is pushed is door. The actor is John.

ACT $\xleftarrow{O}$ PP	John pushed the door.	John $\overset{P}{\Longleftrightarrow}$ PROPEL $\xleftarrow{O}$ Door

5. The R in the rule indicates the relation indicates a recipient–donor pair.

   Example: John gave a flower to Sue. Here, the actor is John, the recipient is Sue, the action is giving and the object that is given is flower.

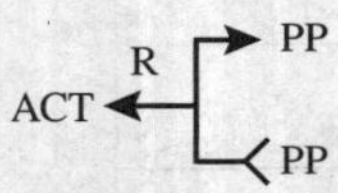

John gave a flower to Sue.

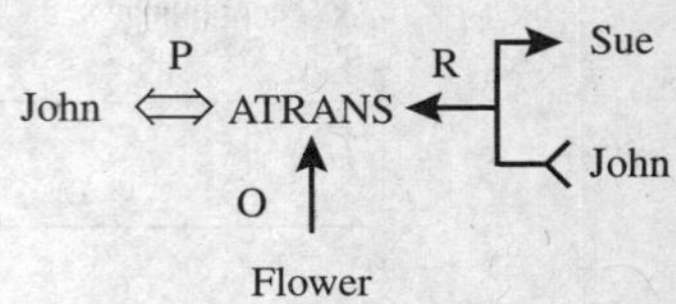

6. The D in the following rule indicates the physical source - destination pair of the object.

   Example: The gardener will water the plants. Here, the actor is gardener, the action is watering, the changes are in the physical location of water from bucket or pipe to plants.

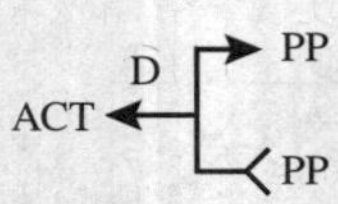

The gardener will water the plants.

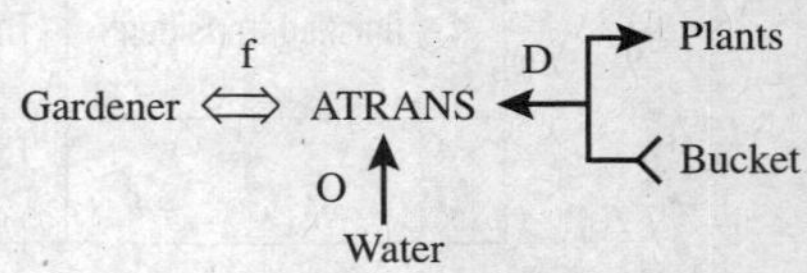

7. PP <≡> PA

   The triple arrow is link but between an object, PP, and its attribute, PA. It represents *isa* type dependencies. *Example:* Dave <≡> lecturer, Dave is a lecturer.

   Primitive states are used to describe many state descriptions such as height, health, mental state, and physical state. There are many more physical states than primitive actions. They use a numeric scale.

John <≡> height (+10)	John is the tallest
John <≡> height (<average)	John is short
Frank Zappa <≡> health (–10)	Frank Zappa is dead
Dave <≡> mental_state (–10)	Dave is sad
Vase <≡> physical_state (–10)	The vase is broken

8. This rule indicates the relation between a conceptualization and the time at which it occurred. → indicates the time of occurrence in the relationship.

   Example: Raghav gave the book to Mauli yesterday.

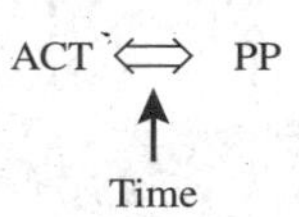

Raghav gave the book to Mauli yesterday

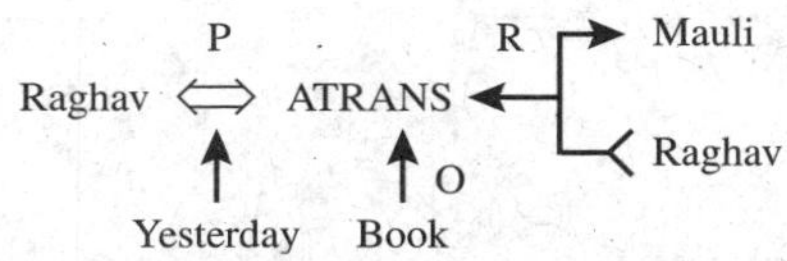

9. This rule specifies the relation between a conceptualization and the place at which it occurred. Example: Raghav will be eating ice-cream in ice-cream parlor tomorrow. The place is indicated by arrow with a double line.

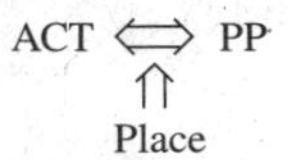

Raghav will be eating ice cream in the ice cream parlor.

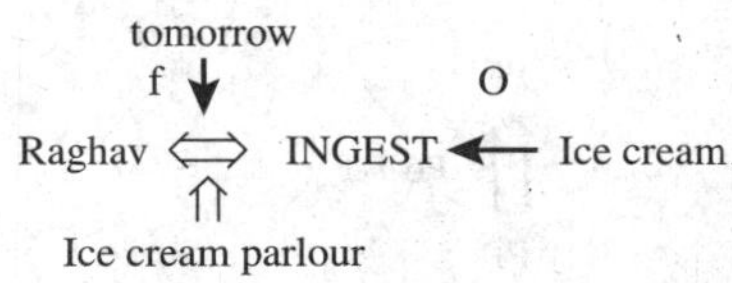

10. This rule describes the relationship between an actor and a state in which it started and another in which it ended.

    Example: The boy fell ill. This can be represented as the change in health of the boy from positive value to negative value.

The boy fell ill.

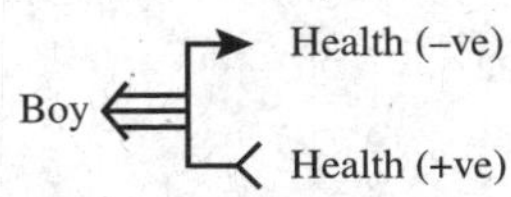

11. The following rule specifies the relationship between one conceptualization and another one that caused it to occur.

    Example: Saurabh became healthy because he used to drink juice. Here, the health of Saurabh improved from say 10 to 50. This occurred because he ingested juice.

Saurabh became healthy because he used to drink juice

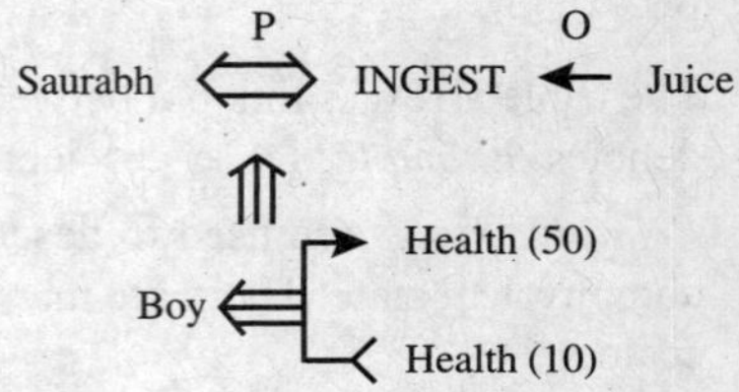

12. The following rule specifies the relationship between one conceptualization and another one that occurred at the time of occurring of the first.
    Example: Usha saw a peacock while going home from garden.

Usha saw a peacock while going home from garden.

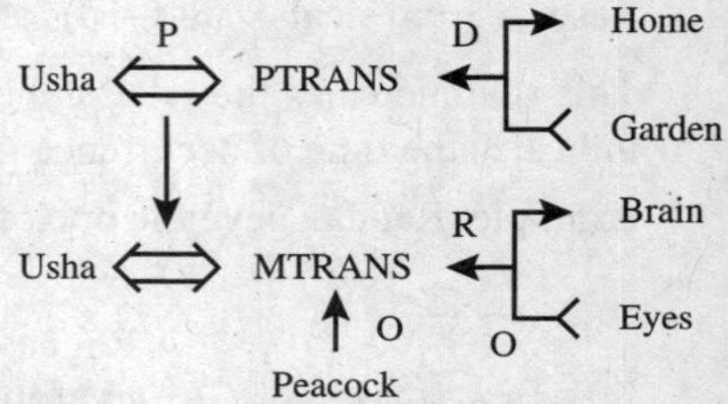

13. When one actor provides some information about the other object, the relation between two actors is indicted by the following rule. This information can be of three types:
    (a) *Possession* (*POSS-BY*)
    Example: Smriti's doll. This means doll is possessed by Smriti.

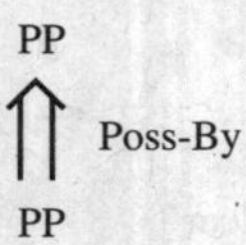

Smriti's doll

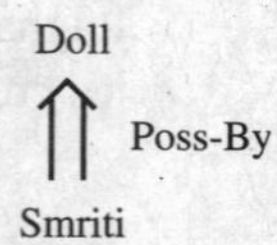

(b) *Location* (*LOC*)
Example: Patiala is located in Punjab. This means Punjab is location of Patiala.

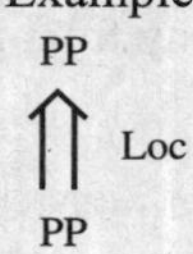

Patiala is located in Punjab.

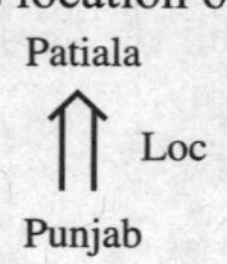

(c) *Physical containment* (*CONT*)
Example: The candy is in the container. This means the container contains the candy.

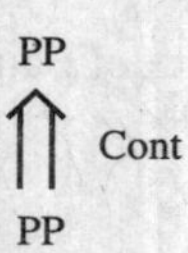

The candy is in the container.

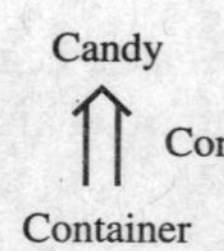

14. This rule specifies the relation between the instruments with which the actor performs the action. Example: Deepak ate curd with the spoon. Here, the action is ingesting the curd and it is done with a spoon.

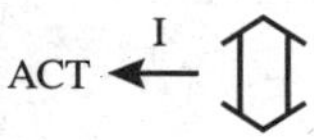

Deepak ate curd with the spoon.

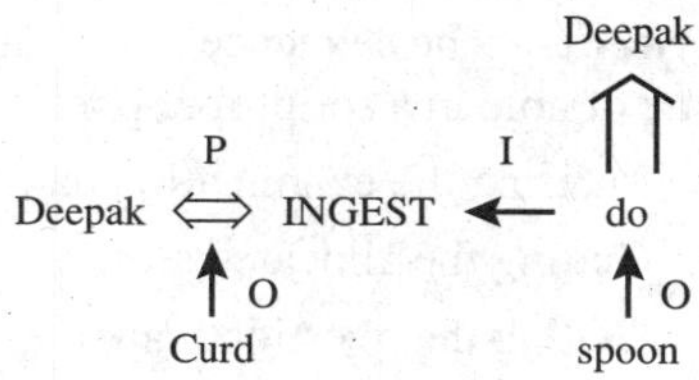

Q. Write the advantages and disadvantages of CDs?

Ans. Conceptual dependencies using these primitives involves fewer inference rules, many inference rules are already represented in CD structure and the holes in the initial structure help to focus on the points still to be established.

Disadvantages of CD are knowledge must be decomposed into fairly low level primitives, impossible or difficult to find correct set of primitives, a lot of inference may still be required. Representations can be complex even for relatively simple actions.

There are many advantages of representing knowledge using conceptual dependencies and there are some disadvantages also. These are summarized in table below:

Advantages	Disadvantages
• Conceptual dependencies involve fewer inference rules because many inference rules are already represented in CD structure	• Using CDs, knowledge must be decomposed into fairly low level primitives which may be impossible or difficult to find
	• Representations can be complex even for relatively simple actions

4.8.2 Scripts

Q. How can we represent knowledge using Scripts?

Ans. A script is a structure that prescribes a set of circumstances which could be expected to follow on from one another. It is similar to a thought sequence or a chain of situations which could be anticipated. It could be considered to consist of a number of slots or frames but with more specialized roles. The components of a script include:

Roles – Persons involved in the events. For example in a script for appearing for exam in an examination hall, the roles are student, instructor.

Props – Slots representing objects involved in events. For example in a script for appearing for exam in an examination hall, the props are pen, student_identity_card, answer_sheet, question_paper, table, desk.

Entry conditions – These are the conditions that must be satisfied before events in the script can occur. For example in a script for appearing for exam in an examination hall, the entry condition is that there is exam scheduled on that day, the student has pen and student_identity_card, the instructor has answer_sheets and question_papers with him/her.

Results – Conditions that will be true after events in script occur. For example in a script for appearing for exam in an examination hall, the student will have question_paper, the instructor will have filled answer_sheets.

Track – Variations on the script. Different tracks may share components of the same script. For example in a script for appearing for exam in an examination hall, it may be centre for AIEEE exam or centre for CAT exam.

Scenes –The sequence of events that occur. Events are represented in conceptual dependency form. For example in a script for appearing for exam in an examination hall, the scenes could be

1. Entering the examination hall.
2. Getting the allocated seat.
3. Getting the question_paper.
4. Attempting the question_paper.
5. Submitting the answer_sheet.
6. Exiting the examination hall.

Q. Write the advantages and disadvantages of scripts.

Ans. Advantages of scripts are that they are able to predict events and a single coherent interpretation may be build up from a collection of observations. Disadvantages are that they are less general than frames and these may not be suitable to represent all kinds of knowledge.

There are many advantages of representing knowledge using conceptual dependencies and there are some disadvantages also. These are summarized in table below:

Advantages	Disadvantages
• Scripts have the property that they are able to predict events	• Scripts are less general than frames
• A single coherent interpretation may be build up from a collection of observations	• Scripts may not be suitable to represent all kinds of knowledge

4.8.3 CYC

Q. Explain CYC.

Ans. CYC is a very large knowledge base project aimed at capturing human commonsense knowledge. In knowledge representation, sometimes some facts are missing if we forget to state them explicitly. This causes some theorems to fail while they are true because of the missing facts. The goal of CYC is to encode a very large body of knowledge which is made so clear that there is nothing left unstated. CYC can be used by multi-users for natural language understanding as it includes a vast knowledge (millions of facts). One user can modify the centralized knowledge base and other users can access the modified shared knowledge. It can also be combined with other specialized knowledge bases to produce systems which are not brittle.

Q. What is CYCL?

Ans. CYCL is LISP like frame-based language in which the knowledge in encoded in CYC. It simplifies the task of inheritance by generalization in inheritance so that properties can be inherited not only using *isa* and *instance* links but along any link. Here slots are full-fledged objects.

Q. How does CYC incorporates a huge amount of knowledge?

Ans. In any knowledge-based system, the knowledge represents entities in the world. In order to identify the kinds of things which can exist, the relationship between them, the properties common in them, the concept of global ontology is used by CYC. The highest level concept is Thing, i.e., everything is an instance of Thing. Below this, there are several distinctions:

(a) *Collection*: Represents a class of objects like Person, Furniture.
(b) *IndividualObject*: Represents an instance of collection like Shrey, Chair.
(c) *Intangible*: Represents things without mass, like numbers, sets, laws, etc.
(d) *TangibleObject*: Represents things with mass, like an apple, a table, etc.
(e) *CompositeObject*: It has two key slots: *physicalExtent* and *intangibleExtent*.
Example: An animal is a CompositeObject whose physicalExtent is its body and whole, intangibleExtent is it heart.
(f) *Substance*: It is subclass of Individual Object. Any subclass of substance is something that retains its properties when it is cut up into smaller pieces, like steel is a metal and bowl Bowl1 (IndividualObject) is made up of steel (Substance).
(g) *Slots*: It is subclass of Intangible.
(h) *Time*: There are two temporal measures used for representing information about events occurring at a particular time.

4.9 ONTOLOGY

Q. What is ontology?

Ans. In problem solving, many different areas may be involved in reasoning simultaneously. We may need to represent Beliefs, Categories, Physical Objects, Composite Objects, Mental Objects, Events, Change, Processes, Substances, Measures, Space, and Time.

In problem solving, many different areas may be involved in reasoning simultaneously. Ontology is the philosophical study of what exists in real world. It is concerned with entities and specifies at a very high level what kinds of things exist and what are their general properties. We may need to represent entities which may be categorized as Beliefs, Categories, Physical Objects, Composite Objects, Mental Objects, Events, Change, Processes, Substances, Measures, Space, and Time.

Q. Discuss categorization and objects.

Ans. Knowledge representation requires the organization of objects into categories: Interaction at the level of the object and reasoning at the level of categories. Categories play a role in predictions about objects based on perceived properties. Categories can be represented in two ways by first-order logic – (1) Predicates: apple (x) and (2) Reification of categories into objects: apples. Category defines the set of its members.

Various categories in first-order logic are:

1. An object is a member of a category:
   Example: FB1 is a member of class Footballs.
   $FB_1 \in$ Footballs implies Member-of (FB_1, Footballs) in first-order logic
2. A category is a subclass of another category:
   Example: all footballs are balls.
   Footballs $\subseteq$ Balls implies Subset-of (Footballs, Balls) in first-order logic
3. All members of a category have some properties:
   Example: all footballs are round.

$\forall x : x \in$ Footballs $\Rightarrow$ Round (x)

4. All members of a category can be recognized by some properties:

   Example: A ball having white and black color and round shape is a football.

   $\forall x$ (White_and_black (x)) $\wedge$ Round (x) $\wedge$ x $\in$ Balls $\Rightarrow$ x $\in$ Footballs
5. Natural kinds: Many categories have no clear-cut definitions, e.g., chair, bush, book.
6. Prototypes: We can write down useful facts about categories without providing exact definitions.

   Example: Tomatoes are sometimes green, red, yellow, black, but are mostly round. We can write a prototype of a typical tomato by defining it to be red in color and round in shape.

   category *Typical (Tomatoes)*

   $\forall x : x \in$ Typical (Tomatoes) $\Rightarrow$ Red (x) $\wedge$ Round (x).

Q. Describe relations between categories.

Ans. Relation between various categories are:

1. Disjoint: Two or more categories c_1 and c_2 are ***disjoint*** if they have no members in common:

   Disjoint (s) $\Leftrightarrow$ ($\forall$ c_1,c_2 $c_1 \in s \wedge c_2 \in s \wedge c_1$ [1] $c_2 \Rightarrow$ Intersection (c_1,c_2) = $\varnothing$)

   Example: Disjoint ({colors, vegetables})
2. Exhaustive decomposition: A set of categories *s* constitutes an ***exhaustive decomposition*** of a category *c* if all members of the set *c* are covered by categories in *s*:

   ED (*s, c*) $\Leftrightarrow$ ($\forall$ i i $\in$ c $\Rightarrow \exists$ c_2 $c_2 \in s \wedge$ i $\in$ c_2)

   Example: ExhaustiveDecomposition ({Americans, Canadian, Mexicans}, North Americans)
3. Partition: A ***partition*** is a disjoint exhaustive decomposition:

   Partition (*s, c*) $\Leftrightarrow$ Disjoint (s) $\wedge$ ExhaustiveDecomposition (*s, c*)

   Example: Partition ({Males, Females}, Persons).

Q. Discuss Composite objects.

Ans. One object may be part of another and hence one is composed of other objects. It is represented using predicate PartOf (object, composite_object). For example, state Punjab is part of country India and is represented as PartOf (Punjab, India). City Patiala is part of state Punjab and is represented as PartOf (Patiala, Punjab). The PartOf predicate is transitive (and irreflexive), i.e.,

$\forall$ x PartOf (x, x)

$\forall$ x, y, z PartOf (x, y) $\wedge$ PartOf (y, z) $\Rightarrow$ PartOf (x, z)

So we can infer that city Patiala is part of country India, i.e., PartOf (Patiala, India)

Q. Discuss measurements.

Ans. Objects have height, mass, cost, etc., as their properties or attributes. These are measured through the values that we assign to these properties or attributes. Some measures have scale while other may not. For example, measures like ease, beauty, and health have no scale for measurement. The measures like length, breadth, and height can be measured in terms of meters and centimeters or inches and feet, while weight can be measured using kilograms and grams or pounds.

Q. Discuss actions, events, and situations.

Ans. Actions, events, and situations are represented using situation calculus. Here the actions are represented as logical terms. Situations are logical terms consisting of the initial situation *s*. All situations resulting from the action *a* on *s* (=*Result (a, s)*). Fluents are functions and predicates that vary from one situation to the next. Eternal predicates are also allowed. Results of action sequences are determined by the individual actions. Projection task is that an agent should be able to deduce the outcome of a sequence of actions. Planning task is to find a sequence that achieves a desirable effect

Q. Describe change.

Ans. Simple situation calculus requires three axioms to describe change:

a. Possibility axiom: when is it possible to do the action
   At (Agent, x, s) $\wedge$ *Adjacent (x, y)* $\Rightarrow$ *Poss (Go (x, y), s)*

b. Effect axiom: describe changes due to action
   Poss (Go (x, y), s) $\Rightarrow$ *At (Agent, y, Result (Go (x, y), s))*

c. Frame axiom: which describe non-changes due to actions
   At (o, x, s) $\wedge$ *(o* $\neq$ *Agent)* $\wedge$ $\neg$*Holding (o, s)* $\Rightarrow$ *At (o, x, Result (Go (y, z), s))*

Q. Discuss mental events and objects in knowledge representation.

Ans. Knowledge base agents can have beliefs and deduce new beliefs using "Epistemic Logic". When there are beliefs and there is some knowledge about the inference process, it is stored in human brain and the brain processes this knowledge. For knowledge base agents, a model of the mental objects in someone's head and the processes that manipulate these objects is needed. For example, Believes (Saurabh, Flies (Doremon)) with Flies (Doremon) being a function is a candidate for a mental object.

Q. Discuss description logics as reasoning system for various categories.

Ans. Description logic is designed to describe definitions and properties about categories. These provide a formal language for constructing and combining category definitions. It provides efficient algorithms to decide subset and superset relationships between categories:

1. *Subsumption*: checking if one category is the subset of another by comparing their definitions.
2. *Classification*: checking whether an object belongs to a category.
3. *Consistency*: checking whether the category membership criteria are logically satisfiable.

SOLVED EXAMPLES

Q. Prove that P → Q is equivalent to ~P V Q.

Ans. In order to prove this, we will compare the truth values of both expressions.

P	~P	Q	P → Q	~P V Q
T	F	T	T	T
T	F	F	F	F
F	T	T	T	T
F	T	F	T	T

Hence, it is proved that P → Q is equivalent to ~P V Q.

Q. Show that the following formulae are logically equivalent using equivalence laws.
1. $(P \land Q) \lor (P \land \sim Q) \cong P$ **2. $P \to (Q \lor R) \cong \sim P \lor Q \lor R$**

Ans.

1. $(P \land Q) \lor (P \land \sim Q) \cong P \land (Q \lor \sim Q)$ (using Distributive law)
 $\cong P \land$ True (Law of excluded middle)
 $\cong P$
2. $P \to (Q \lor R) \cong \sim P \lor (Q \lor R)$
 $\cong \sim P \lor Q \lor R$

Q. Suppose we are to find a proof by resolution of proposition P with respect to a set of axioms: Mary will get her degree only if she registers as a student and pass her exam. She has registered herself as a student. She has passed her exam. Show that she will get a degree.

Ans. Let we symbolize the statements as follows:

R: Mary is a registered student

P: Mary has passed her exam

D: Mary gets her degree

Mary will get her degree only if she registers as a student and pass her exam can be represented as: $R \land P \to D$.

Clausal form of this is: $\sim R \lor \sim P \lor D$

So set F of all propositions in clausal form is $\{R, P, \sim R \lor \sim P \lor D\}$

Goal: Mary will get her degree (D)

Negation is ~D.

So F\` becomes $\{R, P, \sim R \lor \sim P \lor D, \sim D\}$

Let we now resolve theses clauses together to get an empty clause: This proves that Mary does not get a degree s false and hence Mary gets the degree is true (Figure 4.11).

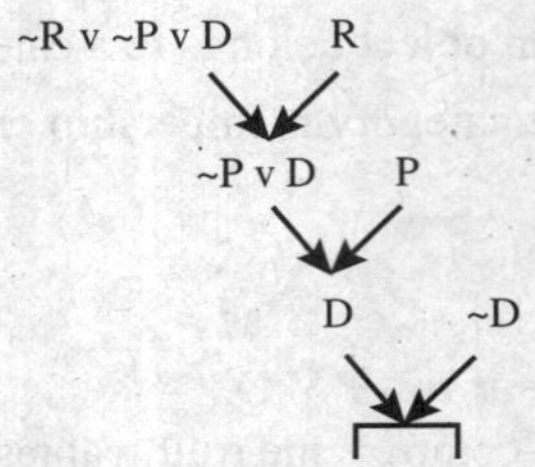

Figure 4.11

Q. Represent the following into first-order predicate logic.
1. Every gardener likes the sun.

Ans. $(\forall x)$ gardener $(x) \geq$ likes (x, Sun)

2. One can fool all of the people some of the time.

Ans. $(\forall x) (\exists t)$ (person $(x) \land$ time $(t) \geq$ can-fool (x, t)

3. All purple mushrooms are poisonous.

Ans. $(\forall x)$ (mushroom $(x) \land$ purple $(x)) \geq$ poisonous (x)

Q. Consider the following set of axioms.

1. Anything anyone eats and is not killed by is a food
2. Noodles are food
3. Burger is food
4. Vishal eats everything, Viraat eats
5. Viraat eats apples and is still alive

Translate these sentences into formulas as predicate logic. Prove that Vishal eats apples using backward reasoning.

Ans. The predicate logic form of the given set of axioms is:

1. $\forall$x, f: eats (x, f) Λ killedby (x, f) $\rightarrow$ food (f)
2. Food (Noodles)
3. Food (Burger)
4. $\forall$ f1: eats (Viraat, f1) $\rightarrow$ eats (Vishal, f1)
5. Eats (Viraat, Apples) Λ alive (Viraat).

This can be written

(5a). Eats (Viraat, Apples)

(5b).Alive (Viraat).

In backward chaining, we start from goal. Goal is: eats (Vishal, Apples).

Eats (Vishal, Apples).

(4) $\uparrow$ {substitution Apples for f1}.

Eats (Viraat, Apples).

(5a) $\uparrow$

Nil.

This implies there is nothing to be proved further. Hence, Vishal eats apple is proved to be true.

Q. Consider the following set of axioms.

1. Sham like easy courses

2. All courses in Arts department are easy

3. All courses in Science department are not easy

4. Physics is a science course

5. Sketching is an Arts course

Find using resolution "Which course does Sham like?"

Ans. In order to use resolution, we will have to represent all clauses into predicate form and then clausal form. First, the representation of all in predicate form is given below:

1. $\forall$ X: easy (X) $\rightarrow$ likes (Sham, X)
2. $\forall$ Y: arts (Y) $\rightarrow$ easy (Y)
3. $\forall$ Z: science (Z) $\rightarrow$ ~easy (Z)
4. science (physics)
5. arts (sketching)

Now the above clauses are converted into clausal form as follows:

1. ~easy (X) V likes (sham, X)
2. ~arts (Y) V easy (Y)
3. ~science (Z) V ~easy (Z)
4. science (physics)
5. arts (sketching)

Goal: (a) ∃ C: likes (sham, C)
In resolution, we need to start with negation of the goal: ~likes (sham, C).
~likes (sham, C) resolves with 1 by substituting X by C and the resolvent is: ~easy (C).
Which is resolved with 2 by substituting Y by C and the resolvent is: ~arts (C).
Which is resolved with 5 by substituting C by sketching.
This produces a null clause, i.e., a contradiction which means the negation: sham does not like any course is false for C = Sketching. Hence, Sham likes sketching is true (Figure 4.12)

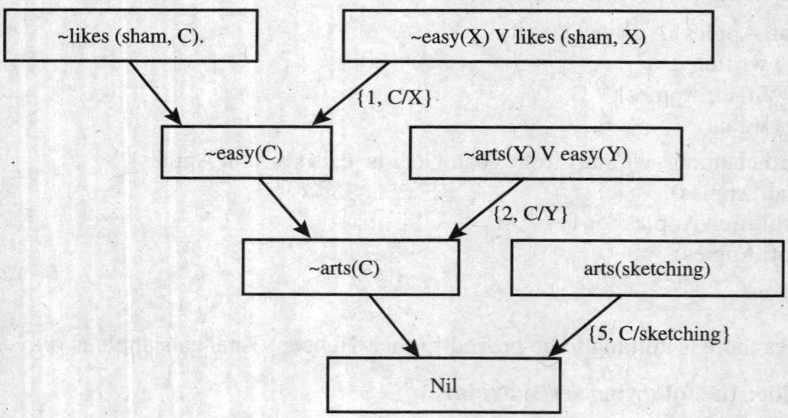

Figure 4.12

Q. Draw a semantic network for representing: Ram was playing with football in the garden.
Ans.

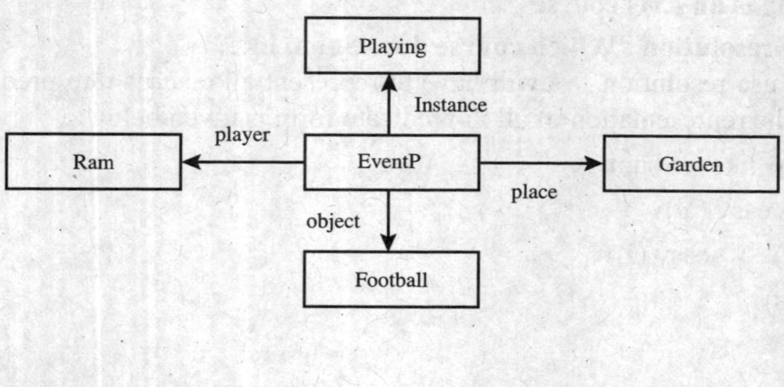

Q. Draw a semantic network to represent: Every teacher likes intelligent students.

Ans. For this sentence, partitioned semantic network will be drawn as shown (Figure 4.13).

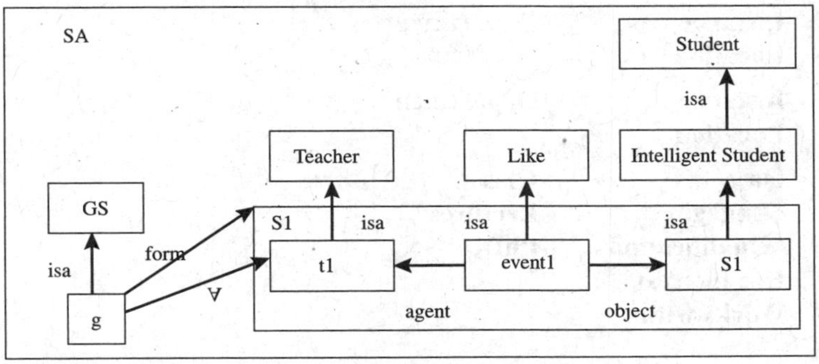

Figure 4.13

Q. Draw a semantic network to represent the following set of knowledge: ABC is a university. CSD, ECD, and MED are three department in it. Sudha works in department of CSD. CSD is located in C block. She is a professor. Every professor engage lectures and has PhD qualification. Sudha's area of interest is AI. Represent the same knowledge in frames.

Ans. the semantic network is drawn in the following (Figure14.4):

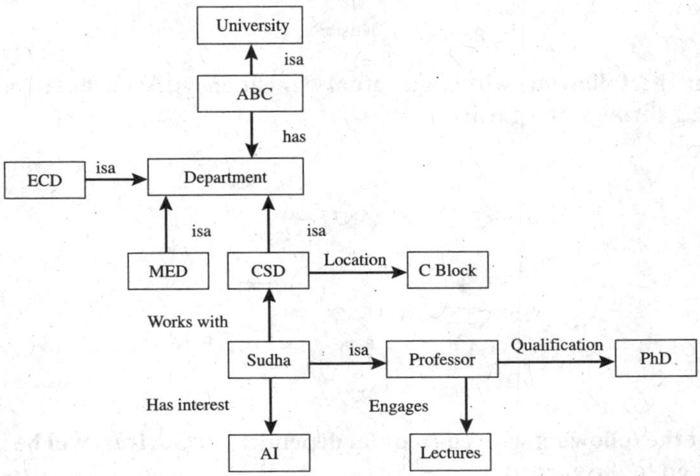

Figure 14.4

University	**Isa**	**Class**	**Slot**		
	***Has**	**Department**	**Sudha**	**Isa**	**Professor**
ABC	**Isa**	**University**		**Has interest**	**AI**
				Engages	**Lectures**
Department	**Part-of**	**University**		**Qualification**	**PhD**
	Location			**Works with**	**CSD**

CSD	**Instance**	**Department**
	Location	**C Block**
MED	**Instance**	**Department**
	Location	
ECD	**Instance**	**Department**
	Location	
Professor	**Isa**	**Class**
	***Engages**	**Lectures**
	***Qualification**	**PhD**
	Has interest	
	Works with	

Q. Represent the following with conceptual dependency: Shikha was listening music in the balcony on Sunday.

Ans.

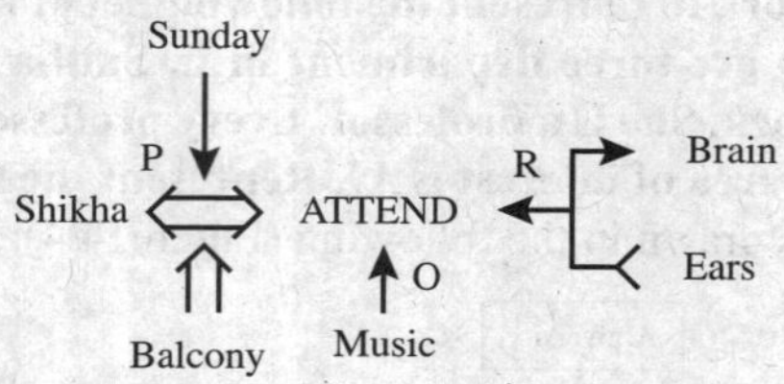

Q. Represent the following with conceptual dependency: Ashu heard a frog in the pond while going through the garden.

Ans.

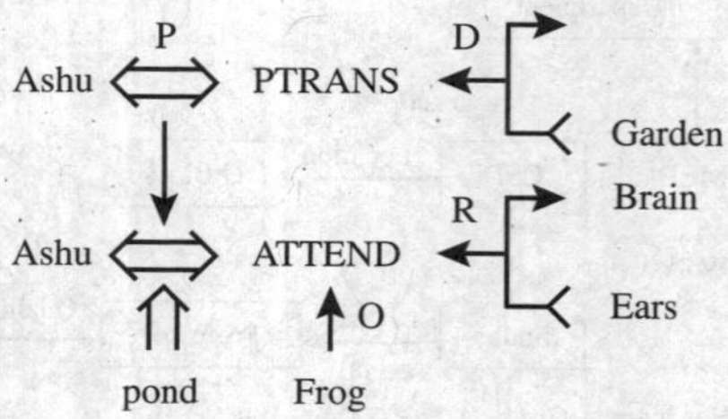

Q. Represent the following with conceptual dependency: Gariyasi will be able to touch roses if she will go to the garden.

Ans.

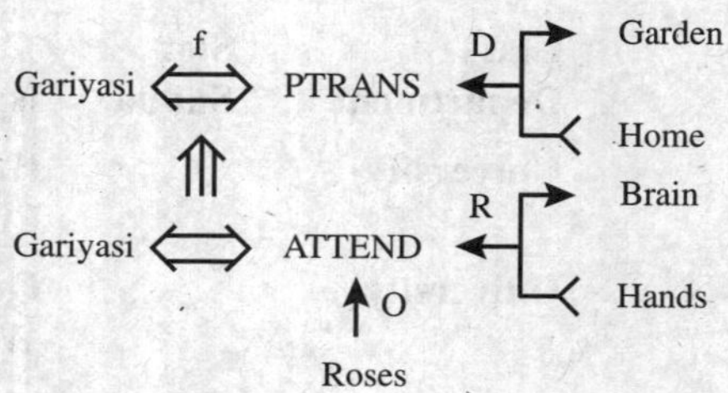

Q. Write a script for Robbing a bank.

Ans. Scripts are useful in describing certain situations such as robbing a bank. This might involve:

- Getting a gun
- Hold up a bank
- Escape with the money

Here the *Props* might be

- Gun, Loot, Bag, Get away in a car

The *Roles* might be: Robber, Cashier, Bank Manager, Policeman.

The *Entry Conditions* might be:

- Robber is poor
- Robber is destitute

The *Results* might be:

- Robber has more money
- Bank Manager is angry
- Cashier is in a state of shock
- Policeman is shot.

There are three scenes: obtaining the gun, robbing the bank, and the get away.

The full script could be described in the following Figure:

<table>
<tr><td>

Script: Robbery   ***Track: ABC Bank***
***Props*:**
G, Gun; L, Loot; B, Bag; D, Door; C, Car.
***Roles*:** R, Robber; M, Cashier; O, Bank Manager; P, Policeman.
***Entry conditions*:** R is poor. R is destitute.
***Results*:**
R has more money
O is angry
M is in state of shock
P is shot

</td></tr>
<tr><td>

***Scene 1: Getting a gun*:**
R PTRANS R into Gun shop
R MBUILD R choice of G
R MTRANS choice.
R ATRANS buys G.
(go to scene 2)

</td></tr>
<tr><td>

Scene 2: Holding up the bag
R PTRANS R into bank
R ATTEND eyes M, O, and P
R MOVE R to M position

</td></tr>
</table>

R GRASP G R MOVE G to point to M R MTRANS "Give the money or else" to M P MTRANS "Hold it Hands up" to R P PROPEL shoots G P INGEST bullet from G M ATRANS L to M M ATRANS L puts in bag B M PTRANS exit O ATRANS raises the alarm (go to scene 3)
Scene 3: The Door M PTRANS M to D M PTRANS M to C

Q. Give an example of a skolem constant.

Ans. Consider the following sentences:

1. Kipper is a dog.
2. There exists a dog who has bitten the king.

The predicate form of these sentences is:

1. dog(kipper).
2. $\forall\chi$ dog(x) Λ bitten(x,king).

   Now in order to eliminate the existential quantifier, if we replace x by kipper, then kipper is called a skolem constant.

Q. Give an example of a skolem function.

Ans. Consider the following sentence: Everyone has a mother.

The predicate form of the sentence is: $\forall\chi\ \exists y$: mother(x,y).

In order to eliminate the existential quantifier y, we can consider it as a function of universally quantified variable x because for any x, we are talking about x's mother. Thus the predicate form becomes: $\forall\chi$: mother(x,m(x)).

MULTIPLE CHOICE QUESTIONS

Select the most appropriate answer for the following questions:

1. Which of the following represents the ability to acquire new information easily?
   (a) Representational adequacy
   (b) Inferential adequacy
   (c) Inferential efficiency
   (d) Acquisitional efficiency
2. Which of the following characters not valid in the alphabet set of predicate calculus symbols?
   (a) #
   (b) a
   (c) _
   (d) 8

3. Which of the following are valid predicate calculus symbols?
   (a) Aman (b) Browny
   (c) Krazzy3 (d) All of these
4. Which of the following strings are not legal predicate calculus symbols?
   (a) 3hats (b) Tsum*
   (c) Percentage % (d) All of these
5. Which of the following symbols do not start with small letters?
   (a) Predicates (b) Variables
   (c) Constants (d) Function
6. Which of the following is not an atomic sentence?
   (a) Equal (plus (two, one), three) (b) Plus (two, three)
   (c) Greater (plus (four, five), plus (eight, three)) (d) None of these
7. Which of the following is not a weak slot and filler structure?
   (a) Conceptual dependencies (b) Frames
   (c) Semantic network (d) None of these
8. Which of the following is not a strong slot and filler structure?
   (a) Conceptual dependencies (b) Frames
   (c) Scripts (d) None of these
9. A general statement class is required in which of the following?
   (a) Frames (b) Semantic network
   (c) Partitioned semantic network (d) All of these
10. Which of the following primitive act is used for transfer of the physical location of an object?
    (a) ATRANS (b) PTRANS
    (c) MTRANS (d) ATTEND

Answers: 1. d 2. a 3. d 4. d 5. b 6. b 7. a 8. b 9. c 10. b

EXERCISES

1. Which of the following pair of expressions are logically equivalent? Show by using truth table.
   (a) (P → Q) → R and P → (Q → R)
   (b) P V ~Q → R and P V (~Q → R)
2. Represent the following statements into propositional calculus:
   It is winter time.
   It is cold.
   If it is winter time, then it is cold.
   A person catches cough if it is cold.
3. Represent the following statements into predicate form.
   a. Rocky and Robin are members of the Lions club.
   b. Every Lions club member is either a swimmer or a mountain climber.

c. Mountain climbers do not like rain.
d. Anyone who does not like rain is not a swimmer.
e. Rocky likes whatever Robin dislikes and dislikes whatever Robin likes.
f. Robin likes rain and water.

Use resolution to answer the question: “What does Rocky dislike?” and “Who is a mountain climber in the Lions club”?

4. Represent the following knowledge using a semantic network: The gardener watered the vegetable plants in the fields on Wednesday.
5. Represent the following knowledge using a partitioned semantic network: All the students hate exams.
6. Represent the following knowledge using a conceptual dependency: John gave a story book to Smith on Sunday morning.
7. Write a script for appearing for a dinner in a restaurant.

5

Uncertain Knowledge and Probabilistic Reasoning

5.1 INTRODUCTION

Most intelligent systems have some degree of uncertainty associated with them due to missing or unavailable data, unreliable or ambiguous data, etc. Sometimes the data representation is also not consistent and precise. Hence some measures should be taken in representing the uncertain data. Inference mechanisms should be used to combine the uncertainty of data in many related items and to draw inferences from such data. Several methods such as probability theory, fuzzy logic, mode, and temporal logic have been proposed by many researchers for handling uncertain information. Bayes' theorem is based on probability theory which formed the basis for Bayesian belief networks. Dempster–Shafer theory is also based on probability theory. Certainty factor theory is also based on probability theory which is used in representing the uncertain information in rule-based expert systems.

5.2 UNCERTAINTY

Q. Define uncertainty.

Ans. Uncertainty is defined as the lack of exact information or knowledge that helps us to find a correct conclusion.

5.2.1 Representing Knowledge in an Uncertain Domain

Q. How can knowledge be represented in an uncertain domain?

Ans. In an uncertain domain, the knowledge can be represented by representing the chance or likelihood of an event. This is done with the use of probability theory. Fuzzy logic can be used to represent uncertain data. Temporal logic also provides a measure to represent uncertain data.

In an uncertain domain, the knowledge can be represented by any of the following ways:

1. Representing the chance or likelihood of an event. This is done with the use of probability theory. For example, the chance of getting a number 5 on rolling a dice is 5/6.

2. Fuzzy logic can be used to represent uncertain data. For example, if we want to classify whether a person can be classified as fat or not based on the given weight of the person. Suppose the criteria is if the weight is more than 40 kilograms but less than 60 kilograms, the person is not fat and fat otherwise. Here for a given weight of 35, the person is not fat (value 0). For a given weight of 75, the person is fat (value 1). For a weight of 55 kilograms, the value will lie between 0 and 1 as it is uncertain.
3. Temporal logic also provides a measure to represent uncertain data. Temporal logic is used to describe any system of rules and symbolism for representing, and reasoning about, propositions qualified in terms of time. In a temporal logic, we can express statements like "I am *always* reading", or "I will be reading *until* I get tired. Always and until represent uncertainty in time.

5.3 PROBABILISTIC REASONING

Q. Define probability.

Ans. Probability is defined as the chance of occurring of an event. It lies between 0 and 1 and it represents the proportion of cases in which the particular event occurs among all the possible cases. In natural language like English, there are some vague words like probably, perhaps, etc. which indicate that the event is not certain, which leads to the definition of probability. So probability of 0 indicate impossibility of an event occurring and 1 indicate complete certainty for an event occurring and the value between 0 and 1 indicates the chance of occurring an event. The chances of an event occurring are called probability of success and the chances of an event not occurring are called probability of failure.

$$\text{Probability (success)} = \frac{\textit{The number of successes for an event}}{\textit{The total in number of possible outcomes}}$$

$$\text{Probability (failure)} = \frac{\textit{The number of failures for an event}}{\textit{The total in number of possible outcomes}}$$

Also, Probability (failure) + Probability (success) = 1

Therefore,

Probability (failure) = 1-Probability (success)

5.3.1 Joint Probability

Q. Define joint probability.

Ans. It is defined as the probability of occurrence of two independent events in conjunction, i.e., occurring together. The joint probability of A and B is written as P(A ∩ B) or P(A and B). It is given as P(A and B) = P(A)*P(B).

Example

An automatic machine fills poly bags with a mixture of beans, potatoes, and other vegetables. Most of the bags contain the correct weight, but because of the variation in the size of the beans and other vegetables, a package might be underweight or overweight. A check of 4,000 packages filled in the past month revealed the following information:

Weight	Event	Number of packages	Probability of occurrence
Underweight	A	100	P(A) = 100/4000
Satisfactory	B	3600	P(B) = 3600/4000
Overweight	C	300	P(C) = 300/4000
		4000(Total)	

5.3.2 Conditional Probability

Q. Define conditional probability.

Ans. Suppose there is a hypothesis H and an evidence E which may or may not support H. P(H) is the probability of H independently, i.e., without any relation to any evidence. This is also called prior probability. Conditional probability of H is represented by P(H|E) and is read as the probability of hypothesis H given that the evidence E is true. It is calculated as:

$$P(H|E) = \frac{\text{(The number of times H and E can occur)}}{\text{The number of times of E can occur}}$$

The numerator, i.e., the number of times H and E can occur indicate the probability that both H and E will occur is called joint probability of H and E and it is denoted by p(H ∩ E). The denominator, i.e., the number of rimes E can occur indicates the probability of occurrence of E denoted by p(E). The conditional probability of H given E has occurred is given as:

$$P(H|E) = \frac{P(H \cap E)}{P(E)} = \frac{P(H \text{ and } E)}{P(E)}$$

5.3.3 Probabilistic Techniques

Q. What are all the various probabilistic techniques?

Ans. These are the techniques which use probability for handling uncertainty in domain. Three types of probabilistic techniques are:

1. Bayesian networks.
2. Dempster–Shafer theory.
3. Certainty factors.

5.3.4 Bayes' Theorem

Q. Define Bayes' theorem.

Ans. Bayes' theorem provides a means to handle uncertain reasoning. It relates the conditional probability and probabilities of events H and E where H is the hypothesis and E is evidence. Bayes' theorem states that:

$$P(H|E) = \frac{P(E|H)*P(H)}{P(E)}$$

In expert systems, the domain experts need to do the following for applying Bayes' theorem:

1. Prior probabilities: The domain expert is required to find the prior probabilities for all the possible hypotheses which is true p(H) and false, i.e., p(~H).
2. Conditional probabilities: The domain expert is required to find conditional probabilities for observing evidence E given hypothesis H is true p(E|H) and if hypothesis is false p(E|~H). This is to be done for all possible combinations of evidences for all hypotheses.
3. Posterior probabilities: The expert system calculates p(H|E) when the user gives information about the observed evidence E, known as posterior probability.

Bayes' theorem can be further extended when there is one hypothesis and two evidences:

$$P(H \mid E1 \text{ and } E2) = \frac{P(E1 \mid H \text{ and } E2) * P(H \mid E2)}{P(E1 \text{ and } E2)}$$

Bayes' theorem can be further extended when there is one hypothesis and more than one evidences which are assumed to be independent of each other:

$$P(H \mid E1, E2, \ldots En) = \frac{P(E1 \mid H) * \ldots * (P(En \mid H))P(H)}{P(E1, E2, \ldots, En)}$$

Bayes' theorem can be further extended when there are more than one hypothesis and single evidence:

$$P(H_i \mid E) = \frac{P(E \mid H_i) * P(H_i)}{\sum_{n=1}^{k} (P(E \mid Hn) * P(Hn))}$$

Bayes' theorem can be further extended when there are more than one hypothesis and more than one evidence:

$$P(H_i \mid E1, \ldots En) = \frac{P(E1, \ldots En \mid H_i) * P(H_i)}{\sum_{n=1}^{k} (P(E1, \ldots, En \mid Hn) * P(Hn))}$$

$$= \frac{P(E1 \mid H_i) * P(E2 \mid H_i) * \ldots * P(En \mid H_i) * P(H_i)}{\sum_{n=1}^{k} (P(E1 \mid H_i) * P(E2 \mid H_i) * \ldots P(En \mid Hn) * P(Hn))}$$

5.3.5 Limitations of Bayes' Theorem

Q. What are the limitations of Bayes' theorem?

Ans. In Bayes' theorem, if there are *n* different propositions being considered, then the size of the set of joint probabilities that is required to compute the conditional probability of a given hypothesis grows as 2^n. This leads to many limitations such as a very large space required to store all the probabilities, very large amount of time required to compute the probabilities; and the most important, it is very difficult to compute all the probabilities.

5.3.6 Bayesian Belief Network

Q. Explain Bayesian belief networks.

Ans. Belief networks define probabilistic independencies and dependencies among the variables in the network. Causality relationship is also reflected in belief networks. So these are also known as causal network or probabilistic network. It contains a directed acyclic graph (DAG) whose nodes are random variables in the given problem. If there is a direct link from node A to node B, then it indicates that node A has direct influence on node B and A is called the parent of B. In the network, a table is created which contains the conditional probability for all nodes along with the effect of their parent nodes. This table contains manageable number of probability values by considering only those conditional probabilities which are actually required for dependent nodes only. Otherwise, in principle, handling uncertainty needs specifying the complete probability distribution over all possible combinations of variable values (2^n-1 for n variables). For example, if X and Y are dependent then, P(XY) = P(X)*P(Y|X). But for those variables, where X and Y are independent, P(XY) = P(X)*P(Y) and there is no need for calculating P(Y|X). Thus Bayesian belief network simplifies the tasks by stating independent variables and eliminating the need for specifying conditional probabilities among all the variables. Also these can easily handle incomplete data sets.

Explain probabilistic independencies and dependencies. Also define causality relationship. If defined earlier, there should be a side note in a shaded box for recapitulation as these are technical terms which need to be understood for proceeding further with the chapter. Give an illustration of a DAG, linked to an example, explain what are nodes, When explaining the dependency formula give an example of a situation illustrating dependency. Elaborate on what is an incomplete data sets as well and how using Bayesian belief networks is an advantage in this situation.

5.3.7 Propagation of Belief

Q. How propagation of belief is done in Bayesian network?

Ans. To propagate the belief in a Bayesian network, the initial DAG is converted into an undirected graph in which the arcs can be used to transmit probabilities in the direction of evidence. For correctness, there should not be any cycle in the graph (Figure 5.1).

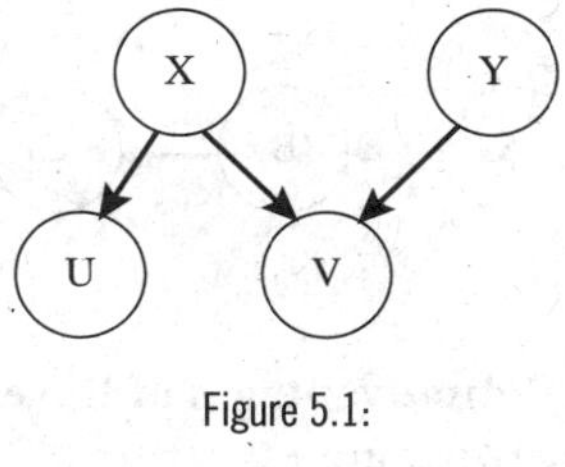

Figure 5.1:

Three algorithms have been proposed for doing these computations:

Q. How do we infer in Bayesian belief networks?

Ans. During reasoning and problem-solving, there is a need to compute the inference of a node on any other node. A network is constructed which stores the probabilities of all independent variables and conditional probabilities of dependent variables. Joint probability distribution of n variables using Bayesian network can be written as the product of the local distributions of each node and its parents such as:

$$P(X1,X2,...Xn)\prod_{i=1}^{n} P(Xi|\text{parent nodes }(Xi))$$

1. Message passing method: This method requires that to compute the probability of a node A, it is necessary to know the total support arriving at A from its parent nodes; the total support arriving at A from its children and the entry in the fixed conditional probability matrix that relates A to its causes. Common causes, i.e., parents or ancestors cause conditional independence: B is common cause of two symptoms A and C (Figure 5.2). The probability is given as: $P(C|A \wedge B) = P(C|B)$

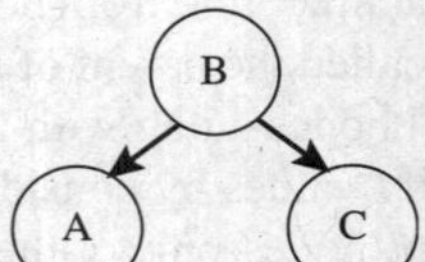

Figure 5.2:

2. A clique triangulation method: In this method, explicit arcs are introduced between pairs of nodes that share a common child. Common effects, i.e., children or descendants cause conditional dependence: B is common child of both A and C (Figure 5.3). The probability is given as $P(A|B \wedge C) \neq P(A)*P(C)$

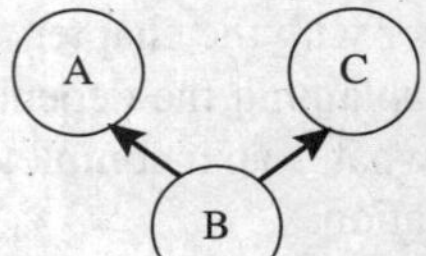

Figure 5.3:

3. Stochastic algorithms: These transform an arbitrary network into a Markov chain to shield a given node probabilistically from most of the other nodes in the network. Causal chain causes conditional independence: A causes B which causes C (Figure 5.4). The probability is given as: $P(C|A \wedge B) = P(C|B)$.

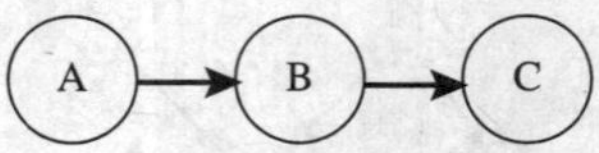

Figure 5.4:

Q. What are the advantages and disadvantages of Bayesian network?

Ans. The advantages of Bayesian network are:

(a) It can easily handle the situations where some data entries are missing Δ

(b) It is easier to handle direct dependencies and local distributions than complete joint distribution

(c) It helps in learning causal relationships.

Following are the disadvantages of Bayesian network:

(a) Reliability of Bayesian network depends on the reliability of prior knowledge.

(b) All branches must be calculated to find the probability of any branch of the network which is difficult for an NO-hard problem.

5.3.8 Belief Interval

Q. Define a belief interval.

Ans. Belief interval is used in Dempster–Shafer theory which is defined as the interval in which the degree of belief must lie. It is defined as the range between two variables Belief and Plausibility (i.e., Belief, Plausibility). Belief (bel) measures the strength of the evidence in favor of a set of propositions and ranges from 0 (no evidence) to 1 (certainty).

Belief is defined as the sum of all masses of subsets of set X of interest and is calculated as:

$$\text{bel}(X) = \sum m(Y) \;\; \forall Y \subseteq X$$

Plausibility (pl) is defined as:

$$\text{pl(X)} = 1 - \text{bel}(\sim \text{X}).$$

It is also calculated as:

$$\text{pl(X)} = \sum m(\text{Y}), \forall \text{ Y such that Y} \cap \text{X} \neq \phi.$$

This is a measure of the extent to which evidence in favor of ~X leaves behind for belief in X. This also lies in the range between 0 and 1. If bel is 1 for X, then bel(~X) will be 0 and hence pl(X) = 1.

5.3.9 Dempster–Shafer Theory of Uncertainty Management

Q. Explain Dempster–Shafer theory of uncertainty management.

Ans. Dempster–Shafer has given a theory of uncertainty management. It is a generalization of the Bayesian theory of probability. It consists of sets of propositions and assigns the degree of belief which lies between an interval [Belief, Plausibility] to each of the propositions. This belief interval measures the level of belief as well as the amount of information present. To define the belief, first the hypotheses must be defined. These hypotheses should be mutually exclusive and are called the frame of discernment, denoted by Θ. The goal is to attach some measure of belief to elements of Θ. There are certain constraints for this. First, only a subset of elements in the set can be supported by all evidence. Second, due to mutually exclusive nature, if evidence is supporting some elements may have an effect on belief in the others. To handle this, probability density function *m* is used which is defined for all elements and subsets of Θ. If there are p hypotheses, then *m*(p) measures the amount of belief currently assigned to these. The value of *m* should be assigned in such a way that the sum of all *m* values assigned to all subsets of Θ is 1. If the set Θ contains *n* elements, then the number of subsets will be 2^n. Due to a large number of subsets, all of these may not be included for belief. If some subset is not considered, then associated value for that subset should be 0.

Q. How can multiple sources of evidence be supported in Dempster–Shafer theory?

Ans. To combine two functions, Dempster's rule of combination can be used to combine any two belief functions. If there are two belief functions *m*1 and *m*2, X and Y are the set of subsets of Θ to which *m*1 and *m*2 assigns a nonzero value, i.e., $m1(\text{X}) \neq 0$ and $m2(\text{Y}) \neq 0$, respectively. Then the combination *m*3 of *m*1 and *m*2 which can be applied to any subset Z of Θ is given as:

$$m3(\text{Z}) = \frac{\sum \text{X} \cap \text{Y} = \text{Z} m1(\text{X}) * m2(\text{Y})}{1 - \sum \text{X} \cap \text{Y} = \varphi m1(\text{X}) * m2(\text{Y})}$$

This belief function gives us a new value when applied on the set Z where Z = X ∩ Y. The combination of two belief functions is called joint mass. *m*3 can be written as (*m*1 o *m*2). The expression $\sum X \cap Y = \varphi(m1(X) * m2(Y))$ is known as normalization factor and is a measure of the amount of conflict between the two mass sets.

Q. What are the advantages of Dempster–Shafer theory over Bayesian network?

Ans. Bayesian network uses prior probabilities which are not used in Dempster–Shafer theory. It allows specification of a degree of ignorance in case of missing prior and conditional probabilities instead of applying prior probabilities forcibly.

5.3.10 Certainty Factor Based Reasoning

Q. Define certainty factor theory.

Ans. Certainty factor theory is based on measuring confidence levels for a number of observations instead of probability. In probability, the sum of the confidence for a relationship and against a relationship must add up to 1. But certainty factor deals with the situations where an expert has a confidence C about a relationship but the absence of that relationship cannot be equal to 1-C because there is no idea or certainty about the falsehood of that relationship. Hence two sides of confidence of a given piece of evidence are measured separately as measure of belief (MB) and measure of disbelief (MD). As these two measures are related to the same evidence, there should be some relation between the two. The measure of belief and disbelief in hypothesis H gives the evidence E, i.e., MB[H,E] and MD[H,E], respectively lies in the range [0,1].

MB[H,E] = 1 if the evidence E fully supports the hypothesis H
MB[H,E] = 0 if the evidence E does not support the hypothesisH
MD[H,E] = 1 if the evidence E does not support the hypothesisH
MD[H,E] = 0 if the evidence E fully supports the hypothesisH

The measure of belief calculates the relative decrement of disbelief in a given hypothesis H due to some evidence E:

$$MB[H,E] = \frac{(1-P(H)) - (1-P(H|E))}{(1-P(H))} = \frac{P(H|E) - P(H)}{(1-P(H))}$$

Similarly, the measure of disbelief calculates the relative decrement of belief in a given hypothesis H due to some evidence E:

$$MD[H,E] = \frac{(1-P(H|E)) - (1-P(H))}{P(H)} = \frac{P(H) - P(H|E)}{P(H)}$$

To avoid getting negative value of belief, the definition for belief can be modified to get positive value of measure in the range [0,1] as:

$$MB[H,E] = 1, \qquad P(H) = 1$$
$$= \frac{\text{Max}\{P(H \mid E) - P(H)\} - P(H)}{(1-P(H))}.$$

Similarly, to avoid getting negative value of disbelief, the definition for belief can be modified to get positive value of measure in the range [0,1] as:

$$MD[H,E] = 1, \qquad P(H) = 0$$
$$= \frac{P(H) - Min\{P(H|E), P(H)\}}{P(H)}, \text{otherwise}$$

The total strength of certainty factor in a hypothesis is given as:
$CF[H,E] = MB[H,E] - MD[H,E]$, where $-1 \le CF[H,E] \le 1$.

If CF is 1, the hypothesis is said to be true and if CF is equal to –1, the hypothesis is considered to be false. If Cf = 0, there is no evidence regarding whether the hypothesis is true or false.

5.3.11 Certainty Factors and Rule-based Systems

Q. How rule-based systems are assigned the certainty factors?

Ans. In rule-based expert systems, the knowledge engineer gathers knowledge from domain experts and formulates the rules in the form of if-then-else rules. The rules are written in natural language like English which may contain ambiguous words such as sometimes, often, rarely, etc. These cause some vague associations present in the rules, which need to be correlated using some numerical certainty factors. A certainty factor is a number which lies between 0 and 1 is used to measure the expert's belief. The value 0 indicates certainly false and the value 1 indicates certainly true.

In expert systems with certainty factors, the knowledge base consists of a set of rules with the syntax given below:

If <evidence E> Then <hypothesis H> {CF}, where CF represents the belief in hypothesis H given that evidence E has occurred. A CF between –1 and 1 reflects the belief in a hypothesis.

In case of more than one conjunctive hypotheses H_1 and H_2 in a rule, the certainty factor was calculated by $CF[H_1 \text{ and } H_2] = Min(CF[H_1], CF[H_2])$.

In case of more than one disjunctive hypotheses H_1 and H_2 in a rule, the certainty factor was calculated by $CF[H_1 \text{ or } H_2] = Max(CF[H_1], CF[H_2])$.

If there are multiple rules leading to the same conclusion, then CFs obtained from multiple rules are combined to get a single certainty factor as $Combine(CF[H_1], CF[H_2])$:

$$Combine(CF[H_1], CF[H_2]) = \{CF[H_1] + CF[H_2] - (CF[H_1]*CF[H_2])\}, \text{ if } \{CF[H_1] > 0 \text{ and } CF[H_2]\} > 0)$$
$$= \{CF[H_1] + CF[H_2] + (CF[H_1]) * CF[H2])\}, \text{if} \{CF[H1] < 0 \text{ and } CF[H2]\} < 0\}$$
$$= \{CF[H_1] + CF[H_2]\} / Min(|CF[H_1]|, |CF[H2]|), \text{ otherwise}$$

5.4 TEMPORAL MODELS

5.4.1 Hidden Markov Model

Q. Define Hidden Markov Model.

Ans. This model was given by a Russian scientist, Andrei Markov. It is based on temporal probability models. According to Markov chain property, the probability of each subsequent state depends only on what was the previous state, i.e., $P(s_{ik}|s_{i1}, s_{i2}, \ldots s_{ik-1}) = P(s_{ik}|s_{ik-1})$.

In a Hidden Markov Model, there is a set of states: $\{s_1, s_2, \ldots s_n\}$. The process moves from one state to another generating a sequence of states: $s_{i1}, s_{i2}, \ldots, s_{ik}, \ldots$. It states that evidence can be observed but the state is hidden.

To define Markov model, three probabilities needs to be specified:

1. Priors or initial probabilities: A vector of initial probabilities $P(S_i)$.
2. State transition model, i.e., transition probabilities, i.e., Transition probability of moving from s_i to s_j is given as $t_{ij} = P(s_i|s_j)$. The matrix of transition probabilities is defined as $T = (t_{ij})$.
3. Evidence observation model, i.e., observable probabilities: A matrix of observable probabilities $O = (o_i(v_m))$ and $o_i(v_m) = P(v_m|S_i)$

The model is represented by M = (T,O,P).

Q. What are the main issues in Hidden Markov Model?

Ans. There are many issues in Hidden Markov Model:

1. *Evaluation*: It is difficult to calculate the probability that the given model M has generated the sequence S.
2. *Decoding*: It is difficult to calculate the most likely sequence of hidden states H is that produced the observation sequence O.
3. *Learning*: It is difficult to find the Hidden Markov Model to best fit the given training examples.

5.4.2 Utility Theory

Q. Define utility theory.

Ans. If X is the outcome of performing action A, whose possible n values are $x_1,\ldots,x_n$ and probability distributions $(p_1,\ldots,p_n)$ and function U of X is a mapping from states to numerical utilities (values), then he expected utility of performing action A is

$$EU[A] = \sum i = 1,\ldots,n\,p(x_i \mid A)U(x_i),$$

where $p(x_i|A)$ is the probability of each outcome and $U(x_i)$ is the utility of each outcome. The properties of utility functions are:

- **Orderability**: Given two states, one or the other should be better, or the agent cannot care.
- **Transitivity**: If A is better than B and B is better than C, then A is better than C.
- **Continuity**: If A is better than B and B is better than C, then you can "interpolate" A and C with some probability p to get an outcome that's equally desirable to B:
  $\exists p : [p, A; 1-p, C] = B$
- **Substitutability:** If there is indifference between A and B, then A can substitute for B in any lottery and the results will be the same.
- **Monotonicity:** If A is better than B, then a lottery that differs only in assigning higher probability to A is better:
  $p \geq q \leftrightarrow [p, A; 1-p, B] \geq [q, A; 1-q, B]$
- **Decomposability:** Compound lotteries can be reduced using the laws of probability.

Decision networks are used to represent utilities.

5.5 FUZZY LOGIC

Q. Explain the fuzzy logic.

Ans. Fuzzy logic is a totally different approach to represent uncertainty. Changes the definitions of set theory and logic to allow this. Traditional set theory defines set memberships as a Boolean predicate.

5.5.1 Fuzzy Set

Q. Define a fuzzy set.

Ans. Fuzzy set theory can be used to represent the uncertainty in natural language. Instead of quantitative measures such as in probability, linguistics measures are used to represent the uncertainty. It focuses on ambiguities in describing events rather the uncertainty about the occurrence of an event. Set theories are used to define the set memberships.

Definition:

Consider the case of "youthness". In this case, the set S (the universe of discourse) is the set of people. A fuzzy subset YOUNG is defined, which answers the question "to what degree is person x young?" To each person in the universe of discourse, we have to assign a degree of membership in the fuzzy subset YOUNG. The membership function based on the person's age is:

$\mu = \{$ 1, if age(x) $\Leftarrow$ 20,

(30-age(x))/10, if 20 < age(x) $\Leftarrow$ 30,

0, if age(x) > 30 $\}$

A graph of this looks like:

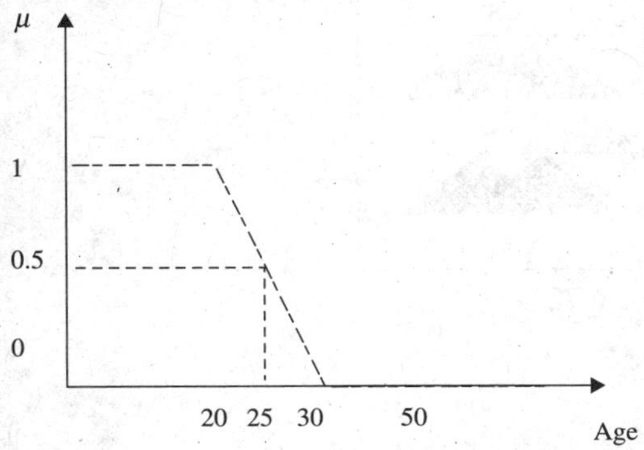

Some of the examples are:

Person	Age	degree of youth
Vishal	10	1.00
Vikas	21	0.90
Vinay	25	0.50
Viraat	26	0.40

Q. Define membership function.

Ans. Membership function essentially embodies all fuzziness for a particular fuzzy set, its description is essential to fuzzy property or operation.

Q. Define features of membership function

Ans. Features of membership functions are:

1. Core: comprises of elements x of the universe, such that $\mu_A(x) = 1$.
2. Support: comprises of elements x of universe, such that $\mu_A(x) > 0$.
3. Boundaries: comprise the elements x of the universe
   $0 < \mu_A(x) < 1$.

A normal fuzzy set has at least one element with membership 1

For fuzzy set, if one and only one element has a membership = 1, this element is called as the prototype of set.

Q. Define fuzzy set operations.

Ans. Fuzzy set operations are defined as:

1. Union: $\mu_{A \cup B}(x) = \mu_A(x) \cup \mu_B(x)$, $x \in U = \max(\mu_A(x), \mu_B(x))$.
2. Intersection: $\mu_{A \cap B}(x) = \mu_A(x) \cap \mu_B(x)$, $x \in U = \min(\mu_A(x), \mu_B(x))$.
3. Complementary: $\mu_{A'}(x) = 1 - \mu_A(x)$, $x \in U$.
4. Containment: $R \subseteq S \rightarrow \mu_R(x) \leq \mu_S(x)\ \forall\ x \in S$.

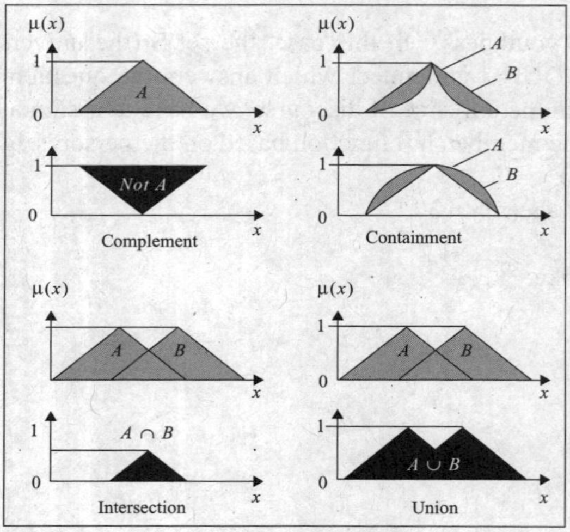

Figure 5.5

De Morgan's Law also holds:

$$v(\tilde{A} \cup \tilde{B})' = (\tilde{A})' \cap (\tilde{B})'.$$

Q. Define properties of Fuzzy sets.

Ans. Properties of Fuzzy sets:

Commutativity:	$\tilde{A} \cup \tilde{B} = \tilde{B} \cup \tilde{A}$	$\tilde{A} \cap \tilde{B} = \tilde{B} \cap \tilde{A}$.
Associativity:	$\tilde{A} \cup (\tilde{B} \cup \tilde{C}) = (\tilde{A} \cup \tilde{B}) \cup \tilde{C}$	$\tilde{A} \cap (\tilde{B} \cap \tilde{C}) = (\tilde{A} \cap \tilde{B}) \cap \tilde{C}$,
Distributivity:	$\tilde{A} \cup (\tilde{B} \cap \tilde{C}) = (\tilde{A} \cup \tilde{B}) \cap (\tilde{A} \cup \tilde{C})$	
	$\tilde{A} \cap (\tilde{B} \cup \tilde{C}) = (\tilde{A} \cap \tilde{B}) \cup (\tilde{A} \cap \tilde{C})$.	
Idempotency:	$\tilde{A} \cup \tilde{A} = \tilde{A}$	$\tilde{A} \cap \tilde{A} = \tilde{A}$.
Others:	$\tilde{A} \cup U = U$	$\tilde{A} \cap U = \tilde{A}$
	$\tilde{A} \cup \emptyset = \tilde{A}$	$\tilde{A} \cap \emptyset = \emptyset$.

Let x be a linguistic variable in universe X, A_1, A_2 and A_3 are three fuzzy sets under universe X. Let y be another linguistic variable in universe Y and B1, B2 and B3 are three fuzzy sets under universe Y. The implication rules can be defined between variables x and y as follows:

Q. Explain inferencing using Fuzzy modus ponens.

Ans. A fuzzy modus ponen inference rule takes the form:

If $\tilde{A}$, $\tilde{A}1$, $\tilde{B}$, and $\tilde{B}1$ be the statements characterized by fuzzy sets. Then one form of the generalized modus ponens is:

Premise: x is $\tilde{A}1$

Implication: if x is $\tilde{A}$ then y is $\tilde{B}$

Conclusion: y is $\tilde{B}1$.

Rule1: IF x is A_1, then y is B_1

Rule 2: If x is A_2, then y is B_2

Rule 3: If x is A_3, then y is B_3

5.5.2 Inverse Fuzzy Relation

Q. Define inverse fuzzy relation.

Ans. The inverse of a fuzzy relation R(X,Y) is denoted by $R^{-1}(Y,X)$ and is defined as a relation on Y x X as:

$$R^{-}(y,x) = R(x,y) \forall x \in X, y \in Y.$$

A membership matrix for $R^{-1}(Y,X)$ is $R^{-1} = [r_{yx}^{-1}]$ and it is equal to the transpose of the matrix R for relation R(X,Y).

Example:

Rule1: IF a banana is Yellow, then it is ripe.

Rule 2: If a banana is very Yellow, then it is very ripe.

Rule 3: If a banana is more-or-less Yellow, then it is more-or-less ripe.

Q. Define fuzzy inverse model.

Ans. A fuzzy inverse model is used in a fuzzy model reference learning controller system. The aim is that such a system will learn to retune itself if it returns to some familiar situation. For this, it needs some feedback which it can utilize to improve learning. The inputs to this system at u(kT) where T is the sampling period. The output of the system is y(kT). There is a reference input to the plant in the system which is denoted by r(kT). Using this numerical data, the system characterizes the fuzzy control system's current performance and automatically adjusts the fuzzy controller to give required performance.

The error in the output is denoted by e(kT) = r(kT) – y(kT).

The change in error is given by $c(kT) = \dfrac{e(kT) - e(kT - T)}{T}$.

The error in output $y_e(kT)$ is denoted by = $y_m(kT)$ – y(kT), where $y_m(kT)$ is smooth, stable response.

The fuzzy inverse model is a fuzzy system to map $y_e(kT)$ and possibly functions of $y_e(kT)$ to necessary changes in the process inputs, i.e., p(kT) to reduce the error $y_e(kT)$.

This is called fuzzy inverse model since information about the plant inverse dynamics is used in its specification.

SOLVED EXAMPLES

Q. Consider the problem of tossing of two coins separately. What is the probability of throwing two successive heads?

Ans. There are two possible outcomes of throwing one coin, one is the head and the other is the tail. The chance of getting a head and a tail is equal to 0.5 each. When two coins are tossed successively, there are four possible outcomes {1-Head 2-Head, 1-Head 2-Tail, 1-Tail 2-Tail, 1-Tail 2-Head} .Out of the four possible outcomes, there is only one case with head on both coins. So the probability of throwing two successive heads is ¼, i.e., 0.25.

Q. Consider the problem of tossing two fair coins. Calculate the probability of getting tail on both coins. What is the probability of getting a tail on tossing one or both coins?

Ans. The probability of getting a tail on first coin P(T1) = 0.5.

The probability of getting a tail on second coin P(T2) = 0.5.

The joint probability of getting tail on first and second coin is given as

P(T1 and T2) = P(T1)*P(T2) = 0.5*0.5 = 0.25.

The joint probability of getting tail on one or both coins is given as

P(T1 or T2) = P(T1) + P(T2) − P(T1)*P(T2) = 0.5 + 0.5 − 0.5*0.5 = 0.75.

This can also be verified that there are three possible outcomes for this situation out of four possible outcomes {1-Head 2-Head, 1-Head 2-Tail, 1-Tail 2-Tail, 1-Tail 2-Head}, where tail is either on one coin or on both coins. Hence probability = ¾ = 0.75

Q. Suppose that the probability of any person chosen at random being Indian is 0.60 and the probability of any person chosen at random having an age more than 70 years is 0.003. What is the probability of the fact that a person chosen at random of age more than 70 years is in Indian.

Ans. P(A is Indian and the age of A > 70) = P(A is Indian)*P(age of A > 70)

= 0.60*0.003 = 0.0018.

$$P(\text{A is Indian} \mid \text{age of A} > 70) = \frac{P(\text{A is Indian and the age of A} > 70)}{P(\text{age of A} > 70)} = \frac{0.0018}{0.003} = 0.60.$$

Q. Consider the given probabilities for an examination to be easy is 0.7 and for an examination to be not easy is 0.3. The probability that Amit and Bharat will pass or not pass in the given an easy or not easy examination is given in the Tables 5.1 and 5.2:

Table 5.1

P(Amit)	Easy = True	Easy = False
Pass=True	0.8	0.1
Pass=False	0.2	0.9

Table 5.2

P(Bharat)	Easy = True	Easy = False
Pass = True	0.7	0.1
Pass = False	0.3	0.9

Draw the Bayesian network for this problem. Find the probability that Amit will pass in the examination. Also find the probability that Bharat will pass. If the evidence is given that Amit has passed, find the probability that the examination was easy.

Ans. The Bayesian network is shown in Figure 5.6:

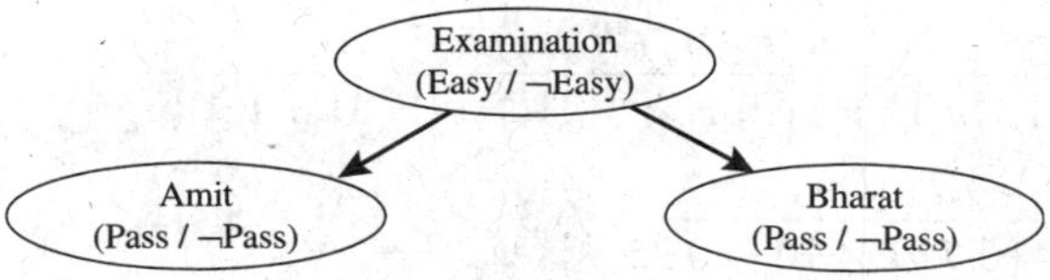

Figure 5.6

$$P(\text{Amit Pass}) = P(\text{Amit Pass} \mid \text{Easy})*P(\text{Easy}) + P(\text{Amit Pass} \mid \neg\text{ Easy})*P(\neg\text{ Easy}).$$
$$= 0.8 * 0.7 + 0.1 * 0.3 = 0.59.$$
$$P(\text{Bharat Pass}) = P(\text{Bharat Pass} \mid \text{Easy})*P(\text{Easy}) + P(\text{Bharat Pass} \mid \neg\text{ Easy})*P(\neg\text{ Easy}).$$
$$= 0.7 * 0.7 + 0.1 * 0.3 = 0.52.$$
$$P(\text{Easy} \mid \text{Amit Pass}) = \frac{P(\text{Amit Pass}|\text{easy}) * P(\text{easy})}{P(\text{Ami Pass})} = \frac{0.8*0.7,\ 0.1*0.3}{0.59} = 0.95,\ 0.05$$

Q. Consider an example in MYCIN with the given rules:
R1: IF blood test result is yes THEN the disease is malaria (CF 0.8)
R2: IF living in malaria zone THEN the disease is malaria (CF 0.5)
R3: IF bit by a flying bug THEN the disease is malaria (CF 0.3)
What is the CF for having malaria (as its calculated by ES), if the first two rules are considered to be true?

Ans. $CF(R1,R2) = CF(R1) + CF(R2) * (1 - CF(R1))$
$= 0.8 + 0.5*(1 - 0.8) = 0.8 - 0.1 = 0.9.$

Q. Consider that there are three hypotheses whose probabilities are given below:
$p(H_1) = 0.40$; $p(H_2) = 0.35$; $p(H_3) = 0.25$.

Suppose there are three evidences E1, E2, and E3 which can cause these hypotheses to be true. The conditional probabilities are given below:

$p(E_1|H_1) = 0.3$; $p(E_1|H_2) = 0.4$; $p(E_1|H_3) = 0.5$;
$p(E_2|H_1) = 0.9$; $p(E_2|H_2) = 0.6$; $p(E_2|H_3) = 0.7$;
$p(E_3|H_1) = 0.6$; $p(E_3|H_2) = 0.3$; $p(E_3|H_3) = 0.9$.
If E3 was observed first of all, calculate the posterior probabilities for all three hypotheses.

Ans. The probability of hypotheses given an evidence is given by:

$$P(H_i|E) = \frac{P(E|H_i)*P(H_i)}{\sum_{n=1}^{k}(P(E|Hn)*P(Hn))}$$

$$P(H_1|E_3) = \frac{P(E_3|H_1)*P(H_1)}{P(E_3|H_1)*P(H_1)+P(E_3|H_2)*P(H_2)+P(E_3|H_3)*P(H_3)}$$

$$= \frac{0.6*0.4}{0.6*0.4+0.7*0.35+0.9*0.25} = 0.34$$

$$P(H_2|E_3) = \frac{P(E_3|H_2)*P(H_2)}{P(E_3|H_1)*P(H_1)+P(E_3|H_2)*P(H_2)+P(E_3|H_3)*P(H_3)}$$

$$= \frac{0.7*0.35}{0.6*0.4+0.7*0.35+0.9*0.25} = 0.34$$

$$P(H_3|E_3) = \frac{P(E_3|H_3)*P(H_3)}{P(E_3|H_1)*P(H_1)+P(E_3|H_2)*P(H_2)+P(E_3|H_3)*P(H_3)}$$

$$= \frac{0.9*0.25}{0.6*0.4+0.7*0.35+0.9*0.25} = 0.32$$

Q. Consider the problem of identifying the naughty group or groups responsible for a certain mischief in a school. Suppose any of the three naughty groups A, B, and C could have been responsible for the mischief. Assume that one piece of evidence support the belief that groups A and B were responsible to a degree of m1{(A,B)} = 0.8 and another source of evidence supports that groups A and C were responsible for the mischief with the belief m2(A,C) = 0.6. Combine the belief functions to generate an m3 function using Dempster–Shafer theory.

Ans. There are nine possible subsets of U. The belief function using m3 is given in Table 5.3:

Table 5.3 Tableau of combined values of belief for m1 and m2

Combination of m1 and m2	m2{A,C}(0.6)	m2(U) = 0.4
m1({A,B}) (0.8)	m3({A}) = (0.8)*(0.6) = 0.48	m3({A,B}) = (0.8)*(0.4) = 0.32
m1(U) (0.2)	m3({A,C}) = (0.2)*(0.6) = 0.12	m3(U) = 0.2*0.4 = 0.08

m1*o* m2 ({A}) = (0.8)* (0.6) = 0.48.
m1*o* m2 ({A,C}) = (0.2)*(0.6) = 0.12.
m1*o* m2 ({A,B}) = (0.8)*(0.4) = 0.32.
m *o* m2({U}) = (0.2)*(0.4) = 0.08.

Q. Consider a case where we are given two states wet and dry with initial probabilities as P(dry) = 0.4 and P(wet) = 0.6 the following transition probabilities:
P(dry|dry) = 0.4; P(wet|dry) = 0.6; P(wet|wet) = 0.3; P(dry|wet) = 0.7.
Using Markov model, calculate a probability of a sequence of states in our example, {dry, dry, wet, wet}.

Ans. P({dry, dry, wet, wet}) = P(wet|wet)*P(wet|dry)*P(dry|dry)*P(dry)
= 0.3*0.6*0.4*0.4 = 0.0288.

Q. Define a fuzzy set for defining a person as tall.

Ans. A person is defined as tall if the height of the person is more than 6' but not below 4'.

$$\text{Tall}(x) = 1 \qquad \text{if height}(x) \geq 6'$$

$$= \left(1+\left(\frac{6-\text{height}(x)}{2}\right)^{-2}\right)^{-1} \qquad \text{if height}(x) < 6'.$$

Q. Suppose the following statements are given: This mango is very yellow. If a mango is yellow, then it is ripe. What will be concluded using fuzzy modus ponens?

Ans. The conclusion will be this mango is very ripe.

MULTIPLE CHOICE QUESTIONS

Select the most appropriate answers for the following questions:

1. Which of the following methods cannot be used for handling uncertainty in expert systems?
   (a) Certainty factors (b) Bayesian networks
   (c) Dempster–Shafer (d) None of these
2. Which of the following method cannot be used when there is difficulty in getting probabilities?
   (a) Certainty factors (b) Bayesian networks
   (c) Dempster–Shafer (d) None of these
3. Which of the probability is needed to use Bayesian network?
   (a) Prior probability (b) Joint probability
   (c) Posterior probability (d) All of these
4. There are two bags, one white and another black. White bag has 2 red balls and 5 blue balls. The black bag has 4 red balls and 3 blue balls. What is the probability of picking a red ball from the white bag?
   (a) 4/7 (b) 2/7
   (c) 6/7 (d) None of these
5. There are three boxes. First box has 2 white, 3 black, and 4 red balls. Second box has 3 white, 2 black, and 2 red balls. Third box has 4 white, 1 black, and 3 red balls. A box is chosen at random and 2 balls are drawn out of which one is white and other is red. What is the probability that they came from the first box?
   (a) 0.237 (b) 0.723
   (c) 0.18 (d) None of these
6. Which of the following methods cannot be used for handling uncertainty in rule-based expert systems?
   (a) Probabilities (b) Fuzzy logic
   (c) Certainty factors (d) None of these
7. Which of the following use temporal reasoning?
   (a) Bayesian networks (b) Decision networks
   (c) Hidden Markov Model (d) All of these
8. Which of the following do not use static reasoning?
   (a) Bayesian networks (b) Decision networks
   (c) Dynamic Bayesian networks (d) None of these

9. If a particular problem has n propositions in a frame of discernment, then how many subset scan be created?

   (a) n (b) $2*n$
   (c) 2^n (d) None of these

10. Which of the following reasoning method uses linguistic approach for handling uncertainty?

   (a) Certainty factors (b) Fuzzy logic
   (c) Dempster–Shafer theory (d) None of these

Answers: 1. b 2. b 3. a 4. b 5. a 6. d 7. c 8. c 9. c 10. b

EXERCISES

1. Consider the problem of throwing two cubical dice separately. What is the probability of getting a number 4 on both dices?
2. Suppose that the probability of any person chosen at random being male is 0.40 and the probability of any person chosen at random having an age more than 60 years is 0.045. What is the probability of the fact that a person chosen at random of age more than 60 years is a female?
3. Consider the following Bayesian belief network:

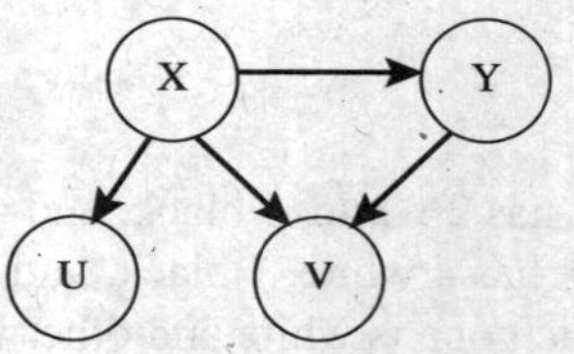

   The probabilities are given as:

   P(X) = 0.4 P(Y|X) = 0.4 P(Y|~X) = 0.1 P(U|X) = 0.6
   P(U|~X) = 0.3 P(V|X,Y) = 0.7 P(V|X,~Y) = 0.3 P(V|~X,Y) = 0.3
   P(V|~X,~Y) = 0.2

   Compute the probability P(X|Y) and P(X,Y,U,V).
4. Suppose by observing evidences E_1 and E_2, the belief in hypothesis H_1 is confirmed with $MB[H_1,E_1] = 0.5$ and $MD[H_1,E_1] = 0.3$, $MB[H_1,E_2] = 0.2$ and $MD[H_1,E_2] = 0.4$.

   Compute the following certainty factors.
   $CF[H_1,E_1]$ (b) $CF[H_1, E_1$ and $E_2]$.
5. Consider the mutually exclusive hypothesis represented by a set U ={viral, measles} in a diagnostic system. Suppose we have a measure of belief function M1 based on evidence of fever as M1({viral}) = 0.6 and measure of belied M2 function based on evidences of fever and headache, respectively. M2({viral, measles}) = 0.45. Combine the given belief functions to generate an M3 function using Dempster–Shafer rule.

6. Consider the problem of identifying the naughty group or groups responsible for a certain mischief in a school. Suppose any of the four naughty groups A, B, C, and D could have been responsible for the mischief. Assume that one piece of evidence support the belief that groups A and C were responsible to a degree of m1 {(A,C)} = 0.4 and another source of evidence supports that three groups A, B, and D were responsible for the mischief with the belief m2(A,B,D) = 0.6. Combine the belief functions to generate an m3 function using Dempster–Shafer theory.
7. Define fuzzy sets that can be used to represent the list of propositions:

   (a) Kunal is very short.
   (b) Smriti is little sad today.

6

Commonsense

6.1 INTRODUCTION

Commonsense indicates the level of knowledge in any human. It is supposed that commonsense should increase with age, i.e., the person is supposed to acquire and use more and more intelligence in doing all the tasks by applying the knowledge. Any machine can be thought to have negligible commonsense. But an intelligent system is supposed to exhibit commonsense, i.e., they possess more than enough knowledge to be able to work in a given environment. In order to do so, any machine needs knowledge representation schemes for acquiring and using knowledge. Since commonsense is related with day-to-day events and tasks, frames can be used as a flexible and efficient way of storing complete descriptions of everyday objects. The objects and events may be related to each other through some sequence that must be specified in order to take any further action. Scripts are a good way of recording typical sequences of everyday events. Default reasoning is an important aspect of commonsense that can be implemented using non-monotonic logic.

It is important to find how to make an intelligent machine understand and predict physical processes, how to model the behavior of materials and how to reason about time and space, how experiences are organized in memory, how these are generalized and used to solve new problems. The model of physical processes contain variables which store information about the physical objects in terms of states which can take a set of discrete values known as quantity space and their rate of change is also defined. Expressions are formed by combining various variables. Both the variables and equations can be linked to each other via equations.

6.2 QUALITATIVE PHYSICS

Q. What is qualitative physics? What are its building blocks?

Ans. Qualitative physics is an area of AI that aims to understand physical processes by building model of physical processes. Many intelligent human can predict the outcome of physical processes but these are difficult to be incorporated into machine. A model is an abstract representation that eliminates irrelevant details for quick and clear understanding of the physical processes. The building blocks of a model are

(a) ***Variables:*** These are used to represent features of objects such as position, velocity, angle, and temperature restricted to a finite set of possible values.

(b) ***Expressions:*** Expressions are formed by combining the variables.
(c) ***Equations:*** These are used to link expressions and variables.
(d) ***Quantity spaces:*** It is the set of discrete values for a variable.
(e) ***Rates of change:*** The rate of change of a variable is the change in the value of the variable with time, which can be modeled qualitatively with the quantity space {decreasing, steady, increasing}.
(f) ***States:*** A state is a single instance in which each variable possesses one value.

Q. Explain how can we reason with qualitative physics?

Ans. Reasoning in qualitative physics is called qualitative simulation. Here, a sequence of discrete episodes is constructed that occur as a result of changes in qualitative variables. The states are linked to other states by qualitative rules. When the system contains more than one object, then the rules must apply to all objects simultaneously keeping into consideration all the constraints that need to be satisfied. To avoid ambiguity, a qualitative simulation must split into two or more possible paths. Each path is called a history. A network of all possible states and transitions for a qualitative system is called an envisionment.

Example of an envisionment: Envisionments are important for many applications since they provide explanations for physical systems that can be used to predict future behavior. In a mechanical device, these can be used to diagnose problems that occur when components could not behave correctly.

6.3 COMMONSENSE ONTOLOGIES

Q. Explain commonsense ontologies.

Ans. Commonsense is used by a computer program when it interacts with the real world. There are three ontologies that can be used to deal with commonsense: time, space, and materials.

1. **Time:** In physical world, one gets the information about time by specifying the events that occur at a particular time. For example, I am doing work since morning, or Kangana died in 1940 and this indicates she was born before 1940. Events are the most basic notion of time that occurs during intervals, i.e., continuous spaces of time. An interval has a start and end point and a duration (of time) between them. For a computer machine or program, intervals can be related to one another using descriptions such as *is-before, is-after, meets, is-met-by, starts, is-started-by, during, contains, ends, is-ended-by,* and *equals*. Axioms can be build with intervals to describe events in time.
2. **Space:** All objects may be placed somewhere that relates them in terms of space. For example, in blocks world problem, block A is placed on the top of block B and block B is on the table indicates the location of both blocks. All objects have a spatial extent while events have a temporal extent. Though all objects are placed in 3D, it is difficult to include that level of abstraction, so these are treated as 2D objects for representation. Also the relevant properties should also be selected at particular levels of *granularity*. For example, we can define relations over spaces such as *inside and adjacent.* Relations for curves, lines, surfaces, planes, and volumes can be defined as *along, across, perpendicular, etc.*
3. **Materials:** There are many types of materials used in physical world, e.g., solids and liquids. All materials have different properties. So in order to represent materials, we need to define properties on the type of materials used in the system. The properties for solid objects could be rigid and flexible. For liquids, the spatial property could be represented as capacity, amount, etc.

6.4 MEMORY ORGANIZATION

Q. Discuss memory organization.

Ans. Memory is the place where every individual stores the knowledge or common sense. It is also the basis for learning. Psychologists have identified two aspects of human memory.

(a) Short-term memory (for storing perceptual information for a short duration).

(b) Long-term memory (capacity for storage is very large and fairly permanent). This further divided into two sections: Episodic memory that contains information about personal experiences and semantic memory that contains general facts like grass is green with no personal meaning.

Similarly, the production system is a computer model which contains working memory for storing the perceptual information for a short duration and the production rules which store the rules for a long duration. For a given query in working memory, the rules in production systems are matched and the answer is obtained. This may lead to updation of the rule in production system.

Memory organization packets (MOPs) are used to store stereotypical sequences of scenes like in a script. MOPs organize scenes and are organized into higher level MOPs. In MOP-based system, if an expectation is repeatedly violated, then the MOP is generalized or broken into two or more MOPs. These MOPs look like scripts but they share scenes with one another.

With MOPs, memory is both constructive and reconstructive process. It is constructive because new experiences create new memory structures. It is reconstructive because even if the details of a particular episode are lost, the MOP provides information about what was likely to have happened. These use case-based reasoning that is based on taking a decision based on analogy. Examples of an MOP-based program are CYRUS, IPP, and MOPTRANS.

6.5 CASE-BASED REASONING

Q. Discuss case-based reasoning.

Ans. In case-based reasoning, a system maintains a large library of cases and is able to solve new problems by finding the analogy with old cases. The success of a case-based reasoning system depends on the organization of cases in the memory, the way of acquiring the cases, the way of adapting previous cases to new problems and the way to retrieve the relevant cases from memory. The components of case-based reasoning systems are:

(a) ***Knowledge base or case base for acquiring the cases:*** A small library of cases can be entered by hand while large set of cases can be acquired through bootstrap from rule-based search into case-based reasoning. The stored cases can be adapted and modified.

(b) ***Random access memory for storing cases in memory:*** In order to use the memory effectively, a rich indexing mechanism must be used. A case can be stored as a monolithic structure when it is possible to get almost perfect match. A case can be stored as piecemeal in complex problem-solving domains.

(c) ***Inference engine for retrieval:*** A set of cases can be retrieved from the memory. Then, the best case is selected and adapted for the current situation. Preference heuristics can be used to choose the best case according to current goal, as per important feature, preference according to specificity, frequently matching cases, recently matched cases or according to ease of adaptation of cases to new situations.

(d) ***Adaptation:*** The adaptation is to be done when the selected case does not match the current situation exactly. The adaptation involves mapping new objects onto old ones. When old cases represent a complete problem-solving episode, the adaptation is difficult.

Q. What are the advantages and disadvantages of case-based reasoning systems?

Ans. The advantage is that these are able to obtain solutions in areas not previously well understood. The disadvantage is that there is very little quality control or guarantee that the solution is optimum and storing all cases are costly.

6.6 MONOTONICITY

Q. Define monotonicity.

Ans. Monotonicity is the property of conventional reasoning systems that the information can change if new facts are added to the database when they become available. Adding new axioms may cause new well formed formulas to become provable but no old proofs will ever become invalid. If these facts are consistent with all the other facts that have already been asserted, then nothing will ever be retracted from the set of facts that are known to be true.

6.7 AXIOMATIC THEORY

Q. What is axiomatic theory?

Ans. The axiomatic system is based on a set of three axioms and one rule of deduction. The axioms are always true are

Axiom 1: $\alpha \rightarrow (\beta \rightarrow \alpha)$

Axiom 2: $[\alpha \rightarrow (\beta \rightarrow \gamma)] \rightarrow [(\alpha \rightarrow \beta) \rightarrow (\alpha \rightarrow \gamma)]$

Axiom 3: $(\sim\alpha \rightarrow \sim\beta) \rightarrow (\beta \rightarrow \alpha)$

The deduction rule is Modus ponen rule which is stated as:

Hypothesis: $\alpha \rightarrow \beta$ and α;

Consequent: β.

In this system, only two logical operators are allowed to form a formula. These are not (~) and implies (→). All other logical operators like and (Λ), or (V) and ↔ are expressed using these two according to the following equivalence laws:

$A \vee B \cong \sim A \rightarrow B$

$A \wedge B \cong \sim(\sim A \vee \sim B) \cong \sim(A \rightarrow \sim B)$

$A \leftrightarrow B \cong (A \rightarrow B) \wedge (B \rightarrow A) \cong \sim[(A \rightarrow B) \rightarrow \sim(B \rightarrow A)]$

6.8 NON-MONOTONIC REASONING

Q. Explain non-monotonic reasoning.

Ans. Monotonic reasoning is not always possible because we cannot anticipate all possible outcomes of a situation or a plan and we need to assume certain things which we do not know explicitly. So, non-monotonic reasoning is used. Non-monotonic reasoning is the reasoning mechanism that allows us to reason when there is incomplete information in the knowledge base. It allows the extension of axioms and/or rules of inference to make it possible to reason with incomplete information. Non-monotonic systems preserve the property of non–monotonicity, i.e., at any given moment, a statement is either true or false or not believed to be either. This is called so because the set of currently valid (believed) facts does not increase monotonically. Adding a new fact might lead to an inconsistency that requires the removal of one of the contradictory facts. Thus, the set of true facts can shrink and grow with reasoning. In classical logic (first-order predicate logic) this does not happen. Once a fact is asserted, it's forever true. This can be implemented using default reasoning. This is a very common form of non-monotonic reasoning.

6.9 NON-ATOMIC REASONING USING MCDERMOTT'S NML-I

Q. How can we use McDermott's non-monotonic logic-I?

Ans. We use non-monotonic reasoning to perform default reasoning where we want to draw conclusions based on what is most likely to be true. This can be done using non-monotonic logic and default logic.

(a) ***Non-monotonic logic:*** A system that provides a basis for default reasoning is NML, which is an extension of first-order predicate logic to include a *modal* operator, *M*. The purpose of this is to allow for consistency.

For example: $\forall x, y$: friend (x, y) ΛMGetAlong $(x, y) \rightarrow$ WillCarefor (x, y) states that for all x and y, if x is a friend of y and x gets along with y is consistent with all other knowledge then we can conclude that x will care for y.

(b) ***Default logic:*** Default logic introduces a new class of inference rule of the form: $\frac{A \bullet B}{C}$, which states if A is deducible and it is consistent to assume B then conclude C.

Now this is similar to non-monotonic logic but there are some distinctions:

i. New inference rules are used for computing the set of plausible extensions. So in the Raman example above Default logic can support both assertions since it does not say anything about how choose between them, it will depend on the inference being made.

ii. In Default logic, any non-monotonic expressions are rules of inference rather than expressions in the language. So, these cannot be manipulated by other rules of inference.

6.10 PROBLEMS WITH NML-I

Q. What are the problems with non-monotonic logic?

Ans. One problem that arises with the use of non-monotonic logic is when there are more than one non-monotonic statement taken alone, suggest ways of augmenting our knowledge that if taken together would be inconsistent. For example, if there are two assertions, A Λ M B → B and ¬A Λ M B → B which are inconsistent.

The solution to this problem is to combine the logical expressions to derive the expression:

M B → B

Second problem with non-monotonic logic is definition is "consistent". In PROLOG, Horn clauses use a decidable theory. According to this, to prove P to be consistent, we try to prove ¬P as false and if so, P is proved to be consistent. But we are to start with first order predicate logic, which does not use a decidable theory. The solution to this problem is to define consistency based on some heuristic.

6.11 REASONING WITH NML-II

Q. What are the various reasoning with non-monotonic logic-II?

Ans. The second type of non-monotonic reasoning is minimalist reasoning. It requires defining a model to be minimal if there are no other models in which fewer things are true. The idea behind using minimal model for non-monotonic reasoning is that there are only a few true statements as compared to large number of false statements. So, it is better to include all true statements in the knowledge base. So, it is assumed that only true statements are those which are necessary to be true in order to maintain the consistency of the knowledge base. The closed world assumption (CWA) is a simple kind of minimalist reasoning. It says that only objects that satisfy any predicate P are those that must. It is useful for reasoning with databases that are assumed to be complete with respect to the properties they describe. For example, a student database can be assumed to list all of the university students. It should be able to say yes/no about a particular student whether it is listed in the database or not. Hence, it is complete. There are some limitations of using CWA. First, it is not possible to close some parts of world realistically. Second, it is purely syntactical reasoning process. Results depend on the form of assertions provided and it assumes all predicates have all of their instances listed which may not be possible in a real situation. The solution to this is found using circumscription. In this method, new axioms are added to existing knowledge base. The effect of these axioms is to force a minimal interpretation of knowledge base, i.e., each specific axiom describes a way that the set of values for which a particular axiom of original theory is true to be circumscribed, i.e., delimited. For example, if we have a predicate A (Value 1) V B (Value 2). If we circumscribe only A, then this assertion describes exactly those models in which A is true of no one and B is true for atleast Value 2. If we circumscribe only B, then this assertion describes exactly those models in which B is true of no one and A is true for atleast Value 1. If we circumscribe both A and B together, then this assertion describes exactly those models in which A is true of only Value 1 and B is true of no one **or** those in which B is true for atleast Value 2 and A is true of no one. Thus, circumscription allows us to describe the logical relationship between A and B.

Q. What is a Truth Maintenance System?

Ans. A Truth Maintenance Systems (TMS) is a dynamic knowledge base that is used to maintain the truth of the atoms present in the knowledge base at any time. In a knowledge base, there are some facts called premises and rules that add some new atoms based on the values of the premises. Change in any one of the atom may lead to changes in the atoms deduced from different rules and further the rules using these changed atoms. It uses dependencies among facts to keep track of conclusions and allow revision or retraction of facts and conclusions. TMS is often based on dependency-directed backtracking to the point in reasoning where a wrong assumption was used. The knowledge base is represented as a spreadsheet with one row and one or more columns. Each column stores a premise/atom or the atoms formed through rules. Since the atoms can be inserted or removed dynamically from the knowledge base, the number of columns for each atom will also increase or decrease, so this structure is called a spreadline.

6.12 CASE STUDY OF TRUTH MAINTENANCE SYSTEM

Q. Discuss various types of TMS.

Ans. A variety of TMS have been developed as a means of implementing non-monotonic reasoning systems. Basically, all the TMSs do some form of dependency directed backtracking and assertions are connected via a network of dependencies. Three types of TMSs are discussed here:

i. Justification-Based Truth Maintenance Systems

This is a simple TMS in that it does not know anything about the structure of the assertions themselves. It uses forward reasoning to make changes in the knowledge base. Each supported belief or assertion has a justification. The formulas entered in the values of the rule cells are called justifications. Each justification has two parts: an IN-List that supports all the beliefs held and an OUT-List that supports beliefs not held. The atoms for which belief is held can have values either 0 (false) or 1 (true). The atoms for which supports belief is not held has no value specified, i.e., the value is missing and the value is represented as empty to indicate that it is not known whether it is true or false. An assertion is connected to its justification by an arrow. A network is created by feeding one justification to another justification. Assertions may be labeled with a belief status. An assertion is valid if every assertion in the IN-List is believed and none in the OUT-List is believed. The justifications are expressed as disjunctive normal form (DNF), i.e., disjunction (OR) of conjunctions (AND). A justification is non-monotonic if the OUT-List is not empty or if any assertion in the IN-List has non-monotonic justification. It uses depth first search and backtracking.

ii. Logic-Based Truth Maintenance Systems

Logic-based truth maintenance systems (LTMS) are similar to Justification-Based Truth Maintenance Systems (JTMS) but here, nodes representing the assertions assume no relationships among them except ones explicitly stated in justifications. In JTMS, P and ¬P can be represented simultaneously but a LTMS would throw a contradiction in this case and will cause the network to be reconstructed. Like JTMS, it also uses depth first search and backtracking.

iii. Assumption-Based Truth Maintenance Systems

Assumption-based truth maintenance system (ATMS) maintains alternative paths in parallel and uses breadth-first search and avoids backtracking. Here, a spreadline is used in a backward direction. We start with a particular cell's formula and try to find which premisses values and other formulas will make that formula cell true. Such premiss values are called the assumptions. The related formulas used in proving a formula are known as background theory. In these systems, the values of the cells are taken to be the formulas called labels expressed in DNF form in terms of the premiss atoms. The label of each atom consists of the various sets of assumptions, i.e., premiss values which together with background theory would make them the atom have true value. However as reasoning proceeds, if contradictions arise, then the ATMS can be pruned. These are used in diagnosis system as it needs backward reasoning.

SOLVED EXAMPLES

Q. Prove the given in axiomatic system:
{B → A, A → C} |- (B → C).

Ans. We can prove the theorem as follows:

Theorem	:	{B → A, A → C} |- (B → C)	Prove
Hypothesis 1	:	B → A	(1)
Hypothesis 2	:	A → C	(2)
Using axiom 1	:	(A → C) → [B → (A → C)]	(3)
From 2 and 3	:	[B → (A → C)]	(4)
Using axiom 2	:	[B → (A → C)] → [(B → A) → (B → C)]	(5)
From 4 and 5	:	[(B → A) → (B → C)]	(6)
From 1 and 6	:	(B → C)	Proved

Hence, the theorem is proved.

Q. Prove the given theorem in axiomatic system: |- (~B → ~A) → (A → B)

Ans. If we can prove **(~B → ~A) |- (A → B) then using deduction theorem, we will prove |- (~B → ~A) → (A → B)**

Theorem	:	(~B → ~A) |- (A → B)	Prove
Hypothesis 1	:	(~B → ~A)	(1)
Using axiom 3	:	(~B → ~A) → (A → B)	(2)
From 1 and 2	:	(A → B)	Proved

Hence, the theorem is proved.

Q. Consider the problem of finding clothes to wear in the morning. To solve this problem, it is necessary to use knowledge such as:
– Wear a sweater if it is cold.
– It's usually cold in the winter.
– Wear sandals if it is warm.
– It's usually warm in the summer.
Build a JTMS style database of the necessary facts to solve this problem.

Ans. Let us first define the knowledge base for the given problem. The atoms in the knowledge base are

C – It is cold; WS – Wear a sweater; W – It is winter; S – It is summer; WN – Wear a sandals; WR – it is warm

The rules in the knowledge base are

C → WS
W → C
WR → WN
S → WR

W	S	WR	C	WS	WN
1	0	0	1	1	0

Another possible spreadline would be

W	S	WR	C	WS	WN
0	1	1	0	0	1

Q. Explain ATMS used in diagnosis with an example.

Ans. Assume that the knowledge base has the following atoms: P Q R

The rules are $P \wedge Q \wedge Z \rightarrow S$ $R \wedge Q \rightarrow W$ $S \wedge W \wedge Z \rightarrow Y$

The background theory is $P \rightarrow Z$

P	Q	R	S	W	Y
P	Q	R	{P,Q}	{R,Q}	{P} {R,Q}

If we want to diagnose for problem S, then it means both P and Q must be false. In order to prove problem Y, then P should be false as well as P and Q together should be false.

MULTIPLE CHOICE QUESTIONS

Select the most appropriate answers to the following questions:

1. Which of the following is not a commonsense ontology?
   (a) Time (b) Space
   (c)Materials (d) None of these
2. What does MOP stands for?
   (a) Memory Optimizer Packet (b) Memory Optimizing Performer
   (c) Memory Organization Packet (d) None of these
3. Which of the following reasoning method stores a library of cases?
   (a) Case-based reasoning (b) Default reasoning
   (c) Non-monotonic reasoning (d) None of these
4. Which of the following reasoning method allows retraction of older rules in case of contradiction with newly added rules?
   (a) Case-based reasoning (b) Default reasoning
   (c) Monotonic reasoning (d) Non-monotonic reasoning
5. Which of the following reasoning method does not need retraction of older rules in case of contradiction with newly added rules?
   (a) Case-based reasoning (b) Default reasoning
   (c) Monotonic reasoning (d) Non-monotonic reasoning
6. Default reasoning is an example of which of the following reasoning methods?
   (a) Monotonic reasoning (b) Non-monotonic reasoning
   (c) Case-based reasoning (d)None of these
7. In which of the following reasoning method, the non-monotonic expressions are rules of inference rather than expressions?
   (a) Monotonic reasoning (b) Default reasoning
   (c) Case-based reasoning (d) None of these
8. Which of the following is not a property of first order predicate logic?
   (a) Consistency (b) Monotonicity
   (c) Completeness (d) None of these
9. Which of the following TMS does not have any relationship among assertions except the ones stated explicitly?
   (a) Justification-based truth maintenance system
   (b) Logic-based truth maintenance system
   (c) Assumption-based truth maintenance system
   (d) All of these
10. Which of the following does not use depth first search and backtracking?
    (a) Justification-based truth maintenance system
    (b) Logic-based truth maintenance system
    (c) Assumption-based truth maintenance system
    (d) None of these

Answers. 1. d 2. c 3. a 4. c 5. d 6. b 7. b 8. d 9. b 10. c

EXERCISES

1. Consider a balloon hooked up to a bottle of compressed air. As the air is released, then the balloon expands. Using qualitative measures, list the quantity spaces of variables and rates of change in this system. Construct an envisionment for the system, and write down one possible history.
2. Explain the similarities between case-based reasoning and learning by analogy.
3. Consider the problem of reasoning in medical diagnosis. Consider the rule such as, "If you have a running nose, then assume that you have a cold unless it is allergy season". Show how a JTMS could be used in this case.
4. Solve the above example using an ATMS.
5. Establish that $A \rightarrow C$ is a deductive consequence of $\{A \rightarrow B, B \rightarrow C\}$.
6. Prove $\vdash \sim A \rightarrow (A \rightarrow B)$ by using deduction theorem.

7 Planning

7.1 INTRODUCTION

In solving a particular problem, in AI, we start with the initial state and move to the goal state by applying one of the applicable rules at any point of time. In case of multiple rules applicable in a given situation, the selection of the rule may decide whether it leads to the goal or not. Sometimes, the selected rule appears to be better than the other rules and later on proves to be unfruitful. This may lead to only a waste of time in case we are allowed to backtrack. Examples of such problems are theorem proving and 8-puzzle problem. But this may even lead to failure in case we are not allowed to backtrack. For example in game playing with two players where none can undo the unwise step, in chemical synthesis where irreversible change takes place once a rule is applied. Though there are many conflict resolution techniques that help in resolving the conflicts when selecting a rule to be applied, another technique called planning is required which can even help in better understanding of the consequences of selecting the current rule and applying it by proper planning in order to win. There are many planning methods that have been discovered by many researchers including goal stack planning, hierarchical planning, non-linear planning, case-based planning, macro-based planning, etc.

7.2 OVERVIEW

Q. What is planning? In which areas is it used in AI?

Ans. Generation of a sequence of actions to achieve a goal is called planning. It involves a representation of time in order to express and reason about the sequences of actions. The steps taken during planning can be expressed using a planning language which will represent the goals, the states, and the actions. In order that it represents goals, states, and the actions in an easy method, it should be easy to manipulate by algorithms.

Q. What are the ways of representing states, goals and actions?

Ans. *State:* A state represents the scenario at any point of time in planning. It is represented with a conjunction of one or more positive literals. It includes closed world assumption, first order logic, and the using clauses.

Goal: A goal is a partially specified state. This is because a proposition is said to satisfy a goal if it contains all the atoms of the goals along with other atoms.

Action: It is represented as a schema that consists of three parts: the action names, preconditions for the action, and the results known as effects.

Q. Give examples of languages used for planning.

Ans. 1. STRIPS: STanford Research Institute Problem Solver
2. ADL: Action Description Languages
3. PDDL: Planning Domain Definition Language

7.3 PLANNING PROBLEM

Q. Define the planning problem

Ans. In order to define planning problem, there are restrictive assumptions:

(a) infinite number of states: new objects and numbers;
(b) partial observability: non-observable variables;
(c) non-determinism: unpredictable action outcomes;
(d) uncontrollable events: not everything is controllable;
(e) extended goals: conditions on the whole execution path;
(f) beyond sequential plans: react to unpredictable outcomes;
(g) explicit time: durations and deadlines.

The classical planning problem is defined as:

Suppose we impose *all* of the restrictive assumptions. Then, a planning problem is $P = (\Sigma, s_0\ S_g)$, where Σ is a finite state-transition system, each node is a state, each edge is a state transition, s_0 is the initial state, and S_g is a set of goal states. The objective is to find a sequence of state transitions that goes from s to a state in G.

7.4 PLANNING WITH STATE SPACE SEARCH

Q. What state space search is used for planning?

Ans. In planning, we need to search through a search space that constitutes a set of states of the world, an action is defined as transitions between states. The planning problem is to find a path from a given start state to the desired goal state in the search graph. Two approaches can be used for searching: forward chaining also called progression that proceeds by actions specified in given state to find the goal state and backward chaining that proceeds starts from goal state and moves towards the start state. This is done by finding the actions whose effects satisfy one or more of the posted goals. Then, the precondition of the chosen actions as goals is posted. This process is called goal regression. The second space used in planning is plan space.

In case of partial panning, we need to search through plan space graph that represents partial plans where arcs denote plan refinement operations. Either a plan with a totally ordered sequence of actions is searched for or a plan with a partially ordered set of actions is searched for.

7.5 COMPONENTS OF A PLANNING SYSTEM

Q. What are the components of a planning system?

Ans. A planning system is used to solve a particular problem from the given knowledge database. It involves selecting a sequence of actions or rules which should be applied in order to solve a problem efficiently. So, the functions that are necessary for the planning system are

1. ***Selection of best rule for application:*** Choosing the best rule to apply next based on the best available heuristic information. The rules can be selected by first identifying the difference between the current state and the desired goal state. Then, the rules that can be applied in the given situation are identified. In case, there is only one rule applicable that is to be applied directly. In case of more than one, the rule can be applied for reducing the difference between current state and goal state and then the heuristic information is to be used for selecting the best rule for application.
2. ***Application of the selected rule:*** Applying the chosen rule to generate the new problem state. Some parts of the problem may be affected by the rule while some parts may remain unchanged. For simple problems, this can be handled by frame axioms have been applied for handling this situation where we need to express only the state which changes on the application of the rule while others do not. For complex problems, the mechanism STRIPS is used. In this, three lists are added with each operator.
   (a) **PRECONDITION**: It contains the predicates that must be true so that the operator can be applied.
   (b) **ADD:** It contains the list of new predicates that will become true when the operator is applied.
   (c) **DELETE:** It contains the list of old predicates that will become false when the operator is applied.

   Any predicate that is not included in either ADD or DELETE list will remain unaffected by the application of the operator.

   When the rules are applied a search tree is generated, which indicates the ADD and DELETE predicates that can be referred in case the current solution leads to a wrong answer and we need to backtrack.
3. ***Detecting the arrival of the solution:*** Checking whether the solution is found and exiting if so. The solution is indicated through a sequence of operators that transform the initial problem state into the desired goal state. For blocks world, the representation scheme used for indicating the solution is predicate logic which uses theorem proving using deduction method to indicate whether the desired goal state has been reached or not using deduction.
4. ***Identifying the dead ends***: In a planning system, when the sequence of operators is applied for finding the desired solution, it may be possible that the sequence of steps is not leading to goal. Reasoning mechanisms should be used to identify the dead ends so that they can be abandoned. In the case of blocks world problem, the goal is subdivided into subgoal and hence any path that leads to conflict between the subgoals should be abandoned. Also, a path that is satisfying only one subgoal and opposite for other subgoals should also be abandoned. In other problems where the solution is found from start state to desired goal state, the path deviating from the goal state should be directly abandoned.
5. ***Repairing an almost correct solution:*** Most of the problems are not completely decomposable in nature but are nearly decomposable. In order to find the solution, we can assume them completely decomposable so that the solution can be found using any of the planning mechanism and then the results can be combined. In case the results are exactly as desired, then the solution can be used as it is received. But in case of a little mismatch, a patch can be applied to correct the points wherever there are deviations.

Q. Define how a blocks world problem can be solved by a robot (STRIPS).

Ans. In the blocks world problem, there is a flat surface on which the blocks can be placed. There are a number of block which are square in shape and of the same size so that they can placed on the top of one another. The process of putting one block on the top of the other is called stacking and removing a block from the top of the other block is called unstacking. This is done be a robot arm that can hold one block at a time. There are many operators that can be applied in blocks world problem:

1. STACK (X, Y): Place block X on the top of block Y. The precondition for this operator is that in order to pick block X for placing it on the top of block Y, the robot arm must be empty and the block Y should have no block on the top of it.
2. UNSTACK (X, Y): This operation can be performed when block X is placed on the top of block Y. The preconditions for these operations are that the robot arm should be empty for picking block X. There should not be any block on the top of block X, only then block X can be picked up by the robot arm.
3. PICKUP (X): If the block X is lying on the table and there is no other block on the top of it, then the robot arm should pick it up and hold it. For picking up the block, the robot arm must be empty.
4. PUTDOWN (X): If the robot arm is holding a block X, then the robot arm is asked to put block X on the table.

The predicates indicate various states of the blocks world problem: There are two possible states for the robot arm. Either it will be empty or it is holding some block. These can be represented as follows:

1. ARMEMPTY: This indicates that the robot arm is holding nothing.
2. HOLDING (X): This indicates that the robot arm is holding a block X.

For any block, there are three possible states. The block can be resting on a table or the block can be resting on some other block. There is nothing on the top of a block or another block is resting on the top of it. These can be represented by the following predicates:

1. ONTABLE (X): Block X is lying on the table.
2. ON (X, Y): Block X is lying on block Y or Block Y has block X on the top of it and hence its top is not clear.
3. CLEAR (X): There is no block on the top of block X.

Inference rules for blocks world problem indicate the rules which can be applied in a given set of conditions.

1. If the robot arm is holding a block, then this indicates that the robot arm is not empty or vice versa.
   $[\exists\ x\text{: HOLDING }(x)] \rightarrow \neg\text{ARMEMPTY}$
2. If a block is on another block, then it indicates that top of first block is not clear.
   $\forall x\text{: }[\neg\exists\ y : \text{ON }(y, x)] \rightarrow \neg\text{CLEAR }(x)$
3. If a block is on the table, then this means that there is no block on the top of it.
   $\forall x\text{: ONTABLE }(x) \rightarrow\ \neg\exists\ y\text{: ON }(x, y)$

Q. Explain STRIPS algorithm.

Ans. STRIPS takes two inputs: start state and goal state and returns a plan of steps taken in order to reach from start to goal. It works on minimizing the difference between start and goal state.

1. Calculate the difference between start state and goal state, call them subgoals.
2. If there is no difference, then return an empty plan.
3. Choose an operator that matches with most of the required subgoals.

4. Add all preconditions of this operator to the list of existing subgoals.
5. Compute new subgoal by applying the selected operator to start state.
6. Maintain a queue of operators selected and applied that will form the plan returned by the program.

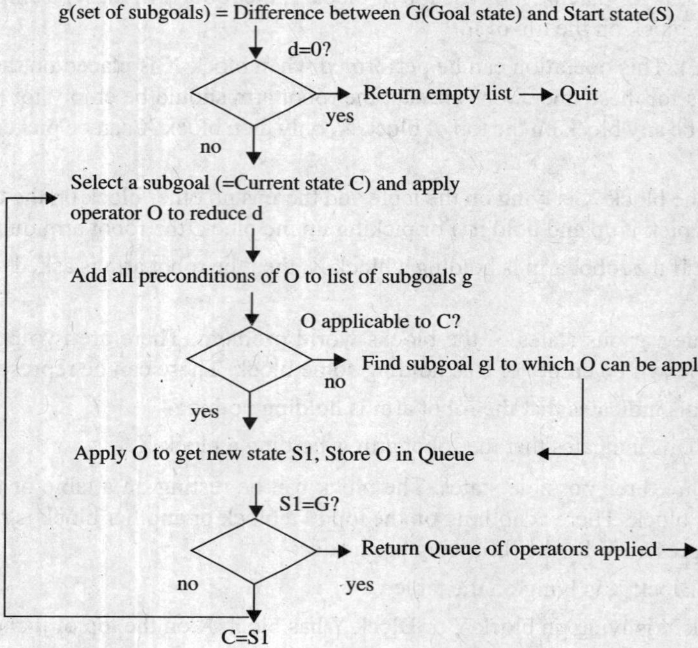

7.6 TYPES OF PLANNING

Q. What are the various types of planning techniques which can be used in artificial intelligence?

Ans. A number of planning techniques have been suggested in artificial intelligence which serves purposes for different conditions:

1. Goal stack planning
2. Conditional planning
3. Partial order planning
4. Non-linear planning
5. Hierarchical planning
6. Reactive systems
7. Triangle tables
8. Metaplanning
9. Case-based planning
10. Macrooperators

7.6.1 Goal Stack Planning

Q. What is goal stack planning?

Ans. Goal stack planning has two words in it. First is the goal and the other is the stack. It is a goal directed approach for finding the solutions to the problem. It involves finding the subgoals for each goal and the operators that need to be solved for solving the subgoal. This is done through a stack where each goal is pushed first. Then each of the subgoals is pushed into the stack one by one. The top most subgoal is popped out of stack and the operators needed to solve it are pushed into the stack. This process is repeated till all the conditions become true. When all the subgoals are satisfied, the main goal is left in the stack. If it only the goal that is left in the stack, then this indicates the solution.

7.6.2 Conditional Planning

Q. What is conditional planning?

Ans. In conditional planning, the rules are of the form:

If <Condition>, <Then part of Plan> or <Else part of plan>

When conditional step is executed, the agent tests the condition against the facts in its knowledge base before execution. If the condition is true, then the agent executes the part of the plan. If the condition is false, then it executes the else part of the plan. In order to execute the conditional plan, the agent may add knowledge from its perception. Sensing actions can be used by the agent in case some information is missing or uncertain. The condition plan may include subplans depending upon the information available to the agent.

7.6.3 Partial Order Planning

Q. What is partial order planning?

Ans. In partial order planning, totally ordered, i.e., linear plans are generated. There are four components in partial order plan:

1. A set of actions {Start, Finish}.
2. A set of ordering constraints {Start $\prec$ Finish}, i.e., Start is before Finish.
3. A set of causal links {$A \xrightarrow{p} B$}, i.e., A achieves p for B.
4. A set of open preconditions {C1 and C2}

The solution of partial order planning is a consistent plan with no open preconditions. A plan is consistent if there are no cycles in the ordering constraints no conflicts in the causal links. The conflicts in the causal link can be achieved through demoting or promoting a conflicting constraint.

Procedure:

1. Setting up an initial plan: This is done by specifying the following:
   (a) Actions which include start and finish.
   (b) Ordering constraints: Start $\prec$ Finish
   (c) Casual links list which is empty initially.
   (d) The set of open preconditions which are to be satisfied.
2. The successor function picks any one of the open preconditions p on an action Y.
3. For every possible consistent action X that achieves p, do the following:
   (a) Generate a successor plan adding the casual link $X \longrightarrow Y$ for condition p and the ordering constraint $X \prec Y$.
   (b) If X was not in the plan, then add Start $\prec$ X and X $\prec$ Finish.

(c) Resolve conflicts between the new causal link all existing actions
(d) Add the successor states for combination of resolved conflicts

4. Repeat the process till there is no precondition left to be satisfied.

7.6.4 Non-linear Planning Using Constraint Posting

Q. Explain non-linear planning using constraint posting

Ans. If the problem is decomposed into a number of subgoals, then in non-linear planning, the solutions to all subproblems are found in a non-linear way, i.e., in any order of subgoals instead of linear sequence of subgoals. This cannot be applied in all situations because all problems are not completely decomposable. Some terms used here are given below:

(a) Promotion: Putting constraints on one step to come before another in a final plan.
(b) Declobbering: Placing one (possibly new) step S2 between two old steps S1 and S3 such that S2 reasserts some precondition of S3 that was neglected (or "clobbered") by S1.
(c) Simple establishment: Assigning a value to a variable, in order to ensure the preconditions of some step.
(d) Separation: Preventing the assignment of certain values to a variable.
(e) Step addition: This means adding new steps for a plan.

Non-linear planning algorithm used in TWEAK:

1. Initialize S to be the set of propositions in the goal state.
2. Remove some unachieved proposition P from S.
3. Achieve P by using step addition, promotion, declobbering, simple establishment or separation.
4. Review all the steps in the plan, including any new steps introduced by step addition, to see if any of their preconditions are unachieved. Add to S the new set of unachieved preconditions.
5. If S is empty, then complete the plan by converting the partial order of steps into a total order, instantiate any variables as necessary.
6. Otherwise, go to step 2.

7.6.5 Hierarchical Planning

Q. Explain hierarchical planning.

Ans. In order to solve hard problems, a problem solver may have to generate long plans. It is important to be able to eliminate some of the details of the problem until a solution that addresses the main issues is found. Then, an attempt can be made to fill the appropriate details. So, in hierarchical planning, all the conditions are assigned a criticality value. The most critical condition is selected and the operator is selected for achieving this while ignoring rest of the less critical conditions at this time. When this condition is fulfilled, then the condition which is most critical in the current list is again selected and an operator is selected for solving it. The results of the application of the earlier operators are used for selecting the operators at the next lower level. Thus, there is a hierarchy of conditions based on criticality forming abstraction levels and the corresponding operators are included in the planning solution. The motivation behind hierarchical planning is to reduce the size of search space, i.e., instead of trying all the possible plan hierarchies, we limit it according to the priority of the goals. It also aims are postponement of details until major steps are in place first. ABSTRIPS, i.e., abstraction-based STRIPS can be used for representing hierarchical planning. Hierarchical task networks are used to find the solution to a complex problem.

The algorithm used in ABSTRIPS is

- First solve the problem completely, considering only preconditions whose criticality value is the highest possible.
- These values reflect the expected difficulty of satisfying the precondition.
- To do this, do exactly what STRIPS did, but simply ignore the preconditions of lower than peak criticality.
- Once this is done, use the constructed plan as the outline of a complete plan and consider preconditions at the next lowest criticality level.
- Because this approach explores entire plans at one level of detail before it looks at the lower level details of any one of them, it has been called length-first approach.

Q. What is HTN?

Ans. In hierarchical planning, a task network is created to indicate the tasks and the constraints which create a hierarchy of tasks. The constraints are designed on the basis of criticality of the tasks.

7.6.6 Reactive Systems

Q. Explain reactive systems.

Ans. In general terms, planning means selecting a set of actions in a sequence to carry out a particular task. A reactive system is the one that reacts to its environment, i.e., that maintains an ongoing interaction with its environment and responds to any changes. A reactive system is a planning system which chooses actions one at a time and does not select a sequence of actions before it does the first thing. It is this property of reactive systems which make them easily operate robustly in domains which are difficult to model completely and accurately, i.e., they can quickly take another step in case first fails as there is no chain of preplanned actions. These are also used in real-time tasks because they avoid wastage of time in deliberative planning and hence are extremely responsive. These are goal directed because they are asked to do some as told by us.

7.6.7 Other Planning Techniques

Q. What are triangle tables?

Ans. These are tables which keep on recording the goals which is to be satisfied by each operator as well as the goals which must be true for it to execute correctly. This table provides required information in case there is a deviation from the plan. In a triangular table, for n operations in the plan, there are $(n + 1)$ rows from 1 to $n + 1$ and $(n + 1)$ columns from 0 to n.

- At the end of the ith row, place the ith component of the plan.
- The row entries for the ith step contain the preconditions for the ith operation.
- The column entries for the jth column contain the add list for the rule on the top.
- The <i,j>th cell (where $1 \leq i \leq n + 1$ and $0 \leq j \leq n$) contain the preconditions for the ith operation that are added by the jth operation.
- The first column indicates the starting state and the last row indicates the goal state.

In searching, triangular tables lead to some amount of fault tolerance in the robot.

Q. Give an example where triangle tables are used.

Ans. Consider the following planning example of STRIPS:

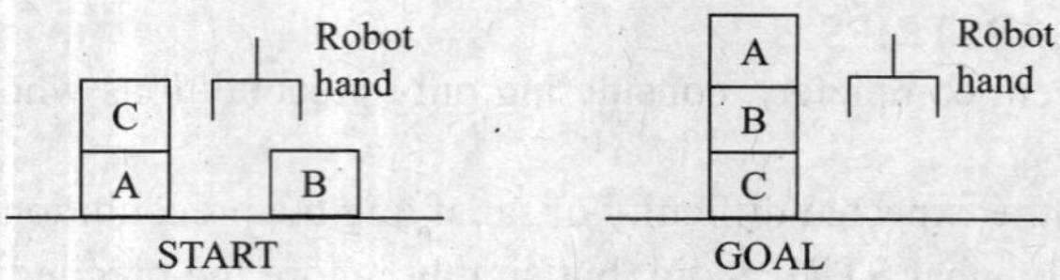

START	GOAL
on(B, table)	on(C, table)
on(A, table)	on(B, B)
on(C, A)	on(A, B)
hand empty	hand empty
clear(C)	clear(A)
clear(B)	

The steps for getting to Goal state from Start state are:

1. Unstack(C,A)
2. Putdown(C)
3. Pickup(B)
4. Stack(B,C)
5. Pickup(A)
6. Stack(A,B)

The execution of the above plan can be depicted using triangular tables:

	0	1	2	3	4	5	6
1	on (C,A) clear(C) hand empty	unstack(C,A)					
2		holding(C)	putdown(C)				
3	on(B,table)		hand empty	pickup(B)			
4			clear(C)	holding(B)	stack(B,C)		
5	on(A,table)	clear(A)			hand empty	pickup(A)	
6					clear(B)	holding(A)	stack(A,B)
7			on(C,table)		on(B,C)		on (A,B) clear(A)

Q. What is meta-planning?

Ans. As the name suggests meta-planning is planning about planning. It is a technique about the planning process as well as the problem solving.

Q. Explain the use of macro-operators in planning.

Ans. Macro-operators are the operators which allow a planner to build new operators which represent commonly used sequences of operators. A macro-operator is a sequence of actions treated as a whole. These were used in problem-solving system STRIPS. It used a learner component. After each problem solving episode/goal G, the learning component used to take the sequence of actions to carry out that plan and store it as a macro-operator (MACROP). Its preconditions are same as preconditions of G and its postconditions are the goals just achieved. These help in creating macros for solving subgoals and hence make compact plans with macros.

Q. What are the common problems faced in planning using macro-operators and how they can be handled?

Ans. There are two problems faced with the use of macro operators:

1. ***Ambiguous generalization:*** If the sequence of operators applied to solve a particular subgoal are taken as constants, then the use of macro is limited. So, it is generalized by replacing constants with variables in sequence of operators in macro, its preconditions and postconditions. But in problems with multiple goals, the preconditions of various subgoals may conflict with the sequence of operators stored in macro. So, generalization should include parameterization in planning. This includes re-evaluation of the preconditions of all subgoals before generalization.
2. ***Non-serializable subgoals:*** When there is sequence of operators defined in a macro, it is possible that the precondition of one subgoal may interfere with the solution required for the other subgoal. So, the use of macro may fail. This can be solved by using non-linear planning.

Q. Explain case-based planning.

Ans. It is a technique to store information about all the plans and then re-using the old plans to make new plans.

SOLVED EXAMPLES

Q. Consider the following blocks world problem: Find the solution using goal stack planning.

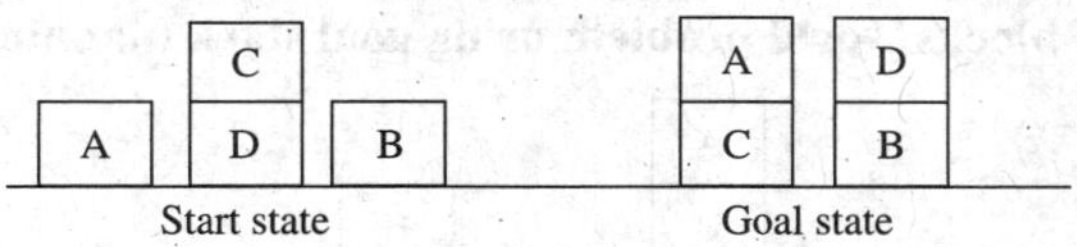

Ans. To start with, goal stack is simply the goal states:

ON(A,C) ∧ ON(D,B) ∧ ONTABLE(C) ∧ ONTABLE(B)

This problem is separate into four subproblems, one for each component of the goal. One of the subproblem ONTABLE(B) and ONTABLE(D) are already true in the initial state.

Alternative 1: Goal stack:

ON(A,C)
ON(D,B)
ON(A,C)∧ON(D,B)∧OTAD

Alternative 2: Goal stack:

ON(B,D)
ON(C,A)
ON(C,A) ∧ ON(B,D) ∧ OTAD

Q. Define Sussman anomaly.

Ans. In blocks world problem, when the goal is ON(C,B) and ON(B,A) and we start from initial state ON(A,C) ∧ ONTABLE(C) ∧ ONTABLE(B) ∧ ARMEMPTY.

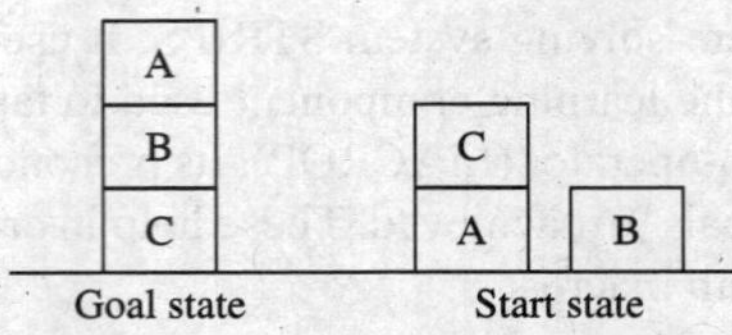

It is an anomaly because a non-interleaved planner cannot solve the problem. This problem can be solved, but it cannot be attacked by first applying all the operators to achieve one goal, and then applying operators to achieve another goal. The problem is that we have forced an ordering the operators. Sometimes, steps for multiple goals need to be interleaved. An example for non-linear plan for the solution of this problem is the following:

- Begin work on the goal ON(C,B) by clearing C, thus putting A on the table.
- Achieve the goal ON(C,B) by stacking C on B.
- Complete the goal ON(B,A) by stacking B on A.

Q. Give an example of a reactive system.

Ans. Thermostat is an example of a reactive system. It needs to control the temperature inside a car or a room to a particular temperature (say room temperature). The possible actions for thermostat are increasing or decreasing the temperature. The thermostat does not plan for actions of increasing or decreasing the temperature of car or room by prediction the weather conditions, rather it acts on a simple pair of situation-action rules. There are two possible rules:

1. If the temperature in car or room is t degrees below the required temperature, then increase the temperature by switching off the air conditioner.
2. If the temperature in car or room is t degrees above the required temperature, then decrease the temperature by switching on the air conditioner.

Q. Solve the given blocks world problem using goal stack planning.

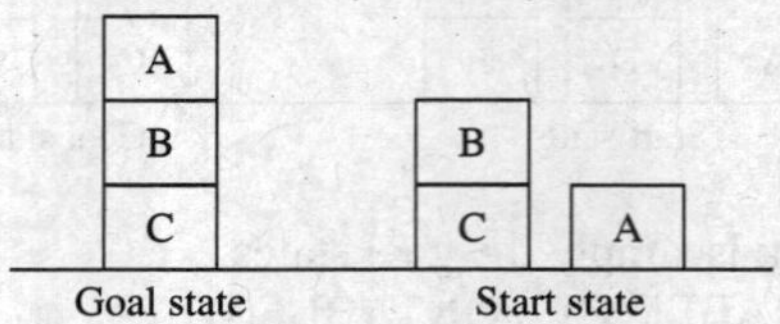

Ans. The goals in goal state required are ON(A,B) Λ ON(B,C) Λ ONTABLE(C). The conditions true in the start state are ON(B,C) Λ ONTABLE(A) Λ ARMEMPTY. In goal stack, the subgoals will be pushed on to the stack corresponding to main goal. Then operators required to solve subgoals will be pushed onto stack and when the conditions become true, the subgoal achieved will be popped. The process will be repeated until the goal stack is empty. The goal stack growth for the current problem is given below:

ON(A,B) Λ ON(B,C) Λ ONTABLE(C)

The subgoals ON(B,C) and ONTABLE(C) are already true. So, the goal stack becomes:

ON(A,B)
ON(A,B) Λ ON(B,C) Λ ONTABLE(C)

To do ON(A,B), the operator required is STACK(A,B), the goal stack becomes:

STACK(A,B)
ON(A,B)
ON(A,B) Λ ON(B,C) Λ ONTABLE(C)

The preconditions for STACK(A,B) are CLEAR(B) and HOLDING(A), the goal stack becomes:

CLEAR(B) Λ HOLDING(A)
STACK(A,B)
ON(A,B)
ON(A,B) Λ ON(B,C) Λ ONTABLE(C)

These are pushed into stack in an order, the goal stack becomes

HOLDING(A)
CLEAR(B)
CLEAR(B) Λ HOLDING(A)
STACK(A,B)
ON(A,B)
ON(A,B) Λ ON(B,C) Λ ONTABLE(C)

The preconditions for HOLDING(A) are CLEAR(A) and ONTABLE(A) and ARMEMPTY, the goal stack becomes

CLEAR(A) Λ ONTABLE(A) Λ ARMEMPTY
HOLDING(A)
CLEAR(B)
CLEAR(B) Λ HOLDING(A)
STACK(A,B)
ON(A,B)
ON(A,B) Λ ON(B,C) Λ ONTABLE(C)

All the three conditions are true and hence popped out of the stack and these are the steps for operator PICKUP(A), the goal stack becomes

PICKUP(A)
CLEAR(B) Λ HOLDING(A)
STACK(A,B)
ON(A,B)
ON(A,B) Λ ON(B,C) Λ ONTABLE(C)

Clear(B) is also true and hence block A will be stacked on B to fulfill goal ON(A,B) and hence the main goal is satisfied. The resulting plan is

PICKUP(A)
STACK(A,B)

Q. Solve given blocks world problem using non-linear planning.

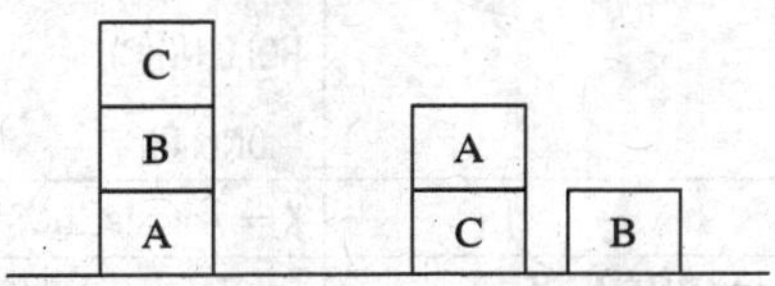

Goal state   Start state

Ans. The goal states are ON(C,B) Λ ON(B,A) Λ ONTABLE(A). The conditions true in the start state are ON(A,C) Λ ONTABLE(B). The two goals taken in parallel (since there is no ordering) are

	CLEAR(B) *HOLDING(C) STACK(C,B) ARMEMPTY ON(C,B) ¬CLEAR(B) ¬HOLDING(C)	CLEAR(A) *HOLDING(B) STACK(B, A) ARMEMPTY ON(B,A) ¬CLEAR(A) ¬HOLDING(B)
To achieve Holding **Step addition →**	*CLEAR(C) ONTABLE(C) *ARMEMPTY PICKUP(C) ¬ONTABLE(C) ¬ARMEMPTY HOLDING(C)	*CLEAR(B) ONTABLE(B) *ARMEMPTY PICKUP(B) ¬ONTABLE(B) ¬ARMEMPTY HOLDING(B)
To achieve CLEAR(B) Promotion step →	Reordering constraint: PICKUP(B)←STACK(C,B)	
To achieve ARMEMPTY Promotion step →	PICKUP(B)←PICKUP(A)	
Declobbering step to achieve ARMEMPTY in PICKUP(A) since PICKUP(B) asserts ¬ARMEMPTY →	PICKUP(B)←STACK(B,A) ←PICKUP(C)	
To achieve CLEAR(C) step addition →	*ON(x,C) *CLEAR(x) *ARMEMPTY UNSTACK(x,C) ¬ARMEMPTY CLEAR(C) HOLDING(C) ¬ON(x,C)	
Simple establishment step →	X = A in step UNSTACK(x,C)	
Promotion step to CLEAR(A) and ARMEMPTY →	UNSTACK(x,C)←STACK(B,A) UNSTACK(x,C)←PICKUP(C) UNSTACK(x,C)←PICKUP(B)	

Declobbering step to achieve ARMEMPTY →	HOLDING(A) PUTDOWN(A) ¬HOLDING(A) ONTABLE(x) ARMEMPTY	
Promotion step to achieve ARMEMPTY →	Ordered as UNSTACK(x,C)←PUTDOWN(A)←PICKUP(B)	
The concrete plan is→	UNSTACK(A,C) PUTDOWN(A) PICKUP(B) STACK(B,A) PICKUP(A) STACK(C,B)	

Q. Draw a triangular table for given blocks world problem.

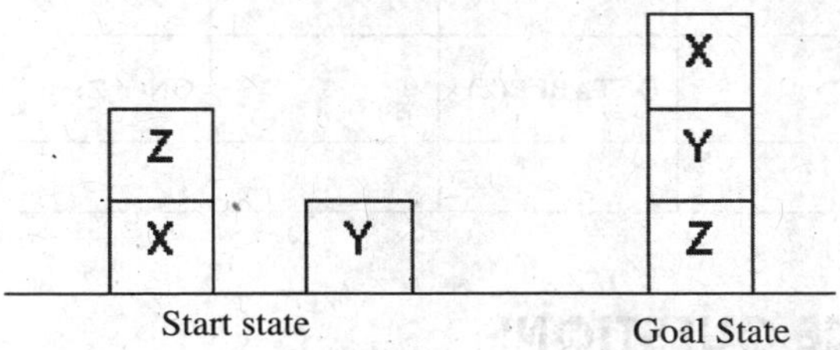

Ans. The start state has the following conditions:

ONTABLE(Y)

ONTABLE(X)

ON(Z, X)

ARMEMPTY

CLEAR(Z)

CLEAR(Y)

The goal state will have the following states:

ONTABLE(Z)

ON(Y, Z)

ON(X, Y)

ARMEMPTY

CLEAR(X)

The steps in solution are: UNSTACK(Z,X), PUTDOWN(Z), PICKUP(Y), STACK(Y,Z), PICKUP(X), STACK(X,Y).

The triangular table is given below:

1	**ON(Z,X) CLEAR(Z) ARMEMPTY**	**UNSTACK(Z,X)**					
2		**HOLDING(Z)**	**PUTDOWN(Z)**				
3	**ONTABLE (Y)**		**ARMEMPTY**	**PICKUP(Y)**			
4			**CLEAR(Z)**	**HOLDING(Y)**	**STACK(Y,Z)**		
5	**ONTABLE (X)**	**CLEAR(X)**			**ARMEMPTY**	**PICKUP(X)**	
6					**CLEAR(Y)**	**HOLDING(X)**	**STACK(X,Y)**
7			**ONTABLE(Z)**		**ON(Y,Z)**		**ON(X,Y) CLEAR(X)**
	0	**1**	**2**	**3**	**4**	**5**	**6**

MULTIPLE CHOICE QUESTIONS

Select the most appropriate answer to following questions:

1. Which is the following planning system does not plan for a sequence of actions?

   (a) Case based (b) Non-linear
   (c) Reactive systems (d) Triangle tables

2. Which of the planning system provide a way of recording the goals?

   (a) Case based (b) Non-linear
   (c) Reactive systems (d) Triangle tables

3. Which of the planning system uses ABSTRIPS?

   (a) Case based (b) Non-linear
   (c) Hierarchical (d) None of these

4. Which of the following was the first true non-linear planner?

   (a) TWEAK (b) MOLGEN
   (c) NOAH (d) STRIPS

5. Which of the planning approach was used by STRIPS?
   (a) Case based (b) Goal Stack
   (c) Non-linear (d) Reactive systems
6. Which of the following is not a part of the list attached with an operator in STRIPS?
   (a) ADD (b) DELETE
   (c) PRECONDITION (d) None of these
7. Constraints are used in which of the following planning approach?
   (a) Goal stack (b) Non-linear
   (c) Reactive systems (d) None of these
8. What is the name given to the process of preventing the assignment of certain values to a variable?
   (a) Promotion (b) Declobbering
   (c) Separation (d) None of these
9. When we place one step s3 between two old steps s1 and s2 such that s3 reasserts some preconditions of s2 that was negated by s1, the process is called:
   (a) Promotion (b) Declobbering
   (c) Separation (d) None of these
10. Which of the planning scheme works on subproblems independently and then combines subplans?
    (a) Partial order (b) Goal stack
    (c) Hierarchical (d) None of these

Ans. 1. c 2. d 3. c 4. c 5. b 6. d 7. b 8. c 9. b 10. a

EXERCISES

1. Consider the blocks world problem. Find the solution using goal stack planning.

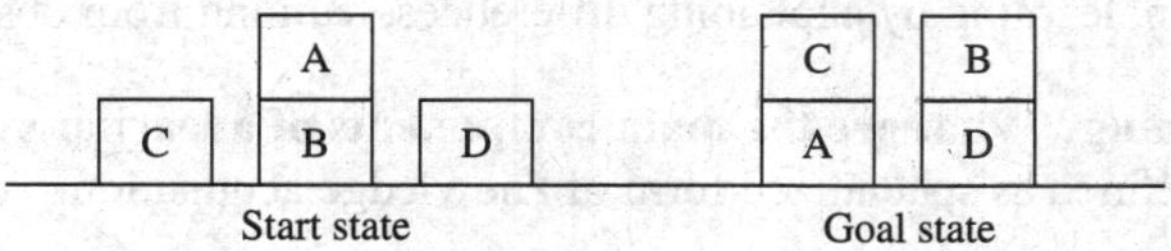

2. Write a set of STRIPS style operators used for the given problems. Write start and goal state descriptions in each case. Generate plans using goal stack planning.
   - Devise a plan for preparing tea for a guest.
   - Devise a plan to pack the lunch in tiffin box.
3. Consider the blocks world problem. Solve it using constraint posting:

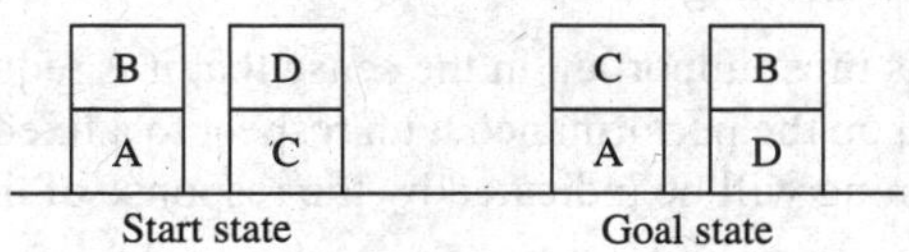

8 Learning

8.1 INTRODUCTION

An AI program is the one that can make a machine intelligent. This is done by introducing the knowledge in the AI program. More the knowledge a system has more is the intelligence of the system. However, knowledge acquisition should not be one time activity. As a human being keeps on updating the older knowledge with newer knowledge, the AI system must also update the knowledge base. This can be done either statically by adding the rules and facts in the database or dynamically, i.e., the AI program itself adds the facts and rules based on the feedback it gets from the environment when it performs some task. This process is called learning. The AI system should be made intelligent by making it learnable. There are mainly two modes of learning –supervised or unsupervised. In case of supervised learning, the system learns with the help of a supervisor who provides it the feedback to improve upon. In case of unsupervised learning, there is no such supervisor available for proving the feedback. There are many ways of learning. Examples are rote learning, learning by examples, learning by taking experience, learning by induction and deduction, learning by explaining differences, learning from observations, etc.

Q. What is learning? What are the main components of a learner system?

Ans. Learning is defined as specialized form of knowledge acquisition. The components of a learning system are

1. Learning component: This is the main component that is to acquire knowledge, make changes or improvements to the system depending on its performance.
2. Performance component: This component performs the task assigned to it by choosing actions that need to be taken.
3. Problem generator: It suggests problems or actions that would lead to generation of new examples or experiences to improve learning
4. Critic: This component is most important in the sense that it is required to give the feedback to the learner component based on the performance with respect to a fixed standard for measuring performance. The level of learning will be indicated by the response of the critic.

5. Environment or teacher: These give input to the learner system and receive the output. Mechanically, this is done through sensors for providing input and effectors for producing output.

8.2 TYPES OF LEARNING

Q. What is rote learning? Give an example.

Ans. Rote learning is defined as learning by copying the knowledge in the same form as told. It is also known as memorization. It requires least amount of inference. Example is to learn the multiplication tables, stories, etc. In computer, when a computed value is stored in cache memory so that it can be referred again without re-computation efforts, then it is known as rote learning. It is used in many AI programs like Checker's game playing to improve performance.

Q. How can learning be done by taking advice?

Ans. A computer learns only by the program it executes. The programmer writes a program and the computer executes it. If the program is written in high level language, then some interpreter or compiler must intervene to change the high level instructions into code that machine can execute directly. In the initial state, a high level advice is given and by using various case analyses and matching, we get an operational rule in the final state. For example, in chess, the advice for the player is "fight for control of the center of the board". A computer program for chess might make use of the advice by adjusting its static evaluation function to include a factor based on the number of centre squares attacked by its own pieces.

Q. What is learning from examples or induction?

Ans. In this type of learning, many positive and negative examples about a particular area of learning are collected and with the use of induction, the results are concluded. Learning by induction uses inductive inference to formulate a new concept after seeing a number of examples or instances of the same concept. Example is to judge the orange as round after being told ball and earth as round objects.

Q. Explain how learning is done by analyzing differences.

Ans. Winston algorithm is an example which learns by analyzing differences.

For a learning procedure L, a positive example helps the leaner to identify the general properties about an example. But when an invalid example is encountered, the learner may not be able to classify it as valid or invalid based on only general concepts learned through positive examples. In order to make it learn more precisely how to classify whether the given example is valid or not, it is trained using negative examples as well. The negative example can be given using a near miss approach where there is only one deviation of the example from the valid example. This can help explain the learner what has made the given example invalid. This can lead to two types of specialization identified, one in positive sense that what was missing in the invalid example, so that property becomes a compulsory property for any valid example. Another is in negative sense that what was wrong in the invalid example and hence should not be a part of any valid examples. This way the learning model will keep on adding the knowledge.

An example is a learning program to judge about which items can cause an allergic reaction to a patient. This can be done by studying the data about several days when the patients eat some things and noting the result. The examples which indicate a reaction has occurred are positive examples. Now the analysis can be done by seeing the difference from those which has negative result. The learning will be done when a new day a patient comes with an allergic reaction. By analyzing the differences, the program should be able to indicate which item caused allergic reaction and should be avoided.

Positive examples:

	Milk	Oranges	Carrot	Fish	Reaction
Day1	Yes	Yes	No	Yes	Yes
Day2	Yes	Yes	No	No	Yes
Day3	No	Yes	Yes	Yes	Yes

Negative examples:

	Milk	Oranges	Carrot	Fish	Reaction
Day4	No	No	Yes	Yes	No
Day5	Yes	No	Yes	Yes	No

The near-miss analysis helps in identifying the causes of reaction. It is clear that consuming milk, oranges and fish together causes reaction. Also eating milk and oranges together can cause reaction. Also eating oranges, carrot and fish together can cause reaction. Thus the program is learning by analyzing the differences between these examples. So, for a given day, if the patient has consumed milk, oranges and carrot, a reaction has occurred. The program can identify the cause of it: consuming milk and oranges together. Hence, it will suggest the patient not to consume milk and oranges together again.

Q. Explain how learning is done by explaining experience.

Ans. In this type of learning, one person can explain the experience to the other person in order to correct the errors and learn.

Q. Explain how learning is done by correcting mistakes.

Ans. Correcting mistakes are very good method for learning. This only needs that learner need to modify the decision taken earlier and update for future use. This is done first by identifying the mistake, then identifying the reasons for committing that mistake (this will help find the point of deviation from goal) and then correcting the mistake known as repairing the mistake.

Q. Explain how learning is done by recording cases.

Ans. In this type of learning, a problem situation is referred to a case. A past case means the situation experienced in past. The current situation is known as the new case whose solution is to be found. Here, learning takes place by using the experience learned from past cases for finding the solution for current cases. The set of all positive examples are stored as cases. In order to find the solution to the current case, the properties of current case are compared against the similar properties in the recorded case. This is done using consistency heuristics that states which of the measures of properties of current case are known and which are unknown. The most similar case according to the known properties helps in identifying the guess for the unknown property. The simplest approach is to use nearest neighbor method for finding the case near to the current case which can be implemented using k-d (distances measured in k dimensions) decision tree.

Q. What is explanation-based learning?

Ans. It is also known as explanation-based generalization. The objective of explanation-based learning (EBL) is to formulate a generalized explanation of the goal concept. The explanation should prove how the training examples satisfy the concept definition in terms of the domain theory. An EBL program needs following inputs:

(a) A training example: The information about the real world given as input to the learning program.
(b) A goal concept: Description of what the program is required to learn.
(c) An operationality criteria: The description of the usable concepts.
(d) A domain theory: A set of rules that describe relationships between objects and actions in a domain.

From all these inputs, an EBL program computes a generalization of the training examples sufficient to describe the concept of goal while satisfying the operationality criteria.

Q. What is analogical learning?

Ans. Analogical learning is defined as learning a new concept through the use of similar known concepts from past experiences. It also needs a lot of inference as to correlate the unknown with the known. Example is problem solving in exams. There are two types of analogical learning:

1. Transformational analogy: In this type of learning, a solution to a previous problem is transformed into a solution for the current problem by identifying the similarity between the two.
2. Derivational analogy: Derivation is the detailed history of the steps taken to solve a problem. If these derivations are taken into considerations for finding a solution to a new problem by analogy, it is called derivational analogy.

Q. What do you understand by formal learning theory?

Ans. Formally, a device learns a concept if it can, given positive and negative examples, produce an algorithm that will classify future examples correctly with probability 1/h. The complexity of learning a concept is a function of three factors: the error tolerance (h), the number of binary features present in the examples (t), and the size of the rule necessary to make the discrimination (f). If the number of training examples required is polynomial in h, t, and f, then the concept is said to be learnable.

Q. What do you understand by neural net learning?

Ans. Neural network model is based on a computational "brain metaphor". Other learning techniques make use of a metaphor based on evolution. Learning occurs through a selection process that begins with a large population of random programs. Learning algorithms that are inspired by evolution are called genetic algorithms.

Q. Learning from observation

Ans. Learning by any program in a particular domain is done in AI by studying examples in that domain. These examples are called observations or patterns. Based on given observations and using some techniques for learning, a task is performed. The common task is classification and inductive learning. Also it is used by learning agents.

Classifiers are functions that use pattern matching to determine a closest match. A classifier can be trained in various ways; there are many statistical and machine learning approaches. The most widely used classifiers are the neural networks, kernel methods such as support vector machine, naïve Bayes classifier and decision trees etc. A classifier's performance depends greatly on the characteristics of the data to be classified.

Q. What is learning by direct instruction?

Ans. This type of learning is used by a teacher in telling a number of facts to the students in an organized manner.

Q. What is learning by deduction?

Ans. It is done through a sequence of deductive inference steps using known facts and new facts or relationships are logically derived from the known facts. Example is proving a theorem from a given set of axioms.

Q. Explain how learning is done using relevance information.

Ans. Relevance-based learning (RBL) is deductive in nature. It needs some prior knowledge about the problem domain. For example, it is prior knowledge that people in a country usually speak the same language. Given a person's nationality we can conclude about its language. This is a form of relevance: determination language is a function of nationality. Determination is really a relationship between the predicates. The corresponding generalization follows logically from the determinations and descriptions. Determinations specify a sufficient basis vocabulary from which to construct hypotheses concerning the target predicate.

A determination $P \succ Q$ says if any examples match on *P*, they must also match on *Q*.

A learner module is required to find the simplest determination consistent with the observations.

8.3 GENERAL MODEL OF LEARNING AGENTS

Q. What is Kohonen Self Organizing Map (SOM) and Kohonen Self Organizing Network(SON)?

Ans. Kohonen's SOMs are a type of unsupervised learning. The goal is to discover some underlying structure of the data. Kohonen's SOM is called a topology-preserving map because there is a topological structure imposed on the nodes in the network. A topological map is simply a mapping that preserves neighborhood relations. A network using Kohonen SOMs are called Kohonen's Self Organizing Networks(SON).

The goal is to train the net so that nearby outputs correspond to nearby inputs. For example, if x_1 and x_2 are two input vectors and t_1 and t_2 are the locations of the corresponding winning output nodes, then t_1 and t_2 should be close if x_1 and x_2 are similar. A network that performs this kind of mapping is called a feature map.

Algorithm for Learning in Kohonen's Self Organizing Map(SOM)

- Assume output nodes are connected in an array (usually 1 or 2 dimensional)
- Assume that the network is fully connected - all nodes in input layer are connected to all nodes in output layer.
- Use the competitive learning algorithm as follows:
  - (i) Randomly choose an input vector x
  - (ii) Determine the "winning" output node i, where wi is the weight vector connecting the inputs to output node i.

$$|\omega_i - x| \le |\omega_k - x| \quad \forall k$$

  - (iii) Given the winning node i, the weight update is

$$w_k(\text{new}) = w_k(\text{old}) + \mu \; \aleph\,(i,k)\,(x - w_k)$$

where $\aleph(i,k)$ is called the neighborhood function that has value 1 when i=k and falls off with the distance $|r_k - r_i|$ between units i and k in the output array. Thus, units close to the winner as well as the winner itself, have their weights updated appreciably. Weights associated with far away output nodes do not change significantly. It is here that the toplogical information is supplied. Nearby units receive similar updates and thus end up responding to nearby input patterns.

The above rule drags the weight vector wi and the weights of nearby units towards the input x.

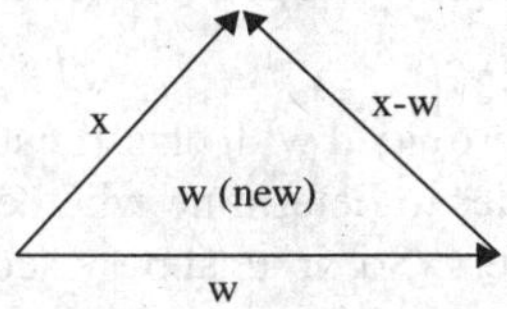

Figure 8.1

Example of neighbouring function is:

$$\aleph\,(i,k) = e^{\left(-|r_k - r_i|^2\right)/(2\sigma^2)}$$

Q. What is supervised learning?

Ans. In supervised learning, both the inputs and outputs can be observed. There is supervision by a supervisor (or a teacher) who provides a set of (x, y) pairs where x denotes the input and y denotes the corresponding output. The learner is given a training set of positive and negative examples of a concept. The learner is to construct a description that will accurately classify whether the future examples are positive or negative through labeling them positive or negative examples. A positive example is an instance of a concept while a negative example is not an instance of the concept. The figure below shows two classes indicate by red and blue dots.

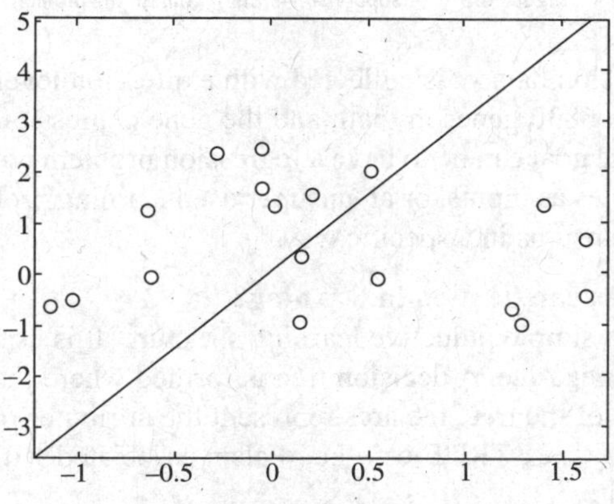

Figure 8.2 Supervised learning

For example, the information from 460 email messages are collected to predict whether the message was a junk email or a spam. The learner is to be built to identify and filter out the spams. The true outcome (email/spam) is available for the training data, as well as the relative frequencies of 60 common words and characters (you / your / free / ! / remove etc.). This words are chosen in such a way that the relative frequencies in the two types differs maximally for them.

In supervised algorithms, the classes are predetermined. In practice, a certain segment of data will be labelled with these classifications. The machine learner's task is to search for patterns and construct mathematical models. These models then are evaluated on the basis of their predictive capacity in relation to measures of variance in the data itself. Many of the methods referenced in the documentation like decision tree, induction, naive Bayes, etc. are examples of supervised learning techniques.

Q. What is unsupervised learning?

Ans. Unsupervised learners are not provided with classifications. Unsupervised algorithms seek out similarity between pieces of data in order to determine whether they can be characterized as forming a group. These groups are termed clusters. So, in unsupervised classification, often known as 'cluster analysis' the machine is not told how the texts are grouped. Its task is to arrive at some grouping of the data. In a very common of cluster analysis (K-means clustering), the machine is told in advance how many clusters it should form - a potentially difficult and arbitrary decision to make. The figure shows many clusters in data:

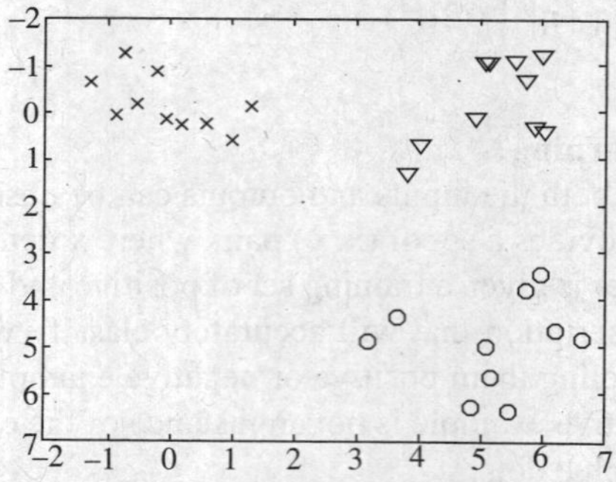

Figure 8.3 Unsupervised learning: Clustering problem

Example: A gene expression dataset is collected with expression levels from 64 cancer tumors from different patients. There are 6830 genes in total, and the gene expression data is displayed in heat map (green - low, red - high). The goal can be to have a regression problem with the gene expressions as output and the genes and samples as inputs, or an unsupervised learning problem where we want to cluster the samples with 6830 dimensions in a specific way.

Q. How decision trees can be used in learning?

Ans. A decision tree is a simple inductive learning structure. It is used for classifying the examples of a concept as positive or negative. A decision tree is formed where the relation between objects and concepts is shown as nodes of the tree, the arcs represent the attributes of objects or concepts. The leaf nodes have a classification (+ i.e., TRUE or – i.e., False) associated with it that is used to classify the example as positive or negative.

Decision tree can be drawn be following given steps:

1. Select an attribute to place at the root of the decision tree and make one branch for every possible value.
2. Repeat the process recursively for each branch.

One common approach to select node on top is based on the information gained by placing a certain attribute at this node.

Entropy of a decision $= -p_1 \times \log p_1 - p_2 \times \log p_2 - \ldots - p_n \times \log p_n$

Where $P_1, P_2, \ldots, P_n$ are the probabilities of the n possible outcomes.

As example, consider the following data:

ID code	Outlook	Temperature	Humidity	Windy	Play
1	Sunny	Hot	High	False	No
2	Sunny	Hot	High	True	No
3	Overcast	Hot	High	False	Yes
4	Rainy	Mild	High	False	Yes
5	Rainy	Cool	Normal	False	Yes
6	Rainy	Cool	Normal	True	No
7	Overcast	Cool	Normal	True	Yes
8	Sunny	Mild	High	False	No
9	Sunny	Cool	Normal	False	Yes
10	Rainy	Mild	Normal	False	Yes
11	Sunny	Mild	Normal	True	Yes
12	Overcast	Mild	High	True	Yes
13	Overcast	Hot	Normal	False	Yes
14	Rainy	Mild	High	True	No

In the weather data example, there are 9 instances of which the decision to play is "yes" and there are 5 instances of which the decision to play is "no'. Then, the information gained by knowing the result of the decision is

$$\frac{9}{14} \times \left(-\log \frac{9}{14} \right) + \left(\frac{5}{14} \right) \times \left(-\log \frac{5}{14} \right) = 0.940 \text{ bits.}$$

Information Further Required If "Outlook" is Placed at the Root =

$$\left(\frac{5}{14} \right) \times 0.971 + \left(\frac{4}{14} \right) \times 0 + \left(\frac{5}{14} \right) \times 0.971 = 0.693 \textit{bits}.$$

The decision tree will look like the following:

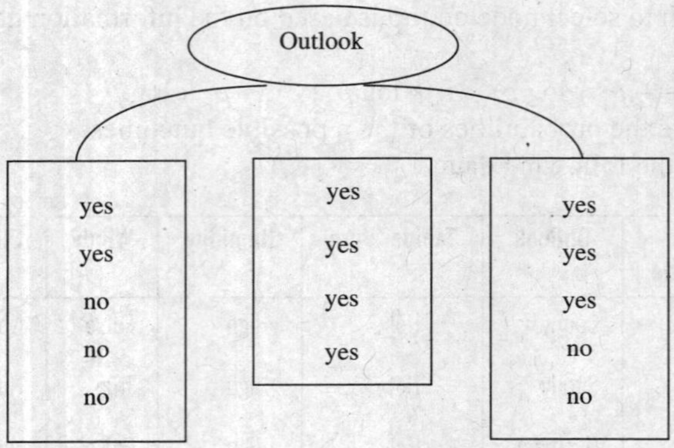

Information Gained by Placing Each of the 4 Attributes

- Gain(outlook) = 0.940 bits – 0.693 bits = 0.247 bits.
- Gain(temperature) = 0.029 bits.
- Gain(humidity) = 0.152 bits.
- Gain(windy) = 0.048 bits.

Select the attribute that gives us the largest information gain. Here, it is the attribute "Outlook".

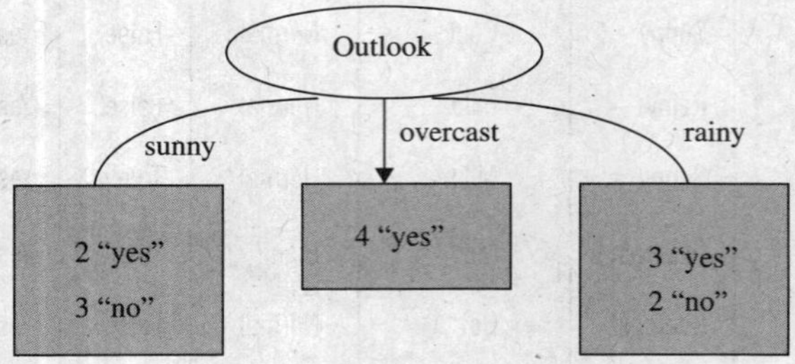

The Recursive Procedure for Constructing a Decision Tree: The operation discussed above is applied to each branch recursively to construct the decision tree.

For example, for the branch "Outlook = Sunny", we evaluate the information gained by applying each of the remaining 3 attributes.

- Gain(Outlook=sunny;Temperature) = 0.971 – 0.4 = 0.571
- Gain(Outlook=sunny;Humidity) = 0.971 – 0 = 0.971
- Gain(Outlook=sunny;Windy) = 0.971 – 0.951 = 0.02

Similarly, we also evaluate the information gained by applying each of the remaining 3 attributes for the branch "Outlook = rainy".

- Gain(Outlook=rainy;Temperature) = 0.971 – 0.951 = 0.02
- Gain(Outlook=rainy;Humidity) = 0.971 – 0.951 = 0.02
- Gain(Outlook=rainy;Windy) =0.971 – 0 = 0.971

The complete decision tree for weather forecast is drawn as shown below:

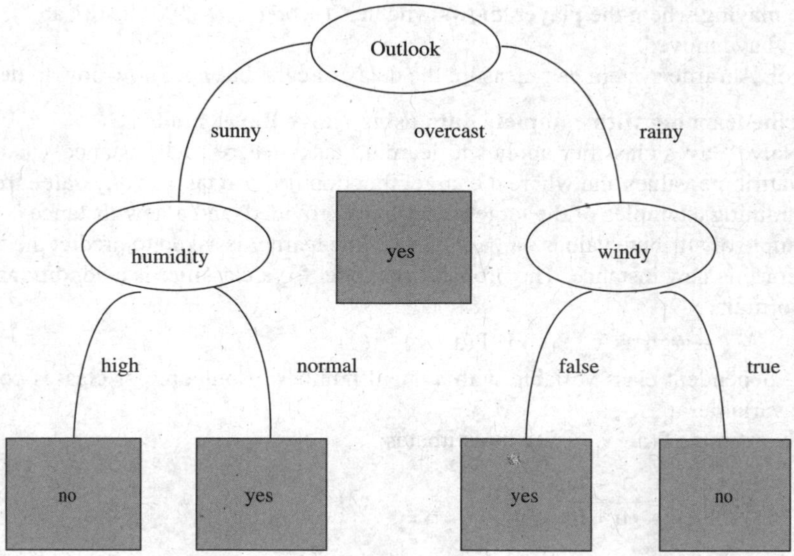

Q. What are the statistical methods for learning?

Ans. There are many models in learning that use statistical equations for learning. Examples are

(i) Bayesian learning formulates learning as a form of probabilistic inference, using the observations to update a prior distribution over hypotheses.

(ii) Maximum a posteriori (MAP) selects a single most likely hypothesis given the data.

(iii) Maximum likelihood (ML parameter learning) simply selects the hypothesis that maximizes the likelihood of the data.

(iv) Expectation Maximization (EM algorithm) can find local maximum likelihood solutions for hidden variables.

(v) Instance-based models use the collection of data to represent a distribution for example, nearest neighbor method.

Q. What is reinforcement learning?

Ans. In reinforcement learning, the decision-making system receives reward for its action at the end of a sequence of steps. If the actions are correct, then reward is given and in case the action is wrong, negative feedback is given. It is done in an environment where the agent cannot directly compare the results of its action to a desired result. So, feedback helps the agent to learn from the feedback whether the action was a good one or a bad one. The aim is to get a successful function using these rewards. Here, there is no direct supervision but learning is through a critic instead of a teacher. It is treated as a credit assignment problem where one would like to assess those individual actions that fetched rewards in past to be recorded for future reference. It also involves exploring many options to select the one which can bring reward. It was first used in Checkers playing program of Arthur Samuel and in cart-pole balancing problem in robotics.

Examples of reinforcement learning are :

(i) Robot juggling: Robot can tell you when you did it wrong.

(ii) Game playing where the player knows whether it won (``yay!") or lost (``ah!"), but not how it should have moved.

(iii) Control: A traffic system can measure the delay of cars, but not know how to decrease it.

Q. Describe learning with complete data using Naive Bayes models.

Ans. The Naive Bayes classifier applies to learning tasks where each instance x is described by a conjunction of attribute values and where the target function f(x) can take on any value from some finite set V. A set of training examples of the target function is provided, and a new instance is presented, described by the tuple of attribute values $<a_1, a_2, \ldots, a_n>$. The learner is asked to predict the target value, or classification, for this new instance. The probability model for a classifier is a conditional model using Naive Bayes Formula:

$$V_{nb} = \text{argmax}_{vj \in V} P(v_j) \Pi P(a_i \mid v_j) \quad (1)$$

Here, v_j is a dependent class variable with a small number of outcome or classes conditional over several feature variables $a_1, \ldots, a_n$.

We generally estimate $P(a_i \mid v_j)$ using m-estimates:

$$P(a_i \mid v_j) = \frac{n_c + m_p}{n + m} \quad (2)$$

where:

n = the number of training examples for which $v = v_j$

n_c = number of examples for which $v = v_j$ and $a = a_i$

p = a priori estimate for $P(a_i \mid v_j)$

m = the equivalent sample size

Consider the problem of classifying whether the car will be stolen or not based on the given attributes?

Suppose the given data set is as shown below:

Example	Origin	Type	Color	Stolen
1	Domestic	Sports	Red	Yes
2	Domestic	Sports	Red	No
3	Domestic	Sports	Red	Yes
4	Domestic	Sports	Yellow	No
5	Domestic	SUV	Yellow	No
6	Imported	Sports	Yellow	Yes
7	Imported	Sports	Yellow	No
8	Imported	SUV	Red	No
9	Imported	SUV	Yellow	Yes
10	Imported	SUV	Yellow	No

The problem is to classify a car : Domestic, SUV and Red in color. Since, it is not in data set, following probabilities are to be computed:

P(Red|Yes), P(SUV|Yes), P(Domestic|Yes) ,
P(Red|No) , P(SUV|No), and P(Domestic|No)

and multiply them by P(Yes) and P(No) respectively. These are calculated as follows:

Yes:	No:
Red: n = 5 n_c= 3 p = .5 m = 3	Red: n = 5 n_c = 2 p = .5 m = 3
SUV: n = 5 n_c = 1 p = .5 m = 3	SUV: n = 5 n_c = 3 p = .5 m = 3
Domestic: n = 5 n_c = 2 p = .5 m = 3	Domestic: n = 5 n_c = 3 p = .5 m = 3

Looking at P(Red | Yes), we have 5 cases where v_j = Yes , and in 3 of those cases a_i = Red. So for P(Red | Yes), n = 5 and nc = 3. Note that all attribute are binary (two possible values). We are assuming no other information so, p = 1 / (number-of-attribute-values) = 0.5 for all of our attributes. Our m value is arbitrary, (We will use m = 3) but consistent for all attributes. The probabilities are calculated as:

$$P(\text{Red} \mid \text{Yes}) = \frac{3 + 3 * 0.5}{5 + 3} = 0.56$$

$$P(\text{Red} \mid \text{No}) = \frac{2 + 3 * 0.5}{5 + 3} = 0.43$$

$$P(\text{SUV} \mid \text{Yes}) = \frac{1 + 3 * 0.5}{5 + 3} = 0.31$$

$$P(SUV \mid No) = \frac{3 + 3 * 0.5}{5 + 3} = 0.56$$

$$P(Domestic \mid Yes) = \frac{2 + 3 * 0.5}{5 + 3} = 0.43$$

$$P(Domestic \mid No) = \frac{3 + 3 * 0.5}{5 + 3} = 0.56$$

We have P(Yes) = 0.5 and P(No) = 0.5, so we can apply equation (2). For v = Yes, we have

P(Yes) * P(Red | Yes) * P(SUV | Yes) * P(Domestic|Yes) = 0.5 * 0.56 * 0.31 * 0.43 = 0.037

and for v = No, we have

P(No) * P(Red | No) * P(SUV | No) * P (Domestic | No) = 0.5 * 0.43 * 0.56 * 0.56 = 0.069

Since 0.069 > 0.037, our example gets classified as 'NO'

Q. Describe learning with hidden data – EM algorithm

Ans. Expectation Maximization algorithm is used for unsupervised learning. The goal is to build a probabilistic model. It is defined by a set of parameters θ. The model parameters can be estimated from a set of training examples x. But some data are hidden:

Consider a probabilistic model where, for observed data x and model parameters θ:

$p(x|\theta) = \sum_y \theta(x, y|\theta)$ where y are "hidden data".

The EM algorithm receives x and parameters θ, and returns new parameters λ^* so that $p(x|\lambda^*) > p(x|\theta)$. The aim of EM algorithm is to find λ^* that maximizes $p(x|\lambda^*) = \sum_y p(x,y|\lambda^*)$. It is found to be equivalent to finding λ^* that maximizes the logarithm $\log p(x|\lambda^*) = \log (\sum_y p(x, y|\lambda^*))$. There are two steps in EM algorithm used in each iteration.

1. E step: Calculate $Q_\theta(\lambda) = \sum y\, p(y|x,\theta) \log p(x,y|\lambda)$.
2. M step: Find λ^* that maximizes $Q_\theta(\lambda)$.

In the next iteration, λ^* is set to θ and the above steps are repeated.

Q. What is adaptive resonance theory?

Ans. Adaptive resonance theory (ART) describes a number of neural network models which use supervised and unsupervised learning methods, and address problems such as pattern recognition and prediction. It was developed by Stephen Grossberg and Gail Carpenter. The basis was how our brain processes information. The primary intuition behind this model is that object identification and recognition generally occur as a result of the interaction of 'top-down' observer expectations with 'bottom-up' sensory information. The model postulates that 'top-down' expectations take the form of a memory template that is then compared with the actual features of an object as detected by the senses. This comparison gives rise to a measure of category belongingness. As long as this difference between sensation and expectation does not exceed a set threshold called the 'vigilance parameter', the sensed object will be considered a member of the expected class.

The basic ART system is an unsupervised learning model consisting of a comparison field and a recognition field composed of neurons, a vigilance parameter, and a reset module. The role of each is discussed below:

Comparison field →	It takes an input vector (a one-dimensional array of values) and transfers it to its best match in the recognition field. Its best match is the single neuron whose set of weights (weight vector) most closely matches the input vector.
Recognition field →	It exhibits lateral inhibition, allowing each neuron in it to represent a category to which input vectors are classified. This is done when each recognition field neuron outputs a negative signal (proportional to that neuron's quality of match to the input vector) to each of the other recognition field neurons and inhibits their output accordingly.
Vigilance parameter →	It has considerable influence on the system: higher vigilance produces highly detailed memories (many, fine-grained categories), while lower vigilance results in more general memories (fewer, more-general categories).
Reset module →	It compares the strength of the recognition match to the vigilance parameter after the input vector is classified. If the vigilance threshold is met, training commences. Otherwise, if the match level does not meet the vigilance parameter, the firing recognition neuron is inhibited until a new input vector is applied; training commences only upon completion of a search procedure. In the search procedure, recognition neurons are disabled one by one by the reset function until the vigilance parameter is satisfied by a recognition match. If no committed recognition neuron's match meets the vigilance threshold, then an uncommitted neuron is committed and adjusted towards matching the input vector.
Training →	(i) In the slow learning method, the degree of training of the recognition neuron's weights towards the input vector is calculated to continuous values with differential equations and is thus dependent on the length of time the input vector is presented. (ii) In fast learning, algebraic equations are used to calculate degree of weight adjustments to be made, and binary values are used.

Q. Discuss various types of ART models

Ans. There are many types of ART models as discussed below:

ART 1	It is the simplest variety of ART networks, accepting only binary inputs
ART 2	It extends network capabilities to support continuous inputs.
ART 2-A	It is a streamlined form of ART-2 with a drastically accelerated runtime, and with qualitative results being only rarely inferior to the full ART-2 implementation

ART3	builds on ART-2 by simulating rudimentary neurotransmitter regulation of synaptic activity by incorporating simulated sodium (Na+) and calcium (Ca2+) ion concentrations into the system's equations, which results in a more physiologically realistic means of partially inhibiting categories that trigger mismatch resets.
FUZZY ART	It implements fuzzy logic into ART's pattern recognition, thus enhancing generalizability. An optional (and very useful) feature of fuzzy ART is complement coding, a means of incorporating the absence of features into pattern classifications, which goes a long way towards preventing inefficient and unnecessary category proliferation.
ARTMAP	also known as **Predictive ART**, combines two slightly modified ART-1 or ART-2 units into a supervised learning structure where the first unit takes the input data and the second unit takes the correct output data, then used to make the minimum possible adjustment of the vigilance parameter in the first unit in order to make the correct classification.
Fuzzy ARTMAP	is merely ARTMAP using fuzzy ART units, resulting in a corresponding increase in efficacy.

SOLVED EXAMPLES

Q. Give an example where reinforcement learning is used.

Ans. Cart-pole balancing problem is a problem that is solved using reinforcement learning. The problem is to control the position of a cart so as to keep a pole balanced on top of it upright, while staying within the limits of the track length.

Q. Give example of learning by analogy.

Ans. Learning by analogy is used when a student appears in an examination. Then, he solves new questions based on the use of similar.

Q. Give an example of deductive learning.

Ans. Theorem proving is the simplest example of learning using deduction. A set of axioms is given along with a theorem that is to be proved. The process proceeds only through deduction, i.e., theorem can be proved only if we are able to deduce it from the given axioms.

Q. Give example of case-based reasoning and learning.

Ans. The most common example of using cases for learning is medical diagnosis and treatment. The history of patient's symptoms identified disease and treatment done is stored as his case history. When a new patient with similar condition is there, the experience (positive or negative) from old cases is used for treatment of the new patient.

Q. Show how can we represent the concept(1) A(1) Λ (∝B(1) V C(1)) using decision tree.

Ans. The decision tree is shown below:

Concept ÷ A ∂ B (∝B • C)

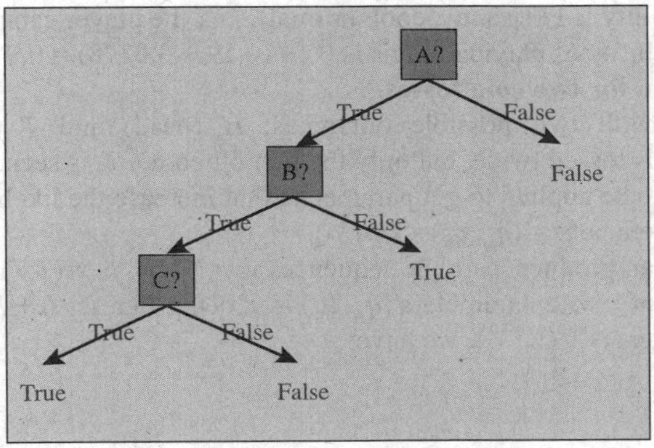

Q. Predict the probability of playing tennis when <sunny, cool, normal> given the following set of probabilities for playing tennis.

Temperature	Humidity	Outlook	Class
Hot	High	Sunny	–
Cool	Normal	Rain	–
Mild	High	Rain	–
Mild	Normal	Sunny	+
Cool	Normal	Sunny	+
Cool	High	Sunny	+
Mild	Normal	Rain	

z. The total number of cases here are 7. The probability of playing tennis is P(+) = 3/7 and the probability of not playing tennis is P(–) = 4/7.

Using Naive Bayes, we need to find P(+|sunny, cool, normal) versus P(-|sunny, cool, normal). For this, we need to create the separate probability tables as follows:

Temp	+	–
Hot	0/3	1/4
Mild	1/3	2/4
Cool	2/3	1/4

Humidity	+	–
High	1/3	2/4
Normal	2/3	2/4

Outlook	+	–
Sunny	3/3	¼
Rain	0/3	¾

P(+|sunny, cool, normal) = P(sunny|+)* P(cool|+) * P(normal|+)* P(+)
= 3/3*2/3*2/3*3/7 = 4/21 = 0.19

P(-|sunny, cool, normal) = P(sunny|–)* P(cool|–) * P(normal|–)* P(–)
=1/4*1/4*2/4*4/7 = 1/56 = 0.0178

The maximum probability is P(+|sunny, cool, normal), i.e., the player can play tennis.

The normalized probability of playing tennis is 0.19/(0.19 + 0.0178) = 0.91.

Q. Use EM algorithm for two coin tosses.

Ans. Given a coin with two possible outcomes: H (head) and T (tail), with probabilities q_H, $q_T = 1 - q_H$. The coin is tossed twice, but only the first outcome, T, is seen. So, the data is $x = (T,*)$.

The EM algorithm is to be applied to get parameters that increase the likelihood of the data.

Let the initial parameters be $\theta = (q_H, q_T) = (1/4, 3/4)$.

The hidden data that can produce x are the sequences $y_1 = (T,H); y_2 = (T,T)$;

Hence, the likelihood of x with parameters (q_H, q_T) is $p(x|\theta) = P(x, y_1|\theta) + P(x, y_2|\theta) = q_H q_T + q_T^2$.

For the initial parameters $\theta = (1/4, 3/4)$, we have:

$$p(x|\theta) = 3/4 * 1/4 + 3/4 * 3/4 = 3/4$$

Calculate $Q_\theta(\lambda) = Q_\theta(q_H, q_T)$.

$$Q_\theta(\lambda) = p(y_1|x,\theta)\log p(x,y_1|\lambda) + p(y_2|x,\theta)\log p(x,y_2|\lambda)$$

$$p(y_1|x,\theta) = p(y_1,x|\theta)/p(x|\theta) = (3/4 \cdot 1/4)/(3/4) = 1/4$$

$$p(y_2|x,\theta) = p(y_2,x|\theta)/p(x|\theta) = (3/4 \cdot 3/4)/(3/4) = 3/4$$

Thus, we have $Q_\theta(\lambda) = 1/4 \log p(x,y_1|\lambda) + 3/4 \log p(x,y_2|\lambda)$.

For a sequence y of coin tosses, let $N_H(y)$ be the number of H's in y, and $N_T(y)$ be the number of T's in y. Then $\log p(y|\lambda) = N_H(y) \log q_H + N_T(y) \log q_T$.

In our example:

$y_1 = (T,H); y_2 = (T,T)$, hence:

$N_H(y_1) = N_T(y_1) = 1, N_H(y_2) = 0, N_T(y_2) = 2$.

Thus,

$$1/4 \log p(x,y_1|\lambda) = 1/4 (N_H(y_1) \log q_H + N_T(y_1) \log q_T) = 1/4 (\log q_H + \log q_T)$$

$$3/4 \log p(x,y_2|\lambda) = 3/4 (N_H(y_2) \log q_H + N_T(y_2) \log q_T) = 3/4 (2 \log q_T)$$

Substituting in the equation for $Q_\theta(\lambda)$:

$$Q_\theta(\lambda) = 1/4 \log p(x,y_1|\lambda) + 3/4 \log p(x,y_2|\lambda)$$

$$= (1/4\, N_H(y_1) + 3/4\, N_H(y_2))\log q_H + (1/4\, N_T(y_1) + 3/4\, N_T(y_2))\log q_T$$

$$Q_\theta(\lambda) = N_H \log q_H + N_T \log q_T$$

Find λ^* that maximizes $Q_\theta(\lambda)$

$$Q_\theta(\lambda) = N_H \log q_H + N_T \log q_T = 1/4 \log q_H + 7/4 \log q_T$$

This is maximized when:

$$q_H = \frac{N_H}{N_H + N_T} = \frac{1/4}{1/4 + 7/4} = 1/8$$

$$q_T = \frac{N_T}{N_H + N_T} = \frac{7/4}{1/4 + 7/4} = 7/8$$

$\lambda^* = (1/8, 7/8)$ and $p(x \mid \lambda^*) = 7/8$

MULTIPLE CHOICE QUESTIONS

Select the most appropriate answers to the following questions:

1. Which of the following is a measure of the ease with which the method can be adapted to different domains of application?
   (a) Efficiency (b) Generality
   (c) Robustness (d) Efficacy
2. Which of the following is a measure of the average time required to construct the target knowledge structures from some specified initial structures?
   (a) Efficiency (b) Generality
   (c) Robustness (d) Efficacy
3. Which of the following defines the ability of a learning system to function with unreliable feedback and training with noisy examples?
   (a) Efficiency (b) Generality
   (c) Robustness (d) Efficacy
4. Which of the following is not a part of the general learning model?
   (a) Knowledge base (b) Learner component
   (c) Performance component (d) None of these
5. Which of the following cannot be a form of the acquired knowledge?
   (a) Facts (b) Rules
   (c) Concepts (d) None of these
6. Which of the following is not a required feature of knowledge?
   (a) Consistency (b) Accuracy
   (c) Redundancy (d) None of these
7. Which of the following is the simplest form of learning?
   (a) Analogy (b) Induction
   (c) Deduction (d) Memorization
8. Perceptrons are pattern recognition devices that make decisions about patterns by which of the following operation on evidence obtained from many small sources?
   (a) Subtraction (b) Addition
   (c) Multiplication (d) None of these
9. When are the Learning Automata not easy to implement?
   (a) Number of states is very less (b) Number of states is more
   (c) Algorithm fails (d) None of these
10. TEIRESIAS is what type of system?
   (a) Learning system (b) Training system
   (c) Intelligent editor (d) None of these

Ans. 1. b 2. a 3. c 4. d 5. d 6. c 7. d 8. b 9. b 10. c

EXERCISES

1. What are various forms of learning?
2. What are the differences between supervised and unsupervised learning?
3. How does past cases help in learning?
4. What is the use of reinforcement learning? Is it supervised or unsupervised form of learning?
5. Differentiate between learning by induction and learning by deduction with a suitable example.
6. Give example of analogical learning.
7. What are the basic concepts in using the decision trees for learning?

9

Neural Networks

9.1 INTRODUCTION

In AI, learning is an important part of intelligent machines. A human brain contains millions of neurons that help in learning. Neural networks are designed by taking inspiration from the human biological neural networks, which provide directions to solve problems arising in natural tasks. Thus, it helps in making the system intelligent. When intelligent tasks are involved, then vast data may be used. This data may observe different patterns as well. These patterns can form a basis for certain declarations of results. Neural networks are designed to extract the relevant features from the input data and perform a pattern recognition task by learning from examples without explicitly stating the rules for performing the task. There are many types of pattern recognition tasks solved using artificial neural networks (ANN). These include pattern classification, pattern storage, pattern association tasks, etc.

9.2 CHARACTERISTICS OF BIOLOGICAL NEURAL NETWORKS

Q. Discuss the characteristics of biological neural networks.

Ans. The characteristics of biological neural networks are

1. Flexibility: The neural network is self-adjusting to a new environment without using any preprogrammed instructions
2. Robustness and fault tolerance: The decay of nerve cells does not affect the performance of the network significantly.
3. Collective or parallel computation: The neural network performs routinely many operations in parallel and distributed fashion.
4. Ability to handle variety of data situations: The network can deal with information that is fuzzy, probabilistic, noisy or even inconsistent.

Q. Discuss historical development of neural networks.principles.

Ans. There was a quest to simulate the human brain into a computer to design an intelligent machine. This was done to design artificial neurons in computer. As there is a network of neurons in human brain, responsible for input, processing and outputting intelligent information, network of neurons was created and is known as neural network. The following are the characteristic of neural networks:

(a) There is a large number of very simple neuron like processing elements.
(b) There are a large number of connections between the processing elements, which are assigned weights that incorporate the knowledge of a network.
(c) Since there are a large number of neurons and processing speed needed is very high, parallel and distributed control is used.
(d) As neurons in human brain learn automatically, emphasis is on learning internal representations automatically.

9.3 ARTIFICIAL NEURAL NETWORKS

9.3.1 Terminology

Q. Explain terminology of ANNs.

Ans. There are four things in an ANN:

(a) ***Processing unit:*** An ANN consists of interconnected processing units each of which consists of a summing part and an output part. The summing part receives *N* inputs (either discrete or continuous), weights each value (either positive or negative), and calculate a weighted sum called the activation value. The output part produces a signal (either discrete or continuous) from the activation value. Both the inputs and outputs can be deterministic or stochastic or fuzzy. The set of all activation states define the activation state space of the network. The set of all possible weight vectors is called the weight space. The set of all output states is called the output state space.
Neural networks are used for learning. So, based on input and output, learning also varies. Deterministic learning is based on optimization of an objective function that can be recomputed many times and always produces the same value given the same weights. Stochastic methods are used when computation of the objective function is corrupted by noise. In particular, basic stochastic approximation is a form of on-line gradient descent learning in which the training cases are obtained by a stationary random process. There are various supervised Adaptive Resonance Theory algorithms that are named with the suffix "MAP", as in Fuzzy ARTMAP. These algorithms cluster both the inputs and targets and associate the two sets of clusters. These include fuzzy inputs.

(b) ***Interconnections:*** The processing units in an ANN are connected through interconnections, which carry weight to define the strength of the connection. If there are *N* units in an ANN, then at any instance of time, each unit have a unique activation value and a unique output value.

(c) ***Operations:*** There are two main operations in an ANN. First is to generate the output from the input values. This is done by activation dynamics that determines the activation values of all the units. Here, the activation state of the ANN is found as a function of time. The second operation is to make the network learn to store a pattern. To do this, it is necessary to adjust the weights of the connections in a network. When the weights are changing, then the synaptic dynamics of the network determines the weight vector as a function of time. The process of adjusting the weights is referred to as learning.

(d) ***Update:*** The updation of the output states of all the units could be performed synchronously or asynchronously. In synchronous updation, the activation values of all the units are computed at the same time, assuming a given output state throughout. In asynchronous update, each unit is updated sequentially and for it, it is required to take the current output state of the network into account.

9.3.2 Models of Neuron

Q. What are various models of a neuron?

Ans. There are three classical models for an artificial neuron that is the main processing unit:

1. McCulloch–Pitts Model;
2. Rosenblatt's Perceptron Model;
3. Widrow's Adaptive Linear Element (Adaline).

Each processing unit needs to define an activation function x from M input values a_i and a bias term q, which is the threshold value. An actual output signal is defined by s. The desired output signal is b and d denotes the error to adjust the weights; and h is the learning rate parameter. For all the three models, these are defined below:

	McCulloch–Pitts Model	Rosenblatt's Perceptron Model	Widrow's Adaptive Linear Element (Adaline) Model
Activation function	$x = \sum_{i=} w_i a_i - \theta$	$x = \sum_{i=} w_i a_i - \theta$	$X = \sum_{i=} w_i a_i - \theta$
Output signal	$s = f(x)$	$s = f(x)$	$s = f(x) = x$
Error	Fixed weights	$\delta = b - s$	$\delta = b - s = b - x$
Weight update	No learning/updation	$\Delta wi = \eta \delta ai$	$\Delta wi = \eta \delta ai$

9.3.3 Topology

Q. Discuss the topology of an ANN.

Ans. The topology of the ANN refers to the arrangement of the processing units, connections, pattern input and outputs. ANNs are organized into layers or processing units. The connections across the layers and among the units within a layer can be organized in two ways: feedforward or feedback.

9.3.4 Basic Learning Laws

Q. Explain the basic learning laws in ANN..

Ans. Learning laws are implementation models of synaptic dynamics that are described in terms of learning equations. The learning equations contain the expressions for the first derivative of the synaptic weights. Learning laws describe the weight vector for the ith processing unit at time instant $(t + 1)$ in terms of the weight vector at time instant (t) as follows:

$$w_i(t + 1) = w(t) + \Delta w_i(t),$$

where $\Delta w_i(t)$ is the change in the weight vector.

There are seven basic learning laws in ANN. These all vary in terms of specifying initial weights, the weight adjustment function, and the learning mode. There are two modes of learning, supervised or unsupervised. The basic learning laws that support unsupervised learning are Hebbian's law and Instar (Winner-take-all) learning law. The learning laws supporting supervised learning laws are Perceptron learning law, Delta learning law, Widrow and Hoff LMS learning law, Correlation learning law, and Outstart learning law.

There are seven basic learning laws in ANN. These all vary in terms of specifying initial weights, the weight adjustment function, and the learning mode. There are two modes of learning, supervised or unsupervised. The laws can be categorized as follows:

Supervised learning laws	Unsupervised learning laws
Perceptron learning law	Hebbian's law
Delta learning law	Instar (Winner-take-all) law
Widrow and Hoff LMS learning law	
Correlation learning law	
Outstart learning law	

9.3.5 Pattern Recognition Problem

Q. Explain pattern recognition problem.

Ans. In any pattern recognition task, we have a set of input patterns and the corresponding output patterns. Depending upon the nature of the output patterns and the nature of the task environment, the pattern recognition problem can be a pattern association problem, a pattern classification problem or a pattern mapping problem. The given set of input-output pattern pairs forms only a few samples of an unknown system. From these samples, the pattern recognition model should capture the characteristics of the system. The patterns can be represented as tensors in multidimensional spaces.

9.3.6 Basic Functional Units

Q. What are the basic functional units of ANN?

Ans. There are three types of ANN:

1. Feedforward neural network
2. Feedbackward neural network
3. A combination of both

The simplest networks of each of these types form the basic functional units. They are functional because they can perform by themselves some simple pattern recognition tasks. They are basic because they form building blocks for developing neural network architectures.

Feedforward neural network: It is a two layer network with *M* input units and *N* output units. Each input unit is connected to each of the output units. A weight indicating the strength of the connection is associated with each connection. The input units are linear while the output units can be either linear or non-linear depending on the task that the network should perform.

Feedbackward neural network: It consists of a set of *N* processing units, each connected to all other units. The connection weights are assumed to be symmetric. Depending on the task, the units of the network could be linear or non-linear.

Combination/Competitive network: It consists of an input layer of units feeding to the units in the output layer in a feedforward manner and a feedback connection among the units in the output layer, including self-feedback. The connection weights of the feedforward path are adjustable by training the network for a given pattern recognition task. The feedback connection weights in the output layer are usually fixed to specific values depending on the problem. The input units are all linear and each unit providing *N* outputs one to each output unit. The output units are either linear or non-linear depending on the task the network should perform.

9.4 FEEDFORWARD NEURAL NETWORKS

Q. What are feedforward neural networks?

Ans. If the graph of a neural network is acyclic, then it is called a feedforward neural network. The information moves only in one direction, i.e., forward from input nodes to output nodes through hidden nodes.

Q. What is multi-layer feedforward neural networks (FFNN)?

Ans. These are neural network that can handle data that is not linearly separable. The examples of linearly separable and non linearly separable classes are shown in figure below: There contain hidden layers between input and output layers. These layers do not directly receive inputs or send outputs to the external environment. It evolves using backpropagation learning method. In FFNN, the derivative of the error function with respect to the network weights is determined. Then the weights are changed accordingly to decrease the margin of error. The activation function should be continuous functions of the weights, so that it is differentiable everywhere. Sigmoid function can be used as an activation function that can be considered as a continuous approximation of the step function. The activation function for a node i can be given as:

$$\varphi(V_i) = \frac{1}{1+e^{(-A*V_i)}}.$$

where $A > 0$, $V_i = \sum Wij * Yj$ such that W_{ij} is a weight of the link from node i to node j and Y_j is the output of node j.

9.4.1 Pattern Association Networks

Q. Explain pattern association problem and analysis of network for solving it.

Ans. Given a set of input-output pattern pairs $(a_1, b_1), (a_2, b_2), \ldots. (a_l, b_l)$, where $a_L = (a_{l1}, a_{l2}, \ldots a_{lM})$ and $b_L = (b_{l1}, b_{l2}, \ldots b_{lN})$ are MXN dimensional matrices.

The pattern association problem is to design a neural network to associate each input pattern with corresponding output patterns. The training involves finding the weights of a network. Apply the operations of network to input patterns and get the output patterns. If the input contains noisy input, then the output will be wrong. This is indicted using a noisy vector $\in$. So, noisy input $a_i = a_l + \in$.

9.4.2 Pattern Classification Networks

Q. Explain pattern classification problem and analysis of network for solving it.

Ans. If some of the input patterns are identical and map to the same output pattern, then these are called a class. The network identifies the class label. During training, a few samples of patterns for each class are given. The problem of pattern classification is to find the class of input patterns that matches to an output pattern. For example, all the fruit elements will be classified as one class and all vegetable elements will be classified as another class. Feedforward neural network is used for solving this as shown in figure below. Here information flows in forward direction only and never in backward direction.

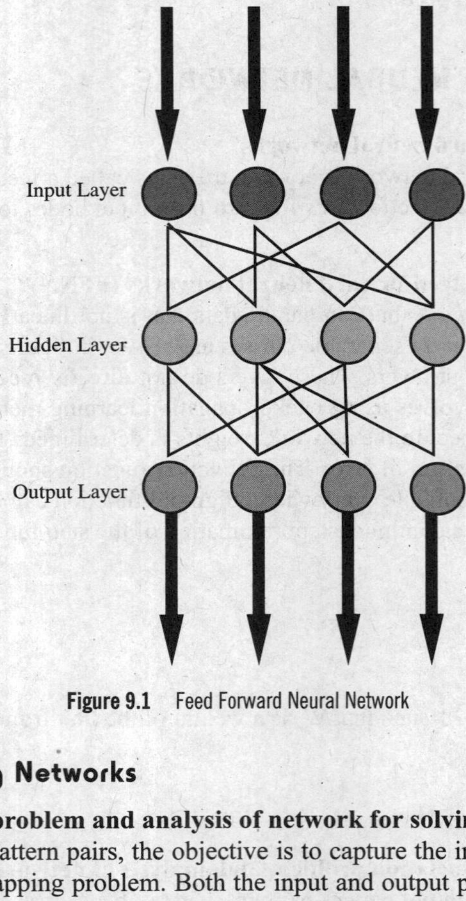

Figure 9.1 Feed Forward Neural Network

9.4.3 Pattern Mapping Networks

Q. Explain mapping problem and analysis of network for solving it.

Ans. Given set of input pattern pairs, the objective is to capture the implied mapping of input to an output pattern is a pattern mapping problem. Both the input and output patterns are only samples from the mapping system. Once the system behavior is captured by the network, the network would produce a possible output pattern for a new input pattern which was not used in the training set. The possible output pattern would be approximately an interpolated version of output patterns corresponding to input training patterns close to the given test input pattern. Feedforward neural network is used for solving this. Example is a neural network which performs elementary arithmetic operation such as bit shifting, multiplication of 2 b-bit numbers etc.

9.5 FEEDBACK NEURAL NETWORKS

9.5.1 Pattern Autoassociative Networks

Q. Explain autoassociative pattern recognition problem and analysis of network for solving it.

Ans. Given a set of input-output pattern pairs (a_1, b_1), (a_2, b_2), …. (a_l, b_l) where $a_L = (a_{l1}, a_{l2}, \ldots a_{lM})$ and b_L=$(b_{l1}, b_{l2}, \ldots b_{lN})$ are MXN dimensional vectors.

The pattern association problem is to design a neural network to associate each input pattern with corresponding output patterns. The training involves finding the weights of a network. Apply the operations of network to input patterns and get the output patterns. If the input contains noisy input, then the output will be wrong. This is indicted using a noisy vector $\in$. So, noisy input $a_i = a_l + \in$. If $a_l = b_l$, then the problem is called autoassociative pattern recognition problem. It is solved using feedback neural network. This is a trivial case where the network merely stores the given set of input patterns. When a noisy input pattern is given, the network receives the same noisy pattern. It is solved using feedback neural networks.

9.5.2 Pattern Storage Networks

Q. Explain pattern storage problem and analysis of network for solving it.

Ans. In an autoassociative problem, if a given input pattern is stored in a network for later recall by an approximate input pattern then the problem becomes a pattern storage problem. Any input vector close to a stored input pattern will recall that input pattern exactly from the network and thus the network displays accretive behavior. Accretive behavior means there is no interpolation by the neural network and the result will be continuous and within the clusters. This problem is also solved using feedback neural network. Example is pattern memorization problem in nonlinear networks. The number of patterns that can be memorized has been referred to as the information capacity and storage capacity.

9.6 COMPETITIVE LEARNING

9.6.1 Introduction

Q. Explain competitive learning.

Ans. It is a form of unsupervised learning in ANN. It works on the principle of increasing the weights of each node in the network to find the clusters. Here is a simple competitive learning algorithm to find *n* clusters within some input data.

1 Let a set of sensors all feed into *n* different nodes, so that every node is connected to every sensor. Let the weights that each node gives to its sensors be set randomly between 0.0 and 1.0. Let the output of each node be the sum of all its sensors, each sensor's signal strength being multiplied by its weight.
2. When the net is shown an input, the node with the highest output is deemed the winner. The input is classified as being within the cluster corresponding to that node.
3. The winner updates each of its weights, moving weight from the connections that gave it weaker signals to the connections that gave it stronger signals.

9.6.2 Pattern Clustering Problem

Q. Explain the problem of pattern clustering problem and analysis of networks for solving it.

Ans. Given a set of patterns, if they are grouped according to similarity of patterns, then the resulting problem is called pattern clustering. It is solved using competitive learning. How it is solved using competitive learning?

9.6.3 Feature Mapping Problem

Q. Explain the feature mapping problem and analysis of networks for solving it.

Ans. In feature mapping problem, similarities of the features of the input patterns have to be retained in the output. A given set of input patterns are mapped onto output patterns in such a way that the proximity of the output patterns reflects the similarity of the features of the corresponding input patterns. When a test input pattern is given, it will generate an output which is in the neighborhood of the outputs for similar patterns. It is solved using competitive learning network (how it is solved using competitive learning network).

9.7 HOPFIELD NETWORKS

9.7.1 Introduction

Q. Explain Hopfield networks.

Ans. Hopfield proposed a neural network as a theory of memory. A Hopfield network has the following features:

1. Distributed representation: In a Hopfield network, a memory is stored as a pattern of activation across a set of processing elements.
2. Distributed, asynchronous control: Every processing element in a Hopfield network can make decisions based only on its own local situation. All theses local actions are added up to a global solution.
3. Content-addressable memory: A number of patterns can be stored in a network. A pattern can be retrieved by only specifying a portion of it. The Hopfield network automatically finds the closest match.
4. Fault tolerance: If a few processing elements misbehave or fail completely, then the network will still function properly.

Q. What are the applications of Hopfield network?

Ans. Hopfield networks can be used to solve a wide variety of constraint – satisfaction problems, optimization problems, pattern classification and these can be used as a content-addressable memory system.

9.7.2 Associative Memory Problem

Q. What is associative memory problem?

Ans. In a Hopfield network, there are problems with associative memory:

1. The invoked pattern is sometimes not necessarily the most similar pattern to the input.
2. Some patterns will be recalled more than others.
3. There are many non-original patterns.

9.8 LEARNIG IN NEURAL NETWORKS

9.8.1 Perceptron

Q. What is a perceptron?

Ans. The perceptron was one of the earliest neural network models invented by Rosenblatt. If includes inputs $x_1, x_2, \ldots x_n$ and assign them corresponding weights $w_1, w_2, \ldots w_n$ like a neuron. It models a neuron by sending the output 1 if the weighted sum of inputs is greater than some adjustable threshold and a 0 otherwise. The values of the weights can be positive or negative real values.

$$g(x) = \sum_{i=}^{n} w_i x_i$$

$$\text{Output function } o(x) = 1 \text{ if } g(x) > 0$$
$$= 0 \text{ if } g(x) < 0$$

Q. What is a multilayer perceptron?

Ans. A multilayer perceptron is a perceptron with multiple layers. It has an input layer, an output layer and two or more layers of hidden neurons. Each neuron computes an activation function. These are called hidden layers because these are not directly accessible to the outside world like input and output layers. The hidden layer neurons extract the required information from the input layer and pass them to the output layers where the output is shown to the outside world through computation nodes.

Q. What are the limitations of perceptron?

Ans. A perceptron can only model linear separable functions. If we are dealing with two classes that are not linearly separable, then a linear separator is required that minimizes the mean squared error. Example is XOR function, it cannot be modeled by a perceptron because it is not linearly separable. An example of classes linearly separable and non linearly separable are shown in figure below.

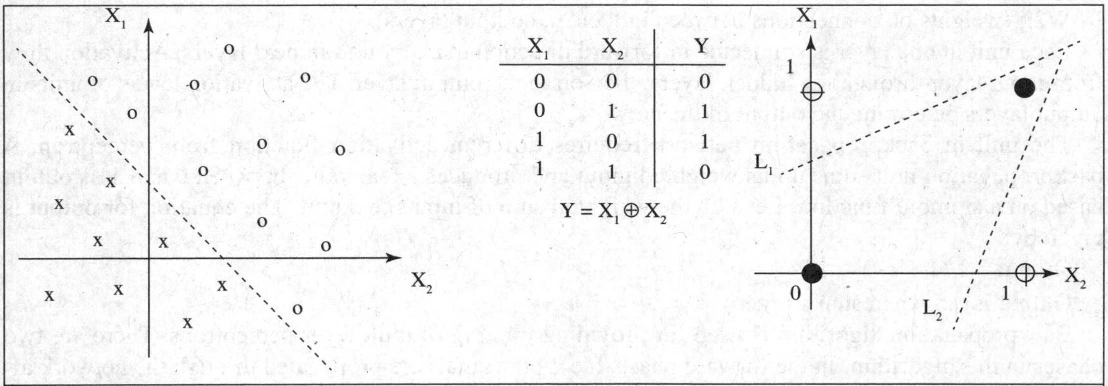

Linearly separable classes | XOR: Non linearly separable

Figure 9.2

Q. Explain the process of learning in neural networks.

Ans. During learning, the error is reported from desired output and actual output produced by the perceptron. The aim of the learning is to reduce this error to zero. For this, the learning rate is defined to make adjustments in the weights. The learning rate indicates how much learning is still required. If output is correct, then learning rate is 0. If the output is too low, that is the direction of weight adjustment should be in positive direction, then A is given a small positive number less than 1. Similarly, if the output is too high, then the learning rate is given a small positive number less than 1 to indicate the weight adjustment should be in decreasing direction. The complete process by which the perceptron learn is through the following process:

1. Initially random weights are assigned to input variables in the range -0.5 to +0.5.
2. Training data is presented to perceptron and its output is noted.
3. If output is incorrect, then the weights are adjusted accordingly using the formula: Wi = Wi + (A*Xi*E) where A is the learning rate which lies between 0 and 1 and E is the error produced.
4. After modification of weights, the next training data is applied with the modified weights and the weights are further adjusted accordingly.
5. Once all the training data has been applied, the process starts again until all the weights are correct and all errors are zero.
6. Each iteration of this process is called an epoch.

Q. What is the capacity of a stochastic network?

Ans. The capacity of a network is the ability to model any function, i.e., the maximum number of patterns that can be stored in the network.

Q. What is a backpropagation networks?

Ans. The neural networks must be able to learn of their own representations. The property of perceptrons that "whatever they could compute, they could learn to compute", is used for a multilayer network using backpropagation algorithm called backpropagation network. It consists of the following:

x_i (the unit activation levels of input)
o_i (the output units)
h_i (the hidden units)
W1ij (weights on connections between input and hidden layers)
W2ij (weights on connections between hidden and output layers)

Each unit in one layer is connected in forward direction to every unit in next layers. Activation flow from input layer through the hidden layers, then on to the output layer. The activation levels of units in output layers determine the output of the network.

The unit in backpropagation network requires different activation function from perceptron. A backpropagation unit sums up its weighted input and produces a real value between 0 and 1 as output based on a sigmoid function. Let *s* be the weighted sum of inputs to a unit. The equation for output is given by:

Output = $1/(1 + e^{-s})$

Output is 0.5 when sum *s* is zero.

Backpropagation algorithm is used for providing training of multilayer perceptrons. There are two phases in this algorithm. In the forward phase, the input signals are propagated through the network after fixing the free parameters of the network. The output from the network is recorded. Along with this, the deviation of the actual output from the desired output is also calculated.

The aim of the backward phase is to identify the deviation of the actual output from the desired one and to apply corrections. So, in this phase, adjustments are applied to free parameters so as to minimize the error in statistical sense.

9.8.2 Generalization

Q. What is generalization in backpropagation learning networks?

Ans. A backpropagation learning network is expected to generalize from the training set data so that the network can be used to determine the output for a new test input. But when the training period is long, then there is a degradation in the performance on test set because the network begins to memorize the individual input-output pairs rather than settling for weights that generally describe the mapping of all cases. This is undesirable. In order to prevent this, a small amount of noise can be added deliberately in the training input set. Also a bottleneck can be created between input and output layers by reducing the number of hidden units. When there is a situation of a plateau, it is better to stop training to avoid memorization. During generalization, do not forget to add exceptions.

Q. What is Boltzmann machine?

Ans. A Boltzmann machine is a variation on the idea of a Hopfield network. The main problem with Hopfield networks is that they settle into local minima. For constraint satisfaction tasks, globally optimal state of the network is required to be found. This state corresponds to an interpretation that satisfies as many interacting constraints as possible. Simulated annealing is a technique for finding globally optimal solutions to combinatorial problems. Boltzmann machines are networks formed with combination of Hopfield networks and simulated annealing.

Q. Explain supervised learning.

Ans. As the name suggests, in this type of learning, there is a supervision in learning process. It is done through the use of a set of training examples including input and output for each one of them. For a given set of *N* examples, the aim of supervised learning is to compute the free parameters of the neural networks so that the output of the neural network is close enough to the desired outputs for all examples in statistical sense, i.e., within the accepted error.

Q. Explain unsupervised learning.

Ans. In unsupervised learning, labeled training examples are not available and little information is available beforehand regarding the object population. This form of learning is known as clustering. In this case, the system must be able to perceive and extract relevant properties from the otherwise unknown objects.

9.9. APPLICATIONS OF ANN

Q. What are the applications of ANN?

Ans. There are many application of ANN including connectionist speech, connectionist vision, and recurrent networks.

Q. Explain connectionist speech.

Ans. Connectionist networks have been applied to a number of problems in speech recognition. In this approach, a network is presented with words and their pronunciations and it is assumed that the network will discover the regularities and also remember the exceptions itself. NETtalk was the first successful connectionist network that learns to pronounce English text using backpropagation network.

Q. Explain connectionist vision.

Ans. The concept of using vision for input in artificial systems is complicated because for interpreting even a single scene, about a hundred computational steps are needed. This is due to the fact that individual neural firing rates lie in milliseconds. The interpretation of one scene needs to be continuously integrated with interpretation of subsequent scenes in order to form the complete input. For an artificial system, the human vision can be treated as a parallel task because there are strong timing constraints, i.e., it seems as if all interpretations are done in parallel. Connectionist vision systems use the concept of parallel relaxation to do visual interpretations assuming there is massive parallel machinery. These use parallel relaxation search as used in Hopfield networks and Boltzmann machines.

Q. Discuss recurrent networks.

Ans. A recurrent network is a network that has loops. By the use of the loops, the response from the real world can be inputted into the network for planning and learning that need temporal reasoning. In this type of network, the input can be given and there are many output units. The state of the network can be changed by training using backpropagation algorithm. At each step, the activations of the output are compared with the desired activations and the errors are propagated backward through the network. Learning in this way, the recurrent network will be able to perform the desired operation when the training is complete. The examples of recurrent networks are Jordan's network that tries to teach how to shoot a basketball through a hoop by continuously taking feedback from the outside world using a mental model.

Q. Discuss how ANN can be used in distributed representations.

Ans. Distributed representations are the class of connectionist networks that use patterns of activations over many units instead of using individual units to represent concepts. This is implemented using Hopfield network in which each structure is stored as a collection of active units. One set of units can store many different objects. The advantages of distributed representations include efficiency and resistance to damage.

Q. Discuss connectionist AI and symbolic AI.

Ans. The connectionist approach in AI deals with the use of uncertainty and neural networks. The symbolic approach in AI uses symbolic manipulation functions. A comparison of the two is given below:

	Symbolic AI	Connectionist AI
Knowledge representation methods	Predicate logic, semantic networks, frames, scripts	Structures stored as distributed patterns of activation, real valued connection strengths
Search	Using traversal through the state space	Using parallel relaxation method
Learning	Using explanation-based learning, version spaces, macro-operators, through discovery	Using backpropagation, Boltzmann machines, unsupervised learning, reinforcement learning
Training examples required	Less	More
Explanation	Easy	Difficult
Search efficiency	Less efficient	More efficient due to parallel relaxation
Modeling human mental processes	Low level modeling	High level modeling

Q. Which optimization problems can be solved using neural networks?

Ans. Traveling salesman problem is a combinatorial problem. Hopfield and Tank showed how a Hopfield network can be programmed to find an approximate solution to traveling salesman problem. The system employs n^2 neural units, where n is the number of cities to be toured. Each row in nXn matrix represents one city. The tour proceeds horizontally across the columns. The starting city is marked by the active unit in column 1, the next city by column 2. This nXn array contains a number of weighted connections like a Hopfield network. The connection weights are initialized to reflect exactly the constraints of a particular problem instance. First of all, every unit is connected with a negative weight to every other units in its column, because only one city at a time can be visited. Second, every unit inhibits every other unit in its row, because each city can only be visited once. Third, units in adjacent columns inhibit each other in proportion to the distances between cities represented by their rows. For example, of city D is far from city G, then the fourth unit in column 3 will strongly inhibit the seventh unit in columns 2 and 4. There is also some global excitation, so that in the absence of strong inhibition, individual units will prefer to be active. Each unit represents some hypothesis about the position of a particular city in a short tour. To find that tour, we start by giving our units random activation values. Once all the weights are set, the units update themselves asynchronously according to the rule. This updating continues until a stable state is reached. Stable states of the network correspond to short tours because conflicts between constraints are minimal. The other optimization problems which can be solved using neural networks are image optimization, weighted matching problem, and graph bipartitioning problem.

SOLVED EXAMPLES

Q. Design a perceptron for Boolean function OR.

Ans.

OR function

Inputs		Output
X	Y	X XOR Y
0	0	0
0	1	1
1	0	1
1	1	0

Q. Explain how linearly inseparable function XOR is implemented using multi-layer feed-forward neural networks?

Ans. XOP function takes two inputs, each with value either 0 or 1. It returns one output either 0 or 1. The output for XOR is 1 when both inputs are different and it returns a 0 when both input values are same.

XOR function

Inputs		Output
X	Y	X XOR Y
0	0	0
0	1	1
1	0	1
1	1	0

Figure 9.3

These cannot be drawn as linearly separable classes when plotting a graph. FFNN uses two hidden nodes that take input from the two inputs and return an output using sign activation function (step function) defined as:

$$\varphi(V) = 0, \text{ if } V \leq \theta$$
$$= 1, \text{ if } V > \theta$$

The connections from input nodes to two hidden nodes are weighted with weight vectors: (1, –1) and (–1, 1) indicating weights from (X to H1 and X to H2) and (Y to H1 and Y to H2), respectively. The weight on connections from hidden to output nodes is 1. The output node is used to combine the outputs of the two hidden nodes with bias as a negative fraction, say –0.5. The working of FFNN is given below:

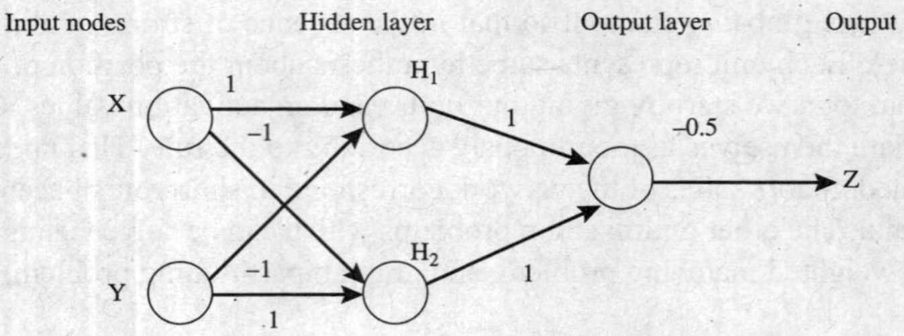

MULTIPLE CHOICE QUESTIONS

Select the most appropriate answers to the following questions:

1. If the output of a perceptron is very low, then what will be the value of learning rate A?
   (a) 0 (b) 1
   (c) Positive value (d) Negative value
2. Which of the following function is not linearly separable?
   (a) OR (b) XOR
   (c) AND (d) None of these
3. Which of the following cannot be used as activation function in a neuron?
   (a) Ramp function (b) Sigmoid function
   (c) Gaussian function (d) None of these
4. Which of the following is a cyclic network?
   (a) Feedforward neural network (b) Feedbackward neural network
   (c) Recurrent networks (d) All of these
5. Which of the following is not an example of non-linearly separable learning problem?
   (a) Face recognition (b) Handwriting recognition
   (c) XOR function (d) None of these
6. Which of the following learning law supports unsupervised learning?
   (a) Hebbian (b) Perceptron
   (c) Delta (d) None of these
7. Which of the model of a neuron cannot learn?
   (a) McCulloch–Pitts model (b) Rosenblatt's perceptron model
   (c) Widrow's Adaline model (d) None of these
8. In which of the following pattern matching problem, implied mapping of input pattern to output pattern is required?
   (a) Pattern mapping problem (b) Pattern clustering problem
   (c) Patten association problem (d) None of these
9. Which of the following pattern recognition problem cannot be solved using feedforward neural network alone?
   (a) Pattern association problem (b) Pattern classification problem
   (c) Pattern clustering problem (d) None of these

10. Which of the following pattern recognition problem can be solved using feedback neural network alone?
    (a) Pattern association problem
    (b) Pattern classification problem
    (c) Pattern clustering problem
    (d) None of these

Ans. 1. c 2. b 3. d 4. c 5. d 6. a 7. a 8. a 9. c 10. d

EXERCISES

1. Give any basic topological structures of ANN.
2. Identify supervised and unsupervised basic learning laws.
3. Design perceptrons for Boolean function AND.
4. Consider a Hopfield network with four nodes and train this for weights for the following input vectors: {[1 1 –1 1], [1 –1 1 1], [–1 1 1 1], [–1 1 1 –1]}.
5. Differentiate between Hopfield network and Boltzmann machine.
6. Given the following Hopfield network with suitable weights, generate mutually all possible stable states of these.

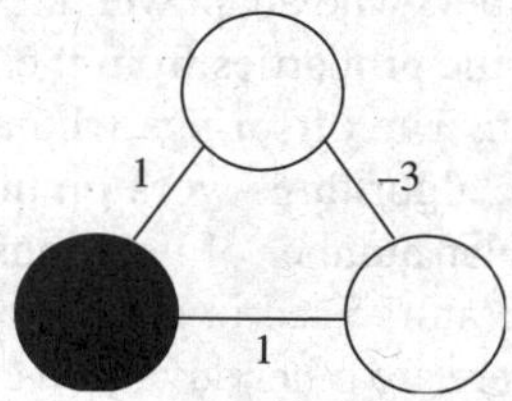

10

Genetic Algorithms

10.1 INTRODUCTION

Genetic algorithms learning methods are based on the models of natural adaptation and evolution. In genetics, there is an initial population that is subject to an environment. Based on the performance, the new population is generated. The members who adapt well are selected for mating and reproduction. As in case of biology, the children inherit the properties from their parents. Thus, only the best performing offsprings are chosen for mating again. The offsprings who are poor in performance will not participate in reproduction. Thus, the genetic algorithms work on the rule of survival of the fittest. This also ensures better learning. After a particular number of iterations, all the population will contain the best offsprings. There are mainly three operators used in genetic algorithms for producing new offsprings, mutation, crossover, and inversion. There are other advanced cycle operators also which can be used for producing even better offsprings.

10.1.1 Robustness of Traditional Optimization and Search Methods

Q. What are genetic algorithms?

Ans. Genetic algorithm was originally developed by John Holland in 1975 to understand the adaptive processes of natural systems and to design some artificial systems based on these. Genetic algorithms can be defined as a class of search algorithms that are inspired by the biological evolution process and use probabilistic optimization algorithms. These are well suited for solving hard problems where we know less about the entire search space and there are huge search spaces. These are kind of evolutionary algorithms, which are using the concept of natural selection and genetic inheritance. The aim is to combine the things in an optimal way possible to find an early solution.

Q. What are the benefits of using genetic algorithms?

Ans. There are many benefits of using genetic algorithms:

1. The concept is similar to natural evolution and hence it is easy to understand.
2. The algorithms can be separated from the complete application as it is modular in nature.
3. It can support optimization in problems that need multiple objectives.
4. It has the capacity to learning and improving, so we can use it in environments where we may have noisy inputs as these will be filtered out.

5. The genetic algorithms always ensure an answer to the problem and that too can improve over time.
6. It can support parallel computing.
7. Many alternatives can be tried at the same time.

10.1.2 Goals of Optimization

Q. What are the goals of optimization?

Ans. The goal of optimization is to find a better solution to a problem.

10.1.3 Traditional Methods versus Genetic Algorithms

Q. Explain the differences between traditional methods and genetic algorithms.

Ans. There are many differences between traditional methods and genetic algorithms as listed in table below:

	Traditional methods	Genetic algorithms
1.	Traditional methods work with parameters	Genetic algorithms work with a coding of the parameter set
2.	Traditional methods may search from a single point	Genetic algorithms always search from a population of points
3.	Traditional methods may involve derivatives or other auxiliary knowledge also	Genetic algorithms use objective function information only
4.	Traditional methods use deterministic rules	Genetic algorithms use probabilistic transition rules

10.1.4 Simple Genetic Algorithm

Q. Give an example of a simple genetic algorithm.

Ans. The simple genetic algorithm is

1. Produce an initial set of population of individuals.
2. Evaluate the fitness of all the individuals in the population using fitness function.
3. Continue in the loop until the terminating condition is not met:
   (a) Select individuals from population which appear to be fitter, i.e., better than the other individuals in the population.
   (b) Recombine among the individuals that are selected in (a).
   (c) Mutate the individuals.
   (d) Re-evaluate the fitness of the individuals modified in step (c) using the fitness function.
   (e) Generate a new population.

The termination condition could be any one of the following:

(a) When the pre-specified number of generations have been completed.
(b) When an individual solution has reached a specified level of fitness value.
(c) When a level of stability has been achieved in variation of individuals from one to the next generation.

Q. What do you understand by similarity templates? What are their uses?

Ans. A good string is the one which is assigned a large value of probability. In order to search in a good direction, we should be able to relate one good string with its fellow good strings. This can be done by a similarity template called schema. It describes a subset of strings with similarities at certain string positions. A meta symbol * can be used to match any similar strings of a particular length and alphabet. For example, if we have a binary alphabet set {a,b}. We can extend this alphabet set by appending * to this alphabet set {a,b, *}. Now the schema matches a particular string if at every location in the schema an "a" matches an "a," a "b" matches with "b" or matches either "a" or "b". Consider the strings and schemata of length 4. The schema ab*a matches two similar strings abaa and abba. These help in implementing implicit parallelism and improve the generation of best population.

Using implicit parallelism, information learned about a single chromosome during fitness evaluation can lend information about other similarly structured chromosomes. This helps in getting more values quickly in parallel. This was proposed by John Holland who proposed genetic algorithms.

Q. Explain learning the lingo in genetic algorithms.

Ans. Genetic algorithms have their roots in both natural genetics and computer science. So, the terminology used should be related in both. The relation between various terminologies used in biological systems and genetic systems in computer science is discussed here:

Biological systems		Correspondence in Genetic Algorithms in computer Science
Chromosomes	→	Strings
Chromosomes are made up of genes	→	Represented as a feature, a character, or a detector
The values that a gene can take on are called alleles	→	Feature values
Position of the gene is called its locus	→	String position
When one or more chromosomes combine to form the total generic package, these are called the genotype	→	The total package of strings is called a structure
The organism formed by the interaction of the total genetic package with its environment is called the phenotype	→	Structures decode to from a particular parameter set, solution alternative, or point
A gene is epistatic when its presence suppresses the effect of a gene at another position. Even when individual genes are not epistatic, i.e., interacting with other genes, there will be "chains of influence". Hence, interaction among genes is unavoidable	→	Implemented using non-linearity

Q. Give the fundamental theorem in mathematics for genetic algorithms.

Ans. The Schema theorem is the fundamental theorem in mathematics for genetic algorithms. It states that short, low-order, above-average schemata receive exponentially increasing trials in subsequent generations of a genetic algorithm.

In order to see how it is derived, consider the following definitions:

- $m(S,t)$ is the number of individuals in the population belonging to a particular schema S at time t (in terms of generations).
- $f_S(t)$ is the average fitness value of strings belonging to schema S at time t.
- $f(t)$ is the average fitness value over all strings in the population.

Under fitness-proportionate selection, the expected number of individuals belonging to schema S at time $(t + 1)$ is

$m(S,t+1) = m(S,t)\,(f_S(t)/f(t))$

Assuming that a schema S remains above average by $0 \le c$, (i.e., $f_S(t) = f(t) + c\,f(t)$),

Then $m(S,t) = m(S,0)\,(1 + c)^t$

This indicates "above average" schema receives an exponentially increasing number of strings in the next generation.

The probability of schema S ($|S| = l$) to survive crossover is

$p_s(S) \ge 1 - p_c(\delta(S)/(l - 1))$

The combined effect of selection and crossover yields

$m(S,t+1) \ge m(S,t)\,(f_S(t)/f(t))\,[1 - p_c(\delta(S)/(l - 1))]$

It signifies that above-average schemata with short defining lengths would still be sampled at exponentially increasing rates.

The probability of S to survive mutation is

$p_s(S) = (1 - p_m)^{o(S)}$

Since $p_m \ll 1$, this probability can be approximated by:

$p_s(S) \ge 1 - p_m o(S)$

The combined effect of selection, crossover and mutation yields

$m(S,t+1) \ge m(S,t)\,(f_S(t)/f(t))\,[1 - p_c(\delta(S)/(l - 1)) - p_m o(S)]$

Hence, it states that short, low-order, above-average schemata receive exponentially increasing trials in subsequent generations of a genetic algorithm.

Q. What is a schema? What is its order?

Ans. A schema is a template consisting of a string composed of the symbols defined in the alphabet set of the given problem. The order of the schema indicates the number of fixed positions in the schema. It is represented as o(S). It is useful for calculating the survival probability of the schema for mutations.

Q. What is the defining length of a schema? What does it signify?

Ans. The defining length of a schema is the distance between the first and last fixed positions in the schema. It is denoted by delta(S). It helps in calculating the survival probability of the schema for crossover operations

Q. State the schema theorem.

Ans. Short, low-order, above average schemata receives exponentially increasing trials in subsequent generations of a genetic algorithm.

Q. Explain the data structures used in implementation of genetic algorithms.

Ans. In a genetic algorithm, the basic unit that is to be manipulated is an individual. It is a biological chromosome which can be represented as a string. All the individuals form the population that is represented as an array of strings. When the organism is formed by the interaction of the total genetic package with its environment, it is called the phenotype. This is represented using a data structure, parameter set and a fitness value.

In C, the data structure used will be an array of individuals where each individual is a structure as defined below:

```
struct individual{
unsigned int individual_no;
char chromosome[30];
```

```
unsigned int phenotype;
float fitness_value;
int others;
};
struct type individual population[100];
```

Q. Explain the 2-armed Bandit problem.

Ans. It is a statistical decision theory. Suppose there is a slot machine with two arms. The aim is to give the tasks to the arm whose performance is better. Initially, we do not know which is better performing. This can be judged by first giving them a fraction of total tasks divided equally between the two arms and watching the output/awards. The arm that proves to be better can be given the rest of the tasks.

Let us assume that one of the arms pays an award μ_1 with variance of σ_1 and the other arm pays an award μ_2 with a variance σ_2 where $\mu_1 \geq \mu_2$. A decision is to be made about which arm to play and which is the better performing arm.

Suppose there are a total of N trails to be allocated among the two arms. Both arms are allocated an equal number of trials, n such that $2*n < N$ during the experimental phase. After the experiment, the remaining $N-2*n$ trials are allocated to the arm which is better.

If q(n) is the probability that the worst arm is the observed best arm, the decision is wrong and the remaining tasks are allocated to an arm that was not better actually, then the expected loss is calculated as

$$L(N,n) = |\mu_1 - \mu_2| * [(N-n)\,q(n) + n(1 - q(n))]$$

This probability can be approximated by the tail of the normal distribution

$$q(n) \cong \frac{1}{\sqrt{2\pi}} * \frac{e - sqr(x) / 2}{x}$$

where $x = \mu_1 - \mu_2 * \sqrt{n}$

$$\sqrt{sqr\sigma(1)} + \sqrt{sqr\sigma(2)}$$

This can be solved by taking the derivative of loss equation and setting it to zero.

Q. Explain the k-armed Bandit Problem.

Ans. The k-armed bandit problem is extension of 2-armed bandit problem. A genetic algorithm may have to consider the simultaneous solutions of many multi-armed bandits. The solution to k-armed bandit was given by Holland. More than one schemata may be defined over the same positions when there are more than two schemata available. These compete with one another for precious population slots. In order to allocate the population slots properly, we need to allocate exponentially increasing numbers to the observed best schemata.

Q. Explain the building block hypothesis.

Ans. Building blocks are the name given to highly fit schemata of low defining length and low order. This is because the performance of genetic algorithms is determined by these building blocks. According to the building block hypothesis, a genetic algorithm seeks near optimal performance through the juxtaposition of short, low-order but high performance schemata. Though this hypothesis is applicable in many cases but the success depends on the representation and genetic operator in use.

Q. Describe the minimal deceptive problem.

Ans. In a minimal deception problem, the aim was to violate the building block hypothesis and make a genetic algorithm to diverge from global optimum. This is done using short, low-order building blocks that lead to incorrect, i.e., suboptimal, longer and higher order building blocks. The introduction of an element of deception is necessary to make this a tough problem for a simple genetic algorithm. The simplest is to use 2-bit problem. Suppose we have a set of four order two schemata over two defining positions, each schema associated with a fitness value as follows:

* * * 0 * * 0 * *	f_{00}
* * * 0 * * 1 * *	f_{01}
* * * 1 * * 0 * *	f_{10}
* * * 1 * * 1 * *	f_{11}

The fitness values are schema averages that are assumed to be constant with no variance. Let us assume f_{11} is global optimum. So, $f_{11} > f_{10}$ and $f_{11} > f_{01}$ and $f_{11} > f_{00}$. In order to introduce deception, we need a problem where 1 or both of the suboptimal order −1 schemata are better than the optimal order −1 schemata.

So, $f(0*) > f(1*) \rightarrow [(f(00) + f(01))/2] > [(f(10) + f(11))/2]$

Or $f(*0) > f(*1) \rightarrow [(f(10) + f(00))/2] > [(f(01) + f(11))/2]$

Without any loss of generality, let us assume that first expression is true. OS the deceptive 2-bit problem is specified by the global condition, i.e., f_{11} is best and one deception condition $f(0*) > f(1*)$.

10.2 SELECTION TECHNIQUES IN GENETIC ALGORITHMS

Q. What are various selection methods in genetic algorithms?

Ans. Genetic algorithms are based on the concept of natural evolution. It selects the fitter individuals from the current population to be used in next reproduction. There are many techniques for selection of individuals which are to be copied over into the next generation:

1. Roulette-wheel selection
2. Rank selection
3. Boltzmann selection
4. Scaling selection
5. Generational selection
6. Elitist selection
7. Fitness-proportionate selection
8. Hierarchical selection

Q. Explain Roulette-wheel selection in genetic algorithms.

Ans. This selection technique has been adopted from the game of roulette. In this game, each individual gets a slice of wheel. The one getting the larger slice of wheel is more fit than those getting the smaller slices of wheel. The limitation of this type of selection is that if the fitness changes by orders of magnitude. In that case, the individual who have higher magnitude of fitness will be the parent of almost every offspring in the next generation. Also in case all the individuals have equal values, then all will be selected with equal probability and hence there will be no optimal solution.

Q. Explain linear-rank selection in genetic algorithms.

Ans. In linear-rank selection method, individuals are assigned subjective fitness based on the rank within the population. If PS is the population size, r_i is the rank of the individual i, then the subjective fitness of individual i based on rank selection is given as:

$Sf_i = (P - r_i) * (Max - Min)/(P - 1) + Min$, where max is the fitness assigned to the best individual and Min is the fitness assigned to the worst individual. The limitation of this method is that population size needs to be stored on each cycle.

Q. Explain Tournament selection rank in genetic algorithms.

Ans. All the other selection methods are based on global population. In tournament selection, the population is reducing to the current tournament, i.e., any k random individuals are chosen to select the best of them using rank selection. The same process is repeated to select more individuals. The advantage of the method is that there is less competition for the individual for selection. However, with an increase in the sample size, the selection pressure increases for each individual. Again, if the unselected individuals can re-participate in the next selection process, then there is less selection pressure. But if the selection is with replacement, then the selection pressure increases.

Q. Explain Elitist selection in genetic algorithms.

Ans. The term Elitism refers to saving the chromosome of the most fit individual in a given generation. In this type of selection, the best individuals are copied in the next generation. If there are N individual in a generation, then only N - 1 individuals are produced by recombining the information from the parents. The last individual is the copy of the best fit individual from the generation. This ensures that the best individual is never lost due to any random operation or event.

Q. Explain fitness-proportionate selection in genetic algorithms.

Ans. In this type of selection, individuals are assigned a probability of being selected on the basis of their fitness, p_i.

$$p_i = f_i / \sum fi$$

Here, f_i is the fitness of the individual i. This selection method has a limitation that it cannot be used on minimization problems.

Q. Explain Boltzmann selection in genetic algorithms.

Ans. This is done using simulated annealing. This method simulates the process of slow cooling of molten metal to achieve the minimum function value in a minimization problem. The cooling process is simulated by controlling a parameter like temperature, which is induced with the help of Boltzmann probability distribution. The system in thermal equilibrium at a temperature has its energy distribution based on the probability defined by

P(DE) = –exp(DE/kT), where k is Boltzmann constant. The expression suggests that a system at a higher temperature has almost uniform probability at any energy state, but at lower temperature, it has a small probability of being at a higher energy state. So by controlling temperature T and assuming that the search process follows Boltzmann probability distribution, the convergence of the algorithm is controlled.

10.3 OPERATORS IN GENETIC ALGORITHMS

Q. Explain the various operators in genetic algorithms.

Ans. There are mainly three operators in genetic algorithms: reproduction, crossover, and mutation.

Q. Explain reproduction in genetic algorithms.

Ans. Reproduction comes after selection of fit individuals. It involves altering the selected individuals randomly so that their fitness is improved in the next generation. There are two ways to reproduce crossover and mutation.

Q. Explain crossover operator in genetic algorithms.

Ans. In crossover, two strings are divided into segments that are exchanged with each other to produce new generation. A random recombination of the chromosomes of the two parents is crossover to produce new offsprings. There are three variations of crossover:

(a) ***Single-point crossover:*** Here, one bit position in the chromosome is chosen. Offspring 1 is produced by combining head of chromosome of parent 1 till the selected bit position with the tail of the second parent after the selected bit position. Offspring 2 is produced by combining the head of chromosome of parent 2 till the selected bit position with the tail of the first parent after the selected bit position.

(b) ***Two-point crossover:*** This is also known as multi-point crossover. Here, two bit positions are selected at random. The offsprings are generated by combining the heads and tails of parents as in single-point crossover.

(c) ***Uniform crossover:*** Here, a random mask is generated that determines which bits are to be copied from one parent and which ones are to be copied from the second parent to form the offspring. The uniform crossover results in only one offspring.

1010|01 $\rightarrow$ 101000
1110|00 $\rightarrow$ 111001

Crossover

101001 $\rightarrow$ 101101

Mutation / Inversion

Q. Explain mutation operator in genetic algorithms.

Ans. In mutation operator, an arbitrary bit of parent is selected and it is inverted. This results in production of a new offspring.

Q. Explain inversion operator in genetic algorithms.

Ans. Order of genes on a chromosome is critical for the building block hypothesis to work effectively. Purpose of inversion/reordering is to find gene orderings that have better evolutionary potential. Inversion is a special form of reordering that reverses the order of genes between two randomly selected positions. Reordering expands the search space.

Q. Explain reordering operators in genetic algorithms.

Ans. There are three reordering operators in genetic algorithms. These all are variations of crossover operator and are binary:

(i) ***Partially matched crossover:*** Here, two strings are aligned and two crossing sites are picked uniformly at random along the strings. These two points define a matching selection that is used to affect a cross through position by position exchange operations. There is a position-wise exchange between strings A and B. New offsprings are formed in which each string contains ordering information partially determined by each of its parents.

Informal procedure for parents P1 and P2:

1. Choose random segment and copy it from P1.
2. Starting from the first crossover point look for elements in that segment of P2 that have not been copied.

3. For each of these i look in the offspring to see what element j has been copied in its place from P1.
4. Place i into the position occupied j in P2, since we know that we will not be putting j there (as is already in offspring).
5. If the place occupied by j in P2 has already been filled in the offspring k, then put i in the position occupied by k in P2.
6. Having dealt with the elements from the crossover segment, the rest of the offspring can be filled from P2.

Second child is created analogously.

(ii) ***Order crossover:*** Here, a matching section is selected. Each string maps to constituents of the matching section of its mate. It uses a sliding motion to fill the holes left by transferring the mapped positions. These holes are filled with a sliding motion that starts following the second crossing site. The holes are then filled with the matching section taken from the mate.

(iii) ***Cycle crossover:*** This ordering operator performs recombination under the constraint that each node comes from one parent or the other. Instead of choosing crossing sites, we start at the left most node and choose a node from the first parent. This is mapped to left most node of the other parent. The next node selected is the node corresponding to this node in the second parent. This process continues till the node is repeated, i.e., the cycle is completed for that node. The remaining nodes are filled from the other string.

The algorithm is

1. Make a cycle of alleles from P1 in the following way.
   (a) Start with the first allele of P1.
   (b) Look at the allele at the *same position* in P2.
   (c) Go to the position with the *same allele* in P1.
   (d) Add this allele to the cycle.
   (e) Repeat step (b) through (d) until you arrive at the first allele of P1.
2. Put the alleles of the cycle in the first child on the positions they have in the first parent.
3. Take next cycle from second parent.

Q. What are the other micro-operators in genetic algorithms?

Ans. There are many micro-operators defined in genetic algorithms, which are used to capture various functions of biological chromosomes.

(i) ***Segregation:*** In biology, there are not only diploids but haploid chromosomes that have more than two chromosomes. A human carries 23 pairs of diploid chromosomes. Holland suggested that multiple chromosome genotypes might be useful in extending the power of genetic algorithms. Segregation is the process of randomly selecting one of each of the haploid chromosomes during gamete formation process. Its purpose is to disrupt any linkage that might exist between genes on different chromosomes. But the genes located on the same chromosome still are linked more or less tightly depending upon the distance separating them. In this way, only highly fit alleles will be used for reproduction and poor alleles cannot because the linkage is destroyed by segregation.

(ii) ***Translocation:*** This is interchromosomal crossover operator. A tagging of alleles with their gene names is needed so that we can identify their intended meaning when they are shuffled from chromosome to chromosome by the translocation operator.

(iii) ***Duplication:*** This is intrachromosomal operator. Duplication is done by duplicating a particular gene and placing it along with its progenitor on the chromosome.

(iv) ***Deletion:*** This operator removes a duplication gene from the chromosome.

Q. What do you understand by A Time to Reproduce, A Time to Cross in genetic algorithms?

Ans. This means creating a new population from an old one. The steps are

1. Start at an individual index $i = 1$ and continue until the population size has been exceeded.
2. Take any two mates m1 and m2 to select.
3. Cross and mutate m1 and m2 using crossover.
4. Decode the pair of chromosomes.
5. Evaluate the objective function values.
6. Increment the population index i by 2.

10.4 OBJECTIVE FUNCTION AND FITNESS SCALING

Q. Explain the process of objective function and constraints.

Ans. A genetic algorithm generates a sequence of parameters that are to be tested using a system model, an objective function and the constraints. The constraints are generally specified in the form of inequalities. If constraints are present in a problem, then the objective function is evaluated and checked to see if any constraints are violated. The solution is called unfit if the constraints are violated with the objective function value. Then it is evaluated again after making changes. But in reality, it is not possible to satisfy all the constraints. So, an error or penalty is associated in terms of cost to a constrained problem to convert it to an unconstrained problem. This cost is included in the objective function evaluation.

If the constrained problem is

minimize $f(x)$

Subject to constraint:

$g_i(x) \geq 0,\ i = 1, 2, \ldots n$ where x is an m vector.

We transform this to unconstrained problem:

$$\text{minimize } f(x) + r * \sum_{i=1}^{n} \Phi g_i(x)$$ where Φ is penalty function and r is penalty coefficient.

Under certain conditions, the unconstrained solution converges to the constrained solution as the penalty coefficient r approaches infinity. The penalty function is generally taken as the square of the function to be violated.

Q. Explain how the objective functions are mapped to fitness form?

Ans. The objective function may have two forms, either it is for minimizing the cost or for maximizing the utility value or profit. So, different mapping to fitness functions can be used with the aim to make the fitness function positive. In case of objective function for minimizing the cost, the corresponding transformation to fitness is given as:

$f(x) = \text{Cmax} - g(x)$ when $g(x) < \text{Cmax}$

$= 0$, otherwise

Here, the coefficient Cmax may be an input coefficient, as the largest g value observed so far, as largest g value in current population or largest of last k generations.

When the objective function is maximizing a utility value, the corresponding transformation to fitness is given as:

$f(x) = u(x) + \text{Cmin}$ when $u(x) + \text{Cmin} > 0$
$= 0$ otherwise

Here, the coefficient Cmin is an input coefficient, as absolute value of the worst u (i.e., utility) value in current or last k generations, or as a function of the population variance.

Q. What is fitness scaling in genetic algorithms?

Ans. The purpose of the fitness function is to select the parent that can be used for production of next generation, i.e., offsprings. In order that only best fit parents are selected, the fitness function should be a measure of convergence toward optimal solution. It should be chosen in such a way that it reflects the value of the chromosome in some real way and there is no significant diversity within the population. In order to scale the fitness function, the values are subtracted or divided so that the worst value is close to 0 and the best value is close to a typical value, say 2. This is because the chances of selection for worst fit individual is 0 and that for the best fit individual is 2 times the average. Linear scaling is the simplest way to do this. Let a raw fitness function is defined as f and scaled function is defined by f'. The relation between f and f' should be linear:

$f' = af + b.$

Here, the coefficients a and b may be chosen in a number of ways, in all cases we want the average scaled fitness f'_{avg} to be equal to average raw fitness f_{avg} because subsequent use of selection procedure will ensure that each average population member contributes one expected offspring to the next generation. To control the number of offspring given to population member with maximum raw fitness, the scale maximum fitness is given as:

$f'_{avg} = \text{Cmult} * f'_{avg}$

where Cmult is the number of expected copies desired for best population number.

There are two problems in scaling - super fit and super unfit. Super fit occurs when the original maximum is very extreme. Super unfit occurs when the original minimum is very extreme.

10.5 CODING

Q. Explain the different terms used during coding in genetic algorithms

Ans. Coding is representation of individuals in genetic algorithms. An individual is characterized by a set of parameters that are called the genes. When these genes are combined together in a string, they form a chromosome. Similar types of chromosome form genotype. The phenotype is representing an organism that is produced using information contained in genotype. The phenotype, i.e., the organism is checked for its fitness in real world.

Q. What are various types of codings in genetic algorithms?

Ans. In genetic algorithms, design alternatives are coded as individuals that are representing chromosomes in nature. Single design choice is encoded as a gene. The design objectives are encoded as fitness function. As an example, consider the processor job scheduling problem where n jobs are to be scheduled on m processors so that maximum span is minimized. The encoding is as follows:

Here, design alternative is job $j = 1,\ldots n$ is assigned to processor $p = 1,\ldots m$.

An individual is a vector Pj = 1, 2,..., m. The design objective is to minimize the maximal span. The fitness function is the maximal span for each processor. The individual's can be encoded as:

(a) Bit strings (01001101010…)
(b) Real numbers (4.12 3.45 -0.78…)
(c) Permutations of element (P1 P4 P12 …)
(d) List of rules (R1 R2 R3…)
(e) Program elements (genetic programming)
(f) Any data structure

Q. Explain binary coding in genetic algorithms.

Ans. Binary coding can be used for any simple problems say, switching problem, where a 0 indicates that the switch is off and a 1 indicate that the switch is on. A string is formed by concatenating a number of 0's and 1's.

Let the string be $S = s_n s_{n-1} \ldots s_1 \ldots s_2 s_1$

Here, s_1 is the lowest order bit and s_n is the highest order bit in the string and n is the total number of bit sin the string.

This is decoded to parameter value $x = \sum si\ 2^{i-1}$

Q. Explain multi-parameter, mapped, fixed-point coding.

Ans. Here, if parameter $x \in [0, 2^n]$, it is decoded linearly from $[0, 2^n]$ to a specified interval $[U_{min}, U_{max}]$. The precision of the mapped coding may be calculated as

$$\Pi = \frac{U_{max} - U_{min}}{2^n - 1}$$

If there is only single parameter and $n = 4$. The decoding is $U_{min} = 0000$ and $U_{max} = 1111$ and all the others map linearly between these two.

In case of multi-parameter coding with five parameters, the decoding is done as:

u1 = 0001
u2 = 0110
…
u5 = 1111

Q. Explain the process of discretization.

Ans. Discretization means having some discrete values of a function, i.e., which are not continuous. In genetic algorithms, many optimization problems have a control function what is continuous, i.e., must be specified at every point in some continuum. It is difficult to code a continuous function. So, discretization is used that reduces the optimization problem to finite parameter before the parameter coding may take place.

10.6 APPLICATIONS OF GA

Q. Discuss the rise of genetic algorithms.

Ans. First of all Fraser simulated the evolution of future string generations and calculated the percentage of individuals with accepted phenotypes with successive generations. Then, Holland and his students applied genetic like operators to artificial problems in adaptation. He recognized the fundamental role of the unnatural selection and artificial survival of the fittest.

Q. Discuss genetic algorithm applications of Historical Interest.

Ans. There are many applications for genetic algorithms, which are of historical interest:

1. Bagley and adaptive game playing program
2. Rosenberg and biological cell simulation
3. Cavichhio and pattern recognition
4. Weinberg, cell simulation and meta-level genetic algorithms
5. Hollstien and function optimization
6. Frantz and positional effect
7. Bosworth, foo and Zeigler, and real genes
8. Box and evolutionary operation
9. Fogel, Owens, and Walsh and evolutionary programming

Q. Explain De Jong and function optimization.

Ans. De Jong devised two measures to quantify the effectiveness of different genetic algorithms:

1. To gauge convergence for offline performance of genetic algorithms.
2. To gauge ongoing performance of genetic algorithms.

Online performance denoted by $x_e(s)$ of a strategy *s* on environment *e* is defined as

$$x_e(s) = \frac{1}{T} \sum_{t=1}^{T} fe(t)$$

where *fe*(*t*) is the objective function value for environment *e* on trial *t*.

The offline performance of a strategy *s* on environment *e* is defined as

$$x_e{}^*(s) = \frac{1}{T} \sum_{t=1}^{T} fe^*(t)$$

where *f*(*e*) * (*t*) is the best value in {fe(1), fe(2)… fe(t)}

De Jong constructed a test environment of five problems in function minimization. The characteristics of the applications were continuous or discontinuous, convex or non-convex, unimodal or multimodal, quadratic or non-quadratic, low dimensionality or high dimensionality and deterministic or stochastic. He constructed a version called R1 (reproduce plan 1) that considered three operators, Roulette wheel selection, simple crossover, and simple mutation.

Q. Discuss current applications of GA.

Ans. There are various areas in which applications of genetic algorithms are used:

1. Combinatorial optimization: It includes applications like traveling salesman problem, set covering, routing, bin packing, graph coloring, and partitioning.
2. Control: The applications are gas pipeline, missile evasion, pole balancing, etc.
3. Design: The applications are in aircraft design, communication networks, keyboard configurations, semiconductor layout, etc.
4. Game playing: The applications of genetic algorithms are in solving checkers, poker, and prisoner's dilemma.
5. Machine learning: Genetic algorithms are used in classifier systems, classification algorithms, and designing neural networks.
6. Scheduling: In scheduling, genetic algorithms can be used in resource allocation, facility scheduling, and manufacturing.
7. Signal processing: Filter design is an example where genetic algorithms can be used.

10.7 ADVANCED OPERATORS AND TECHNIQUES IN GENETIC SEARCH

Q. What are haploid and diploid chromosomes?

Ans. When a single chromosome (string) is capable of storing all the information about an individual, it is called a haploid. Diploid chromosomes are used to represent the individual with double-stranded chromosomes.

Q. Define dominance.

Ans. In diploid chromosomes, the paired chromosomes store or encode information related to the same gene or the same characteristic. But on each of the chromosomes, the gene may have different values or same values. These values on each chromosome are called the alleles. Each allele may code for a different phenotypic characteristic. In order to find a stable and consistent phenotypes, the allele is defined as dominating allele if it is expressed in the phenotypic when paired with some other. An allele x dominates y if it is at least as good on all criteria and better on at least one.

Q. Define diploidy.

Ans. According to Goldberg, diploidy provides a mechanism for remembering alleles and allele combinations that were previously useful and the dominance provides an operator to shield those remembered alleles from harmful selection in a currently hostile environment.

Q. Define abeyance.

Ans. Abeyance is the process so that one solution is not over selected.

Q. What is the importance of diploidy and dominance?

Ans. Diplody and dominance affect a kind of long-term memory in genetic algorithms. They allow alternate solutions to co-exist. Using dominance and diploidy, only one solution is expressed as the other ones are held in abeyance.

Q. Explain Niche and Speciation.

Ans. There are various methods for Niche selection in genetic algorithms:

1. Preselection: It state that if fitness function f(child) > f(parent), then make child the parent.
2. Crowding: In this method, the replacement is done on the basis of string similarity. Each individual is compared to random subpopulation say of two or three members. The new strings are replaced with the subpopulation individual with closest similarity.

Speciation: In nature, different species adapt to occupy different environmental niches. As there are limited resources, so all species are in competition with each other. There are mating restrictions due to which the species can reproduce only with other members of the same species. These forces result in phenotypic homogeneity within species, but differences between species.

Q. Explain multi-objective optimization.

Ans. In problem where the solution can be generated by a single quality function, they can be transformed into a single fitness function and optimised via genetic operators. There are problems where several criteria must be considered simultaneously and cannot be solved by a single fitness function. Such problems are known as multi-criteria or multi-objective optimisation problems (MOPs). The definition of the fitness function requires a different definition in the multi-criteria case, which integrates all the separate criteria.

Q. What are the approaches for solving MOPs.

Ans. There are three general approaches for MOPs.

1. Preemptive optimization: Here, the optimization objectives of all problems are considered in the order of priority. The solution for highest priority function is then fixed and the solution to rest of the objectives is found based on that constraint. The process is repeated for function with next higher priority till the optimization solution to all the problems is found.
2. Composite objective function: This approach works on creating a composite function on the basis of the weighted sum of all the problems. The weights are assigned to the functions of all the problems according to some predefined criteria. The functions with maximizing and minimizing function will get the opposite signs.
3. Purely multi-objective: Population-based solutions can be used for pure multi-objective optimization problems, which are based on Pareto optimality.

Q. Explain Pareto optimality.

Ans. Pareto optimality theorem is used for multi-objective optimization. If $C1,\dots, Cn$ are n criteria requiring simultaneous optimisation.

Then, if $X = (x1, \dots, xn)$ and $Y = (y1, \dots, yn)$ be two vectors defined on $C1$ ´ ¼ ´ Cn

Let < and <= be defined on each Ci as "strictly better" and "at least as good," respectively.

Then, X is said to be partially better than Y, denoted by $X <\_p\ Y$, if and only if, for all $1 <= i <= n$, $xi <= yi$ and for at least one such i, $xi < yi$.

If $X <\_p\ Y$, then X is said to dominate Y. If a vector is not dominated by any other, then it is said to be non-dominated.

The set of non-dominated answers is called the Pareto optimal set. In general, the Pareto optimal set contains more than one element and there is no "automatic" way of selecting a single alternative. The user needs to select the most appropriate one.

Q. Explain knowledge-based techniques in genetic algorithms.

Ans. The genetic algorithms are blind search algorithms. But they need to deploy knowledge in order to find the solution in a better way. There are many different knowledge-based techniques that can be used in genetic algorithms:

1. ***Approximate function evaluation:*** In some problems, the cost of computing the actual fitness function may be prohibitive but with sufficient domain knowledge, an approximate model of the problem at hand can be used effectively to replace the actual function. It allows more efficient computations of fitness values
2. ***Knowledge augmented operators:*** In addition to using knowledge to speed up search, it is possible to use domain-specific knowledge to augment random choice in operators like mutation and crossover.
3. ***Punishment or reward schemes:*** It is sometimes possible to add knowledge into GAs by explicitly modifying the fitness function used. This is done through the use of punishment or reward mechanisms can be used to incorporate knowledge. To do this, the raw fitness function F is modified as follows:

   $$F' = F + f,$$

   where f is a function used either to decrease the fitness of particular solutions (punishment) or to increase it (reward). The undesirable reproduction of individuals with high fitness values can be reduced by punishing these individuals whose number of prototypes is large.
4. ***Simulated annealing terminology:*** This exploits an analogy between the physical annealing process and the search for an optimal solution in any general system.

Q. Explain parallel processes and genetic algorithms

Ans. Grefenstette examined parallel implementations of genetic algorithms. He outlined four prototypes:

(i) ***Synchronous master-slave:*** A single master process coordinates k slave processes that controls the selection, mating, and performance of genetic operators. The slave processes perform the function evaluations given to it by master process. The model is easy to implement but depends on the reliability of the single master process. There is also a wastage of time due to synchronous mode whenever there is a variance in the time for function evaluations by various slave processes.

(ii) ***Semi-synchronous master-slave:*** The disadvantage of synchronous master-slave is overcome by not waiting for all the slaves to complete simultaneously. The slave process if selected whosoever complete their work by the master process.

(iii) ***Asynchronous concurrent:*** In this model, the system has a common shared memory that is accessed by k identical processes which are performing both generation of operations and function evaluations independently of each other. It is reliable since there is no single master process but it needs a process to avoid simultaneous hits on identical memory locations

(iv) ***Network:*** In this system, k independent simple genetic algorithms run with independent memories, independent genetic operations and independent function evaluations. This is very reliable.

Goldberg has outlined two prototypes for parallel processing in genetic algorithms:

(i) ***Community mode:*** Here, a genetic algorithm is mapped to a set of interconnected communities. The communities consist of a set of homes connected to the centralized interconnected towns. Parents give birth to offspring in their homes and perform function evaluations there. The children are sent to a centralized singles bar where they meet up with prospective mates. After mating, the couples go to town's real estate broker to find a home. Homes are auctioned off to completing couples. If the town is currently crowded, then the couples may also consult the broker about homes in other communities and if necessary they may go to the bus station to move to another community.

(ii) ***Plant pollination:*** This parallel model consists of a series of plant nodes connected by a pollination network. Seeds grow up to become full plants that generate pollen that is cast out on the pollination network. Associated with each pollination network link is a probability of pollen transmission. This capability permits plant subpopulations to be more or less isolated from one another. Plant pollen fertilizes mature plants, creating more seeds. Selection occurs locally by selecting the local best seeds to become mature plants in a probabilistic fashion.

SOLVED EXAMPLES

Q. Give example of an allele.

Ans. Consider a diploid consisting of eight upper and small case letters each representing a gene. Different alleles are aBcDeFgh and ABcDeFgh.

Q. Give an example of a schema processing at work.

Ans. Consider the representation of string sin binary form, i.e., the possible values are 0 and 1. The symbol alphabet of this representation problem is defined as: {0,1,#}. # is wildcard character that can be equated to any one of the value 0 or 1. If the schema is [01##1], then it will match with the binary strings 01001, 01011, 01101, and 01111.

Q. What is the order of the schema [011*] where * is a wildcard character? Calculate the survival probability of the schema for mutation?**

Ans. The order of a schema is the number of fixed characters in the string. So, the answer is 3.

Q. Give an example of single-point crossover.

Ans. If given parents are 1010 001101 and 0011 010010, then the bit position selected is 4. The offsprings after crossover are 1010 010010 and 0011 001101.

Q. Give an example of two-point crossover.

Ans. Parents: 1010 0011 10 and 0011 0100 10 (bit positions are 4 and 7). Offsprings: 1010 0100 10 and 0011 0011 10.

Q. Give an example of mutation operator.

Ans. The parent string is 11010101. If the bit position selected for mutation is 3, then the offspring produced is 11110101.

Q. Give an example of genetic algorithm.

Ans.

```
Procedure GA{
t = 0;
Initialize P(t);
Evaluate P(t);
While (not done)
{
Parents(t) = Select_Parents(P(t));
        Offspring(t) = Procreate(Parents(t));
        Evaluate(Offspring(t));
        P(t + 1) = Select_Survivors(P(t),Offspring(t));
        t = t + 1;
}
```

Q. Give an example of knowledge augmentation in genetic algorithms.

Ans. The Crossover scheme proposed for TSP (by Grefensttete et al., 1985). It makes use of knowledge about distances in the parents to choose the better of two parental edges for the offspring:

This operator constructs an offspring from two parent tours as follows:

Pick a random city as a starting point for the child's tour. Compare the two edges leaving this starting city in the parents and choose the shorter edge. Continue to extend the partial tour by choosing the shorter of the two edges in the parents that extends the tour. If the shorter parental edge would introduce a cycle into the partial tour then extend the tour by a random edge. Continue until a complete tour is generated."

Good results up to 200 cities.

Q. Give example of binary coding.

Ans. Optimization of function $f(x, y, z)$, assume that x,y,z ³ 0 and x,y,z £ 63

Phenotype: $x = 46$, $y = 24$, $z = 13$

Genotype: 0 1 1 1 0 1 | 0 0 0 1 1 0 | 1 0 1 1 0 0

Q. Consider the following strings with the fitness values. Find which string will be selected using Roulette wheel selection?

S. No.	Fitness value	Running total
1	8	8
2	4	12
3	10	22
4	7	29
5	11	40

Ans. A random number to be generated between 1 and 40. Let it be 20. So, the string no. 3 is selected. If the number generated would have been 30, then string no. 4 would have been selected.

Q. Give an example of partially matched crossover.

Ans. Consider the two strings:

A: 1 4 5 | 3 2 9 | 7 10 6 8

B: 2 4 3 | 1 5 6 | 7 8 9 10

Here, 1 and 3 are mutually exchanged, 2 and 5 are mutually exchanged, and 9 and 6 are mutually exchanged and the resulting strings are

A': 3 4 2 | 1 5 6 | 7 10 9 8

B': 5 4 1 | 3 2 9 | 7 10 6 8

Q. Give an example of an order crossover.

Ans. Consider the two strings:

A: 1 4 5 | 3 2 9 | 7 10 6 8

B: 2 4 3 | 1 5 6 | 7 8 9 10

For substrings matching with 1, 5, and 6, holes will be inserted for 3, 2, and 9 as H and the resulting B string is

B': H 4 H | 1 5 6 | 7 8 H 10

Now the holes will be ordered and the resulting B string is

B': 1 5 6 | H H H | 7 8 10 4

Now, these will be replaced by substring for which the holes were inserted as 3, 2, and 9.
The resulting string B is

B': 1 5 6 | 3 2 9 | 7 8 10 4

Performing the operation and completing the complementary cross, we get string A' as

A': 3 2 9 | 1 5 6 | 7 10 4 8

Q. Give an example of cycle crossover.

Ans. Consider the two strings:

1 2 3 4 5 6 7 8 9 and 9 3 6 5 7 2 1 4 8 using the cycle crossover, we start from bit 1 in first string and match it with the number in first bit position in string 2 and cycle this matching from string 1 and string 2 till we reach number 1 again.

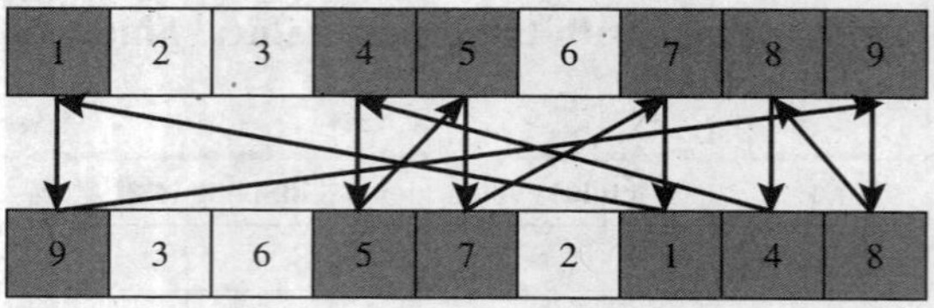

The numbers highlighted indicate the freezed bits. Next, we start with number at bit 2 in string 1 and match it to corresponding bit in string 2 and so on till again the cycle is complete.

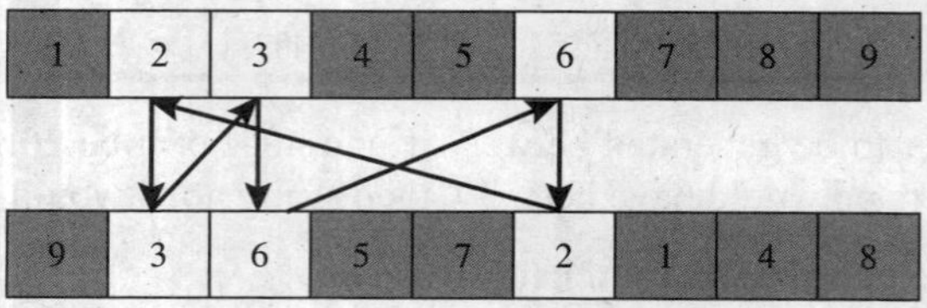

Thus, the resulting offspring after the cycle crossover are

1	3	6	4	5	2	7	8	9

9	2	3	5	7	6	1	4	8

Q. Give an example of MOP is real life.

Ans. Buying a vehicle while optimizing cost, speed, strength, and reliability.

MULTIPLE CHOICE QUESTIONS

Select the most appropriate answers to the following questions:

1. What is the order of the schema S1 = [01##1#10] for binary string representation where # is the wild card character.
   (a) 8 (b) 5
   (c) 3 (d) None of these
2. Which of the following micro-operator destroys the linkage between genes?
   (a) Translocation (b) Segregation (c) Delete (d) None of these
3. Which of the following operators use holes during crossover?
   (a) Partially matched crossover (b) Cycle crossover
   (c) Order crossover (d) All of these
4. Which of the model for parallel processes in genetic algorithm is most reliable?
   (a) Synchronous master-slave (b) Semi synchronous master-slave
   (c) Network (d) None of these

5. Which of the operators was not included in De Jong's reproduction plan 1?
   (a) Roulette wheel selection (b) Simple crossover
   (c) Simple mutation (d) None of these
6. Which of the following was proposed by Goldberg for parallel processing in genetic algorithms?
   (a) Community model (b) Synchronous master-slave
   (c) Semi synchronous master-slave (d) None of these
7. Which of the following specify the building blocks hypothesis in genetic algorithms?
   (a) Schemata of long length, low-order, and above average fitness value
   (b) Schemata of short length, low-order, and above average fitness value
   (c) Schemata of long length, high-order and above average fitness value
   (d) None of these
8. Strings in genetic algorithm are analogous to which of the following in biological systems?
   (a) Chromosome (b) Genotype
   (c) Allele (d) None of these
9. A structure in genetic algorithm is analogous to which of the following in biological systems?
   (a) Chromosome (b) Genotype
   (c) Allele (d). None of these
10. Which of the following is the characteristic of a genetic algorithm?
   (a) Direct manipulation of a coding (b) Search from a population
   (c) Search via sampling (d) All of these

Answers. 1. b 2. b 3. c 4. c 5. d 6. a 7. b 8. a 9. b 10. d

EXERCISES

1. There are six strings with the fitness functions values given as: 10, 20, 30, 40, 50, and 60. Under Roulette wheel selection, calculate the expected number of copies of each string in the mating pool if a constant population size, $n = 6$ is maintained.
2. A population contains the following strings and fitness values as generation 0:

S. No.	String	Fitness
11	0001	20
2	11100	10
3	00011	5
4	01110	15

The probability of mutation is pm = 0.01 and the probability of crossover is pc = 1.0. Calculate the expected number of schemata of the form 1***** in generation 1. Estimate the expected number of schemata of the form 0**1* in generation 1.

3. Perform partially matched crossover for the following strings:

   A: 1 4 5 | 2 7 3 | 6 8 9

   B: 2 4 6 | 1 8 7 | 3 5 9

4. Perform order crossover for the following strings:

   A: 2 3 5 | 1 7 4 | 9 8 6

   B: 2 4 6 | 1 8 9 | 3 5 7

5. Perform cycle crossover for the following strings:

   A: 1 3 5 | 2 7 4 | 6 8 9

   B: 1 2 3 | 4 5 6 | 7 8 9

11

LISP Programming

11.1 INTRODUCTION

LISP was first written by John McCarthy in 1958. He wrote an algebraic list processing language for AI work. McCarthy's graduate student wrote an interpreter for it. LISP is a family of languages developed mainly from Common LISP which is an ANSI Standard written in the 1980s. Other variants of LISP are Scheme, LISPWorks, Allegro, SBCL, and CLisp Functional, which is the most natural to write. LISP programming has very simple syntax and is consistently represented using lists. A language is a strongly typed if it contains compile time or run time type constraints violations. A language is strongly typed if type annotations are associated with variable names, rather than with values. A programming language is said to be dynamic when the majority of its type checking is performed at run-time. A variable can refer to a value of any type. LISP is strongly and dynamically typed language. Here values of many types can be defined such as numbers, strings, functions, lists, and other data structures. The basic building blocks are atoms and lists also known as symbolic expressions or s-expressions. There are many built-in functions for list, logical, and numeric processing. The users can easily define a new function using defun. Any number of arguments can be passed as parameters and value returned can be passed easily to other functions. Using lambda, anonymous functions can also be defined which can be used for one time only. LISP provides many functions for easy declaration and manipulation of arrays. Objects in real life can be modeled using property lists in LISP.

Q. What is LISP?

Ans. LISP is functional programming language. LISP is one of the oldest computer programming languages. It was invented by John McCarthy during late 1950s. LISP is particularly suited for AI programs because of its ability to process symbolic information effectively. It is a language with a simple syntax, with little or no data typing and dynamic memory management.

11.2 DIALECTS OF LISP AND BUILDING BLOCKS

Q. What are various dialects of LISP?

Ans. There are many dialects of LISP such as FRANZLISP, INTERLISP, MACLISP, QLISP, COMMON LISP, LISPWorks, and SCHEME.

Q. What are the basic building blocks of LISP?

Ans. The basic building blocks of LISP are the atom, list, and the string. These three are the only valid objects in LISP. They are called symbolic-expressions or s-expressions.

Atom: It is a number or string of contiguous characters, including numbers and special characters, e.g., bill, 1200, a100, rock*, etc.

List: It is a sequence of zero or more symbolic-expressions (atoms and/or other lists) enclosed within parentheses, e.g., (a b c), (a, (j, i), (e, g, h)), (), (sat, sun), etc.

String: It is a group of characters enclosed in double quotation marks, e.g., "hello LISP", "∧&∧%%fbdfdbfds" etc.

Q. How a LISP program is executed?

Ans. LISP programs run either or an interpreter or as compiled code. The interpreter examines source programs in a repeated loop, called the read–evaluate–print loop. This loop reads the program code, evaluates it and prints the values returned by the program. The comments can be written and may be placed anywhere after a semicolon.

The symbol -> indicates the prompt for getting the input from the user. The input is always in the form of a function written in prefix form and enclosed in parentheses. LISP tries to evaluate everything, including the arguments of the function.

The syntax of a function call is:

(function-name arg1 arg2…),

where any number of arguments may be used. When a function is called, the arguments are evaluated from left to right (unless with quotation marks) and then the function is executed using the evaluated argument values. The quotation marks inform the interpreter that the atom or list should not be evaluated, but should be taken literally as atom or list.

Q. Which elements always return their own values in LISP?

Ans. There are three special types of elements which are constant and always evaluate to themselves, returning their own value. They are numbers, the letter t (for logical true), and nil (for logical false). So if we evaluate any one of these, the answer is the element itself:

```
->60
60
->t
T
->nil
NIL.
```

Q. What are the top elements of a list?

Ans. The list may contain either atoms or lists. The basic elements are called the top elements of the list. For example, if the list is (a (b c) d (e f g)) then the top elements of the list are atom a, list (b c), atom d and the list (e f g).

11.3 USER-DEFINED LIST MANIPULATION FUNCTIONS

Q. How user-defined functions can be defined in LISP?

Ans. The user can define their own functions using the following syntax:

(defun name (param1 param2….) body).

(defun sum2(a b) (+ a b))

The function named sum2 takes two arguments a and b. It evaluates the sum of two arguments passed and returns that value.

Defun does not evaluate its arguments. It builds a function which may be called like any other pre-defined function. Defun takes three arguments: the new function name, the parameters for the function, and the function body or LISP code which performs the desired function operations. When the function is called, the arguments supplied in the call are evaluated unless they are in quotation marks and bound to function parameters. The function arguments are bound to the parameters in the same order they were given in the definition.

Q. Explain mapping functions and their use in LISP.

Ans. Mapping functions are used to map one operation or function to a number of elements in any given list. In LISP, mapcar is a mapping function. The syntax of mapcar is

(mapcar <function> <list of elements>)

The first argument is the function that is to be mapped, which can be named or unnamed. The remaining argument(s) are the lists of elements to which the mapped function is to be applied.

Q. Explain Lambda function and its use in LISP.

Ans. Lambda functions are used to write unnamed functions that are evaluated only when they are encountered in a program. This saves memory for storing the named functions and for writing the functions that are to be used once in a program.

(lambda (arguments) <function-body>)

Generally, lambda is used with ***mapcar*** functions. Whenever a function is called by another function, it should be preceded by the character '#' to indicate that the next term is a function.

11.4 INBUILT LIST PROCESSING FUNCTIONS

Q. What are the basic numeric functions in LISP?

Ans. The basic numeric function defined in LISP are +, –, *, /. Please refer Table 11.1.

Table 11.1 Basic Numeric Functions in LISP

Function	Explanation
(+ argl arg2…)	+ takes zero or more arguments and returns their sum. The sum of zero arguments is 0. Example: (+2 3) will return 5.
(– argl arg2)	- takes two arguments and returns the difference argl-arg2. Example: (- 4 7) will return -3.
(* argl arg2…)	* takes zero or more arguments. The product of no arguments is 1 and the product of 1 argument is the value of the argument. Example: (* 34 2) will return 78.
(/ argl arg2)	/ takes two arguments and returns argl/arg2. Example: (/ 72 3) will return 24.
(rem x y)	rem takes two arguments and returns remainder of x/y. Example: (rem 45 4) will return 1.
(abs x)	abs takes one argument and returns its absolute value. Example: (abs -5) will return 5.
(max $x_1,x_2,\ldots x_n$)	max takes any list of arguments and returns the maximum value. Example: (max '(1 34 56 78)) will return 78.
(min $x_1,x_2,\ldots x_n$)	min takes any list of arguments and returns the minimum value. Example: (min '(1 34 56 78)) will return 1.

Q. What are the basic list manipulation functions in LISP which take only one argument?

Ans. The following list manipulation functions in LISP take only one argument:

- ***car***: It takes one argument, a list and returns the first element of the list. For example, ***(car '(a b c))*** will return ***A***.

- ***cdr***: It takes one argument, a list and returns a list with the first element removed or tail of the list. For example, ***(cdr '(a b c))*** will return ***(B C)***.
- ***last***: It takes one argument, a list and returns a list containing the last element. For example, ***(last '(a b c d))*** will return ***(D).***
- ***reverse:*** It takes one argument , a list and returns a list with top elements in reverse order. For example, ***(reverse '(a (b c) d))*** will return ***(D (B C) A)***.
- ***list-length:*** It takes one argument, a list and returns the number of elements in the list. For example, ***(list-length '(a b c d e f))*** with return **6**.

Q. What are the basic list manipulation functions in LISP which take two arguments?

Ans. The following list manipulation functions in LISP take two arguments:

1. ***cons***: It takes two arguments, an element and a list and returns a list with the element inserted at the beginning. For example, ***(cons 'a '(b c))*** will return ***(A B C)***.
2. ***member***: It takes two arguments, an element and a list and returns remainder of second argument list starting with element matching first argument. For example, ***(member 'b '(a b b c d b))*** will return ***(B B C D B)***.
3. ***nth:*** It takes two arguments, an element and a list and returns the *N*'th member of list *L,* assuming that the elements are numbered starting from 0. For example, ***(nth 0 (1 2 3))*** will return **A**.

Q. What are the basic list manipulation functions in LISP which take any number of arguments?

Ans. The following list manipulation functions in LISP take variable number of arguments:

- ***append***: It takes two or more lists as arguments, and return a list by merging all of these into a single list. For example, (append '(a) '(b c) '(e)) will return ***(A B C E)***.
- ***list***: It takes any number of arguments and returns a list with the arguments as elements. For example, ***(list 'b '(a b)(d c e))*** will return ***(B (A B) (D C E))***.

Q. What are in built predicates in LISP?

Ans. Predicates are functions that test their arguments for some specific condition. All predicates return true (t) or false (nil), depending on the arguments.

The most common predicates can be divided into various categories:

(a) ***evenp***: It returns true if the argument passed is an even number. For example, ***(evenp 4)***will return **T(true)** and ***(evenp 5)*** will return **false,** i.e., NIL.

(b) ***oddp:*** It returns true if the argument passed is an odd number. For example, ***(oddp 41)*** will return **T(true)** and ***(oddp 50)*** will return **false,** i.e., NIL.

(c) ***numberp:*** It returns true if the argument passed is a number. For example, (numberp 11) will return **T(true)** and ***(numberp '(a))*** will return **false,** i.e., NIL.

(d) ***zerop***: It returns true if the argument passed is zero. For example, ***(zerop 0)*** will return **T(true)** and ***(zerop 0.001)*** will return **false,** i.e., NIL.

(e) ***greaterp:*** It returns true if the arguments passed are successively larger, from left to right ***greaterp(1 2 3)*** will return ***true*** and ***(greaterp 4 1 2)*** will return **false,** i.e., NIL. It can also be written using >sign instead of greaterp.

(f) **>=*:*** It returns true if the arguments passed are successively larger or equal , from left to right (>= *1 1 2 3)* will return ***true*** and *(>= 41 1 2)* will return **false,** i.e., NIL.

(g) ***lessp:*** It returns true if the arguments passed are successively smaller, from left to right ***lessp(21 20 3)*** will return ***true*** and ***(lessp 4 3 21)*** will return **false,** i.e., NIL. It can also be written using < sign instead of greaterp.

(h) *<=:* It returns true if the arguments passed are successively smaller or equal , from left to right *(<= 12 10 10 3)* will return ***true*** and *(<= 41 11 20)* will return **false,** i.e., NIL.

(i) ***equal:*** It returns true if the two arguments passed are equal. For example, ***(equal 'a (car '(a b))*** will return ***T*** and ***(equal 'a (car '(b a b))*** will return **false,** i.e., NIL.

(j) ***null:*** It returns true if the argument passed is an empty list. For example, ***(null nil)*** will return T (true) and ***null('a)*** will return **false**, i.e., NIL.

(k) ***atom:*** It returns true if the argument passed is a valid atom. For example, ***(atom 'aabb)*** will return **true** and ***(atom '(a))*** will return **false,** i.e., NIL.

(l) ***listp:*** It returns true if the argument passes is a valid list. For example, ***(listp '(a))*** will return true and ***(listp 'b)*** will return **false,** i.e., NIL.

Q. What are the various logical functions in LISP?

Ans. Logical functions are like predicate functions which return true (t) or false (nil) or some value. There are three logical functions as explained in Table 11.2:

Table 11.2 Logical Functions in LISP

Logical Function Explanation	Example	Value returned
or takes any number of arguments and evaluate them from left to right. The first argument which evaluates to non-nil is returned else nil is returned.	***(or (member 'e '(a b c) (member 'e '(a e c)))***	(E C)
and takes any number of arguments and evaluate them from left to right. If all the arguments evaluate to non-nil then the value of last argument returned else nil is returned.	***(and(member 'e '(a b c) (member 'e '(a e c))))***	Nil
not takes one argument and returns t if the argument evaluates to nil else nil.	***(not (atom '(a b c))***	T

11.5 VARIABLE DECLARATION

Q. How can we define variables in LISP?

Ans. Variables in LISP are symbolic (non-numeric) atoms. They may be assigned values, i.e., bound to values with the function setq. There is no assignment operator used in LISP. Setq takes two arguments, the first of which must be a variable. It is never evaluated and should not be in quotation marks. The second argument is evaluated (unless in quotation marks) and the result is bound to the first argument. The variable retains this value until a new assignment is made. When the variables are evaluated, they return the last value bound to them. If we try to evaluate an undefined variable, then the error - unbounded variable – is displayed by the interpreter. For example:

```
->(setq a 100)
100                          ; a is bounded with value 100 and same value is returned.
->a
100                          ;displays the value bound to variable a.
->x
Unbounded variable: X        ; no value is bound to variable x.
```

Q. What are the constructs for defining local variables in LISP?

Ans. There are three functions which we can be used for defining local variables whose scope is local, i.e., within a function only.

1. ***local-var:*** Setq function is used to make global assignments to variables. If we need local variables in a function, we can define a function local-var to define local variables.

Example: Consider the variables x and y:

```
->(setq x '(a b c))
(A B C)
->(setq y '(d e f))
(D E F)
->(defun local-var (x)
   (setq y (cons x y)))
LOCAL-VAR
->(local-var 5)
(5 D E F)
->x
(A B C)
->y
(D E F)
->
```

2. ***let:*** let function allows us to create more than one variable in a single function. The format is (let ((var$_1$ val$_1$) (var$_2$ val$_2$)….<s-expressions>) where each var$_i$ is a different variable name and each val$_i$ is evaluated and assigned to corresponding variable and the s-expressions are evaluated in order. The value of last expression evaluated is returned. If no initial value is included with a vari, it is assigned nil.
   Example: To take two local variables and make a list using them:

```
->(let ((x 'a)
        (y 'b))
        (cons x (list y)))
(A B)
->
```

3. ***prog:*** prog executes list s-expressions in sequence and returns nil unless it encounters a function call named return. Prog allows the use of unconditional go statements and labels to identify the go-to transfer locations.
   Example: implementation of member function:

```
->(defun memb(element list1)
    (prog ()
     start
     (cond ((equal element (car list1))(return list1)))
     (setq list1 (cdr list1))
     (go start)))
MEMB
->
```

11.6 PROGRAMMING CONSTRUCTS

Q. Which construct in LISP can be used for permitting branching?

Ans. For branching, cond for if..then..else construct is used. The syntax is given below:

```
(cond (<test1><action1>)
      (<test2> <action2>)
      (<testm> <actionm>))
```

Each (<test$_1$> <action$_1$>), $i = 1 \ldots m$ is called a clause. <test$_i$> indicates the test and <action$_i$> indicates the result. The first clause following the cond is executed by evaluating <test$_1$>. If this evaluates to non-nil, the action1 is evaluated, its value is returned and the remaining clauses are skipped over. If <test$_1$> evaluates to nil, control passes to the second clause without evaluating <action$_1$> and the procedure is repeated. If all tests evaluate to nil, cond returns nil.

Q. Which construct can be used for iteration in LISP?

Ans. do construct can be used to write an iterative program in LISP. The syntax for do is given below:

(do (<var$_1$ val$_1$ ><var-update$_1$>)
    (<var$_2$ val$_2$ > <var-update$_2$>)
    .
    .
    .
    (<test> <return-value>)
    (<s-expressions>))

The val$_i$ are initial values which are all evaluated and then bound to the corresponding variables var$_i$ in parallel. Following each such statement are optional update statements which define how the var$_i$ are to be updated with each iteration. After the variables are updated during an iteration, the test is evaluated and if it returns non-nil, the return-value is evaluated and returned. The s-expressions forming the body of the construct are optional. If present, they are executed each iteration until an exit test condition is encountered.

Example: Write a function in LISP to find factorial of a number:

```
->(defun factorial (n)
(do ((count n (- count 1))
            (product n (* product (- count 1))
((equal 0 count) product)))
FACTORIAL
->(factorial 5)
120
->
```

Q. How can we implement looping in LISP?

Ans. loop function is used for implementing looping in LISP. The syntax is given below:

(loop <s-expressions>) where the s-expressions are evaluated repeatedly until a call to a return is encountered.

Q. How can we implement recursion in LISP?

Ans. A recursive function is one which calls itself successively to reduce a problem to a sequence of similar steps. Recursion requires a stopping condition and a recursive step.

Example: to find the factorial of a number using recursion:

```
->(defun factorial(n)
        (cond ((zerop n) 1)                    ;terminating condition factorial of n is 1
                (t (* n factorial (- n 1))))))  ;recursively call factorial of n-1 and ;
                                                ;multiply with n
FACTORIAL
->(factorial 4)
24
->
```

11.7 INPUT AND OUTPUT

Q. Write various functions which can be used for input in LISP.

Ans. There are various functions used for input and output in LISP. The most commonly used input function is **read**. This function takes no arguments. The read takes as input the s-expression entered from the keyboard by the user.

Example: we are using read in an arithmetic expression to read two values and find their sum.

```
->( + (read) (read))
8                % first value entered by the user
11      % second value entered by the user
19         %value returned by the function
->
```

Q. Write various functions which can be used for output in LISP.

Ans. There are various functions used for output: print ,princ, and prin1. The format of these is given below:

print: It takes one argument and prints the argument and the returns the same argument. The arguments are preceded by the carriage-return and line-feed characters (to start a new line) and are followed by a space.

Example: let us use print function to print a list

```
->(print '(sun mon tue wed thu fri sat))
(SUN MON TUE WED THU FRI SAT)            % prints the list passed
(SUN MON TUE WED THU FRI SAT)            % returns the list passed
->
```

prin1: It is same as print but the new-line characters and space are not provided.

Example: let us use prin1 function to print a list

```
->(prin1 '(sun mon tue wed thu fri sat))
(SUN MON TUE WED THU FRI SAT)(SUN MON TUE WED THU FRI SAT)
->
```

princ:It is same as prin1 except that it does not print the unwanted quotation marks.

princ function to print a string

```
->(prin1 "sun mon tue wed thu fri sat")
SUN MON TUE WED THU FRI SAT "SUN MON TUE WED THU FRI SAT"
->
```

Q. Which functions are used for formatting the output in LISP?

Ans. There are two functions used for formatting the output:

1. Example: let us use *terpri*: It takes no arguments and is used to introduce a newline whenever it appears and then returns nil.
2. Format: It has the format (format <destination><string> arg1 arg2 …). Function *destination* specifies where the output is to be directed (monitor or some external file). *String* is the desired output string, but intermixed with format directives which specify how each argument is to be represented. Directives appear in the string in the same order the arguments are to be printed. Each directive is preceded with a tilde character (~) to identify it as a directive. Common directives are:

   ~A: The argument is printed as if princ function were used

   ~S: The argument is printed as if prin1 function were used

~%: A new line is printed
~C: The argument is printed as character output
~D: The argument which must be an integer is printed as a decimal number
~F: The argument which must be a floating point number is printed as a floating point number
Example: format the output of the program which has x = 3.5 and y = 4.

```
->(format t "X = ~2F~% Y = ~3D" x y)     %~2F indicates the width for floating point is 2.
"X = 3.5
Y = 4"
->
```

11.8 ARRAY HANDLING

Q. How are arrays created in LISP?

Ans. In LISP, a single or multiple dimension array can be defined using **make-array** function. The items stored in the array may be any LISP object. **setf** or **setq** function is used to bind the unquoted name to an array and a specification of the number of cells.

Example:

```
->(setf array1 (make-array '(5)))
#A (NIL NIL NIL NIL NIL)
->
```

Here, the name of the array is array1. The function setf returns the pound sign (#) followed by an A and the array cells are initially set to nil.

Q. How can the array elements be accessed?

Ans. The array elements can be accessed using the function **aref** which takes names of the array and the index value as arguments. The index value for array elements starts from 0.

Example:

```
->(aref array1 3)
NIL
->
```

Q. How can we assign the values to array elements?

Ans. Using setf, the individual array elements can be assigned values. They can take values of any LISP object.

Example:

```
->(setf (aref array1 0) 10)
10
->(setf (aref array1 1) 100)
100
->(setf (aref array1 2) 1)
1
->(setf (aref array1 3) 1000)
1000
->(setf (aref array1 4) '(sun mon tue wed thu fri sat))
(SUN MON TUE WED THU FRI SAT)
->
```

11.9 PROPERTY LISTS

Q. What is a property list and how it is used in LISP?

Ans. Property list is a function used for assigning, retrieving, replacing, or removing some property to atoms as required. For example, the object student is an atom, who can have many properties such as name, marks, and result. Putprop function can be used to assign the values of these properties to the object and change as required. The values can be retrieved using putprop. The values may be any LISP object.

Q. Explain putprop function with example.

Ans. putprop function takes three arguments: an object name, a property pr attribute value, and a property or attribute name and returns the value of the property assigned or retrieved.

Example:

```
->(putprop 'student 'raghav 'name)
RAGHAV
```

Q. How can we read the value of an attribute of an object?

Ans. Using get function which takes two arguments: object name and property or attribute name and returns the value.

Example:

```
->(get 'student 'name)
RAGHAV
->
```

Q. How can we remove the values from some attributes of an object?

Ans. remprop function can be used to remove the values of attributes.

Example:

```
->(remprop 'student 'name)
RAGHAV
->(get 'student 'name)
NIL
->
```

Q. How can we define the function for implementing putprop when it is not supported in Common LISP?

Ans.

```
-> (defun putprop(object value property)
(setf (get object property) value))
PUTPROP
->
```

11.10 INTERNAL STORAGE

Q. How are elements of a list stored in internal memory?

Ans. Lists are flexible data structures which can grow when more elements are there and shrink when the elements are less. This can be implemented using linked list in memory. It can be visualized as storage boxes or cells having two components which corresponding to car (i.e., first elements) of the list and cdr (i.e., tail) of the list. The cells are called cons-cells because they are constructed using the cons (i.e., concatenation) function. The left component pointer in cons-cell points to the first (i.e., car) element of the list and the right component points to the remainder of the list (i.e., cdr). For example, if the list is (a b c). It will be represented as shown in Figure 11.1:

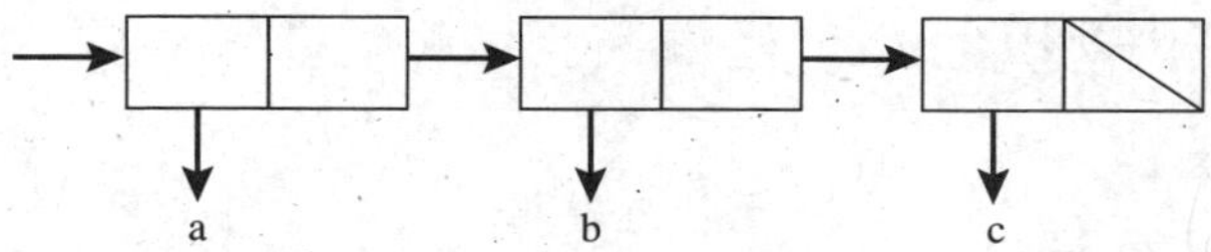

Figure 11.1 Internal representation of list in memory

SOLVED EXAMPLES

Q. Define a function that finds the maximum of two numbers.

Ans.
```
-> (defun max2(a b)
        (cond ((>a b) a)                    ; if a>b return the value of a
                    (t b)))                        ; else return b
MAX2                                               ; function name is returned
->
-> (max2 (15 4))                            ; function call to max2
15
->(max2 (30  400))                          ; function call to max2
400
->
```

Q. Define a function that takes a list as its argument and returns the first top element of the list.

Ans.
```
->(defun top(list1)
     (return car(list1)))
  TOP
  ->(top(1 2 3))
  1.
```

Q. Define a function that finds the maximum of any three numbers.

Ans.
```
-> (defun max3(a b c)
        (cond ((> a b)(cond ((>a c) a)      ; if a>b and a>c then return a
                                  (t c)))          ; else return the value of c
                   ((>b c) b)                ; if a<b and b>c then return b
                   (t c)))                         ; else return c
MAX3                                               ; function name is returned
 -> (max3 23 12 25)
25
```

Q. Define a function called first_element that takes a list as its argument and returns the first top element of the list.

Ans.

```
-> (defun first_element (lst)
         (cond (null lst) nil)
             (t (car (lst)))))
)
FIRST_ELEMENT
->(first_element (12 23 34 45))
12
```

Q. Define a function in LISP which implements union of two lists.

Ans.

```
->(defun union (set1 set2)
   (cond
     ((null set1) set2)
     ((member (car set1) set2)
      (union (cdr set1) set2))
   (t (cons (car set1)
     (union (cdr set1) set2)  )) ) )
UNION.
->(union (1 2 3) (3 4 5))
(1 2 3 4 5)
```

Q. Define a function in Lisp for implementation of list-nth function.

Ans.

```
->(defun list-nth (n L)
        "Return the n'th member of a list L."
        (cond
        ((null L)   nil)
        ((zerop n)  (first L))
        (t        (list-nth (1-n) (cdr L))))).
LIST-NTH
->(list-nth (2 (1 2 3 4)))
3
```

Q. Define a recursive function that implements member function.

Ans. ->(defun newmember (e lst)

```
    (cond ((null lst) nil)
            ((equal e (car lst)) lst)
            ((t (newmember e (cdr lst)))))
NEWMEMBER
->(newmember 5 '(1 3 5 7))
(5 7)
```

Q. What will be the output of the function call (fun2(3,14, 45)) where fun2 is defined below in LISP:

```
-> (defun fun2(a b c)
      (cond ((>a b)(cond ((>a c) a)
   (t c)))
   ((>b c) b)
(t c)))
```

Ans. 45

Q. Write a mapcar function to multiply each element of the given list of elements by 10.

Ans.
```
->(mapcar '10* '(1 2 3))
(10 20 30)
->
```

Q. Write a lambda function to find the square of a number.

Ans. (lambda (n)(* n n)).

Q. Define a function in LISP which finds the square of all the elements of a list of integers.

Ans. This can be done using mapcar function.

```
->(defun sqlist(list1)
(mapcar # '(lambda (n)(*n n)) list1))
SQLIST
->(sqlist (10 15 25))
(100 225 625).
->
```

MULTIPLE CHOICE QUESTIONS

Select the appropriate answer to the questions:

1. Which of the following construct in LISP allows us to create multiple variables:
   (a) setq (b) cond
   (c) let (d) All of these
2. Which of the following function can be used to change the value of an attribute in a list?
   (a) get (b) putprop
   (c) remprop (d) None of these
3. What will be value returned by the predicate (atom '(a b c))?
   (a) A (b) B
   (c) C (d) None of these
4. Which of the following when evaluated will return the same value?
   (a) 47 (b) t
   (c) Nil (d) All of these

5. What will be the value returned by the function member(b '(a a b b c b))?
   (a) (B B C B) (b) (B C B)
   (c) (B) (d) None of these
6. Which construct can be used to write an iterative program in LISP?
   (a) loop (b) do
   (c) defun (d) All of these
7. What value will be returned by the function (or (member 'e '(a b e)) (member 'e '(a e c)))?
   (a) (E) (b) (E C)
   (c) T (d) None of these
8. What value will be returned by the function: (reverse '((a b) (b c) d))?
   (a) (D C B B A) (b) (D (C B) (B A))
   (c) (D (B C) (A B)) (d) None of these
9. What value will be returned by the function: (lessp 15 4 3 20)?
   (a) (15 4 3) (b) T
   (c) Nil (d) None of these
10. What value will be returned by the function: (list 'a '(b c) e)?
   (a) (A B C E) (b) (A (B C) E)
   (c) (A E (B C)) (d) None of these

Answers. 1. c 2. b 3. d 4. d 5. a 6. b 7. a 8. c 9. c 10. b

EXERCISES

1. What will be the output of the function call (and (member 'e '(a b c) (member 'e '(a e c))))?
2. Which function of LISP is implemented by the following:

```
->(defun fun1(element list1)
  (prog ()
   start
   (cond ((equal element (car list1))(return list1)))
   (setq list1 (cdr list1))
   (go start)))
```

3. What will be the output of the function call (≥ 4 5 15 6)?

Q. Define functions in LISP to do the following:

1. A function that finds the largest of given five numbers
2. A function that takes two arguments, any atom and a list and return the list with the first argument appended in it as the last element.
3. A function that finds and prints the number of top elements in a given list passed as an argument.
4. A function that represents an object student with properties name, age, and course. It should be able to read and display the values from the property list.

12

Prolog Programming

12.1 INTRODUCTION

Logic programming is a declarative approach of writing computer programs based on logic. PROLOG stands for PROgramming in LOGic. The program in Logic represents facts about the real world objects like constants represented as functors and numbers and compounded structures like lists and trees. A program in PROLOG consists of various Horn clauses. A Horn clause follows the rules of first-order predicate logic. The proof of any goals is done using backtracking. An select linear definite (SLD) tree is generated during proof generation of the queries. There are two types of queries in PROLOG. A ground query which results in true or false answer. For ground query, a proof tree is generated. A non-ground query results in finding solution to one or more variables. For this type of query, a search tree is generated. The PROLOG interpreter is using stack implementation for finding solutions to the queries. There is an in-built predicate cut (!) which is used to prune backtracking. This helps in reducing the number of branches to be explored for finding the solution to a query. The in-built predicate fail is used to represent the failure and is mainly used for representing the negative aspects of any sentence.

12.2 LOGIC PROGRAM

Q. What is a logic program?

Ans. A logic program is a finite sequence of program clauses. A program clause is of the form $A \leftarrow B_1, B_2, \ldots, B_n$ that contains precisely one positive literal. It is also called as conditional rule. In a program clause, A is called Head and $B_1, B_2, \ldots, B_n$ is called body of the rule. The semantics of the program clause in logic is that "for all interpretations, if $B_1 \land B_2 \land \ldots \land B_n$ is true, then A is true".

12.3 SYNTAX OF PROLOG PROGRAM

12.3.1 Horn clause

Q. What is a Horn clause?

Ans. A Prolog program is based on Horn clause. A clause is represented as:

A: $-B_1, B_2, \ldots B_n$.

Here, A is the positive atom and $B_1, B_2, \ldots, B_n$ are negative atoms. The clause is interpreted as "A is true if B_1, $B_2, \ldots,$and B_n" are simultaneously true. A fact is always true and is represented by A. :-$B_1, B_2, \ldots B_n$. means a conjunctive query "if B_1, B_2, …, and B_n are true, what is the consequent?" All B_1, B_2 …, and B_n are sub-goals.

12.3.2 Constants, Variables, String, Function, Predicate, and Operators

Q. Describe the syntax of Prolog program.

Ans. A Prolog program consists of a set of Horn clauses. Each Horn clause is terminated by a full stop(.).

Q. How are constants used in Prolog?

Ans. Constants are numerals and symbols such as 56, raghav, etc. These are either number or name starting with small case letter.

Q. How are variables used in prolog?

Ans. Variables are names formed by using lower case letters, numerals, and underscore (_), but it must start with upper case letter. Normally we use capital letters like X, Y, Z, etc. For variables, other examples may be Name, Value, etc.

Q. How do we use string in prolog?

Ans. String is a string of characters and is enclosed within single quotes, for example, "this is a string".

Q. How is function or predicate name represented in prolog?

Ans. Function or predicate names are formed using lower case letters, numerals, and underscore (_), but must start with lower case alphabet. For example, likes, father, etc.

Q. How an assignment is made in Prolog?

Ans. An arithmetic assignment is done by writing the goal "X is Expression" and is performed by first evaluating the Expression and then unifying the left-hand side variable X. All variables on the right-hand side of predicate '**is**' must be known at the time of execution otherwise the assignment will fail.

Q. Explain various operators available in Prolog.

Ans. Arithmetic operators: In Prolog various arithmetic operators used are:

X+Y, X-Y, X*Y, X/Y, X mod Y with usual meanings in arithmetic.

Relational operators: In Prolog various relational operators used are given below. Here, the values of X and Y are compared and the goals succeed or fail as described below:

X < Y succeeds if X is less than Y

X > Y succeeds if X is greater than Y

X =< Y succeeds if X is less than or equal to Y

X >= Y succeeds if X is greater than or equal to Y

X = Y (X equals to Y) succeeds if the terms X and Y match. This is called Equality operator.

X \= Y (X is not equal to Y) succeeds if X = Y fails, otherwise it fails. This is called Non-equality operator.

Q. Explain how to define a user defined operator in Prolog.

Ans. Prolog provides facility for defining new operator (symbol or name) which is recognized by interpreter with the help of built –in predicate named '**op**'. Operator definition must be given in the beginning of the program. The general format of operator definition is:

:-op(P,S,O), where P, S and O are variables and have the following meanings:

P- precedence class, an integer value within range [1,1200]
O- symbol or name representing an operator to be defined
S- specification representing associativity by special atoms given below:

Prefix operator	Postfix operator	Infix operator
The operator f comes before the argument {fx, fy} 'x' and 'y' represent arguments. The choice of 'x' and 'y' in the positions mentioned above convey associativity information: 'x' means that the operator '0' in the argument must have strictly lower precedence value than that of operator 'f'. 'y' means that the operator '0' in the argument must have same or lower precedence value than the operator 'f'. fx- non associative (prefix) fy – right associative (prefix)	The operator f comes after the argument {xf, yf} 'x' and 'y' represent arguments. The choice of 'x' and 'y' in the positions mentioned above convey associativity information: 'x' means that the operator '0' in the argument must have strictly lower precedence value than that of operator 'f'. 'y' means that the operator '0' in the argument must have same or lower precedence value than the operator 'f'. xf- non associative (postfix) yf – left associative (postfix)	The operator f comes in between the arguments For infix operators, possible values of specification s are: xfx : non associative xfy : right associative yfx : left associative

12.4 UNIFICATION OF GOALS

Q. How does unification of goals take place in Prolog?

Ans. According to equality theory, X equals Y if X is an unbound variable or Y is an unbound variable or X and Y are (bound to) the same constant or X and Y are terms with the same functor and arity.

Example: X is *term*(V1, …,V*n*) and Y is *term*(U1, …,U*n*) and for all arguments 1 =< *i* =< *n*: V*i* equals U*i*.

A substitution is a function *Subst: Var -> Term.* Substitutions can be applied to terms or substitutions and also to formulas. A substitution may be represented as a conjunction of simple equalities x = t where a variable x occurs on the left-hand side at most once or as a set {x/t | x = t} meaning a function that replaces x with t for each x/t in the set.

A unifier is a substitution s such that *s*s ° *t*s, i.e., applying s to *s* and to t creates identical terms. A unifier s is more general than a unifier d if there exists another unifier w such that s w ° d.

A unifier s is the most general unifier of two terms if s is more general than any other unifier of the two terms.

Example: t(X,Y,Z) and t(U,V,W) are unified by {X/a,Y/b,Z/c, U/a,V/b,W/c}. The mgus in this case are {X/U,Y/V,Z/W} and {U/X,V/Y,W/Z}.

An algorithm that constructs most general unifiers for two terms in an environment is a *unification procedure*. As the most general unifier is unique (modulo renaming of variables), unification can also be understood as a function *unify: Subst x Term x Term -> Subst*

12.5 SLD RESOLUTION

Q. How SLD resolution is done in Prolog?

Ans. SLD resolution is an inference mechanism which is defined as:

<- A1,...,A(i-1),Ai,A(i+1),...,Am B0 <- B1,...,Bn
<- (A1,...,A(i-1),B1,...,Bn,A(i+1),...,Am) σ

Where *P* is a program, A1,…., A*m* are atomic formulas (goals), B0 <- B1,…., B*n* is a (renamed) clause in *P* and unifier function σ = mgu(A*i*,B0).

It involves unification. An SLD derivation of goal *G*0 (using *P* and <) is a finite or infinite sequence of goals: g0->g1->g2…->gn ….

SLD-refutation: a finite derivation of the goal g0

Failed derivation: a derivation of the goal g0 with the last element that is not empty and cannot be resolved by any clause of the program.

A goal selection function specifies which goal A*i* is selected by the SLD rule. The order in which clauses are chosen is determined with a clause selection rule.

12.5.1 SLD Tree

Q. How is an SLD tree drawn in Prolog?

Ans. To draw an SLD tree, the goal is root of the tree. All the possible rules whose left-hand side match with the goal become the children of the root node. The interaction between the sub-goals is indicated by the OR or AND arcs. An OR arc indicates more than one answers of all of the OR arcs give a solution. An AND arc implies all the sub-goals must be solved to get the answer to the goal. This process is repeated at each level with each of the sub-goals till either all solutions are found or there are no more rules possible to be applied. The solution is indicated by an empty child.

12.6 SCENE INTERPRETATION AND FLOW OF SATISFACTION

12.6.1 Scene interpretation

Q. Explain how a scene is interpreted using a PROLOG program?

Ans. In a PROLOG program for scene interpretation, three things need to be specified for the current scene. These are

- objects in the domain specified as predicates
- the domains of all possible values which the objects can take (variables are indicated as capital letters or words starting with capital letter, constants are indicated as words with small letters)
- the clauses indicating the relations between the objects

Example: Consider the given scene at school where a student plays guitar sitting on a chair.

- ***Domains in this database are:***

  S, O, X, Place, sumita, guitar, school, chair

- ***Predicates in this database are:***

  Student (S)
  Plays (S, guitar, Place)
  Equal (Place, school)
  Sits-on (S, chair, Place)
  Person(1).

- ***Clauses in this database are:***

  Object (guitar). 1
  Plays (sumita, guitar, school). 2
  Sits-on (sumita, chair, school). 3

Person (sumita). 4
Equal (Place, school). 5
Student(X):- Person(X), Plays(X, guitar, Place), Equal (Place, school), Object (guitar).6

In a PROLOG program, only the facts in the program are written and no procedure to solve the problem of scene interpretation is given. Now, suppose, the user makes a query:

(i) Who plays guitar at school?
Goal: Plays(X, guitar, school)?
System prompts: Plays(sumita, guitar,school).
This flow of satisfaction is illustrated using backtracking. It is matched with clause 2 and variable X is equated with the value sumita.

(ii) Is the place playground?
Goal: Equal (Place, playground) ?
System prompts: No.
The predicate is directly matched with predicate Equal(Place, school) and constant school does not match with constant playground.

(iii) Who is the student?
Goal: Student(X).
System prompts: sumita
This flow is satisfied using backtracking for clause 6. X is matched with sumita and Plays(sumita, guitar, Place) is true. Then Equal (Place, school) matches with Plays (sumita, guitar, school). Lastly Object (guitar) is also true. Hence the answer is X = sumita.

12.6.2 Flow of Satisfaction Program (flow of satisfaction diagram)

Q. What is flow of satisfaction diagram?

Ans. Flow of satisfaction diagrams are used to illustrate how backtracking is done in finding the solutions in scene interpretation:

Let us now concentrate on the query: Student (S)?

Since Student (S) □ Person (S), Plays (S, guitar, school). To satisfy the Goal: Student (S), one has to satisfy the sub-goals: Person (S), Plays (S, guitar, school). Now, PROLOG searches a sub-goal Person ( ) for the predicate Person (X). At clause 4, it fi nds a match and X is instantiated to Sumita. PROLOG puts a marker at clause 4. Now, it continues searching Plays (Sumita, guitar, school) in the remaining clauses. But it fails to fi nd so, as Plays (S, guitar, school) is at 2nd position in the list of clauses. So, it has to trace back above the marker place and then ultimately it fi nds Plays (S, guitar, school). As the sub-goals are succeeded, the goal also succeeds, yielding a solution: Student (sumita). This is represented using figure 12.1 given below:

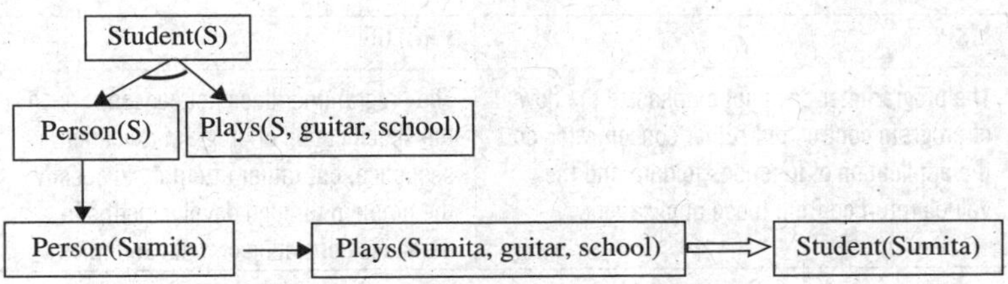

Figure 12.1 Diagram for flow of satisfaction program

12.7 ITERATION

Q. Explain how to do iterative programming in Prolog?

Ans. To implement iterative algorithm, one requires the storage of intermediate results, Prolog predicates are augmented with additional arguments called accumulators. These are similar to local variables in procedural languages. A Prolog program is iterative if it contains only unit clauses and iterative clauses. Recursive call, if any, should be the last call.

Example: To find factorial of a number *N* and store it in a variable *F*.

factorial(N, F):- fact(N,F,0,1). (1)
*fact(N,F,I,Temp):- I<N, J is I+1, Temp1 is J*t, fact(N,F,J,Temp1).* (2)
fact(N,F,N,F). (3)

Here, *N* is the input variable, *F* is output variable, *I*, *J*, Temp, and Temp1 are accumulators for storing intermediate values.

12.8 RECURSION

Q. Explain how to do recursive Programming in Prolog?

Ans. Recursion is one of the most important execution control techniques in Prolog. When the same function calls itself with different arguments, it is called a recursive function. To write a recursive function, one must give terminating condition and a general recursive rule.

Q. What is the use of cut predicate in Prolog?

Ans. Prolog is non-terminating in nature due to backtracking. Cut predicate is used for pruning the backtracking. It is represented as !. The advantages of using Cut predicate is that program using cut operates faster because it does not waste time in satisfying those sub-goals which will never contribute to the solutions. Program may occupy less of memory space because search tree is cut down and does not generate redundant branches.

Q. Explain the use of Cut predicate with an example.

And. Consider the following program:
goal(a):-!. (1)
goal(b). (2)
goal(X):- f(X). (3)
Answer the query ?- goal(X).

There are three rules which match the goal query. The rule order matters and the first rule is matched which succeeds by generating an empty clause and unifying the variable X with value a (Figure 12.2). Table for difference between LISP and PROLOG

LISP	PROLOG
The programmer does not emphasize the flow of program control, but rather concentrates on the application of functions to data and the values returned from these applications	The programmer does not concentrate on the specification of program execution sequence, but rather attempts to specify the problem through development of a database consisting of facts and rules

12.9 OBJECTS

Q. Explain how can we represent objects in Prolog?

Ans. Object is a collection of attributes. All the related information about an object is to be represented together. In Prolog, we can define predicates for describing any object and its attributes. One predicate may be nested in other predicate also.

Example: address (House_number, City, Zipcode, Country) represents the predicate which represents the address with attributes House_number, City, Zipcode, and Country. This can be nested in representing another object person which is defined by the predicate person (Name, Age, address (House_number, City, Zipcode, Country), Hobbies).

12.10 CONTROLLING BACKTRACKING USING CUT

12.10.1 Command Use of CUT

Q. What is the use of cut predicate in Prolog?

Ans. Prolog is non-terminating in nature due to backtracking. Cut predicate is used for pruning the backtracking. It is represented as !. The advantages of using Cut predicate is that program using cut operates faster because it does not waste time in satisfying those sub-goals which will never contribute to the solutions. Program may occupy less of memory space because search tree is cut down and does not generate redundant branches.

Q. Explain the use of Cut predicate with an example.

Ans. Consider the following program:

goal(a):-!. (1)
goal(b). (2)
goal(X):- f(X). (3)
Answer the query ?- goal(X).

There are three rules which match the goal query. The rule order matters and the first rule is matched which succeeds by generating an empty clause and unifying the variable X with value a (Figure 12.2).

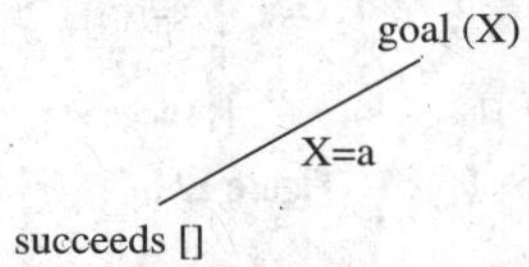

Figure 12.2

As rule 1 has cut predicate and goal(a) has succeeded, so rest of the matching rules are pruned. The program answer only one answer as X = a.

Example: Consider the following program for calculating the factorial of a number using recursion.

fact(0,1). *(1)*
*fact(N,F):- N1 is N-1, fact(N1, F1), F is F1*N.* *(2)*

This program is non-terminating. To prune backtracking, cut predicate is used in first clause.

fact(0,1):-!.

12.10.2 Implementation of Backtracking Using Stack

Q. How does backtracking takes place using stack?

Ans. Consider the following program:

goal(a). (1)
goal(b). (2)
goal(X):- f(X). (3)

Answer the query? - goal(X).

Ans. There are three rules which match the goal query. The rule order matters and the first rule is matched which succeeds by generating an empty clause and unifying the variable X with value a (Figure 12.3).

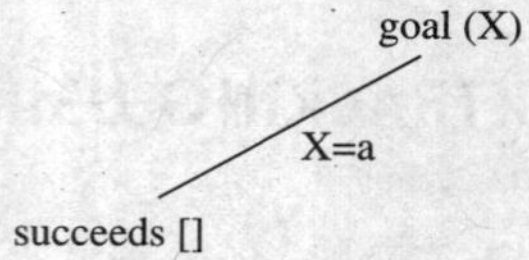

Figure 12.3

On backtracking, the goal(X) is matched with rule no. 2. This also succeeds by generating an empty clause and unifying the variable X with value b (Figure 12.4).

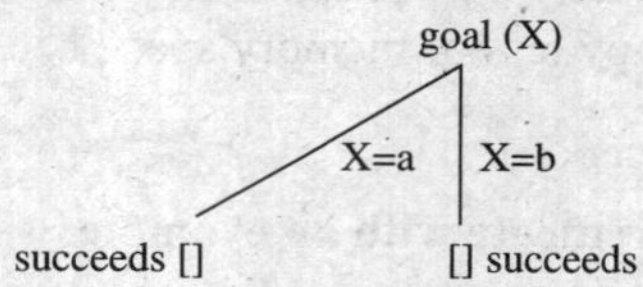

Figure 12.4

On backtracking again, the goal(X) is matched with rule no. 3 generating a sub-goal f(X). Now, the subgoal f(X) is to be solved, but it fails because there is no value with which X can be unified. So the answers using backtracking are X = {a,b} (Figure 12.5)

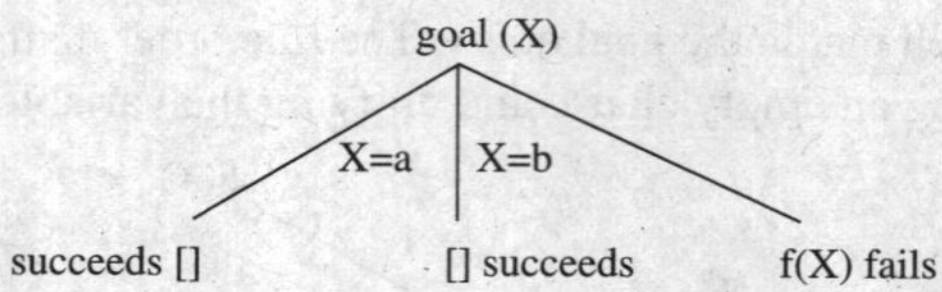

Figure 12.5

12.10.3 Risk of Using CUT

Q. What is the risk of using CUT?

Ans. A cut predicate improves the efficiency of a program but it makes it difficult to prove the correctness of concepts. Cut should be used only when it cannot be avoided. It should not be added in an unknown large program. The cut predicate can make programs wrong if predicates are called with unexpected binding patterns. Example: The predicate for the absolute value can also be written as follows:

abs(X,X):- X > = 0,!. *(1)*
abs(X,Y):-Y is –X. *(2)*

As the second rule is executed only when the first rule is not applicable, it might seem that the test X = < 0 used earlier is superfluous.

abs(3,-3). The cut must be exactly at the point where it is clear that this is the right rule.

12.10.4 Types of CUT

Q. Explain the types of cut predicate in PROLOG.

Ans. There are two types of cut predicates in PROLOG.

(a) Green cut: Green cut does not affect the solution but affects the efficiency of the Prolog program. Removal of green cut does not change the meaning of the program.

Example of green cut: A program to find minimum of given two numbers.

minimum (A,B,Min):- A =< B, !, Min is A. ***(1)***
minimum (A,B,B):- A > B. ***(2)***

Here, if cut is removed from rule (1), we get the same answer in all cases.

(b) Red cut: Red cut is that cut which if removed from the program changes the meaning of the program.

Example of red cut: A program to find minimum of given two numbers.

minimum (A,B,Min):- A =< B, !, Min is A. ***(1)***
minimum (A,B,B). ***(2)***

Here, if cut is removed from rule (1), we get wrong answer in case A < B.

12.11 FAIL PREDICATE

Q. What is the use of fail predicate in prolog?

Ans. The built-in predicate *fail* is used to make the clause in which it appears fail explicitly. It is used to represent the negation. Predicate fail tells Prolog interpreter to fail a particular goal and subsequently forces backtracking. All the sub-goals defined after fail will never be executed. So, it should be the last predicate in a rule. For example, if the sentence is "John does not like pasta" can be represented using fail predicate as:

like(john, pasta):-fail.

12.12 Application of Cut-fail Combination

Q. Give an application of cut–fail combination.

Ans. If cut is used in conjunction with fail predicate and of control reaches fail in the body of a rule after crossing cut, then the rule fails and no solution is displayed. The cut–fail combination is a technique that allows early failure. Consider the following definitions of the rules using cut and fail combination:

G:- A, !, fail. ***(1)***
G:- B. ***(2)***

Query: ?- G.

If A succeeds, then rule (1) fails and rule (2) will not be tried. If A fails, then rule (2) will be tried on backtracking.

Q. Give an example to show how we can replace cut–fail by not.

Ans. One application of cut–fail combination is implementation of negation as failure.

Consider the implementation of logical operator not.

```
not(Goal):- Goal, !, fail.      (1)
not(Goal).                      (2)
```

Here, if Goal is true, then clause (1) will make it return false and use of cut will prune the use of clause (2). If Goal is false, then cut is not crossed and fail is also not executed and hence on backtracking clause (2) will return true.

?- not(4>3).
(1)↓4>3 is True,!, fail
Returns fail, i.e., No.

12.13 LISTS

Q. Discuss list manipulation in Prolog.

Ans. A list is a common and very useful recursive data structure in non-numeric programming. It is an ordered sequence of elements that can have variable length. The first element of the list is called head and the remaining list is called tail. Processing of a list is always done sequentially by inspecting head of the list. In Prolog, the list is represented by elements separated by commas and enclosed in square brackets. For example: A = [1,3,56,78]. The list element may be a sub-list also. For example: B = [1,2, [4,5], 7]. The empty list is represented by [ ] and is useful for terminating recursive programs for list.

Recursive definition of a list:

```
list([ ]).                   (1)    %and empty list is a list
list([H|T]): - list (T).     (2)    %the list is a list if tail T is also a list.
```

12.14 DISTINCTION BETWEEN LISP AND PROLOG

In LISP, the programmer does not emphasize the flow of program control, but rather concentrates on the application of functions to data and the values returned from these applications. In PROLOG, the programmer does not concentrate on the specification of program execution sequence, but rather attempts to specify the problem through development of a database consisting of facts and rules.

SOLVED EXAMPLES

Q. Write a program in Prolog to check whether the two numbers are equal or not.

Ans. The program takes two arguments, the numbers and return TRUE or FALSE.

```
equal(X,Y):- X = Y.
```

Q. Write a program in Prolog to find the length of a given list.

Ans. The program takes two arguments, first a list and then the variable to hold the length of the list.

```
len([],0).                                (1)
len([H|T], L):- len(T,L1), L is L1+1.     (2)
```

Q. Write a program in Prolog to find the sum of all the elements of a given list.

Ans. The program takes two arguments, first a list and then the variable to hold the sum of the list.

```
sum_list([],0).                                    (1)
sum_list([H|T], S):- sum_list (T,S1), S is S1+H.   (2)
```

Q. Write a program in Prolog to add the contents of one list at the end of the second list.

Ans. The program takes three arguments, first and second as given lists and then the variable to hold the concatenation of the two lists.

append(L,[],L). (1)
append([],L,L). (2)
append(L1, [H2|T2], [H2|T3]):- append(L1, T2, T3). (3)

Q. Write a Prolog program to reverse a list.

Ans. The program takes three arguments; first two are the lists to be appended and third is a list to store the resultant list.

append([],L,L). (1)
append(L,[],L). (2)
append([H1|T1],L2,[H|L3]):-append(T1,L2,L3). (3)
rev([],[]). (4)
rev([H|T],R):- rev(T,T1),append(T1,H,R). (5)

Q. Write a program to find the sum of all the elements of the list passed as argument.

Ans. The program takes two arguments, first is the list and second is the variable to store the sum of all the elements.

sum_list([],0). (1)
sum_list([X],X). (2)
*sum_list([H|T],S):- sum_list(T,S1), S is H*S1.* (3)

Q. Write a program in Prolog to check if a given number is a member of the list, i.e., whether it is present in the given list or not.

Ans. The program takes two arguments, first the element or the number to be searched in a given list and second is the list. It returns true or false depending upon whether the number is present in the list or not. The logic is implemented using recursion. If the number is the same as the head of the list, it is present in the list; else if it is a member of its tail, it is a member.

member(N,[N|T]). (1)
member(N,[H|T]):- member(N,T). (2)

Q. Represent a binary tree in Prolog.

Ans. Binary tree is an example of recursive data type and can be implemented as a list. It has three components or sections to be specified: the value of the root of the tree; the left sub-tree which is again a binary tree; and A right sub-tree which is also a binary tree. Due to this symmetry, it can be represented as the ternary functor in Prolog:

binary_tree(Value, Left_subtree, Right_subtree).

The Value of the tree indicates the root value of every sub-binary tree. The Left_subtree and Right_subtree are again represented in a similar manner.

The binary tree in Figure 12.6 will be represented as follows:

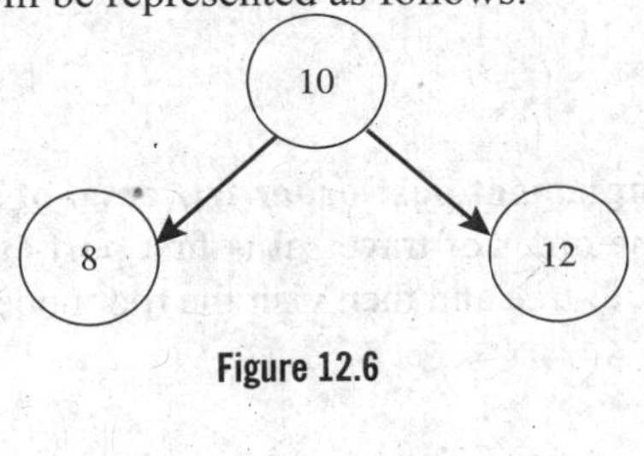

Figure 12.6

binary_tree(10, binary_tree(8,void,void), binary_tree(12,void, void)).
The atom void indicates the branch of the binary tree as empty or NULL.

Q. Write a program to implement pre-order, post-order, and in-order traversal of a binary search tree.

Ans. The traversals of a binary tree can be done using recursion.

(i) Pre-order traversal: The order of traversal is first visit root node, then pre-order traversal of left sub-tree and then pre-order traversal of the right sub-tree.
pre(void, []). *(1)*
pre(binary_tree(Root, Left, Right), PRE):- pre(Left, L1), pre(Right, R1), append([Root|L1], R1, PRE). *(2)*

Example: Do pre-order traversal of binary tree (Figure 12.7):

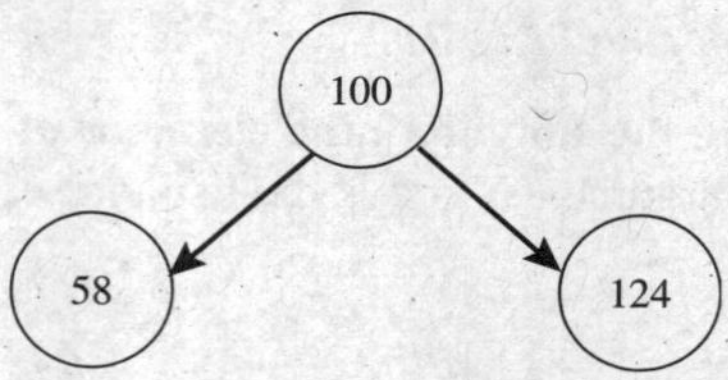

Figure 12.7

?- pre(binary_tree(100, binary_tree(58,void,void),binary_tree(124,void,void)), PRE).

(ii) ↓ {Root = 100, Left = binary_tree(58,void,void),
Right = binary_tree(124,void,void)}

?- pre(binary_tree(58,void,void), L1), pre(binary_tree(124,void,void), R1), append([100|L1],R1,PRE]).

(2) ↓ {Root = 58, Left = void, Right, void}

?- pre([],L2), pre([], R2), append([58|L2],R2,L1), pre(binary_tree(124,void,void), R1), append([100|L1],R1,PRE]).

(1) ↓ {L2 = [], R2 = [], L1 = [58]}

?- pre(binary_tree(124,void,void), R1), append([100|58],R1,PRE]).

(2) ↓ {Root = 124, Left = void, Right, void}

?- pre([],L3), pre([], R3), append([124|L3],R3, R1), append([100,58],R1,PRE]).

(1) ↓ {L3 = [], R3 = [], R1 = [124]}

?- append([100, 58], 124, PRE).

↓PRE = [100,58,124].

Succeeds.

Ans. PRE = [100,58,124].

Q. Write a program to implement post-order traversal of a binary search tree.

Ans. Post-order traversal: The order of traversal is first post-order traversal of left sub-tree. Then post-order traversal of the right sub-tree and then visit the root node of the tree.

post(void, []). *(1)*

post(binary_tree(Root, Left, Right), POST):- post(Left, L1), post(Right, R1), append(R1,[Root], P1), append(L1,P1,POST). (2)

Q. Write a program to implement in-order traversal of a binary search tree.

Ans. In in-order traversal, the order of traversal is first in-order traversal of left sub-tree. Then visit the Root node and then in-order traversal of the right sub-tree.

```
in(void, []).                                                        (1)
in(binary_tree(Root, Left, Right), IN):- in(Left, L1), in(Right, R1),
append(L1,[Root|R1], IN).                                            (2)
```

Q. Write a program to count the number of nodes in a tree.

Ans. The number of nods in a tree can be counted using recursion. It will be given as the number of nodes in left sub-tree + number of nodes in right sub-tree + 1 for root node.

```
count(void, 0).                                                           (1)
count(t(N, L, R),N):- count(L, N1), count(R, N2), N is N1 + N2 + 1.       (2)
```

Q. Write a program to implement if-then-else in Prolog.

Ans. The program takes three arguments. First is the condition hat is to be evaluated. Second is the expression that needs to be executed if the condition is true and third is the expression that is to be evaluated if the condition is false.

```
if_then_else(Cond, T, F):- Cond, !, T.        (1)
if_then_else (Cond, T, F):-F.                 (2)
```

Q. Write a program in PROLOG to implement quick sort.

Ans. The quick sort can be implemented using recursion:

```
qsort([], []).                                                             (1)
qsort([X|Xs], Ys) :-  partition(Xs, X, Littles, Bigs), qsort(Littles, Ls),
                      qsort(Bigs, Bs), append(Ls, [X|Bs], Ys).             (2)
partition([], _, [], []).                                                  (3)
partition([Y|Ys], X, [Y|Ls], Bs) :- X > Y, partition(X, Ys, Ls, Bs).  (4)
partition([Y|Ys], X, Ls, [Y|Bs]) :- X =< Y, partition(X, Ys, Ls, Bs).      (5)
```

Q. Consider the following PROLOG program:

```
not(P):- call(P), !, fail.
not(P).
man(amitabh).
man(abhishek).
wife(amitabh, jaya).
bachelor(X):- man(X), not (wife(X,Y)).
```

What will be the output of the query: bachelor(X).

Ans. X = abhishek.

Q. Consider the following database: Amit eats banana. Amit likes apple. Rahul likes apple. A person likes a food if he eats it. A person likes somebody if that person also likes the same food. Draw SLD tree to find what does Amit like?

Ans. The given facts and rules are presented in PROLOG as Horn clause as follows:

```
eats(amit,banana).          (1)
likes(amit,apple).          (2)
```

likes(rahul,apple). *(3)*
likes(Person,Food):- eats(Person, Food). *(4)*
likes(Person,Somebody):- likes(Person, Food), likes(Somebody, Food). *(5)*

The goal is?- likes(amit, X).

The answer to the query is X = apple and X = rahul using backtracking. The SLD tree is shown in Figure 12.8:

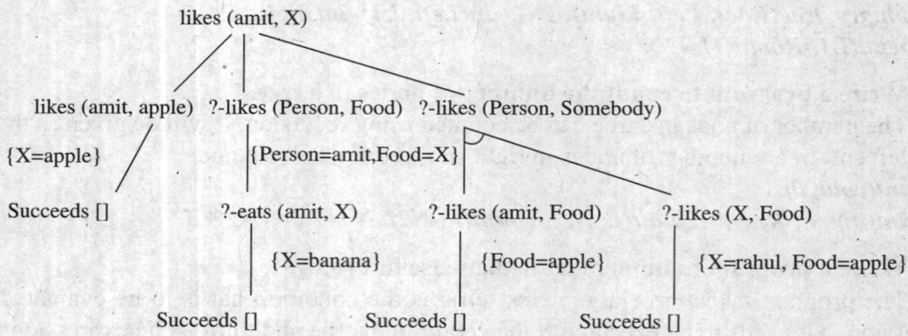

Figure 12.8

MULTIPLE CHOICE QUESTIONS

1. Consider the following Prolog program:

```
not(G):- G,!, fail.                          (1)
not(G).                                      (2)
illiterate(X):- person(X), not(literate(X)). (3)
person(raju).                                (4)
person(juhi).                                (5)
literate(juhi).                              (6)
```

   What will be the output of the query? –illiterate(raju).

   (a) True (b) False
   (c) raju (d) None of these

2. Consider the following Prolog program in Question 1:

   What will be the output of the query? –illiterate(X).

   (a) X = raju, juhi (b) X = juhi
   (c) X = raju (d) None of these

3. Consider the following Prolog program:

```
person(X):- man(X),!.     (1)
person(X):- woman(X).     (2)
man(mohit).               (3)
man(shobhit).             (4)
woman(shalu).             (5)
```

woman(sangeeta). (6)

What will be the output of the query? –person(P).

(a) P = mohit, shobhit, shalu, sangeeta (b) P = mohit, shobhit
(c) P = mohit (d) None of these

4. Fail should be the last predicate in any Horn clause.

(a) TRUE (b) FALSE

5. Which of the predicate is used for pruning backtracking in PROLOG?

(a) stop (b) cut
(c) fail (d) All of these

6. Which of the predicate is used for making a clause return false?

(a) stop (b) fail
(c) cut (d) All of these

7. Which of the following is the right associative specification for user-defined infix operators in Prolog?

(a) xfx (b) xfy
(c) yfx (d) All of these

8. Which of the following is the non-associative specification for user-defined infix operators in PROLOG?

(a) xfx (b) xfy
(c) yfx (d) All of these

9. Which of the following is similar to local variables in PROLOG?

(a) Predicates (b) Accumulators
(c) Functions (d) None of these

10. What will be the output of the following program in PROLOG?

Factorial(0,1).
Factorial(N,F):- N1 is N-1, factorial (N1, F1), F is N*F1.
?-factorial(5).

(a) 120 (b) 1200
(c) Infinite loop (d) None of these

Answers. 1. a 2. c 3. c 4. a 5. b 6. b 7. b 8. a 9. b 10. c

EXERCISES

1. Write a program in Prolog to delete an element from a given list.
2. Write a program in Prolog to concatenate two lists represented in the form of difference lists.
3. Write a program in Prolog to insert a given element in the beginning of a given list.
4. Write a program in Prolog to merge two ordered lists.
5. Write a program in Prolog to check whether a given number is present in a given binary tree or not.

6. Write a program in Prolog to find the sum of first *N* natural numbers using recursion.
7. Write a program in Prolog to check if the given number is in a given valid range or not.
8. Consider the following program in Prolog:

   display(Name, Department): - employee(Name, Department).
   Employee(smith, computer).
   Employee(saurabh, electrical).
   Employee(saraansh, civil).
   What will be the output of the following query?- display(Name, Department).
9. Consider the following program in Prolog:

   likes(joe, fish).
   likes(joe, mary).
   likes(mary, book).
   likes(john, book).
   What will be the output of the following query?- likes(joe, money).
10. Consider the following program:

    top(X, Y):- p(X, Y).
    top(X, X) :- s(X).
    p(X, Y) :- true(1), q(X), true(2), r(Y).
    p(X, Y) :- s(X), r(Y).
    q(a).q(b).r(c).r(d).s(e).
    true(X).
    What will the answer to the query?- top(X, Y). Draw the SLD tree.
11. Consider the program given which creates a small set of facts and rules on who is the ancestor of whom.

    ancestor(A, X) :- parent(A, X).
    ancestor(A, X) :- parent(A, C), ancestor(C, X).
    ancestor(bobby, suman).
    parent(fantom, sandy).
    parent(katrina, sandy).
    parent(sandy, diane)
    parent(sam, bill).
    What will be the output of the following queries after program?
    (a) ancestor(fantom, sally).
    (b) ancestor(katrina, diane).

13

Intelligent Agents

13.1 INTRODUCTION

An intelligent agent is an AI system that is capable of doing an intelligent task. It is capable of performing tasks on behalf of a business process, a software application, or an intelligent human being. For this, it needs to incorporate the knowledge which is stored in a knowledge database. It should be able to take the queries or tasks as input from the environment which is done with the help of sensors. The effectors are used to get the output from the intelligent agent. An intelligent agent has many capabilities as that of an intelligent human being. It is capable of drawing inferences and reasoning to intercept the perceptions. It is capable of selecting the rules for solving a given problem. Also, the communication with environment and other agents is an integral part of an intelligent agent. An intelligent agent if can think rationally like a human is called a rational agent while an agent who is executing a set of programs like automatic mail search program is called a software agent.

13.2 AI INTELLIGENT AGENTS

Q. What is an intelligent agent?

Ans. Intelligent agents execute tasks on behalf of a business process, computer application, or an intelligent individual. An intelligent agent is capable of reason to interpret perceptions, representing knowledge, drawing inferences, solve problems using the environment that is provided to it for finding the solution to the problem. For example, corporate use of monitoring software based on agents can be a key component in cutting support costs and increase computer efficiency. Intelligent agents can learn or use knowledge to achieve their goals.

Q. What tasks can be performed by an intelligent agent?

Ans. There are many tasks which an intelligent agent can perform:

(a) *Planning*: It involves agents which find a set of actions that achieve a certain goal.
(b) *Interpretation*: Inferring situation description from sensory data.
(c) *Diagnosis*: Finding the areas of mal functions based on given observations.
(d) *Prediction*: Inferring likely consequences of given situations.

(e) *Design*: Configuring the objects keeping design constraints into picture.
(f) *Monitoring*: Comparing observations to expected outcomes.
(g) *Debugging*: Prescribing remedies for malfunctions.
(f) *Repairing*: Executing plans to administer prescribed remedies.

13.3 STRUCTURE OF INTELLIGENT AGENTS

Q. What is the structure of intelligent agents?

Ans. An intelligent agent consists of a knowledge base and a problem-solving engine. The knowledge base stores the information about the problem domain in terms of rules, constraints, and laws to represent and operate objects. The problem-solving engine implements a general method of interpreting the input problem based on the knowledge from the knowledge base.

Every intelligent agent needs to have the following:

1. Accept percepts from the environment;
2. To generate actions to maximize the performance measures;

For performing first step, the contents from static memory are used. The memory is updated based on the selection of action in the second step for future use of perceptions learned.

13.4 AGENTS AND ENVIRONMENTS

Q. What is the relation between an agent and its environment?

Ans. An agent is to learn perceptions provided to it through the environment. Based on this, an agent develops a history of perceptions for actions. For a given action, which it is suppose to perform, it maps that perception to corresponding action and runs on the physical architecture to perform that action. An agent cannot have complete control over its environment. So, the success of the intelligent agent lies on the completeness of the environment provided to it, so that it can map its actions correctly.

Q. Discuss various types of environments for agents.

Ans. There are a number of environments possible for agents:

1. *Fully observable or partially observable*: An agent's sensors give it access to the complete state of the environment at each point in time.
2. *Deterministic or stochastic*: If the environment has a single guaranteed effect of any action, and there is no uncertainty, it is deterministic. The next state of the environment is completely determined by the current state and the action executed by the agent. In stochastic or non-deterministic environment, some probabilistic model is used for selecting the actions.
3. *Episodic or sequential*: The agent's experience is divided into atomic "episodes" (each episode consists of the agent perceiving and then performing a single action), and the choice of action in each episode depends only on the episode itself. Here, the agent need not remember the past actions and need not to bother about the next episodic ahead.
4. *Static or dynamic*: The environment is unchanged while an agent is deliberating (the environment is semi-dynamic if the environment itself does not change with the passage of time but the agent's performance score does).
5. *Discrete or continuous*: A limited number of distinct, clearly defined percepts, and actions.
6. *Single-agent or multi-agent*: In this type of environment, an agent is operating in an environment by itself.

13.5 TYPES OF AGENTS

Q. What are the various types of agents in AI?

Ans. Intelligent agents can be divided into two categories: Physical agents and software agents. There are four types of agents in AI:

1. *Simple reflex agents*: Simple reflex agents are based on condition-action rules and implemented with an appropriate production system. They are stateless devices which do not have memory of past world states. Model based reflex agents, history is stored along with current actual percept to produce the action.
2. *Goal-based agents*: These are the agents which in addition to state information have a kind of goal information which describes desirable situations. Agents of this kind take future events into consideration.
3. *Utility-based agents*: There can be several possible answers that can be taken for current situation. The utility of next achieved state is used to arrive at a consideration. These agents base their decision on classic axiomatic utility-theory in order to act rationally. A simple utility function can be used to map given situation onto a real number. This value can be used to give relative importance to competing goals.
4. *Model-based learning agents*: These are agents that keep track of the world. These can become competent over a period of time. These have a learner component, a performance component, and evaluator component and a problem generator component.

Q. What is Wumpus world problem that is solved by agents?

Ans. In Wumpus world, following are the objects, actions and senses:

- **Objects** -
  1. **Wumpus** - a beast that eats anyone that enters its room.
  2. **Agent** - the player that traverses the world in search of gold and while trying to kill the wumpus.
  3. **Bats** - creatures that instantly carry the agent to a different room.
  4. **Pits** - bottomless pit that will trap anyone who enters the room except for the wumpus.
- **Actions** - There are six possible actions:
  - A simple move **Forward**.
  - A simple **Turn Left** by 90°.
  - A simple **Turn Right** by 90°.
  - The action **Grab** can be used to pick up gold when in the same room as gold.
  - The action **Shoot** can be used to fire an arrow in a straight line in the current direction the agent is facing. The arrow continues until it hits and kills the wumpus or hits a wall.
  - The action **Climb** can be used to climb out of the cave but only when in the initial start position.
- **Senses** - There are five senses, each only gives one bit of information:
  - In the square containing the wumpus and in the directly (not diagonal) adjacent squares, the agent will perceive a **Stench**.
  - In the squares directly adjacent to the bats, the agent will perçeive the **Bats**
  - In the squares directly adjacent to a pit, the agent will perceive a **Breeze**.
  - In the square where gold is, the agent will perceive a **Glitter**.
  - When the agent walks into a wall, the agent will perceive a **Bump**.
  - When the wumpus is killed, it emits a **Scream** that can be perceived anywhere in the cave.

In this problem, there are twenty rooms, each connecting to three others, arranged like the vertices of a dodecahedron, or the faces of an icosahedron (which are identical in layout). There are many hazards like bottomless pits, super bats (which drop the player in a random location) and the Wumpus itself. The Wumpus is described as having sucker feet (to escape the bottomless pits) and being too heavy for a super bat to lift. A player of the game move through the rooms or to shoot "crooked arrows" along a tunnel into one of the adjoining rooms. When the player has deduced from hints which chamber the Wumpus is in without entering the chamber, he fires an arrow into the Wumpus's chamber to kill it. The player wins the game if he kills the Wumpus. However, firing the arrow into the wrong chamber startles the Wumpus, which may cause it to move to an adjacent room. The player loses if he or she is in the same room as the Wumpus (which then eats him or her) or a bottomless pit.

Q. What is a physical agent?

Ans. A physical agent is a programmable system that can be used to perform a variety of tasks. A robot is an example of a physical agent. A human agent has eyes, ears, mouth, and other body parts to do the tasks. Similarly, robotic agents have infrared range finders for sensors, cameras, actuators, etc., for doing various tasks. Simple robots can be used in manufacturing to do routine jobs such as assembling, welding, or painting. Mobile robots are used underwater to prospect for oil. A humanoid robot is an autonomous mobile robot that is supposed to behave like a human.

13.6 COMMUNICATION AS ACTION

Q. What is the role of communication for an intelligent agent?

Ans. Communication is an important way for an intelligent agent to interact with other agents or human beings. The communication takes place through the use of an agent-communication language. Using this communication language, the intelligent agent can get the request from the user and decide independently to execute the required commands for action. It may have the ability to modify the requests or may even deny the specific request. The agent can also use communication language to ask clarification questions. The communication language should be as natural to human users. The speech act of agent may be required for communication in order to produce language. Example is a speaker agent that produces a speech act.

Q. What are the types of communicating agents?

Ans. There are two types of communicating agents:

(i) Communicating using Tell and ask: These agents share a common internal representation language and the agents are capable of communicating without any external language at all.

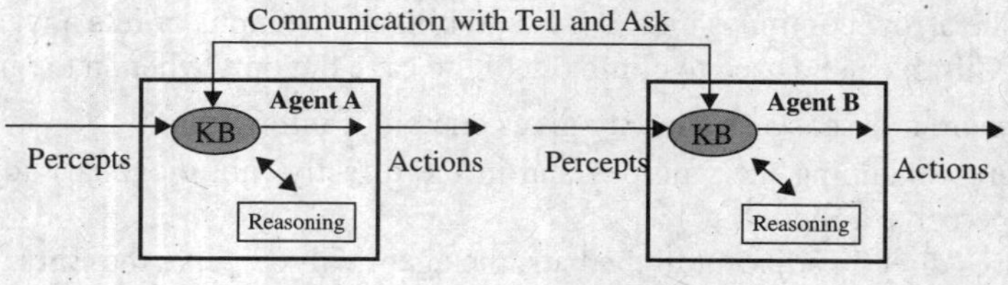

Here, agent A can tell about any percept to agent B and agent B can tell agent A about what is the action taken for the percept. These use TELL( ) and ASK( ) commands.

(ii) Communicating using Formal Language: Here agents make no assumptions about each other's internal language and they share a communication language that is a subset of English

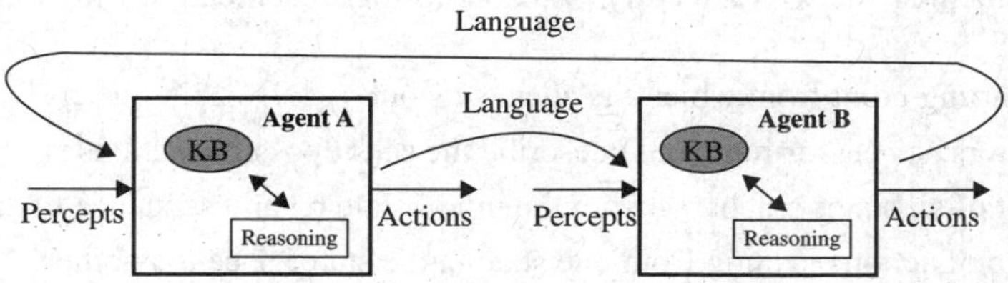

Here, agent A and agent B use formal languages to communicate about the percept and action taken.

Q. What are problem-solving agents?

Ans. There are four types in which problem solving agent can be categorized as:

(i) *Single-state problems*: In this type of problems, accessible world and knowledge of its actions allow the agent to know which state it will be in after a sequence of actions. All the necessary information of the world can be accessed using sensors. The consequences of actions are known to the agent. For each initial state that is known, there is a unique goal state that is guaranteed to be reachable via an action sequence. Thus, the prediction is exact. Example is vaccum world.

(ii) *Multiple-state problems*: In this type of problems, the world is only partially accessible, and the agent has to consider several possible states as the outcome of a sequence of actions. All the essential information of the world cannot be obtained through sensors. Reasoning can be used to determine the set of possible states. Also, the consequences of actions are not always or completely known to the agent. The actions or the environment might exhibit randomness goal due to ignorance. So there may be no fixed action sequence that leads to the goal. Thus the prediction here is semi-exact. Example is vacuum world but here the agent has no sensors. It cannot deal with changes in world during execution.

(iii) *Contingency problems*: In this type of problems, at some points in the sequence of actions, sensing may be required to decide which action to take; this leads to a tree of sequences.

Here, the state is unknown in advance and may depend on the outcome of actions and changes in the environment. Some essential information of the world may be obtained through sensors only at execution time. The consequences of actions may not be known at planning time. Instead of single action sequences, there are trees of actions. Here contingency is the branching point in the tree of actions. Here the agent must act on incomplete plans. Example: vacuum world . Here the effect of a suck action is random. There is no action sequence that can be calculated at planning time and is guaranteed to reach the goal state. But the agent can't deal with situations in which the environment or effects of action are unknown.

(iv) *Exploration problems*: In this type of problems, the agent doesn't know the outcome of its actions, and must experiment to discover states of the world and outcomes of actions. Here the set of possible states may be unknown. some essential information may be obtained through sensors only at execution time consequences of actions may not be known at planning time. Goal can't be completely formulated in advance because states and consequences may not be known at planning time. What states exist is discovery. The outcomes of actions is experimentation. When the agent remember and evaluate experiments, it is learning.

A well defined problem is one with a readily available formal specification which includes the following:

(a) initial state: starting point from which the agent sets out

(b) actions (operators, successor functions):describe the set of possible actions

(c) state space: set of all states reachable from the initial state by any sequence of actions

(d) path : sequence of actions leading from one state in the state space to another

(e) goal test: determines if a given state is the goal state

(f) solution: path from the initial state to a goal state

(g) search cost:time and memory required to calculate a solution

(h) path cost:determines the expenses of the agent for executing the actions in a path, sum of the costs of the individual actions in a path

(i) total cost:sum of search cost and path cost, overall cost for finding a solution

A problem-solving agent selects states by identifying distinguishable stages during the problem-solving process. Actions move the agent from one state to another by applying an operator to a state which is dependent on states, capabilities of the agent, and properties of the environment. The choice of suitable states and operators can make the difference between a problem that can or cannot be solved.

Q. What is rationality?

Ans. Rationality is selecting the best possible actions among the current possible actions in order to maximize a particular goal. It does not mean that the person or agent has infinite knowledge (i.e., omniscience). The knowledge available till date is considered in the form of perceptions, and it is used to select the best possible action. The actions which can maximize the current goal can be used as an experience to learn in future. Also, if an agent is able to perform rationally by its own experience, it is autonomous which is important for it to be learnable and adaptable. The rationality depends on the knowledge about the task environment, the experience gathered so far, the performance measures that are required to be satisfied and the actions which can be taken.

Q. What is a rational agent?

Ans. There are a fixed performance measures that evaluates the sequence of activities in environments. An agent is rational if it tries to maximize the expected value of the given performance measure. It should be able to select the best possible solution among all possible ones. To design a rational agent, the task environment must be specified. This task environment requires the specification of PEAS, i.e., performance measures, environment, actuators, and sensors.

Satellite image analysis system.
Performance measure: correct image categorization
Environment: downlink from orbiting satellite
Actuators: Display categorization of scenes
Sensors: Color pixel arrays

Q. Discuss PEAS representation for an agent.

Ans. An intelligent agent is successful if it can act rationally. For this, the task environment must be specified. There are four components of a task environment defined using PEAS. It stands for specifying four things: Performance measures, Environment, Actuators, and Sensors.

Q. What is a software agent?

Ans. A software agent is a set of programs that are designed to do particular tasks. For example, a software agent can browse the world wide web, check the contents of received e-mails, and classify them into different categories (spam, less important, important, very important, and so on). Software agents offer various benefits to their end users by automating complex or repetitive tasks.

Q. What are the characteristics of a software agent?

Ans. A software agent acts on behalf of a person or another program. The characteristics of a software agent are as follows:

1. *Autonomy*: A software agent should have autonomous control, i.e., it should be able to operate independently without the any human help. It should be able to control its internal state and actions by itself. For example, a software agent which fill out forms on the web automatically for you, storing information about you for future reference.
2. *Reactivity*: The software agent must be able to react to its environment based on its perception and the current states. Example is agents used in managing telecommunications networks and in business process management.
3. *Pro-activity*: The software agent should be able to take useful actions by foreseeing the possible states ahead. Example is agent-based WWW information manager.
4. *Sociability*: The software agent should be able to interact with other program, agents, or humans for input and output. Example is the Ringo / HOMR system which is a personalized recommendation system for music albums and artists which uses interface agents that work by social filtering. If a user's agent finds other agents which are correlated, then it recommends whatever films their users like to its own users.
5. *Mobility*: The software agent must be able to be used across many applications. Example is java applets, programs in Telescript.
6. *Veracity*: The software should not communicate false information intentionally. Example: JACK intelligent agents provide a message-based communication framework which allow messages to be passed to another named agent in the system. It is also proactive and benevolent.
7. *Benevolence*: The agents must not have conflicting goals and should be able to whatever they are asked to do. For example, a query agent which is a web agent. It searches the Web to find an answer to a user's request, and in so doing it may visit many sites and databases. When asked, a benevolent query agent would freely share its query results with other agents on the Web, even though it may have consumed substantial resources to get this knowledge and might have to consume more to share it.

13.7 AGENT TOPOLOGY OR AGENT ARCHITECTURE

Q. Define agent architecture.

Ans. According to Patti Maes, "The architecture of an agent proposes a methodology for building an autonomous agent. It specifies how the construction of the agent can be decomposed into the construction of a set of component modules and how these modules should be made to interact. The total set of modules and their interactions has to provide an answer to the question of how the sensor data and the current internal state of the agent determine the actions (effector outputs) and future internal state of the agent. An architecture encompasses techniques and algorithms that support this methodology." There are three types of agent architectures:

- *Reactive approach*: Here, the agent selects the action based on the inputs it gets from the sensors, generates the state, and takes action to produce the output to effectors (Figure 13.1). Example of reactive architecture is Brooks: subsumption architecture.

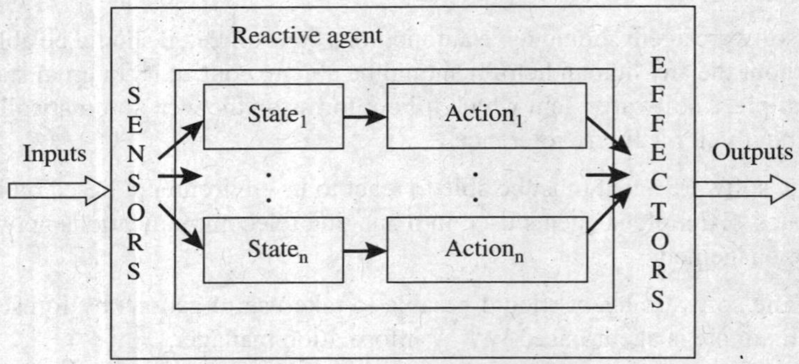

Figure 13.1 Agent architecture – Reactive approach

- *Deliberative approach*: Here, the agent takes input from the sensors, applies world knowledge using symbolic manipulation and pattern matching, plans for the action, and then executes the action to produce the outputs to effectors (Figure 13.2). Example of deliberative agent architecture is Belief-Desire-Intension (BDI) software model.

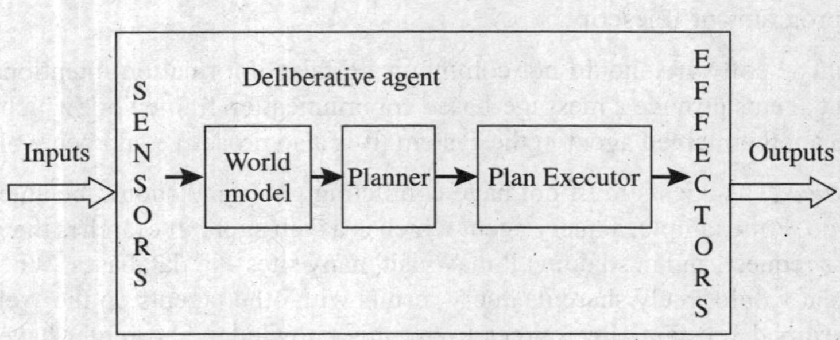

Figure 13.2 Agent architecture – Deliberative approach

- *Hybrid approach*: It has both types of components in the agent system. Reactive component takes actions quickly and deliberative component plans by judging the appropriate situation and then executing the actions (Figure 13.3). Example of hybrid agent architecture is InterRap.

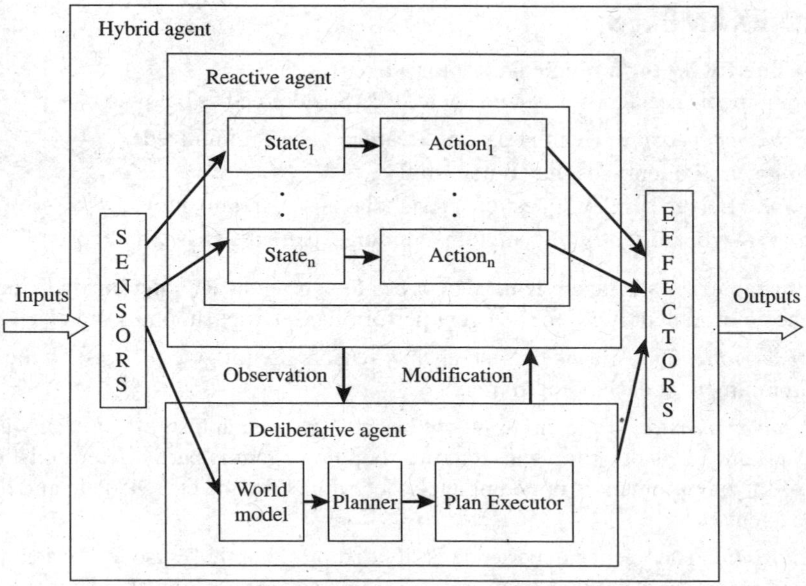

Figure 13.3 Agent architecture – Hybrid approach

13.8 AGENT-ORIENTED PROGRAMMING

Q. Discuss agent-oriented programming.

Ans. Agents are processes that can execute a procedure for general purpose functions. Open Agent Architecture is a standard group for agent-oriented programming. Agent-oriented programming is different from object-oriented programming. Here, individual separate modules communicate with each other and each has individual ways of handling incoming messages. Here, the modules are called agents which have a fixed state called mental state which consists of beliefs and capabilities. The methods between agents are constrained, i.e., they can either inform, request, decline, offer to other agents. The messages have the constraints of being honest and consistent.

There are three components of agent-oriented programming framework:

1. Formal language with clear syntax and semantics for describing mental state.
2. Interpreted language in which to define and program agents.
3. An "agentifier" to convert neutral devices into programmable agents.

Agent is an entity consisting:

(a) Beliefs $B^t_a\varphi$:a = agent, t = time, φ = sentence
(b) Commitments: $CMT^t_{a,b}\varphi$
(c) Commitment rules: to add new commitments
(d) Capabilities: what agent can do

Some formalisms used are:

-Belief revision function: brf: $\delta(Bel) \times Per \rightarrow \delta(Bel)$
-Deliberation process: deliberate: $\delta(Bel) \rightarrow \delta(Int)$
-Means-ends reasoning: plan: $\delta(Bel) \times \delta(Int) \rightarrow Plan$

SOLVED EXAMPLES

Q. Define PEAS for a medical diagnosis agent.

Ans. For a medical diagnosis system agent, PEAS is defined as below:

- *Performance measure*: Healthy patient, treatment costs minimized
- *Environment*: Patient, hospital, nurse, staff
- *Actuators*: Screen display (questions, tests, diagnoses, treatments)
- *Sensors*: Keyboard (entry of symptoms, findings, patient's answers, reports)

Q. Characterize all the environment types for an agent who performs Internet shopping.

Ans. The environment types for an agent performing internet shopping are:

(i) ***Not observable:*** This means that the agent's sensors do not give it access to the complete state of the environment at each point in time

(ii) ***Partly deterministic:*** If the environment has a single guaranteed effect of any action, and there is no uncertainty, it is deterministic. Internet shopping agent is partly deterministic because the next state of the environment is not completely determined by the current state and the action executed by the agent

(iii) ***Not Episodic:*** The agent's experience is divided into atomic "episodes" (each episode consists of the agent perceiving and then performing a single action), and the choice of action in each episode depends only on the episode itself. This is not true for internet shopping agent.

(iv) ***Semi static:*** The environment is changing a little while an agent is deliberating

(v) ***Discrete:*** A limited number of distinct, clearly defined percepts and actions exist for the agent.

(vi) ***Multi agent:*** In this type of environment, an agent is not operating alone in an environment itself.

Q. Give example of a well-defined problem for a problem-solving agent.

Ans. Consider the vacuum world problem in which each vacuum –cleaner agent which is to clean a room which can be considered as a grid of n X n square. As hindrance to the agent, the room contains furniture which is considered as wall. The dirt is distributed uniformly around the room, but it is dominating in certain locations such as in front of the couch. The agent gets a three-element percept vector on each turn. There is a touch sensor which will have value 1 if the machine has bumped into something and a value 0 otherwise. The second element of the percept is a photosensor under the machine, which gives a value 1 if there is dirt and a value 0 otherwise. The third value of the percept vector comes from an infrared sensor, which gives a value 1 when the agent is in its home location and a value of 0 otherwise. The other variables are defined as follows:

States: dirty, clean

Initial state: any state

Successor function (operators or actions): go forward, turn left by 90°, turn right by 90°, suck up dirt and turn off.

Goal test: To clean up all squares and go home

Path cost: 100 points for each piece of dirt vacuumed up, minus one point for each action taken and minus 1000 points if it is not in the home location when it turns itself off.

Q. Give example of a goal-based agent.

Ans. The agents who choose action by reasoning to solve a particular goal are called goal-based agents. State allows that an agent can keep track of unseen parts of the world using the state, but the agent must update state based on knowledge of changes in the world and of effects of own actions. An example of a goal-based agent is the one which decides to put a list of grocery items in a bag depending on the knowledge of list of things to be put in the bag. It also needs knowledge about the type of things which can be piled on others and which on cannot.

Q. Give example of a utility-based agent.

Ans. The desired utility function of the goal state is specified in terms of real numbers. The agent needs to evaluate the competing goals and select the goals to map to the utility values. An example is an agent who finds the list of items with least price during shopping. The utility here is to minimize the price.

Q. Give example of a model-based agent.

Ans. These are the agents who keep track of the world. According the perception and the current state, the agent updates the internal state and the actions taken. This updation of internal states requires two kinds of encoded knowledge—knowledge about how the world changes and knowledge about how the agents' actions affect the world. Example of model-based agent is given below.

function Reflex-Agent-With-State (*percept*) **returns** action

static: *rules*, a set of condition-action rules

state, a description of the current world

state ← Update-State(*state*, *percept*)

rule ← Rule-Match(*state, rules*)

action ← Rule-Action[*rule*]

state ← Update-State(*state*, *action*)

return *action*

Q. Give example of a reflex agent.

Ans. A simple reflex agent uses a rule-based system for storing the conditions and corresponding actions. It works by taking a perception as a state and finding a rule whose condition matches the current situation. Then, it executes that action and returns the result of the action taken.

function Simple-Reflex-Agent(location, status) returns action
if status = dirty then return Suck
else if location = R then return Right
else if location = L then return left

Q. Give examples of software agents.

Ans. Examples of software agents are

1. Buyer agents, who travel around the Internet finding information about goods and services.
2. Data mining agents, who are helpful in finding useful information from many different sources using data-mining techniques.
3. Monitoring and surveillance agents, who are used to do monitoring on some computer system and give the prediction based on the analysis.
4. User or personal agents, who act on your behalf like checking your mail, selecting the moves in a game.

Q. Is software same as an intelligent agent?

Ans. No, an intelligent agent or rational agent is a machine or human being who can perform goal-directed behavior while software agent is a set of programs.

MULTIPLE CHOICE QUESTIONS

Select the most appropriate answers to the following questions:

1. What does E stands for in PEAS?
   (a) Efficiency (b) Evaluation
   (c) Environment (d) None of these
2. A rational agent tries to maximize which of the following?
   (a) Efficiency (b) Expected value
   (c) Evaluation (d) None of these
3. Which of the following cannot be handled by an intelligent agent?
   (a) Learning (b) Decision making
   (c) Uncertainties (d) None of these
4. What does an intelligent agent map to actions?
   (a) Rationality (b) Perception
   (c) Environment (d) None of these
5. Consider an agent for automated taxi, which of the following will be a performance measure?
   (a) Accelerator (b) Keyboard
   (c) Safety (d) None of these
6. Consider an agent for automated taxi, which of the following will be an actuator?
   (a) Accelerator (b) Keyboard
   (c) Safety (d) None of these
7. Consider an agent for automated taxi, which of the following will be a sensor?
   (a) Accelerator (b) Keyboard
   (c) Safety (d) None of these
8. Which of the following has discrete environment?
   (a) Backgammon (b) Solitaire
   (c) Taxi (d) None of these
9. Which of the following has continuous environment?
   (a) Backgammon (b) Solitaire
   (c) Taxi (d) None of these
10. Which of the intelligent agent keeps track of the state of the real world?
    (a) Reflex (b) Utility-based
    (c) Goal-based (d) None of these

Answers. 1. c 2. b 3. d 4. b 5. c 6. a 7. b 8. c 9. c 10. a

EXERCISES

1. Define PEAS for an automated taxi.
2. Give an example of a multi-agent system.

14

Expert Systems

14.1 INTRODUCTION

Expert systems solve problems that are normally solved by humans who are experts in a particular domain. In order to solve expert-level problems like an expert, knowledge needs to be provided to the expert system. This is done through a knowledge database. These are given initial states and various conditions and are required to give expert advice for which these need some reasoning mechanism. The human expert can be trusted for the advice he/she is providing because he/she knows the ***consequences*** of giving a wrong advice. But a machine or a program if gives some advice, then some explanation is required in order to validate whether the advice is according to the correct reasoning or not. So an explanation module is always present in an expert system. Initially, the expert systems were developed by hand using LISP dialects. If-Then statements were used to solve most of the problems. These form the set of rules which could be stored in a knowledge base. Working memory was the area in the knowledge base which was used to store the partial or intermediate conclusions. Rule based expert systems were most common because they could handle uncertainty in knowledge by using certainty factors, fuzzy reasoning and Bayesian probabilities. Case based and model based expert systems were also developed. Now a days there are expert system shells available which are AI tools for designing the expert systems. These shells ease the process of design of expert system because the problem solving processing is included in these. The user is required to fill in the knowledge.

Q. What is an expert system?

Ans. A system that draws upon the knowledge of human experts captured in a knowledge base to solve problems that normally require human expertise. A domain engineer gathers information from the human expert in a particular domain and knowledge engineer code that in the form of rule-based expert system. This is capable of taking inputs from the user, match the conditions given by the user and give conclusion based on the rules matching. It has also an explanation module to check how it has reached a particular conclusion.

14.2 MAIN COMPONENTS OF AN EXPERT SYSTEM

Q. What are the main components of an expert system?

Ans. An expert system has the following components:

1. *Knowledge database*: It contains domain-specific facts and rules for solving problems in the domain. There are two sections of the knowledge base. First, for storing the case history for the current query and the general part containing all the facts and rules for the given domain.
2. *Inference engine*: This acts as the brain of the expert system and is also called the interpreter. It performs deductions using facts and rules in the knowledge base for the submitted queries.
3. *User interface for query*: Acquires information from the user and the expert system and also displays results. This is used by both users and expert systems for input and output.
4. *Explanation sub module*: This is very important part of expert system because it helps to interact with the expert systems to know its internal processing. It should have the capabilities for explaining the how and why of the results produced by it.

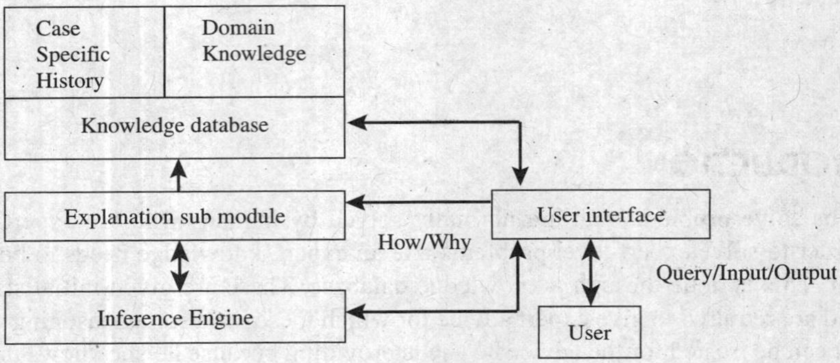

14.3 REPRESENTING AND USING DOMAIN KNOWLEDGE

Q. How is domain knowledge represented and used in expert systems?

Ans. There are various ways of representing domain knowledge in an expert system. The most common method is in the form of rule-based production system. The reasoning mechanisms used are forward chaining, backward chaining, or a combination of these two.

14.4 EXPERT SYSTEM SHELLS

Q. What are expert system shells? What do they do?

Ans. An expert system contains a knowledge base which contains a set of declarative set of facts and rules and an interpreter to find answers to queries given by the users. In an expert shell, an interpreter can be separated from these declarations (i.e., domain-specific knowledge) which act as a separate system. The expert system shell can be used to construct a new system by adding new knowledge corresponding to new domain. The advantage of expert system shell is that it provides flexibility in representing knowledge and in reasoning by supporting rules, frames, and reasoning mechanisms.

14.5 EXPLANATION

Q. What is the important of explanation in an expert system?

Ans. An expert system is designed for use by people as they interact with a human expert. The interface of an expert system should be easy to interact for users. When an expert system performs a task like giving an advice, diagnose a problem. etc., it is required to explain the reasons why it did so. For this, explanation for steps taken must be explained. In case the users are satisfied with the explanation, they will accept the advice or problem diagnosed given by the expert system, otherwise they will lose faith in the expert system. Also, as human expert keeps on updating its knowledge through a learning process called experience, an expert system should update the knowledge by modifying the old knowledge by adding new knowledge and improving the reasoning through some learning process. TEIRESIAS is an example of explanation system.

14.6 KNOWLEDGE ACQUISITION

Q. What is knowledge acquisition? What are the issues in knowledge acquisition?

Ans. A person is called an expert if he/she has high level of knowledge. An expert system will be successful when it has high domain knowledge. Initially, a knowledge engineer collects knowledge from domain engineer through questionnaires or interviews. Then, he/she represents this knowledge in the form of rules, frames, etc., which forms the knowledge database for the expert system. Automatic knowledge acquisition tools may also be used to update the knowledge database. Example of knowledge acquisition system is MOLE which is used for heuristic classification problems such as diagnosing diseases.

14.7 CHARACTERISTICS OF EXPERT SYSTEMS

Q. Discuss all the characteristics of an expert system.

Ans. The expert system is required to perform like a human expert, so it possesses the following characteristics:

1. It needs huge amount of knowledge. So a large efforts and cost is required to design an expert system.
2. It contains domain specific knowledge, i.e. all the knowledge in a specific area to do the expert task in that domain.
3. A justification mechanism: In order to be useful, it must be able to justify its advice/conclusions.
4. The expert system must be able to propagate uncertainties in knowledge and should provide a range of conclusions for the actions taken by it.
5. A refinement mechanism: As the knowledge needs to be updated, it must provide some method to refine the knowledge base.

Q. Discuss the characteristics of expert systems which differentiate expert systems from conventional computer systems.

Ans. There are many characteristics which differentiate expert systems from conventional computer systems:

	Conventional Computer Systems	Expert Systems
1.	Uses data to control the solution process	Uses knowledge to control the solution process
2.	Data is stored along with the control program	Knowledge is stored in encoded form and is maintained as a separate entity from the control program
3.	Usually do not have how and why explanation modules	Expert systems are capable of explaining how a particular conclusion was reached and why requested information is needed during a consultation

4.	Use data in numeric, alphabetic, audio or video form	Expert systems use symbolic representations like rules, networks or frames for representing knowledge
5.	Meta data may or may not be present	Expert systems can reason with meta knowledge about their own knowledge limits and capabilities but inclusion of high level meta knowledge is required

14.8 APPLICATIONS OF EXPERT SYSTEMS

Q. What are the applications of expert systems?

Ans. There are a number of applications in all aspects of human life:

- Different types of medical diagnosis.
- Diagnosis of software development projects.
- Diagnosis of automobiles.
- Forecasting of weather.
- Identification of chemical compound structures and chemical compound.
- Selection and management of stock and bond portfolio.
- Military applications like ocean surveillance.
- Assessment of geologic structures from dip meter logs.
- Career consultation system for students.
- Design of VLSI systems.

14.9 EXISTING SYSTEMS

Q. Discuss existing expert systems.

Ans. The following are existing expert systems:

- DENDRAL (1967) for determining molecular structure based on mass spectrograms.
- MYCIN (1976) for diagnosis and therapy recommendation for blood diseases.
- PROSPECTOR (1978) for mineral exploration.
- XCON (1984) to configure VAX and PDP-11 series computer systems.
- FocalPoint (TriPath Imaging) screens ~10% of all pap smears in USA (2002).
- American Express uses an expert system to automatically approve purchases.
- Mrs. Field's cookies use an expert system to model the founder's operational ideas.
- TaxCut uses an expert system to give tax advice.

Q. Write a note on expert system DENDRAL

Ans. Carl Djerassi and Edward Feigenbaum devised a system called DENDritic ALgorithm (Dendral) that was able to generate possible chemical structures corresponding to the mass spectrometry data as an output in 1960s. It is considered the first expert system because it automated the decision-making process and problem-solving behavior of organic chemists. The project consisted of research on two main programs Heuristic Dendral and Meta-Dendral, and several sub-programs. Heuristic Dendral is a program that uses mass spectra or other experimental data together with knowledge base of chemistry, to produce a set of possible chemical structures that may be responsible for producing the data. Meta-Dendral is a machine learning system that receives the set of possible chemical structures and corresponding mass spectra as input, and proposes a set of rules of mass spectrometry that correlate structural features with processes that produce the mass spectrum. Heuristic Dendral is a performance system while Meta Dendral is a learning system. It was written in AI language LISP.

The approach used was generate and test with human feedback.

Steps are:

1. Generate a hypothesis: a possible chemical compound
2. Test the hypothesis: use a series of heuristics and subprograms to determine if the chemical compound generated is plausible, given the data
3. If so, show it to the user – the user can *change* the direction that DENDRAL takes next by suggesting what chemical elements should be added or removed from the generated hypothesis compound
4. DENDRAL repeats until an answer is found acceptable which does not violate the constraints as dictated by the data

Many expert systems were derived from DENDRAL, including MYCIN, MOLGEN, PROSPECTOR and XCON.

Q. Write a note on expert system MOLGEN.

Ans. Expert system MOLGEN developed in 1981 by Stefik is used for planning experiments in molecular genetics. It is a software tool that is used for chemical education and research. It allows to generate and visualize all the constitutional formulae corresponding to a given gross formula. It also allows to compute all configurational isomers to a given structural isomer along with their realizations in space.

Q. Write a note on expert system PROSPECTOR.

Ans. PROSPECTOR is a consultation system that assists in evaluation of the mineral potential of a geological site. It can also work in structure control, kinds of rocks, minerals and alteration products present or suspected. It was developed in 1980's by Hart and Duda. Since the target user was prospect, i.e. geologist who is in early part of investigating an exploration site, the system was named as PROSPECTOR.

14.10 ADVANTAGES AND LIMITATIONS OF EXPERT SYSTEMS

Q. What are the advantages and disadvantages of expert systems?

Ans. There are many advantages of expert systems. Along with these, there are many disadvantages also as discusses here:

Advantages	Disadvantages
• With the help of expert systems, the availability of the expert knowledge is increased, specially in his absence	• There is lack of common sense, inflexible and sometimes difficulty in modification due to lack of learning ability
• The expert knowledge can be used for training future experts	• Also as the domain of expertise is restricted , it can be used only in limited area
• It can deal with uncertainty as well as it is cost effective i.e. once the knowledge is with the expert system, multiple copies can be made which reduces the need to refer to the human expert	• In case human life is involved like in medical diagnosis and treatment, it cannot always be relied on

• As the knowledge is acquired and stored, it gives consistent answers based on rule based systems for storing the knowledge and it can give explanations also	• These cannot be used where sensory input is required. These can manipulate only symbolic input.
• An expert system can review all transactions while a human being can review only a sample of all transactions	• Expert systems cannot respond creatively to unusual situations as human experts can do

SOLVED EXAMPLES

Q. Why is inference engine separated from knowledge database?

Ans. Inference engine is kept separate from knowledge database so that

-Expert system builder can focus on capturing and organizing problem-solving knowledge than the details of code implementation

–Changes can allowed to be made easily

–Same control and interface software can be allowed to be used in different systems

–Knowledge can be represented in a more natural fashion

Q. Explain DENDRAL.

Ans. The DENDRAL system (DENDRitic ALgorithm) was the first expert system, developed in the 1960s. It was used to identify the chemical composition based on the given mass spectrogram data. The approach used in DENDRAL was plan-generate-and-test with human feedback.

This is a constrained search technique whose steps are

1. *Generate a hypothesis:* a possible chemical compound.
2. *Test the hypothesis:* Use a series of heuristics and subprograms to determine if the chemical compound generated was plausible given the data. If so, it was told to the user. The user was allowed to *change* the direction that DENDRAL could take next by suggesting what chemical elements should be added or removed from the generated hypothesis compound.

The process was repeated until an answer was found acceptable that did not violate the constraints as dictated by the data.

Q. Give examples of rules in MYCIN.

Ans. MYCIN (1976) was developed at Stanford University. It performs bacteriological diagnosis which includes disease identification and treatment. When MYCIN was tested against doctors, interns, medical teachers, and medical students, it outperformed them all in an experiment of approximately 80 different cases. Main characteristics of MYCIN are

- rule-based
- backward reasoning (from a specific goal back to known facts)
- performs depth first, exhaustive search of all rules
- utilizes write this out as certainty factor CF

MYCIN contains a working memory which stores a number of premises of the form

<(condition list), (conclusion), Certainty Factor>

These are placed into a hash table for easy lookup based on the conclusion.

The process used by MYCIN is to identify all rules that can provide the conclusion currently sought (the initial conclusion is called diagnose-and-treat). Any rule that can conclude this is added to a list of rules to test. Each of these rules is used to match their premises against working memory. Any rules that are true are "fired" – that is, their conclusion is an action used to modify the hash table. This can cause either addition of a new piece of knowledge to the hash table or it finds and removes a piece of knowledge which is no longer needed or it finds and modifies a piece of knowledge now that more specific information is known.

Sample rule:

IF: (1) The stain of the organism is gram-positive,
(2) The morphology of the organism is coccus, AND
(3) The growth confirmation of the organism is clumps,

THEN: there is suggestive evidence (0.7) that the identity of the organism is Staphylococcus.

The idea behind MYCIN is that there are thousands of such rules. If the premises allow one rule to be selected, that will modify working memory which in turn might let another, more specific, rule to be selected. How certain is the next rule in the chain of logic?

MYCIN used following rules to compute CF for hypotheses

1. Find rules whose conclusions match the hypothesis
2. Obtain CF's for premises and compute the CF for the conclusion
3. Combine CF's obtained from all applicable rules.

The rules for combining the CF are

1. CF (P1 & P2) = minimum (CF(P1), CF (P2))
2. CF (P1 $\wedge$ P2) = maximum (CF(P1), CF (P2))
3. CF (R1 $\rightarrow$ R2) = CF (R1)* CF (R2)
4. Assume R1 concludes C1 and R2 concludes C1, what is our conclusion of C1 given R1 and R2?

CF (C1) = CF (R1)+CF (R2)–CF(R1)*CF(R2)
if CF (R1)>0 and CF (R2)>0

Consider two rules:

(R1)hasHAIR $\rightarrow$ mammal CF (R1)=0.9

(R2)forwardEyes & sharp Teeth $\rightarrow$ mammal CF (R2)=0.7

Suppose you have determined that:

(CF)(hasHair)=0.8 CF (forwardEyes)=0.75 CF (sharp Teeth)=0.3

Given multiple premises, how do you combine into one CF?

CF (P1 $\vee$ P2) = max (CF(P1), CF (P2))

CF (P1 $\wedge$ P2) = min (CF(P1), CF (P2))

So, CF(forwardEyes $\wedge$ sharp Teeth) = min (0.75,0.3)=0.3

Given the premise CF, how do you combine with the CF for the rule?

CF (H,Rule) = CF (Premise),* CF (Rule)

So, CF (mammal,R1) = CF (hasHair),* CF (R1)=0.8*0.9=0.72

CF (mammal,R2) = CF (forwardEyes$\wedge$sharp Teeth),* CF (R2)
=0.3*0.7
=0.21

CF(H, Rule&Rule2)=CF(H,Rule1)+CF(H,Rule2)*(1–CF (H,Rule1))

So,

CF (mammal,R1 & R2)
=CF (mammal,R1)+CF (mammal,R2)*(1–CF(mammal,R1))
=0.72+0.21*0.28
=0.72+0.0588
=0.7788

Q. Discuss EMYCIN.

Ans. EMYCIN (for empty MYCIN or essential MYCIN) is an expert system shell which was developed as a pattern matching system that would mimic MYCIN's problem-solving process without the domain-specific rules. So, when EMYCIN was used to build a new expert system, only a new knowledge base (the rules) was needed to be supplied. EMYCIN was used to develop following new expert systems

(a) *R1*: To configure VAX computers.
(b) *Puff and centaur*: To diagnose pulmonary disorder.
(c) *GUIDON*: A tutorial system to teach students how to reason like MYCIN.
(d) *SACON*: A structural engineering design and analysis advising system.

Q. Explain XCON/R1 (computer).

Ans. This expert system configures DEC's VAX, PDP11, and VAX computers. DEC offers the customer a wide choice of components when purchasing computer equipment, so that client achieves a custom-made system. For a given customer's order, configuration is made, perhaps involving component replacement or addition. It has a challenging task of configuring a computer system when there is rapidly changing information.

John P. McDermott in 1978 wrote a production-rule-based system called R1 in OPS5. The purpose was to assist in the ordering of DEC's VAX computer systems by automatically selecting the computer system components based on the customer's requirements. Later, it was called XCON for eXpert CONfigurer.

Before XCON, every cable, connection and each bit of software had to be ordered separately. There were delays and errors in configurations as sales people were not always very technically expert. XCON handled this by asking sales person critical questions before printing out a final specification or order slip.

In 1980, when XCON was used for first time in DEC's plant in Salem, New Hampshire, it had about 2500 rules. By 1986, it had processed 80,000 orders, and achieved 95-98% accuracy. It was estimated to be saving DEC $25M a year by reducing the need to give customers free components when technicians made errors, by speeding the assembly process. This also resulted in increased customer satisfaction.

Another version of XCON intended for use by DEC's salesforce to aid a customer in properly configuring their VAX was named XSEL. Another version of XCON, XSITE was developed to handle location problems and configurations.

Q. Give some examples of more expert systems used in real life.

Ans. There are many expert systems used in real life. Some of these are:

- American Express uses an expert system to automatically approve purchases: The expert system named Authorizer's Assistant(AA) was developed in early 1990s. AA is an integral part of AMEX's Credit Authorization System (CAS) transaction processing system for receiving credit requests from merchants, processing those requests, and transmitting the approval or denial back to the merchant. AA analyzes the small percent of requests requiring human attention, and it uses business rules to simulate the decision process of experienced credit agents.
- Mrs. Field's cookies use an expert system to model the founder's operational ideas: The expert system called ROI-Retail Operations Management was designed by pink city group in 1990. It used to take input as weather conditions, along with special events to project production and sales. The expert system was able to predict the daily sale of cookies as well as suggest some moves for better sales.
- TaxCut uses an expert system to give tax advice: In 1977, McCarthy developed TAXMAN, the tax application of an expert system. It was designed in LISP. The main domain of the expert system was rudimentary legal

reasoning. Many experts system were developed after this, including TAXCUT in 1991, by Brown and Philips which helped in tax preparation.

Q. Give examples of rules in R1.

Ans.

IF: the most current active context is assigning a power supply
and an SBI module of any type has been put in a cabinet
and the position it occupies in the cabinet is known
and there is space in the cabinet for a power supply
and there is no available power supply
and the voltage and frequency of the components is known

THEN: find a power supply of that voltage and frequency and add it to the order

Q. Discuss human resource management.

Ans. Human resource management (HRM) is an expert system which facilitates the most effective use of employees to achieve organizational as well as individual goals. It forms part of overall strategy including decision support system and enterprise information system. It helps decision making for HRM managers with heuristic knowledge in unstructured and semi-structured problems (job placement and pay rises). It is used for HR planning, recruiting, compensation, and labor–management relations.

MULTIPLE CHOICE QUESTIONS

Select the most appropriate answer to the following questions:

1. Which of the following is not included in general expert system problem categories given by Waterman?
   (a) Interpretation (b) Prediction
   (c) Design (d) None of these
2. Which part of expert system holds the set of rules of inference that are used in reasoning?
   (a) Inference engine (b) Knowledge base
   (c) User interface (d) All of these
3. Who developed the first well-known medical diagnosis system MYCIN?
   (a) Shortliffe (b) Alan Turing
   (c) Samuel (d) Fillmore
4. Which of the following was not a subsystem of MYCIN expert system?
   (a) Consultation system (b) Explanation system
   (c) Rule acquisition system (d) None of these
5. What does EMYCIN stands for?
   (a) Electronic MYCIN (b) Extra MYCIN
   (c) Empty MYCIN (d) None of these
6. Which of the following expert system assists geologists in the discovery of mineral deposits?
   (a) MYCIN (b) R1
   (c) DENDRAL (d) PROSPECTOR

7. Which of the following expert system was used by Digital Equipment Corporation to select and configure components of complex computer systems?
   (a) MYCIN (b) R1
   (c) DENDRAL (d) None of these
8. Which of the following type of architecture uses a form of opportunistic reasoning?
   (a) Frame based (b) Associative network
   (c) Blackboard (d) Decision tree
9. What will be the category of an expert system who is capable of comparing the observed behavior of a system to its expected behavior?
   (a) Prediction (b) Monitoring
   (c) Interpretation (d) All of these
10 Which of the following cannot be the part of the case-specific data of an expert system?
   (a) Dead ends in search process (b) Partial conclusions
   (c) Confidence measures of conclusion (d) None of these

Answers. 1. d 2. b 3. a 4. d 5. c 6. d 7. b 8. c 9. b 10. d

EXERCISES

1. Discuss limitations of expert systems.
2. What is the role of inference engine in an expert system?
3. What is the use of storing general information in a knowledge base of an expert system along with case-based knowledge?
4. Give example of an expert system used in interpretation.
5. Give example of an expert system used in planning.

15

Natural Language Processing

15.1 INTRODUCTION

Language is the means by which one person communicates with the other person and hence the whole world. One can communicate with other in a particular language only when one can understand the language spoken by the other person. There are many languages in this world. Since computers are common to the whole world, the global communication language English is used for developing the language understanding programs in AI, although multi-lingual applications are also being developed in the whole world today. All the AI programs which are required to take input need some understanding of the input, after which they can perform the task and produce the output. There are many complications in processing the text. First is to represent the appropriate grammar for the language and then parsing the sentence. This includes parsing using lexical, syntactic, semantic, and pragmatic levels. The applications which take input as spoken English still use complicated processes.

15.1.1 Levels in Natural Language Understanding

Q. What are various levels in language understanding?

Ans. A language understanding program in AI must have knowledge about the possible set of words, how they can be combined together to form phrases and sentences. The rules represent the structure of the language. If the structure of the sentence formed from the words is correct, does it convey the right meaning must also be known which also require the knowledge about the meaning of all the words. A sentence may be used in many contexts. The language understanding program must be able to relate whether the context within which it is used is correct or not. The following levels are required in understanding of natural language processing (NLP):

1. *Phonological analysis*: It is formed from the word phoneme. A phoneme is the smallest unit of sound. Many phonemes when combined form words. Phonological analysis deals with relating sounds to the words so that they can be recognized during speech recognition.
2. *Morphological analysis*: It is formed from the word morpheme. A morpheme is the smallest unit of meaning. Morphological analysis is lexical knowledge which deals with forming words from morphemes. The words formed are called lexicons. In natural language English, the types of lexicons are verb, noun, adjective, pronoun, etc.

3. *Syntactic analysis*: Syntactic analysis deals with the syntax of the sentence formed from the combination of the words according to the rules of the grammar.
4. *Semantic analysis*: Semantic analysis deals with the meaning of the sentence which is syntactically correct.
5. *Pragmatic analysis*: Pragmatic analysis deals with high-level knowledge which relates to the use of sentences in different contexts and how the context affects the meaning of the sentences. The structure representing what was said is reinterpreted to determine what was actually meant.
6. *Discourse integration*: The meaning of the individual sentence may depend on the sentences that precede it and may influence the meanings of the sentences that follow it.
7. *World knowledge*: It relates to the language to a user must have in order to understand and carry on a conversation. It must include an understanding of the other person's belief and goals.

15.1.2 Issues in NLP

Q. What are the issues inNLP?

Ans. There are many issues in NLP. In syntax analysis, the issue is to identify part of the speech, parsing, proposition attachment, and in understanding the knowledge correctly because the words are ambiguous. During semantics, the difficulty is in learning the different meaning of words. There are difficulties during machine translations like text-to-text machine translation or speech-to-speech machine translation.

15.2 GRAMMARS

Q. What is a grammar?

Ans. A grammar is a metalanguage used to define the syntax of a language. It contains a finite set of terminal symbols, a finite set of non-terminal symbols, a finite set of production rules, and a start symbol. The language is formed using the grammar and is the set of all sequences of symbols which can be formed by applying all possible production rules in the grammar to the start symbol.

Q. How the sentence generation and translation is done using a grammar for a language?

Ans. A language L is defined as a set of strings formed by concatenating symbols taken from the alphabet set or vocabulary of the language. The length of the string may be finite or infinite. The possible sentences called well-formed sentences are constructed using set of rules defined in the grammar of the language. To generate a sentence, the rules from set of production rule are applied sequentially starting with starting symbol S and proceeding until all non-terminal symbols are eliminated and the sentence is generated using terminal symbols.

15.2.1 Chomsky Hierarchy of Grammar

Q. Explain Chomsky hierarchy of grammars.

Ans. In Chomsky hierarchy of grammars, there are four types of grammars defined:

1. *Regular grammars*: These contain regular expressions and are equivalent to finite-state automata. These are used to define lexical structure of the language.
2. *Context-free grammars*: These are used to define the syntax of the language and are equivalent to non-deterministic pushdown automata.
3. *Context-sensitive grammars*: These include more than one non-terminal on the left-hand side.
4. *Unrestricted grammars*: These are recursively enumerable languages and are equivalent to Turing machines.

15.2.2 Context-free Grammar

Q. What is a context-free grammar?

Ans. A context-free grammar allows rules of grammar to have only a single non-terminal on their left-hand side. So, the rule can be applied to any occurrence of that symbol, regardless of its context. Words from the dictionary that may appear on the right-hand side of the rules are called terminal symbols. Terms that describe higher-level linguistic concepts (sentence, noun, etc.) are called non-terminal symbols. Non-terminals appear on the left- and right-hand sides of the rules. A legal sentence is any string of terminals that can be derived using the rules of the grammar. Any intermediate stages of the derivation consisting of both the terminal and non-terminal symbols are called sentential form.

15.2.3 Transformational Grammar

Q. What are transformational grammars?

Ans. When we use generative grammars, different structures are produced from sentences having the same meaning. For example, John gave a book to Mary and Mary was given a book by John are two sentences with the same meaning. As they are differing in active voice and passive voice, they produce different structures using grammars. Chomsky extended the generative grammars by incorporating two components, namely, a semantic component and a phonological component. They are used to interpret the output of the syntactic component by producing meanings and sound sentences. This extended grammar is called a transformational generative grammar. The transformations are essentially tree manipulation rules which depend on the use of an extended lexicon (dictionary) containing a number of semantic features for each word.

Q. How does transformational grammar produce same structure for sentences with same meaning?

Ans. Using a transformational grammar, a sentence is analyzed in two stages. In one stage, the basic structure of the sentence is analyzed to determine the grammatical constituent parts, which reveals the surface structure of the sentence, the way the sentence is used in speech or in writing. This structure can be transformed into another one where the deeper semantic structure of the sentence is determined.

15.3 SYNTACTIC PARSING

Q. What is parsing?

Ans. Parsing is the process of analyzing a sentence by considering the words separately and determining its structure from its words. The structure of a sentence can be represented with a syntax tree. It is the inverse of sentence generation process because it aims to find a grammatical sentence structure from an input string. The lexicon from the words in input string is identified along with its meaning. The information is used to build a tree.

15.3.1 Top down and Bottom Up Parsing

Q. Explain various parsing techniques.

Ans. There are two types of parsing techniques. Top-down and bottom-up parsing. In top-down parsing, we start with sentence S until a string of terminal symbols is reached. Scan the string from the left to the right until a non-terminal is reached, replace it using a rule, and repeat until no non-terminals are left. In case of more than one rule for replacing a particular non-terminal exists, any rule can be applied. When the string contains only terminals, these are called well-formed sentences. In bottom-up parsing, we start with the words, i.e., the terminal symbols and end up with S. Parsing can also be done using transition networks and augmented transition networks (ATN).

15.3.2 Transition Networks or Nets

Q. What is a transition net? How it is drawn?

Ans. Transition net is also known as transition network. It is based on the application of directed graphs and finite-state automata. It consists of a number of nodes and labeled arcs. The nodes represent various states in traversing a sentence. The states can be initial states, final states and intermediate states. The arcs represent rules to make transition from one state to another. If a transition network can successfully traversed till final state, then the sentence is parsed. The transition network is drawn for each non-terminal symbol in the grammar. All the rules for one non-terminal are shown in one transition network for that non terminal symbol. The labeled arcs could be non-terminal symbols or terminal symbols. The arcs are tested in a clockwise order.

Q. What is a recursive transition network?

Ans. It is a transition network which permits arc labels to refer to other networks and they in turn may refer back to the referring network.

15.3.3 Augmented Transition Nets

Q. What is an augmented transition net? Explain its use.

Ans. An interpreter for an AI language should be able to create the required knowledge entities along with simple accepting or rejecting the sentences after parsing. Also, the data structure should be such that both syntactic as well as semantic information can be represented by it. This is done using ATN parsers which are an extension to recursive transition networks. In order to find possible semantics of a sentence, additional tests should be performed on a sentence. Since this will lead to many different structures generated and all of them may also not be valid, the intermediate results of tests are stored in registers as temporary storage. As we are dealing with semantics also here, a number of different registers based on constituents of a sentence are used to hold different sentence constituents. Examples of sentence constituents are verb phrase (VP), noun phrase (NP), etc. One constituent in one register is connected to other constituents by arcs in the ATN. In case the parse of the sentence is successful, the contents of the registers are combined to form the final sentence data structure required for output. In case of failure during parsing, the partial structures generated are discarded by clearing the registers.

The arcs in the transition network are labeled. The type of arc and its purpose helps in understanding the meaning of the arc and the work that should be matched with it. The arc labels used are

Type of Arc	Meaning
WORD:	Indicates a label for a specific word.
CAT:	Indicates a test label for the current category of the word.
TST:	Indicates a label for an arbitrary test.
JUMP:	An unconditional jump to any arc with no test.
CALN:	Indicates a label for a call to a network.
SUCC:	Indicates a label for the end of a network.

The specification language for ATN is given below:

```
<transition-net>→     (<arc set><arc set>*)
<arc set>→            (<state><arc>*)
<arc>→                (CAT <category name><test><action>*<term action>)|
                      (CALN <state><test><action>*<term-action>)|
                      (TST <arbitrary label><test><action>*<term-action>)|
                      (SUCC <form><test>)
<action>→             (SETR <register><form>)|
                      (SENDR <register><form>)|
                      (LIFTR <register><form>)
<term action>→        (TO <state>)|
                      (JUMP) <state>)
<form>→               (GETR <register>)|
                      @ |
                      (GETF <feature>)|
                       (BUILDQ <fragment><register>*)|
                      (LIST <form>*)|
                      (APPEND <form><form>)s
                      (QUOTE <arbitrary structure>)
```

An action can be either setting the register values equal to the current value of the form (using SETR) or send the current value of the form to next lower level of computation (using SENDR) or returning an information to the next higher level of computation (using LIFTR). GETR function returns the value of the indicated register and GETF returns the value of a specified feature for the current input word. The value of @ is an input word. BUILDQ function takes lists from the indicated registers and builds the sentence structures.

15.4 SEMANTIC ANALYSIS

Q. What do you understand by semantic analysis?

Ans. Once a syntactic parse of the sentence is done, it ensures that the sentence is correct as per grammar rules. Now, semantic analysis is done to produce the meaning of the sentence. The main purpose of semantic processing is the creation of the target language representation of a sentence's meaning. First, we identify the meanings of individual words in the sentence called the lexicons. Since one word may have many meanings, so we need to relate the meaning of each word with all the other words in the sentence. Semantic grammar, case grammar, and conceptual parsing can be used for doing semantic analysis.

15.4.1 Semantic Grammars

Q. What are semantic grammars?

Ans. Semantic grammars encode semantic grammars into a syntactic grammar. These use context-free rewrite rules with non-terminal semantic constituents. The constituents are categories or meta-symbols such as attribute, object, etc., rather than NP, VP, etc. This becomes the disadvantage of such a grammar, and a range of sentences which can be generated are restricted and require a large number of rewrite rules. Semantic grammars are suitable for use in systems with restricted grammars because computation is limited. A semantic grammar can be used by a parsing system in the same ways in which a strictly syntactic grammar could be used.

15.4.2 Fillmore's Case Grammar

Q. What are Fillmore's grammar or case grammars?

Ans. The case grammar was given by Charles Fillmore and is also known as Fillmore's grammar. He tried to include the verb sense or meaning so that the use of the verb is clarified in the sentence. This is done by associating a set of cases to represent the verb sense. A case relates to the semantic role that an NP plays with respect to verbs and adjectives. Case grammars use the functional relationships between NPs and verbs to reveal the deeper case of a sentence.

In case grammars, a sentence is defined as $S \leftrightarrow M + P$, where proposition P, a tenseless set of relationships among verbs and NPs, consists of one or more distinct cases $C1, C2, \ldots, Ck (P \leftrightarrow C1 + C2 + L + Ck)$ and a modality constituent M, composed of mood, tense, negation, aspect, etc. Case frames are provided for verbs to identify the allowable cases. They specify the relationships which are required and are optional. These are used to parse incomplete or noisy sentences. For example, while Shalini gave flower is not correct grammatically, it is still possible to create an appropriate case grammar parse of this string of words.

15.5 DISCOURSE AND PRAGMATIC PROCESSING

Q. Discuss discourse and pragmatic processing.

Ans. Discourse and pragmatic processing refers to the process of relating to the meaning of the sentence in a given context. It is very important in understanding the use of the sentence. For this understanding, we need to relate a sentence to many things like actions, the entities, the objects, the events, the beliefs, the intensions, the plans, etc. So, we need to focus on relevant parts of the available knowledge base and use this knowledge to resolve the ambiguities if any. For example, there is a difference in the meaning of caught in two sentences: Raghav caught cold and Saurabh caught the thief. This can be identified for the current sentence only through the use of context in detail and relating it with the scenes before and after this sentence and the objects used.

15.6 GRAMMAR FREE ANALYZERS

Q. What are various grammar-free analyzers in NLP?

Ans. The parser for a grammar often uses a separate lexical analyzer to create tokens from the sequence of input characters. The parser acts as a compiler which parses a sentence in any programming language to create some form of internal representation. Programming language is specified in terms of context-free grammar. The lexical analyzer splits the input into a set of meaningful symbols defined by a grammar.

15.7 SENTENCE GENERATION AND TRANSLATION

Q. How does sentence generation and translation takes place in NLP?

Ans. A language L is defined as a set of strings formed by concatenating symbols taken from the alphabet set or vocabulary of the language. The length of the string may be finite or infinite. The possible sentences called well-formed sentences are constructed using set of rules defined in the grammar of the language. To generate a sentence, the rules from set of production rule are applied sequentially starting with starting symbol S and proceeding until all non terminal symbols are eliminated and the sentence is generated using terminal symbols. The example is given in solved examples. The translation of one sentence is done using semantic analysis of the sentence.

SOLVED EXAMPLES

Q. Give an example of a regular grammar.

Ans. Let the alphabet set, i.e., set of terminals of the grammar be {c,d}
Let the set of non-terminals be {C,D}
Let S be the starting symbol.
Let the set of production rules be:
S → cS
S → cCD
CD → DC
cC → cd
cC → cc

Q. Consider the context-free grammar given below:

S ↔ NP VP
NP ↔ Art N
NP ↔ N
VP ↔ V
VP ↔ V NP
Art ↔ a
Art ↔ the
N ↔ teacher
N ↔ student
V ↔ taught
V ↔ thanked

Draw the top-down parse tree for the sentence "The teacher taught the student".

Ans.
S ↔ NP VP
S ↔ Art N VP
S ↔ Art N V NP
S ↔ Art N V Art N
S ↔ the N V Art N
S ↔ the teacher V Art N
S ↔ the teacher taught Art N
S ↔ the teacher taught the N
S ↔ the teacher taught the student

Q. Consider the context-free grammar given below:

S ↔ NP VP
NP ↔ Art N

NP ↔ N
VP ↔ V
VP ↔ V NP
Art ↔ a
Art ↔ the
N ↔ man
N ↔ dog
V ↔ bites
V ↔ likes
Draw the bottom-up parse tree for the sentence "The dog bites the man".

Ans.
S ↔ the dog bites the man
S ↔ the dog bites the N
S ↔ the dog bites Art N
S ↔ the dog V Art N
S ↔ the N V Art N
S ↔ Art N V Art N
S ↔ Art N V NP
S ↔ Art N VP
S ↔ NP VP

Q. Give an example system where semantic grammar is used.

Ans. Semantic grammars are suitable for use in systems with restricted grammars. The use of semantic grammar is done in a tutorial system named SOPHIE which is used to teach the debugging of circuit faults. Rewrite rules in these systems are

S → What is <OUTPUT-PROPERTY> of <CIRCUIT-PART>?
OUTPUT-PROPERTY → the <OUTPUT-PROP>
OUTPUT-PROPERTY → <OUTPUT-PROP>
CIRCUIT-PART → C12
CIRCUIT-PART → D11
OUTPUT-PROP → current
OUTPUT-PROP → voltage

Q. Represent the following sentence using case grammar: Did Maria break the vase?

Ans. In case grammar, the sentence is represented as S → **M + P**.In this sentence, the modality is interrogative in the past. The verb is break. The agent is Maria who is treated as the first case C1 of verb and the object is Vase which is treated as second case C2. This is represented in case grammar as the following tree:

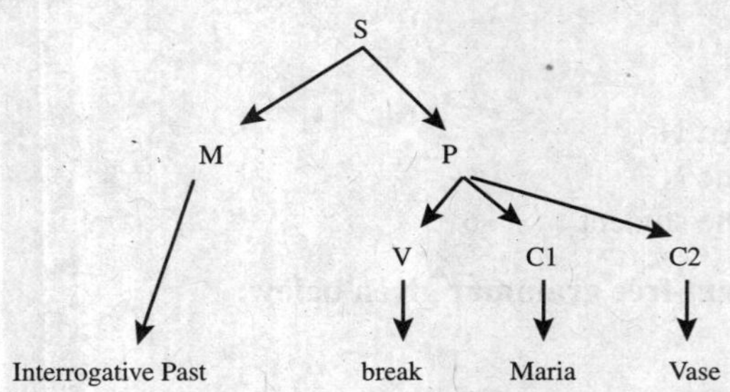

Q. Consider the following context-free grammar:

S ↔ NP VP
NP ↔ Art N
NP ↔ N
VP ↔ V
VP ↔ V NP
Art ↔ the
N ↔ police
N ↔ killer
V ↔ chases
V ↔ kills

Draw a transition network parser for parsing the sentence: "The police chases the killer".

Ans. First, we need to draw the transition network for all the non-terminal in the given grammar.

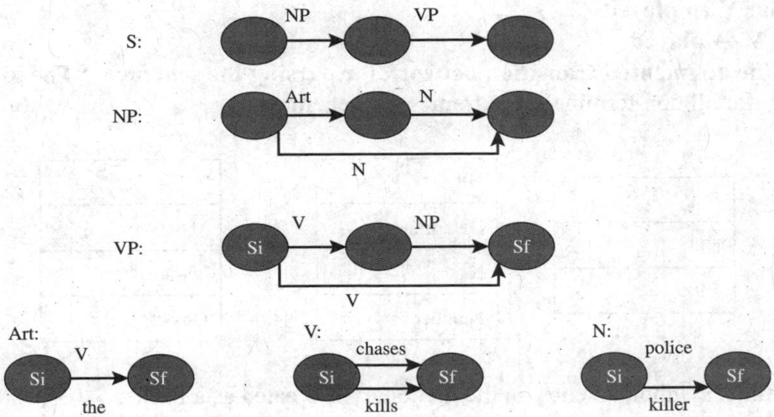

Now the transition network for parsing the sentence: "The police chases the killer".

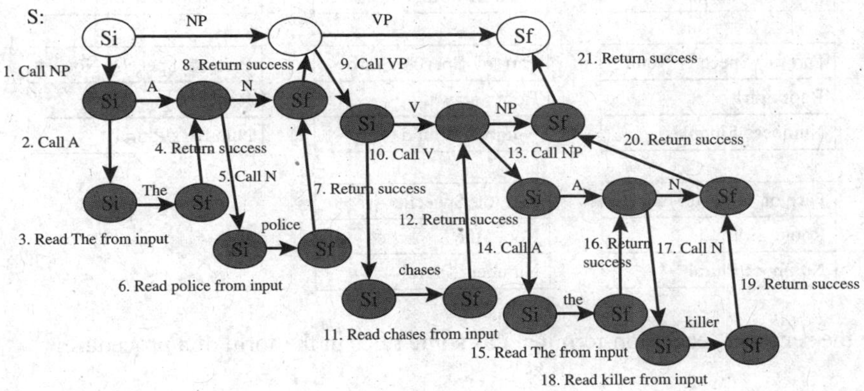

Q. Consider the given context sensitive grammar:

S ↔ NP VP
NP ↔ Art Number N
NP ↔ Number N
Number ↔ Singular
Number ↔ Plural
Art Singular ↔ a Singular
Art Singular ↔ the Singular
Art Plural ↔ the Plural
Singular VP ↔ Singular V
Plural VP ↔ Plural V
Singular N ↔ girl Singular
Singular N ↔ doll Singular
Plural N ↔ girls Plural
Plural N ↔ boys Plural
Singular V ↔ played
Plural V ↔ played

Draw the augmented transition network for parsing the sentence: "The girls played."

Ans. Initially for all non-terminals, the frames are generated:

S
NP
VP

NP
Determiner
N
Number

VP
V
Number
Object

For each terminal symbol, an entry in the dictionary is created as a frame:

Part_of_Speech : Art
Root : the
Number : Singular

Part_of_Speech : Verb
Root : played
Number : Singular

Part_of_Speech : Noun
Root : boy
Number : Singular

Part_of_Speech : Noun
Root : girl
Number : Singular

Part_of_Speech : Verb
Root : played
Number : Plural

Part_of_Speech : Noun
Root : boys
Number : Plural

Part_of_Speech : Noun
Root : girls
Number : Plural

Part_of_Speech : Art
Root : the
Number : Plural

To parse the sentence, each non-terminal has some rules in the form of a procedure:

For starting symbol S, the transition network and procedure is given below:

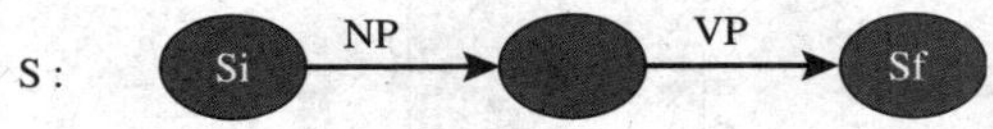

Procedure S-1;
NP: = structure returned by NP network;
S.SUBJECT: = NP;
Function S-2;
VP: = structure returned by VP network;
If NP.NUMBER = VP.NUMBER
{S.VP: = VP;
Return S}
Else fail

The transition network for NP and the procedures for navigation are

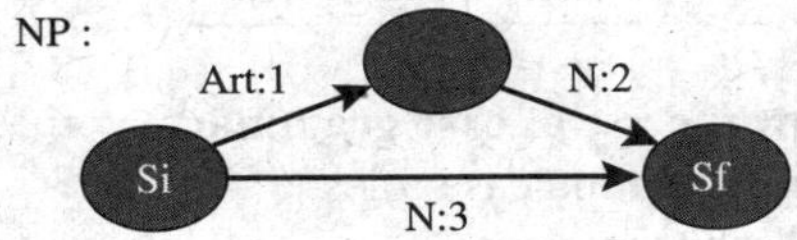

Procedure ART-1; ART: = Definition frame for next word of input; If ART.PART_OF_SPEECH = article NP. DETERMINER: = ART else fail	Procedure N-2; N: = Definition frame for next word of input; If N.PART_OF_SPEECH = verb and N.NUMBER agrees with NP.DETERMINER. NUMBER {NP. NOUN: = N; NP.NUMBER=N.NUMBER return NP} else fail.	Procedure N-3; N: = Definition frame for next word of input; If N.PART_OF_SPEECH = noun {NP. DETERMINER = unspecified; NP. NOUN: = N; NP.NUMBER=N.NUMBER} else fail.

The transition network for VP and the procedures for navigation are

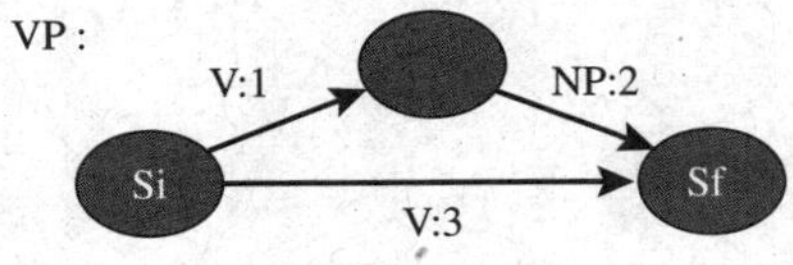

Procedure V-1; begin V: = Definition frame for next word of input; If V.PART_OF_SPEECH = verb {VP. V = V; VP.NUMBER = V.NUMBER}	procedure NP-2; NP: = structure returned by NP network; VP.OBJECT = NP; return VP	Procedure V-3; V: = Definition frame for next word of input; If V.PART_OF_SPEECH = verb {VP. V = V; VP.NUMBER = V.NUMBER VP.OBJECT = unspecified; return VP;}

The ATN parsing for the sentence is given in figure below.

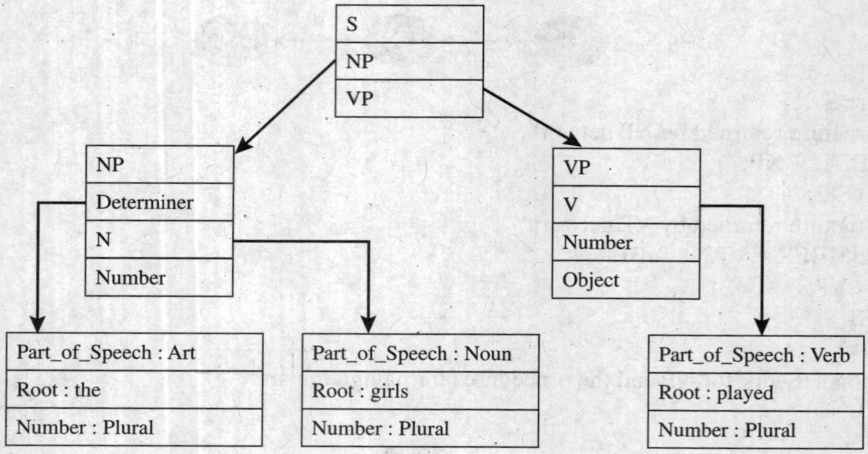

Q. Give an example to show the use of case grammars.

Ans. Sample sentences with their relating case roles:

AGENT: Peter broke the glass.
PATIENT: Peter broke the glass.
INSTRUMENT: Peter broke the glass with a hammer.
SOURCE: Peter left prison. Peter traveled from Denver to Hawaii.
GOAL: Peter went to Africa.

Q. Explain the use of transformational grammar.

Ans. These reflect the active and passive voice of a sentence.

Consider the grammar:

S → NP VP
NP → N
NP → Art N
VP → V
VP → V NP
VP → VERB PP
VP → V NP PP
VP → V ADJ
VERB → AUX V
PP → PREP NP
N → Bobby
N → Somil
V → hit
Art → the
PREP → by
AUX → was

Given the sentence is "Bobby hit Somil". It will be transformed as "the ball was hit by Bobby". It is represented by the following:

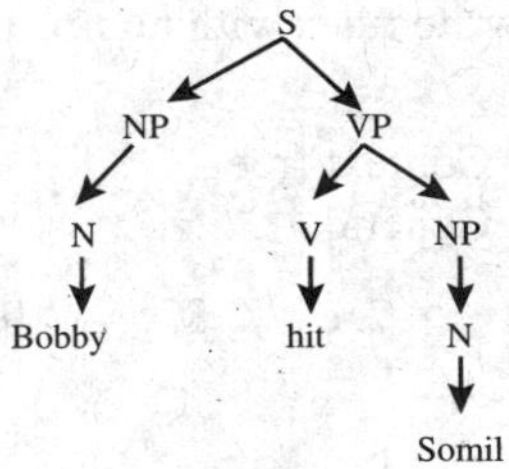

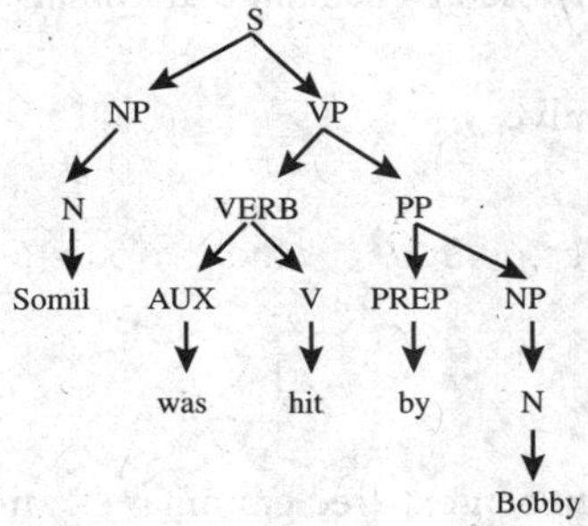

MULTIPLE CHOICE QUESTIONS

Select the most appropriate answers for the following questions:

1. Which is the basic element of language for NLP?
   (a) Character (b) String
   (c) Word (d) Sentence
2. Which analysis is done to form grammatically correct sentences?
   (a) Phonological analysis (b) Syntax analysis
   (c) Semantic analysis (d) None of these
3. Which phase of NLP is used to relate the use of sentence in different contexts?
   (a) Semantic analysis (b) Pragmatic analysis
   (c) Syntax analysis (d) Morphological analysis
4. How many types of grammar are defined by Chomsky hierarchy?
   (a) One (b) Two
   (c) Three (d) Four
5. Which is also known as context-free grammar in Chomsky hierarchy?
   (a) Type 0 (b) Type 1
   (c) Type 2 (d) Type 3
6. Which of the following represent regular grammar in Chomsky hierarchy?
   (a) Type 0 (b) Type 1
   (c) Type 2 (d) Type 3
7. In which of the grammars, a sentence is composed of a proposition and a modality?
   (a) Systemic (b) Semantic
   (c) Case (d) Transformational
8. Who introduced systemic grammars?
   (a) Fillmore (b) Chomsky
   (c) Michael Halliday (d) Alan Turing
9. Which of the following functions are included in systemic grammar?
   (a) Ideational (b) Interpersonal
   (c) Textual (d) Conceptual

10. Which grammar is used by semantic grammars to rewrite rules with non-terminal semantic constituents?
    (a) Context sensitive (b) Context free
    (c) Regular (d) General

Answers. 1. d 2. b 3. b 4. d 5. c 6. d 7. c 8. c 9. d 10. b

EXERCISES

1. Consider the given context-free grammar example:
   S ↔ NP VP
   NP ↔ Art N
   NP ↔ N
   VP ↔ V
   VP ↔ V NP
   Art ↔ a
   Art ↔ the
   N ↔ man
   N ↔ dog
   V ↔ bites
   V ↔ likes
   Parse the sentence: "The dog bites the man" using top-down parsing and bottom-up parsing.
2. Using the grammar given in Q1, draw a transition network for parsing the sentence: "The dogs bite".
3. Consider the given context sensitive grammar example:
   S ↔ NP VP
   NP ↔ Art Number N
   NP ↔ Number N
   Number ↔ Singular
   Number ↔ Plural
   Art Singular ↔ a Singular
   Art Singular ↔ the Singular
   Art Plural ↔ the Plural
   Singular VP ↔ Singular V
   Plural VP ↔ Plural V
   Singular N ↔ man Singular
   Singular N ↔ dog Singular
   Plural N ↔ men Plural
   Plural N ↔ dogs Plural
   Singular V ↔ bites
   Plural V ↔ bite
   Parse the sentence: "The dogs bite".
4. Using the grammar given in Q.3, draw augmented transition network for parsing the sentence: "The dog bites the men".

16

Pattern Recognition

16.1 INTRODUCTION

Pattern recognition is an AI research area which studies the operation and design of systems which can recognize a pattern in data. There are many applications of pattern recognition that are used in practical. These include face recognition, handwriting recognition, fraud detection, prevention, etc.

In face recognition, the face of a human is used to unlock the machine without the need to enter a password via keyboard. This reduces the chances of forgetting the passwords as well as its leakage to an unauthenticated person. This also prevents others from using the computer because their faces are not likely to match the original user's stored face model.

Handwriting recognition is one of the most promising methods of interacting with small portable computing devices, such as personal digital assistants, and is the use of handwriting in AI. To make this communication method more natural, they proposed to observe visually the writing process on an ordinary paper and to automatically recover the pen trajectory from numerical tablet sequences.

Q. Define pattern recognition problem.

Ans. Pattern recognition is the science that concerns the recognition of measurements. The three terms used here are pattern, recognition, and classification. These are defined as:

A pattern is an object, process, or event that can be given a name.

A pattern class (or category) is a set of patterns sharing common attributes and origin.

A classifier is a machine which performs classification, i.e., assigns given objects to prescribed classes.

For pattern recognition, first a physical object or event is assigned to one of several possible pre-specified pattern categories or classes based on either *a priori* knowledge or on statistical information extracted from the patterns. Then, the pattern recognition problem can be defined as the act of taking in raw data and taking an action based on the category of the data.

16.1.1 Design Principles of Pattern Recognition System

Q. Discuss design principles of a pattern recognition system.

Ans. Pattern recognition aims to classify data (patterns) based on either *a priori* knowledge or on statistical information extracted from the patterns. The patterns to be classified are usually groups of measurements or observations, by defining points in an appropriate multidimensional space. A complete pattern recognition system consists of

1. *Sensors*: These are used to gather the observations to be classified.
2. *Description tasks*: It is a feature extraction mechanism. It is a method which computes the numeric or symbolic information from the observations. The task is to transform the data collected from environment to features. It involves three tasks: preprocessing of data, feature extraction, and reduction of features using feature selection. It produces a feature vector which is actually a representation of data for pattern recognition.
3. *A classification task*: This scheme is used to classify observations based on the extracted features. A classifier is used to map a feature vector to a group. A mapping can be formulated using a training phase to induce the mapping from a collection of feature vectors in training set and then it can be used to assign an identification to each unlabeled feature vector subsequently presented to the classifier.

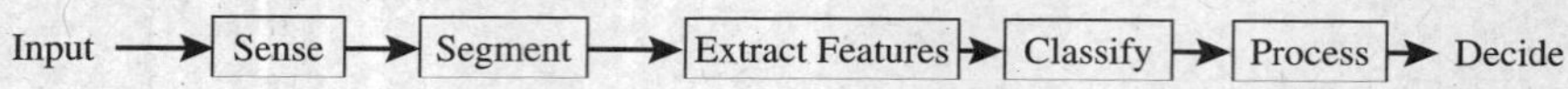

Figure 16.1

16.1.2 Structured or Syntactic Description

Q. How is structure represented in pattern recognition system?

Ans. Syntactic pattern recognition or structural pattern recognition is a form of pattern recognition. In this form, the items are presented as pattern structures which can take into account more complex interrelationships between features. Simple patterns are modeled in terms of primitives and their relations. These are usually represented as strings, trees or graphs. Recognition of an unknown pattern is performed by finding the most similar sample from a database of known objects using error-tolerant string or graph matching.

16.1.3 Symbolic Description

Q. Explain symbolic description of pattern recognition system.

Ans. Various symbols are used to represent the patterns. AI is used to analyze scenes by computing a symbolic representation of the scene contents after the images have been processed to obtain features. Examples are alphabet sets, special symbols, graphical images, etc.

16.2 STATISTICAL PATTERN RECOGNITION

Q. Define statistical pattern recognition.

Ans. Statistical pattern recognition is based on statistical characterizations of patterns, assuming that the patterns are generated by a probabilistic system. It uses concepts in statistical decision theory to discriminate among data from different groups based upon quantitative features of the data. There are a wide variety of statistical techniques that can be used within the description task for feature extraction, ranging from simple descriptive statistics to complex transformations. It includes problems like medical diagnosis and character recognition. A pattern is represented as a set of d features or attributes, viewed as a d-dimensional feature vector $X = (x_1, x_2, \ldots, x_d)^{\mathrm{T}}$

16.2.1 Parameter Estimation Methods

Q. Explain parameter estimation methods in pattern recognition system.

Ans. There are three parameter estimation methods in pattern recognition system:

1. *The method of moments*: It is used to find the estimate of a range of a uniform density. If we are given n samples $x_1, x_2, \ldots, x_n$. Then, this method allows us to find the range estimate variables $\hat{a}$ and $\hat{b}$. The steps are
   (a) Compute the sample mean as: $\bar{x} = E(x') = \sum_{i=1}^{n} xiP(xi) = \frac{1}{n}\sum_{i=1}^{n} xi$
   (b) Calculate the sample variance as: $\sigma_{x'}^2 = \sum_{i=1}^{n} (x_i - E(x'))^2 P(x_i)$
   (c) Solve the two equations: $\mu = (\hat{a} + \hat{b})/2$ and $\sigma_{x'}^2 = (\hat{b} - \hat{a})^2 / 12$ to get the values of $\hat{a}$ and $\hat{b}$.
2. *Maximum likelihood estimates:* It is that value which produces the distribution which maximizes the probability of distribution in the entire observed set of samples.
3. *Unbiased estimators*: An unbiased estimate $\hat{\theta}$ is an estimate for θ that satisfies $E(\hat{\theta}) = \theta$.

$$E(\bar{x}) = E\left(\frac{1}{n}\sum_{i=1}^{n} x_i\right) = \frac{1}{n}\sum_{i=1}^{n} E(x_i) = \frac{1}{n}(n\mu_x) = \mu_x$$

where $\bar{x}$ is always an unbiased estimate of μ_x, regardless of the type of distribution or density.

16.2.2 Principle Component Analysis

Q. Explain PCA.

Ans. It is a form of unsupervised machine learning algorithm which uses a classical linear approach. It is a popular dimensionality reduction technique. Principal component Analysis (PCA): The idea here is to find important variance in the feature matrix. The data is projected into lower dimension feature space where the variables are transformed into a smaller set of principal components. The aim is to get a smaller set of variables that explain most of the variance in the original data, in more compact and insightful form.

Here, the dimensionality reduction is done:

1. The original space representation is given as
   $x = a_1v_1 + a_2v_2 + \cdots + a_nv_n$, where $v_1, v_2, \ldots, v_n$ are the bases in the original N-dimensional space.
2. The lower dimensional sub-space representation is given as
   $\hat{x} = b_1u_1 + b_2u_2 + \cdots + b_nu_n$, where $u_1, u_2, \ldots, u_n$ are the base in the K-dimensional sub-space, where $K < N$.

Areas of variance in data are where items can be best discriminated and key underlying phenomena are observed. The goal of principle component analysis (PCA) is to reduce the dimensionality of the data while retaining as much as variation possible in the dataset, i.e., $\min \| x - \hat{x} \|$. This method is named so because it chooses principal components, i.e., the best eigenvectors (with largest eigenvalues) which help in identifying the best low-dimensional space.

An eigenvector of a square matrix A is a non-zero vector v that, when multiplied by A, yields the original vector multiplied by a single number λ; that is, $Av = \lambda v$. The number λ is called the eigenvalue of A corresponding to v. It is shown in figure below:

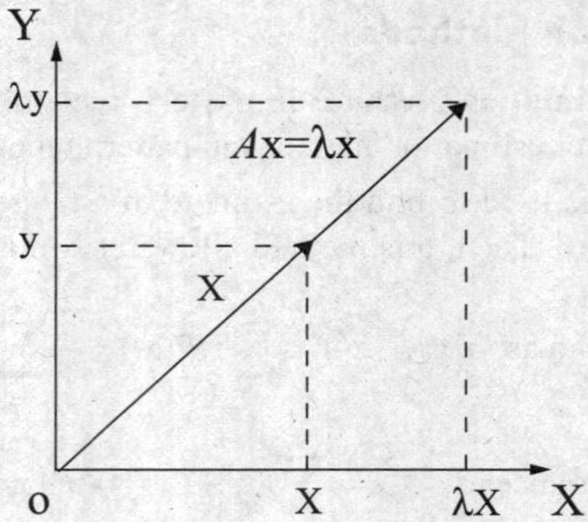

Figure 16.2

Steps during PCA are: Suppose $x_1, x_2 \ldots, x_m$ are $N \times 1$ vectors.

1. Find the mean, $\bar{x} = \left(\sum_{1}^{M} x_i\right) \Big/ M$.
2. Subtract the mean $\Phi i = x_i - \bar{x}$.

Q. What are the main applications of PCA?

Ans. The main application areas for principle component analysis (PCA) are visualization, classification and clustering, feature selection or reduction, data representation or filtering.

(i) Visualization: Data visualization is the study of the visual representation of data, i.e. information that has been abstracted in some systematic form. The attributes or variables for the units of information are also included in data visualization. According to Friedman (2008) the "main goal of data visualization is to communicate information clearly and effectively through graphical means". There are many approaches for data visualization which include statistical graphics and thematic cartography. Statistical graphics include pictorial representation of quantitative data. Examples are histograms, scatter plots, probability plots etc. Thematic cartography includes data visualization through thematic maps. Thematic maps are sometimes referred to as graphic essays. These portray spatial variations and interrelationships of geographical distributions. Location, of course, is important to provide a reference base of where selected phenomena are occurring.

(ii) Classification: Suppose we have a given set of training data for which we can define a function which maps into the training examples. For any new value, we wish to classify to which class the new value belongs to. The classification may have two classes or there can be many classes to which the new data example may belong to. For example, an e-mail program might attempt to classify an e-mail as "spam" or as "legitimate".

(iii) Clustering: This is an example of unsupervised learning. Here unlike classification, no classes are identified before with training examples. Here the problem is to identify the cluster to which the given example belongs to. Each time, the cluster may be different and new. For example, a jeans manufacturing company may need to find the new sizes of jeans based on different clusters of customers in market.

(iv) Feature selection and reduction: This is an important process in handling any problem in real life and writing a program in machine learning. This indicates that for a single problem, there are many features which are to be considered before making a decision or for a prediction. It is easier to handle a small set of features as these can be easily projected into a hyperplane. But as the number of features considered increase, it becomes difficult to project all the features. So the method used is feature reduction. Here the non significant features are eliminated and only important or significant features are retained for projection. For example, consider a bank who wishes to check whether the loan should be given to a particular customer or not. A number of features are inputted from customer like name, address, age, monthly salary, total cost of assets, mobile number, email id etc. The most important features can be considered are monthly salary and total cost of assets for required prediction for loan approval. Thus all others will be reduced to these two features.

(v) **Data representation or filtering:** It is used to filter useful information or data. It involves collaboration among multiple agents, viewpoints, data sources etc. So it is also called collaborative filtering. Applications of collaborative filtering typically involve very large data sets. Collaborative filtering methods have been applied to many different kinds of data including: (a) in electronic commerce and web applications, where the focus is on user data, (b) sensing and monitoring data, such as in mineral exploration, (c) environmental sensing over large areas or multiple sensors and (d) financial data, such as financial service institutions that integrate many financial sources etc.

16.2.3 Linear Discriminant Analysis

Q. Discuss LDA.

Ans. Linear discriminant analysis (LDA) performs dimensionality reduction while preserving as much of the class discriminatory information as possible. It seeks to find directions along which the classes are best separated. It takes into consideration the scattering *within-classes* and scattering *between-classes*.

Assume that there are C classes. Let μ_i be the mean vector of class i, $i = 1,2,...C$. Let M_i be the number of samples within class i, $i = 1,2,...C$.

If M is the total number of samples, then $M = \sum_{l=1}^{C} M_i$

Within-class scatter matrix is given as:

$$S = \sum_{i=1}^{C}\sum_{j=1}^{M_i}(x_j - \mu_i)(x_j -)$$

Between-class scatter matrix is given as:

$$S_b = \sum_{i=1}^{C}(\mu i - \mu)(\mu_i - \mu)^T \frac{-b \pm \sqrt{b^2 - 4ac}}{2a}$$

,

where mean of entire data set $\mu = (1/C) * \sum_{i=}^{C} \mu i$

LDA computes a transformation that maximizes the between-class scatter while minimizing the within-class scatter:

$\max \frac{|U^T S_b U|}{|U^T S_w U|} = \max \frac{|\tilde{S}_b|}{|\tilde{S}_w|}$, where and are the scatter matrices of the projected data y. $\left(y = U^T x\right)$

The LDA solution is given by the eigenvectors of the generalized eigenvector problem:
$S_b u_k = \mu_k S_w u_k$

The linear transformation is given by a matrix U whose columns are the eigenvectors of the above problem

$$\begin{bmatrix} b \\ b \\ \dots \\ b_k \end{bmatrix} = \begin{bmatrix} u \\ u \\ \dots \\ u_k \end{bmatrix} (x-\mu) = U \; (x-\mu)$$

Q. Compare PCA and LDA.

Ans. There has been a tendency in the computer vision community to prefer LDA over PCA because LDA deals directly with discrimination between classes, whereas PCA does not pay attention to the underlying class structure. When the training set is small, PCA can outperform LDA. When the number of samples is large and representative for each class, LDA should be used as compared to PCA.

16.3 CLASSIFICATION TECHNIQUES

16.3.1 Nearest Neighbor Rule

Q. Explain NN rule.

Ans. It is a non-parametric pattern classification technique. Consider a two class problem where each sample consists of two measurements (p, q). For a given query point q, assign the class of the nearest neighbor (NN). Compute the k NNs and assign the class by majority vote. Simplest form is k NN where we have the set of stored records, distance metric to compute distance between records and the value of k, the number of NNs to retrieve. Here, the distance d between any two points p and q is computed as Euclidean distance

$$d(p,q) = \sqrt{\Sigma(p_i - q_i)^2}$$

To classify n unknown record, first the distance to other training records is computed and then k NNs are identified. Class labels of NNs are used to determine the class label of unknown record. The weighted factor is calculated as $1/d^2$ to find the class.

Q. Suppose we have the following data points using 3NN rule:

Point	X1	X2	Class
1	4	3	A
2	1	1	B
3	2	2	A
4	5	1	B

The data points given are X1=3, X2=1. How it should be classified using k=3?

Ans. Using 3NN rule, first compute the distances

Point	X1	X2	Class	Distance
1	4	3	A	$\sqrt{(4-3)2+(3-1)2}$ $=\sqrt{5}=2.23$
2	1	1	B	$\sqrt{(1-3)2+(1-1)2}$ $=\sqrt{4}=2$
3	2	2	A	$\sqrt{2-3)2+(2-1)2}$ $\sqrt{2}=1.414$
4	5	1	B	$\sqrt{5-3)2+(1-1)2}$ $=\sqrt{4}=2$

The three closest points are 2,3 and 4. 2 and 4 are of class B while 3 is of class A. So the new example given is of class B.

Q. What are the issues in NN rule?

Ans. Though simple to understand, there are many issues in NN rule:

(i) *Cost*: It is expensive to determine the NN of a query point *q*. It must compute the distance to all *N* training examples. One way to reduce the cost of computations is to compute only an approximate distance.

(ii) *Storage requirements*: In order to find the NN, all the training data need to be stored at all time. This can be reduced by removing the redundant data.

(iii) *Increasing dimensionality of data*: Required amount of training data increases exponentially with dimension and hence computational cost also increases.

16.3.2 Support Vector Machine

Q. Explain SVM.

Ans. It is supervised learning method. It was developed at AT&T Bell labs. The idea is to select a set of functions (called the hyperplane) that can minimize the sum of the empirical risk and VC dimensions. VC stands for Vapnik–Chervonenkis theory. Support vector machine (SVM) is based on statistical learning and VC theory with an efficient training algorithm. These can represent nonlinear functions.

SVM Steps in greater detail

1. Prepare data matrix {(*xi*,*yi*), i=1 to m}

   These are training examples that are used to get the classification function. Consider there are m training examples.

2. Select a Kernel function

   The Kernel function is very important in SVM. It helps in applying different functions and getting the classification function. Different type of Kernel functions can be used.

3. Select the error parameter C

   The error parameter helps to get the classification function which is at widest distance apart
4. Train the system (to find all αi)
5. New data can be classified using αi and support vectors.

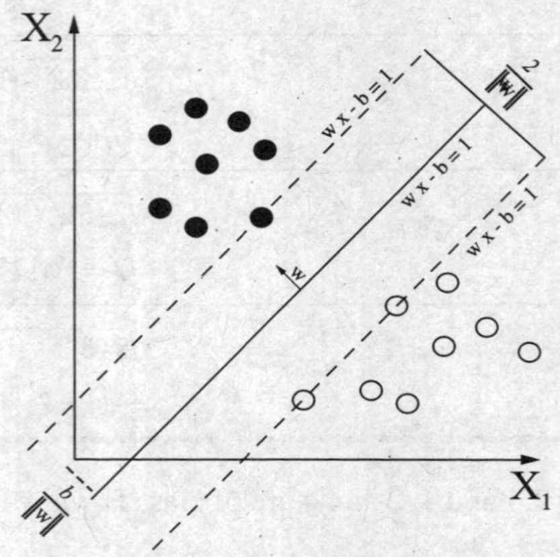

Figure 16.3 Support Vector Machine

16.3.3 K-Means Clustering

Q. Explain clustering.

Ans. Cluster analysis is the formal study of algorithms and methods for grouping objects. The objective of cluster analysis is to fi nd a convenient and valid organization of the data. An object is described either by a set of measurements or by relationships between the object and other objects. There are a number of clustering algorithms which can be grouped into two categories:

1. Hierarchical Clustering : It refers to a clustering process that organizes the data into large groups which further contain smaller groups and so on. It can be drawn as a tree or dendrogram. The top of the dendrogram has all the samples grouped into one cluster and the bottom of the dendrogram contains the final cluster. The hierarchical clustering algorithms include single linkage, complete linkage, average linkage and Ward's (variance) method of clustering.
2. Partitional Clustering : The goal of partitioning clustering is to create a set of clusters that partition the data into similar groups. The advantage of partitioning clustering is that only top part of the dendrogram is needed. The methods in this category are Forgy's algorithm, k-means clustering, isodata and self organization maps.

Q. Explain Forgy's algorithm.

Ans. Let K be the number of clusters to be constructed. K samples are called the seed points. The algorithm steps are as given below:

1. Initialize the cluster centroids to the seed points.
2. For each sample, find the cluster centroid nearest it. Put the sample in the cluster identified with this nearest cluster centroid.

3. If no sample changed clusters in step 2, stop.
4. Compute the centroids of the resulting clusters and go to step 2.

Q. Write algorithm for k-means clustering.

Ans. Algorithm for *K*-means clustering:

Given *N* vectors $x1, x2, \ldots, x\ N$ and *K*, the number of expected clusters in the range [*K*min, *K*max]

1. Randomly choose K vectors as cluster centers
2. Classify the remaining N–K (or N) vectors by the minimum mean distance rule
3. Update K new cluster centers by maximum likelihood estimation
4. Repeat steps (2), (3) until no rearrangements or M iterations
5. Compute the performance index P, the sum of squared errors for the K clusters
6. Do steps (1) to (5) from K = Kmin to K = Kmax, plot P vs. K and use the knee to pick up the best number of clusters.

Q. Explain Self-Organization Map.

Ans. SOM (Self-Organization Map): A self organizing map is like an artificial neural network (ANN) that is trained using unsupervised learning to produce a two-dimensional discretized representation of the input space of the training samples, called a **map**. Self-organizing maps are different from other artificial neural networks in the sense that they use a neighborhood function to preserve the topological properties of the input space. The model was first described as an artificial neural network by the Professor Teuvo kohonen, so it is sometimes called a Kohonen map or network.

Like most artificial neural networks, SOMs operate in two modes: training and mapping. "Training" builds the map using input examples while "Mapping" automatically classifies a new input vector. A self-organizing map consists of components called nodes or neurons. A weight vector is associated with each node of the same dimension as the input data vectors and a position in the map space. The usual arrangement of nodes is a two-dimensional regular spacing in a hexagonal or rectangular grid. The self-organizing map describes a mapping from a higher dimensional input space to a lower dimensional map space. The procedure for placing a vector from data space onto the map is to find the node with the closest weight vector to the data space vector.

Q. Explain Isodata algorithm for partitional clustering.

Ans. Isodata algorithm is an enhancement of the approach taken by Forgy's algorithm and the k-means algorithms. Here steps are:

1. Cluster centers are randomly placed and pixels are assigned based on the shortest distance to center method
2. The standard deviation within each cluster, and the distance between cluster centers is calculated
   - Clusters are split if one or more standard deviation is greater than the user-defined threshold
   - Clusters are merged if the distance between them is less than the user-defined threshold
3. A second iteration is performed with the new cluster centers
4. Further iterations are performed until:
   i) the average inter-center distance falls below the user-defined threshold,
   ii) the average change in the inter-center distance between iterations is less than a threshold, or
   iii) the maximum number of iterations is reached.

Advantages are that it is very effective at identifying spectral clusters in data. The drawback is that algorithm can spiral out of control leaving only one class.

Q. Give an example of Forgy's algorithm for partitional clustering.

Ans. Consider the following samples:

Sample	(4,4)	(8,4)	(15,8)	(24,4)	(24,12)
Nearest Centroid	(4,4)	(8,4)			
First iteration	(4,4)	(8,4)	(8,4)	(8,4)	(8,4)
Second iteration	(4,4)	(4,4)	(17.75,7)	(17.75,7)	(17.75,7)
Third iteration	(6,4)	(6,4)	(21,8)	(21,8)	(21,8)

Thus, Forgy's algorithm terminates since none of the samples changed clusters.

16.3.4 Machine Perception

Q. Explain machine perception.

Ans. Machine perception refers to building a machine that can recognize patterns like speech recognition, fingerprint identification, DNA sequence identification and optical character recognition. All these in detail include line interception, edge detection etc. Machine perception is a term that is used to identify the capability of a computer system to interpret data in a manner that is similar to the way humans use their senses to relate to the world around them. The basic method that the computers take in and respond to their environment is through the attached hardware. Both hardware and software allow computers to take in sensory input in a way similar to humans and with greater accuracy.

It is done using computer vision, machine hearing and machine touch. In computer vision, there are methods for acquiring, processing, analyzing, and understanding images and producing numerical or symbolic information, e.g., decisions. Computer vision has many applications such as facial recognition, geographical modeling, and aesthetic judgment. In machine learning, sound data such as music or speech is taken as input and processed data is the output. The applications including music recording and compression, speech synthesis, and speech recognition. Machine touch is an area of machine perception where tactile input from a user or from the environment can be processed by a machine or computer. Applications for this could allow for more direct communication with mechanical devices like touch pads on devices like phones and laptops.

SOLVED EXAMPLES

Q. Suppose the sample values given are $x = 1,2,4,5,7,8$, which come from a uniform distribution. Find the parameters a and b that determine the range.

Ans. To estimate the range, method of moments can be used

$$\bar{x} = 4.5 \text{ and } \sigma^2_{x'} = \left[(1-4.5)^2 + (2-4.5)^2 + (4-4.5)^2 + (5-4.5)^2 + (7-4.5)^2 + (8-4.5)^2\right]/6$$

$$= 37.5$$

$$(a+b)/2 = 4.5$$

$$(b-a)^2/12 = 6.25$$

Solving these two, we get $a = 0.17$ and $b = 8.83$.

Q. Calculate the maximum likelihood estimate of the range of a uniform distribution. The samples given are $x1 = 2.1$, $x2 = 4.2$, $x3 = 8.4$, $x4 = 16.8$.

Ans. The maximum likelihood estimate $\hat{a}$ for parameter a is the smallest sample value = 2.1. The maximum likelihood estimate $\hat{b}$ for parameter b is the largest sample value = 16.8.

Q. Perform a partitioning clustering using *K*-means clustering algorithm. Given the following sample data.

	x	y
1	1	1
2	2	1
3	2	3
4	5	4

Ans. Let we take $k = 2$ and let the two seed points be (1,1) and (2,1).
First cluster $c1$ = (1,1) and second cluster $c2$ = (2,1).
Distances are D

	1	2	3	4
x	0	1	2.25	5
y	1	0	2	4.24

Next we calculate the new centroid as $c1(1,1)$ and $c2 = \{(2+2+5)/3, (1 + 3 + 4)/3\} = (3,2.67)$
Then again new distances are calculated.

MULTIPLE CHOICE QUESTIONS

Select the most appropriate answer to the following questions:

1. Which of the two will perform better when the training set is small?
   (a) PCA (b) LDA
   (c) Both of these (d) None of these
2. Which of these is preferred by the computer vision community?
   (a) PCA (b) LDA
   (c) Neural Networks (d) None of these
3. Which of the following is not a partitioning clustering method?
   (a) *K*-means (b) Self-organizing map
   (c) Isodata (d) None of these
4. *K*-means clustering supports which of the following learning?
   (a) Supervised learning (b) Unsupervised learning
   (c) Formal learning (d) None of these
5. LDA stands for
   (a) Linear discriminant analysis (b) Logical discriminant analysis
   (c) Layer discriminant analysis (d) All of these

6. Which of the following is used to classify observations based on the extracted features?
   (a) Feature extractor
   (b) Classification scheme
   (c) Sensors
   (d) None of these
7. Which of the two does not need the complete dendrogram for clustering?
   (a) Hierarchical clustering
   (b) Partitional clustering
   (c) Both of these
   (d) None of these
8. What is the goal of SVM in selecting a set of functions?
   (a) Minimize the sum of the empirical risk and VC dimensions
   (b) Minimize the product of empirical risk and VC dimensions
   (c) Maximize the benefit and VC dimensions
   (d) Maximize the benefit and minimize the VC dimensions
9. Which of the following is not an application of SVM s?
   (a) Bioinformatics
   (b) Machine vision
   (c) Text categorization
   (d) All of these
10. Which of the parameter estimation methods estimates the range of a uniform density?
    (a) Maximum likelihood estimates
    (b) Unbiased estimates
    (c) Method of moments
    (d) All of these

Answers. 1. a. 2. b 3. d 4. b 5. a 6. b 7. b 8. a 9. d 10. c

EXERCISES

1. Suppose the sample values given are $x = 2,3,5,6,8,9,11$, and 12 which come from a uniform distribution. Find the parameters a and b that determine the range.
2. Find the maximum likelihood estimate for estimating the number of cards in a numbered deck, given only one draw.
3. Perform a partitioning clustering using K-means clustering algorithm. Consider the dataset as follows:

	x	*y*
1	2	2
2	4	2
3	7	4
4	12	2
5	12	6

Index